Why African Autocracies Promote Women as Leaders

Why African Autocracies Promote Women as Leaders

Aili Mari Tripp

OXFORD
UNIVERSITY PRESS

Oxford University Press is a department of the University of Oxford.
It furthers the University's objective of excellence in research, scholarship,
and education by publishing worldwide. Oxford is a registered trade mark of
Oxford University Press in the UK and in certain other countries.

Published in the United States of America by Oxford University Press
198 Madison Avenue, New York, NY 10016, United States of America.

CIP data is on file at the Library of Congress.

ISBN 9780197828977

ISBN 9780197828960 (hbk.)

DOI: 10.1093/9780197829004.001.0001

Paperback printed by Integrated Books International, United States of America

The manufacturer's authorized representative in the EU for product safety is
Oxford University Press España S.A. of Parque Empresarial San Fernando de Henares,
Avenida de Castilla, 2–28830 Madrid (www.oup.es/en or product.safety@oup.com).
OUP España S.A. also acts as importer into Spain of products made by the manufacturer.

Contents

List of Figures

List of Tables

Acknowledgments

I cannot even begin to express how grateful I am to the many people who helped me in various ways in writing this book. They shaped my thinking and pushed me to consider alternative and deeper explanations.

This book could not have been written without the help of my fantastic research assistants, including Namata Tendo (Uganda), Oubeid Imijine (Mauritania), Kudzai Madziwa (Zimbabwe), Kago Motlhalamme (Botswana), and Gina Tibinyane (Namibia). I relied heavily on them when I was forced to do the interviews over WhatsApp and Zoom because of the Covid-19 pandemic. I was extremely fortunate to receive assistance from Kaden Paulson-Smith, Monica Komer, and Valeria Umanets at the University of Wisconsin–Madison in the United States.

I am deeply appreciative to those who provided invaluable feedback on chapters, wrote letters of recommendation, and provided other kinds of support. These include Timothy Longman, Jennie E. Burnet, Oubeid Imijine, Khaled Esseissah, Cédric Jourde, Moses Khisa, Rudo Gaidzanwa, Glanis Changachirere, Josephine Ahikire, Marwa Shalaby, Myra Marx Ferree, Laurel Weldon, Jess Wang, Henriette Müller, Nevine El Nossery, Scott Straus, Pär Zetterberg, the two reviewers of the book manuscript, and the countless others not mentioned here. I am indebted to Angela Chnapko, who deserves special mention as the executive editor at the Oxford University Press who shepherded the book through the publication process.

I benefited enormously from the extensive feedback I received from colleagues after presenting my work at the Comparative Politics Colloquium at the University of Wisconsin–Madison; Milwaukee Area Political Science Seminar at the University of Wisconsin–Milwaukee and Marquette University; the Women in Legislative Studies Conference at the University of Wisconsin-Madison; the Comparative Politics Colloquium at Princeton University; the African Studies Association annual conference; the American Political Science Association annual conference; the Kellogg Institute at Notre Dame University; the International Studies Association conference at Al Akhawayn University (Ifrane, Morocco); the Resistance Bureau video conference; the European Conference on Politics and Gender (Ljubljana, Slovenia); the Department of Political Science at the University of Witwatersrand (South Africa); the Stellenbosch Institute for Advanced Studies

(South Africa); the Council on Foreign Relations; the Program on Governance and Local Development at University of Gothenburg (Sweden); the Uppsala Forum for Democracy at the University of Uppsala (Sweden); the Nordic Africa Institute in Uppsala (Sweden); the Centro de Estudos Africanos at Universidade Eduardo Mondlane (Maputo, Mozambique); the University of Juba (South Sudan); the International Conference on Gender Studies in Africa at Makerere University (Uganda); the University of Nebraska–Lincoln; and the Wilson Center (Washington, DC).

I spent 2020–2021 at the Wilson Center, where a handful of scholars and I fended for ourselves in an empty building during Covid-19. There, I was sustained by the close friendship of fellow Africanists Khalid Medani and Maria Repnikova as well as several other dear colleagues in our "pod," including Andrew Oros, Thomas Whatley, Elizabeth Chalecki, Sergey Radchenko, Regina Smyth, Amy Holmes, and Asher Orkaby. I spent the spring of 2022 at the Stellenbosch Institute for Advanced Study in South Africa. The excellent food and wine, beautiful surroundings, and community of brilliant scholars nourished me. My husband and I enjoyed the company of other fellows, including Moses Khisa, Freedom Mazwi, Gibson Ncube, Edwin Malala, Jonathan Kingdon, Barbara König, William Beinart, and the late Thomas Hylland Eriksen. It was a real treat to spend time later that year with Elin Bjarngård and Per Zetterberg, who were fabulous hosts at Uppsala University in Sweden. Working on similar issues allowed me to test my ideas in a welcoming intellectual environment and to work in a political science department with as many as fifteen gender scholars!

I am enormously grateful for the support I received from the University of Wisconsin–Madison through the Vilas Research Professorship and, before that, the Wangari Maathai Professorship for Political Science and Gender & Women's Studies along with a chair's leave and sabbatical. I am also extremely appreciative of the aforementioned residencies I held at the Wilson Center in Washington, DC, the Stellenbosch Institute of Advanced Studies in South Africa, and the Uppsala Forum for Democracy in Sweden.

While working on this book, I taught at the University of Wisconsin–Madison when I was not on a residential fellowship. I also edited the *American Political Science Review* as part of a team of eleven feminist scholars while I was carrying out research and writing. The experience of editing the journal was life changing, and I had the privilege of learning a tremendous amount from my talented colleagues and the scholarship of others in my field.

Last but not least, I am indebted to my family. My sister, Eva Swantz, drew a beautiful map of Africa for use with this book, as she has done for all my books, and I am greatly appreciative of this. My husband, Warren Tripp, cheered me on throughout the process. Having recently retired, he was able to accompany me on my residencies in Washington, DC, South Africa, and Sweden, which made these experiences all the more enjoyable.

List of Abbreviations

AFD	French Development Agency
ANT	Alliance for National Transformation (Uganda)
APP	All People's Party (Namibia)
AWI	al-'Adl wal-Ihsane / Justice and Charity Association (Morocco)
AWLN	African Women Leaders Network
BCP	Botswana Congress Party
BDP	Botswana Democratic Party
BMD	Botswana Movement for Democracy
BNF	Botswana National Front
CCP	Chinese Communist Party
CDV	Christian Democratic Movement (Namibia)
CEDAW	UN Convention on the Elimination of All Forms of Discrimination Against Women
COPAC	Constitution Parliamentary Selection Committee (Zimbabwe)
DALFA-Umurinzi	Development and Liberty for All (Rwanda)
DP	Democratic Party (Uganda)
DRC	Democratic Republic of Congo
DTA	One Democratic Turnhalle Alliance (Namibia)
EU	European Union
FDC	Forum for Democratic Change (Uganda)
FDI	foreign direct investment
FFRP	Rwanda Women Parliamentary Forum
FLN	Front de libération nationale / National Liberation Front (Algeria)
GBV	gender-based violence
GGGI	Global Gender Gap Index
GMO	Gender Monitoring Office (Rwanda)
GNU	Government of National Unity
HCE	Haut Conseil d'État / Council of State (Mauritania)
ICESCO	Islamic World Educational, Scientific and Cultural Organization
IMF	International Monetary Fund
IPU	Inter-Parliamentary Union
IRA	Initiative for the Resurgence of the Abolitionist Movement (Mauritania)
LEGCO	Legislative Council (Uganda)
LGBTQ	lesbian, gay, bisexual, transgender, and queer
MDC	Movement for Democratic Change (Zimbabwe)
MDC-T	Movement for Democratic Change–Tsvangirai
MDC-A	Movement for Democratic Change Alliance
MENA	Middle East and North Africa

MND	National Democratic Movement (Mauritania)
NCW	National Council of Women (Uganda)
NEC	National Electoral Commission
NEFF	Namibia Economic Freedom Fighter
NRM	National Resistance Movement (Uganda)
NUDO	National Unity Democratic Organisation (Namibia)
NUP	National Unity Platform (Uganda)
OCRS	Organization Commune des Regions Sahariennes /Organization of Common Saharan Regions
ODA	official development assistance
PDM	Popular Democratic Movement (Namibia)
PJD	Parti de la justice et du développement / Party for Justice and Development (Morocco)
PKM	Parti des Kadihines de Mauritanie / Party of the Kadihines of Mauritania
PPM	Parti du peuple mauritanien / Mauritanian People's Party
PRDR	*Parti républicain pour la démocratie et le renouvellement* / Republican Party for Democracy and Renewal (Mauritania)
PRDS	Parti républicain démocratique et social / Democratic and Social Republican Party (Mauritania)
PRM	Parti du regroupement mauritanien / Mauritanian Regroupment Party
PSC	Personal Status Code
PSF	Private Sector Federation (Rwanda)
PSI	party system institutionalization
PSJN	Parti du sursaut de la jeunesse pour la nation / Burst of Youth for the Nation Party (Mauritania)
RDP	Rally for Democracy and Progress (Namibia)
RFD	Rassemblement des forces démocratiques / Assembly of Democratic Forces (Mauritania)
RPA	Rwandan Patriotic Army
RPF	Front patriotique rwandais / Rwandan Patriotic Front /
RSB	Rwanda Standards Board
SADC	Southern African Development Community
SDG	Sustainable Development Goals
SRH	sexual and reproductive health
SWANU	South West African National Union (Namibia)
SWAPO	South West Africa People's Organisation (Namibia)
UDP	Union pour la démocratie et le progrès / Union for Democracy and Progress (Mauritania)
UFA	Uganda Federal Alliance
UFP	Union des forces du progrès / Union of the Forces for Progress (Mauritania)
UN	United Nations
UNAIDS	UN Programme on HIV/AIDS
UNDP	UN Development Programme
UNESCO	UN Educational, Scientific, and Cultural Organization

UNFPA	UN Population Fund
UNICEF	UN Children's Fund
UPC	Uganda People's Congress
UPM	*Union progressiste mauritanienne* / Mauritanian Progressive Union
UPR	Union pour la république / Union for the Republic (Mauritania)
USAID	US Agency for International Development
UWOPA	Uganda Women's Parliamentary Association
WAG	Women's Action Group (Zimbabwe)
WCoZ	Women's Coalition of Zimbabwe
WIPSU	Women in Politics Support Unit
ZANLA	Zimbabwe African National Liberation Army
ZANU	Zimbabwe African National Union
ZANU-PF	Zimbabwe African National Union–Patriotic Front
ZAPU	Zimbabwe African People's Union
ZEC	Zimbabwe Electoral Commission
ZimPF	Zimbabwe People First
ZWPC	Zimbabwe Women's Parliamentary Caucus

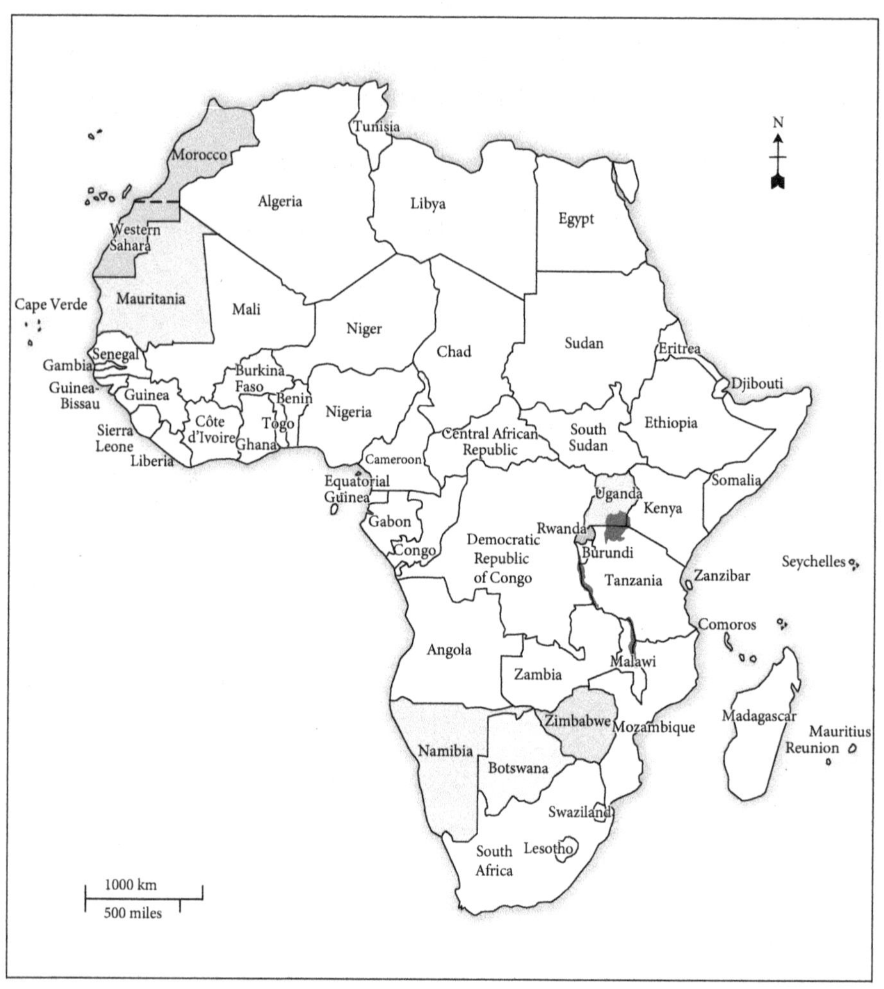

Credit: Eva Swantz

PART I
OVERVIEW

Preface

I carried out most of the interviews for this book while I lived between the White House and the United States Capitol during a time of turmoil from 2020 to 2021. I had a fellowship at the Wilson Center, which is housed in the Ronald Reagan Building, next to the White House. Covid-19 was tearing through the population, and the vaccine wasn't available to us until April 2021. Black Lives Matter protests were a common occurrence on the streets of DC as revelations of police brutality surfaced. Right-wing protests were equally frequent. The Proud Boys militia stayed in the Harrington Hotel, two blocks from our Lansburgh apartment building, and we often passed them on the street. They freely walked around in their tactical vests. Soon, over twenty-five thousand National Guard troops descended on our neighborhood after the violent insurrection at the Capitol on January 6, 2021. Storefront windows were boarded up, shelves in grocery stores were empty, and walls of barricades were erected around the Capitol.

I remember how surreal it was at the time to be carrying out interviews in Zimbabwe with people who had a long experience with authoritarianism. I listened to their horror at the revelations of police brutality against Blacks in the United States and the extent to which democracy was being eroded before our very eyes. To them, the stature of the United States globally was fast diminishing. I concluded writing this book as Trump prepared to embark on his second administration, which he promised would take us even further down the authoritarian path, making the subject of this book, unfortunately, all too relevant. There is much the world can learn from the experiences of African women and men with authoritarianism, including how to resist it and how to bring about change amid terrible odds.

Having studied gender and women's rights in nondemocratic countries, from Algeria to Zimbabwe, for my entire academic career of thirty-five years, I remember being stunned when a prominent European scholar of gender and politics in a public seminar claimed that there was nothing to discuss when it came to women's rights in authoritarian countries since she felt that by definition these regimes were hostile to women's rights. Having witnessed women's rights activists in African authoritarian countries pressing

Why African Autocracies Promote Women as Leaders. Aili Mari Tripp, Oxford University Press. © Oxford University Press (2025). DOI: 10.1093/9780197829004.003.0001

for and succeeding in obtaining constitutional and legislative reforms and increases in women's representation, her comment sparked my curiosity to better understand the role of regime type in advancing women's rights. In many parts of the world, autocracies today do no worse than democracies when it comes to advancing female political representation, and sometimes they do even better. Moreover, there are few differences in general between these regime types when it comes to many other women's rights, so much so that regime type does not feature in most discussions about women's progress today. How, then, does authoritarianism matter for women's leadership and rights? This question is the focus of this book in the African context.

There are some who treat autocracies as all the same and take Afghanistan and Iran to be emblematic of authoritarian regimes. Some throw all authoritarian regimes into the same basket, claiming that they are all ruled by despots intent on running women into the ground. Simultaneously, there is a large literature on gender and politics from a comparative perspective that treats women's leadership in authoritarian countries uncritically or in a neutral fashion, focusing on descriptive representation or some aspect of gender equality but not as much on the nondemocratic reasons for promoting women as leaders in the first place. This perhaps has to do with the historic link that has been drawn between democracy and women's rights and the belief that the adoption of women's rights is an indicator of an aspect of democracy or a pocket of democracy within an otherwise autocratic context.

There are still others who don't consider regime type when studying outcomes for women's status because it does not account for much statistical variance or because their focus is almost entirely on a particular aspect of women's rights and representation. However, the lack of political rights and civil liberties in authoritarian regimes influence women's possibilities for advocating for equality in important ways. It is this tension that motivated the writing of this book.

More recently, there has been an effort to treat women's leadership in authoritarian countries simply as window dressing and as manifestations of "genderwashing" and "gender bashing." Some extrapolate from the context of autocratizing democracies that are clawing back women's rights in critical areas like LGBTQ and abortion rights and argue that this is a worldwide trend. Added to the mix is the literature on would-be autocrats in far-right parties in Europe who may uphold women's rights to defend their racist and anti-immigrant policies.

How, then, do we make sense of these various approaches? I would suggest that we need to avoid getting stuck in simplistic zero-sum binaries, which equate democracies with women's rights and characterize autocracies by their absence of women's rights. We need, instead, an accurate understanding of specific authoritarian contexts and histories that allow some autocrats to promote women's rights and women leaders as well as an understanding of autocrats' limits and the ways in which autocrats instrumentalize women leaders and rights by using them for purposes other than to advance gender equality.

This book wades into this complex terrain to ask some tough questions in the African context, which bears similarities to other parts of the world but has some distinctive historical features. I ask, Why do autocrats today instrumentalize women leaders? Is it similar to or different from how democracies instrumentalize women's rights? What does this mean for women's rights activists? Why do some autocrats promote women as leaders and others don't? Are they complying with international goals set by the United Nations, or are they succumbing to domestic pressures, or both? Are they using women's rights as a signal to other countries to gain favor in status, foreign direct investment, trade, or aid? Is the promotion of women leaders all window dressing? Why do some regimes that don't support major forms of human rights also seek to advance women's rights? How do we reconcile the autocratic promotion of gender equality with the fact that women's movements have also pressed for more women in power? Under what circumstances do autocratic leaders try to spruce up their image using women leaders? How are the African experiences similar to or different from other parts of the world?

I believe we have much to learn from women leaders and women's rights activists in authoritarian countries about both the limits and the possibilities of advocating for women's rights in such contexts. They operate within challenging confines and at great personal risk. Some women leaders become co-opted in the designs of autocratic leaders. Others even try to play the authoritarian patriarchal game to their own advantage. The fact that advancing women's rights can lend legitimacy to an authoritarian regime both internally and externally poses a conundrum for women's rights activists. It can be a "double-edged" sword, as Miria Matembe puts it (see Chapter 3, on Uganda): It can advance women's rights, but simultaneously, it can also contribute to the longevity of a brutal dictatorship.

A closer look at authoritarian practices and policies regarding women's rights reforms reveals a complex landscape. It is full of ambiguities and uncomfortable contradictions. We saw this early on in the case of the Soviet Union and the former communist countries in Eastern Europe that had provided women with job security, child care, abortion in many cases, and political representation. At the same time, they severely curtailed human rights and political rights. In Africa today, women's rights are sometimes instrumentalized to divert attention away from human rights abuses, to create a softer look for the regime, to paper over repression of the opposition, and to give countries a modern gloss. But if standard measures are to be used in evaluating political representation, education, health, economic opportunities, and legal reform in key areas, then authoritarian countries often come out no worse and, sometimes, rank more favorably when compared with democracies. Since 2003, Rwanda has had the highest percentage of women in Parliament in the world (IPU 2024). Ethiopia and Madagascar have among the highest levels of women in cabinets, and Uganda and Senegal are among the top ten countries globally when it comes to women's representation in subnational deliberative bodies (UN Women n.d.b.).

What complicates these strategies is that they are not all simply a ruse to gain international favor. As I will argue, they are also a response to internal pressures, often the product of pressure from women's coalitions that have fought hard for women's rights reforms, as Alice Kang and I discovered in our study of how quotas were introduced in Africa (Kang and Tripp 2018). These autocratic strategies are also ways to enhance power domestically. Being able to point to international acclaim strengthens the hand of rulers at home. However, not all leaders seek international recognition or recognition all the time or in all areas. Most countries in Africa promote women for internal purposes to maintain vote share to extend ruling party hegemony, as we see in the case of Uganda. There, the instrumentalization of women has little to do with external strategies, particularly as Uganda's leaders appear to be little moved by international condemnation of their 2023 antihomosexuality law, which is one of the most repressive in the world. But even as Uganda snubs Western states in its discussion of this law, it continues to promote women leaders and seeks to improve its gender rankings.

Women in authoritarian systems may have few options other than to work with the existing ruling party, not only because of the repression against opposition parties but also because of the hegemonic dominance of the ruling party. One can't fault them for the limited constraints within which they work and the difficult decisions they have to make. There may be little choice but to cooperate with the ruling party if one wishes to advance women's rights. At the same time, they risk co-optation and inadvertently legitimizing authoritarian rule. Agency, as we see in Chapter 4, on Zimbabwe, is not simply about women's movements. Female patrons also operate within the political elite and can behave just like male leaders. Certainly, one can identify women whose agency and use of party patronage ties to women's organizations serve the purpose of enriching themselves at the expense of others through various forms of abuse of power and corruption. But how does one distinguish between women politicians who act to perpetuate the longevity of a corrupt regime by aligning themselves with the ruling party and those who serve the aims of promoting women's status?

This book asks questions that take ambiguity as its starting point. This is not a comfortable place to start a book because social scientists generally seek parsimony and clarity. However, we must recognize that one can simultaneously embrace two contradictory truths. This project has forced me to come to terms, for example, with the fact that Grace Mugabe in Zimbabwe could be someone who simultaneously fought to improve the status of women *and* used the women's movement to serve her own personal ambitions of claiming power. She used patriarchy to benefit herself, played patronage and factional politics to suit her own power grab, *and* was marginalized as a woman and labeled a "whore" in the process. Does this mean that all women leaders in Zimbabwe did this? No. However, some women in the ruling party were complicit with the authoritarian agenda of the ruling party and simultaneously challenged aspects of it. However, many of the demands of independent women's organizations would not have succeeded without the cooperation of ruling party women and men. Often people ask with an element of suspicion, Were the women's rights policies adopted under authoritarian rule transformative from a feminist point of view, fundamentally reshaping norms and institutions? To answer this question adequately, one has to move away from simplistic zero-sum categories and think more about policies as part of an incremental process of empowerment, not just in autocracies but also in democracies. Rarely, even in democratic regimes, are policies totally transformative.

Most studies of authoritarian regimes and women's representation focus on individual countries or involve global cross-national studies. However, only some look at women's leadership at the regional level, as I do in this book, where one can see more clearly how patterns of representation and women's status diverge, thus allowing for middle-range theorizing.

This book is grounded in the literature on African politics, gender, political institutions, parties, and party systems. It shows the similarities and differences between authoritarian and democratic regimes. In particular, I focus on the persistence of dominant hegemonic parties in Africa, in both authoritarian and some democratic regimes, which results in similar outcomes in terms of levels of women's representation. However, democratic and authoritarian regimes differ in important ways, especially when it comes to the treatment of the opposition.

The book situates the cases historically to show how authoritarian regimes came to be interested in women's representation in Africa and how their strategies have changed over time. It also looks comparatively to show why some authoritarian regimes have adopted this strategy while others have not. The book looks not only at parliamentary representation at the national level but at other forms of leadership at the subnational level, within the cabinet, and in other areas. In all these ways, the book differs from existing literature on authoritarianism and women's rights.

Finally, this study looks at why women's rights are pursued in contexts in which political rights and civil liberties are generally weak. Many believe erroneously that women's movements don't have much impact in such contexts and that these regimes are not interested in women's rights. Indeed, not all authoritarian regimes are interested, and many actively repress civil society, including women's rights activists. However, women's movements have some impact, even in many of these restrictive environments. This is partly because the regimes seek internal legitimacy by promoting women leaders, but it is also because many of these countries seek international approval, which some believe assists foreign trade, foreign aid, military, and other international support. This is especially true where regimes have a problematic human rights record to address. I show how these factors affect the promotion of women leaders. Also, the political costs of adopting women's rights are less than the costs of ensuring civil rights and clean elections, which might threaten the regime more directly. I look at the conditions under which women's rights are adopted when human rights are otherwise not a priority.

1
Introduction

The face of African politics has changed significantly since the mid-1990s as more women have entered politics. Women's movements and organizations have successfully lobbied for and won more leadership roles for women. At the same time, this has created a conundrum in authoritarian countries, which constitute the majority of African regimes. These successes in attaining leadership roles for women help strengthen the very regimes that violate human and women's rights in other ways. This creates a paradox that is not easily resolved.

On the one hand, it makes sense for women's rights activists to demand power because, with power, they are in a better position to influence women's rights and democratic reforms. On the other hand, women's increased representation may simultaneously enhance the longevity and entrenchment of the ruling party in authoritarian countries. Moreover, it is often the case that women activists find themselves persecuted by the same autocratic regime that purportedly claims to support women's rights.

By women's rights, I am referring to a subset of human rights that are fundamental to people identifying as women. These include the right to live without violence and discrimination regardless of gender or sexuality, the right to be educated and have access to quality health care, the right to control one's body, the right to freedom of movement, the right to own property, the right to vote and run for office, and the right to earn fair and equal wages, among many other concerns.

It is widely recognized today that there is little difference between authoritarian and democratic regimes when it comes to women's political representation in Africa (Hughes and Tripp 2015; Stockemer 2011; Tripp and Kang 2008) and globally (Kenworthy and Malami 1999; Luciak 2005, Paxton 1997; Reynolds 1999; Stockemer 2009). In Africa, authoritarian regimes have successfully promoted women as leaders, adopted women's rights provisions more generally, and made extensive constitutional and legislative reforms, as explored in Chapter 10.

Why African Autocracies Promote Women as Leaders. Aili Mari Tripp, Oxford University Press. © Oxford University Press (2025). DOI: 10.1093/9780197829004.003.0002

For example, one authoritarian country, Rwanda, has the highest rate of legislative representation of women in the world (63.8 percent) and the highest level of female cabinet representation in Africa (55 percent). Women also hold 40 percent of the local executive committee positions in Rwanda. In Tunisia, President Kaïs Saied suspended the Parliament and the constitution, fired the prime minister, and then in 2021 appointed a woman, Najia Bouden, as prime minister. In Uganda, after a brutal election in which the opposition was severely repressed, President Yoweri Museveni appointed women to the positions of vice president, prime minister, and deputy prime minister. The Parliament—which is dominated by Museveni's party—elected a female speaker of the house after the untimely death of her predecessor. None of these appointments and electoral outcomes in Rwanda, Tunisia, or Uganda is an accident, nor is the fact that they are taking place primarily in authoritarian contexts in Africa.

However, these countries are far from alone. Zimbabwe, Burundi, Ethiopia, South Sudan, and Somalia—all authoritarian regimes—have passed constitutions with extensive provisions for women's rights. Moreover, authoritarian countries like Rwanda, Burundi, and Eswatini have some of the lowest gender gaps in education, health, political empowerment, and economic opportunities, according to the World Economic Forum (2024). While it might be easy to explain away legal measures like the use of gender quotas as mere window dressing, similar outcomes in these other areas are harder to dismiss.

This book is a comparative Africa-wide study that examines why authoritarian regimes promote women as leaders, what strategies they adopt to increase women's representation, the conditions under which authoritarian regimes are more likely to advance women, and the consequences of women's political representation for regime longevity as well as for women's rights and welfare. I focus on Uganda, Rwanda, and Zimbabwe as authoritarian countries and Morocco and Mauritania as semiauthoritarian countries (also referred to as electoral autocracies or hybrid regimes). I include comparisons with Botswana and Namibia as democracies.

The book looks at why the longer authoritarian countries have been in power and the more entrenched their ruling parties are, the more inclined they are to promote women's rights. It focuses on state strategies that instrumentalize women leaders—that is, using the advancement of women representatives for purposes other than to advance gender equality. It also looks at the role of women's movements in pressing for women's rights reforms. The book shows how women's movement successes in gaining leadership positions for women in authoritarian contexts may paradoxically end up strengthening and legitimizing a regime that violates human rights. Women's rights activists risk being co-opted or repressed by a regime that seeks virtually total dominance over its adversaries. Moreover, the state claims the authority to control how it implements women's rights and may do so in ways that only sometimes take into consideration women's interests.

This chapter investigates the reasons behind autocracies' promotion of women leaders in Africa and beyond. It engages with existing scholarship on women's leadership in authoritarian regimes and argues that the advancement of women in African autocracies is primarily driven by the imperative to maintain power, maintain legitimacy, and solidify the dominance of ruling parties. After outlining the various strategies that enable this process, the chapter highlights how the instrumentalization of women became a key tactic for party entrenchment—particularly following the introduction of multiparty politics, the resolution of major conflicts across the continent, and the evolution of international gender norms beginning in the mid-1990s and accelerating in the early 2000s. Women's movements capitalized on these openings to demand increased political representation and broader rights. The chapter also examines the constraints on promoting women leaders, considers alternative explanations for women's political representation in Africa, details the study's research design and methodology, and concludes with an overview of the book's structure.

Prior Literature

A substantial body of comparative and cross-national research on gender and politics examines women's parliamentary representation without reference to authoritarianism, often with an explicit focus solely on democracies. In a somewhat neutral fashion, this literature often focuses on descriptive representation of women as a dependent or independent variable. It tends to overlook the issue of underlying nondemocratic motives for promoting women as leaders in authoritarian and hybrid regimes and their consequences for women.

Schwindt-Bayer and Mishler (2005, 415) explain why the neutral treatment of women's representation might be the case: "Formal representative structures may exist in nondemocracies, but they are usually subsumed by authoritarian leaders and do not operate as functioning representative institutions. Therefore, there is little reason to examine representation in nondemocratic states." When women's representation in autocracies is discussed, it is dismissed as serving only symbolic purposes, as in the socialist states (Waylen 2007). As Pitkin (1967, 2–3) suggested, the expectation is that political representation is closely linked to democracy and that democracy can deliver better outcomes for women's representation than authoritarian regimes. Moreover, survey data shows that people are more likely to value gender equality in democracies than in autocracies (Inglehart and Norris 2003a). Democratization is seen as strengthening parties and institutions, which facilitates women's representation (Thomas and Wilcox 2005). Some also have strong normative expectations that since women are equal citizens in democracies, they should share in public decision-making (Tremblay 2007).

Most studies of authoritarian regimes and women's representation in Africa focus on individual countries (Allan 2019; Burnet 2012; Disney 2008; Kang 2015; Wing 2008), but they do not focus on regime type per se. Numerous global and Africa-wide cross-national studies of women's representation reference regime type (Kenworthy and Malami 1999; Hughes and Tripp 2015; Luciak 2005; Paxton 1997; Reynolds 1999; Stockemer 2011; Tripp and Kang 2008; Viterna et al. 2007; Yoon 2004), but with only a few exceptions (e.g., Kroeger and Kang 2022; Stockemer 2009), this is not the focus of most of these studies. This book looks at women's leadership in Africa at the regional level over time, which is not as common in book-length studies. This perspective allows one to see more clearly specific patterns of variance in women's representation and women's status, thus allowing for middle-range theorizing.

This book contributes to several literatures. It complicates the view that "women's equality is being rolled back at the same time that authoritarianism is on the rise" (Chenoweth and Marks 2022). The book shows that the story is more complex in countries that use women's rights to strengthen authoritarian rule. Certainly, the rise of illiberalism in countries like Hungary is going on hand in hand with a rollback in women's rights, particularly reproductive and lesbian, gay, bisexual, transgender, and queer (LGBTQ) rights (Roggeband and Krizsán 2024). In the United States, the repeal of abortion rights by the Supreme Court in 2022 is also seen as part of a more general illiberal trend of using democratized institutions for authoritarian ends (Erdman and Bergallo 2024). Similarly, Russia, China, and Iran often adopt visibly aggressive policies that undermine women's status, taking aim at women's rights activists.

Most authoritarian countries, however, have been found historically and today to promote women's rights to one degree or another, as we have seen in so many socialist countries and African autocracies. Even the United Arab Emirates (UAE), an autocratic monarchy—and a seemingly unlikely advocate for women's rights—seeks to become a "shining example" of gender equality to the world by appointing women to half the seats in Parliament and one-third of the cabinet positions.

The book draws on, but also diverges somewhat from, those who focus on "genderwashing" state strategies and regard the adoption of women's rights by autocrats as simply another set of top-down initiatives that lack citizen input (Bjarnegård and Zetterberg 2022; Noh 2024). Bjarnegård and Zetterberg (2022) focus on three types of legitimation strategies: ones that are used to manipulate electoral processes to give the appearance of inclusivity while controlling the political opposition, reforms to boost the regime's image to attract foreign aid and reduce external pressures for democratic reform, and finally gender-based projects aimed to appease citizens and co-opt civil society, portraying the government as responsive without making real democratic reforms.

I argue that not all women's rights reforms in authoritarian countries are hollow or devoid of citizen input, especially when reforms in education, health, economic, and political empowerment are considered. I look at the interaction between the women's movement and the state and the ways in which women's movements have fought for women's representation. I look at the consequences of these reforms for regime longevity. The reforms may be underfunded, and their implementation may be lackluster, especially when it comes to accounting for concerns of the women's movement. State capacity is often weak. However, comparatively authoritarian countries in Africa generally are not worse than most democracies in this regard (Donno and Kreft 2019; Komer and Tripp 2025). Moreover, democracies also engage in forms of instrumentalization of women's rights, although they may differ in their goals. It is difficult to interpret the exact intent of leaders in adopting women's rights, especially since their goals may serve multiple purposes.

The main problem with the way authoritarians instrumentalize women's rights is not that they are trying to deceive others with their gender policies. Instead, it has to do with the need for authoritarian regimes to repress the opposition and suppress civil liberties and political rights, using women and women's rights to legitimize and entrench a regime that does this.

There is a strong emphasis in the literature on authoritarianism on the ways in which leaders seek support internationally for their gender policies (Donno et al. 2022) and, in particular, quota legislation (Bush 2011; Bush and Zetterberg 2021, Bush and Zetterberg 2024; Edgell 2017). Donno et al. (2022) find that international aid is related to women's rights legislation but not to politically costly areas like political pluralism, elections, or repression. This book looks primarily at the internal factors that give rise to the promotion of women leaders, although some attention is devoted to external factors in Part III, with the cases of Rwanda and Morocco. However, even in these countries, based on my case studies, it appears that the main factors giving rise to gender policy are internal.

The book also examines historical trajectories in Africa and beyond. The focus of the small but growing literature in this area has tended to treat the authoritarian instrumentalization of women as a recent phenomenon in response to United Nations (UN) policies starting in the 1990s. However, the Chinese Communist Party (CCP) had already adopted quotas as early as 1933. In 1935, the Turkish Republican People's Party of Atatürk set aside seats for eighteen women who were nominated to run for Parliament in a soft quota arrangement. From 1945 to 1985, on average, the socialist East Europe and the Soviet Union had more women in their parliaments than top-performing democratic countries in the Nordic countries. In Africa, populist President Thomas Sankara in Burkina Faso used women's rights in the 1980s to gain popularity in rhetoric and his policies. The 1990s heightened global awareness and interest in women's representation, but this was not a new phenomenon in authoritarian countries.

The book explains why certain types of autocracies in Africa—those with entrenched political parties that have remained in power for decades—are more likely to advance women as leaders. It shows how military autocracies and autocracies experiencing instability and coups are less likely to promote women leaders, as are regimes that alternate parties in power and hybrid regimes. Hybrid or electoral authoritarian regimes are neither fully authoritarian nor democratic. They combine elements of both and can lean toward being either semiauthoritarian or semidemocratic. They are ultimately authoritarian and correspond crudely to Freedom House's "partly free" categorization.

This study contrasts African democracies with authoritarian regimes in promoting women as leaders. Women may have more influence in democracies, but the impact of women in authoritarian regimes can also be consequential, as becomes evident in the case studies. This study shows how there isn't much difference between democracies and autocracies in Africa in terms of female descriptive representation in legislative and subnational governance bodies. Since 1980 there has been a small but growing gap between democracies and autocracies in the appointment of women to ministerial position. In other respects, particularly when it comes to human rights and the treatment of the opposition and even women activists, the two regime types are worlds apart. Moreover, those countries—both authoritarian and democratic—that advance women leaders are equally likely to improve other aspects of gender equality along key dimensions (e.g., education, health, economic empowerment). However, authoritarian regimes in Africa fare less well when it comes to LGBTQ and abortion rights.

Argument of the Book: Why African Autocracies Promote Women Leaders

Why do autocracies promote women leaders? Authoritarian leaders want to stay in power at all costs. Many states have become rather adept in using women leaders and various quota systems to achieve this goal. Hegemonic ruling parties have been able to entrench themselves in power. Authoritarian ruling parties with the longest staying power also tend to have the highest rates of female political representation. While the literature shows that more competitive democracies seem to do better in terms of women's representation globally, for authoritarian regimes, it is the opposite: The ability of authoritarian dominant parties to constrain the opposition makes it easier to adopt women's rights (see Chapter 2).

This book looks at the variety of strategies authoritarian regimes have used to entrench themselves (see summary in Table 1.1). I argue that three major developments gave rise to significant numbers of women leaders in autocracies in Africa: the shift from one-party to multiparty rule in the early 1990s, the end of major conflicts starting in the early 1990s with the end of the Cold War, and changing international gender norms (see Figure 1.1). Although these regimes did not generally democratize, they liberalized aspects of their rule, as is evident in the case of Mauritania, which shifted from a military regime to an electoral semiauthoritarian regime and improved on some aspects of civil liberties and political rights. The ruling parties liberalized in ways that further legitimized and extended the duration of political parties in power.

It is not simply party entrenchment that explains the promotion of women as political representatives, since there was party entrenchment and regime institutionalization also under one-party rule. However, in this period prior to the 1990s, African autocracies did not promote women in large numbers to political office. They appointed a few wives and relatives of ruling party elite to leadership positions, generally placing them in key posts heading up women's wings and mass organizations tied to the ruling party or regime (e.g., the Better Life Movement in Nigeria, and the 31st December Movement in Ghana). Some female elite leaders served as willing beneficiaries of patronage in these positions and organizations, winning salary, opportunities to travel,

Table 1.1 Toward party entrenchment: Why women leaders are instrumentalized

	Economic	Political
International	Expand trade Encourage foreign direct investment Obtain foreign aid	Soften a country's image after civil war, jihadist activity, or military rule Seek legitimacy against a dismal human rights record Comply with international and regional targets for women's representation Indicate status to assert global or regional leadership
National	Expand industrial production Expand export-oriented agriculture Diversify the economy, especially in oil-based economies Increase childbirth to offset the effects of an aging population	Preserve/expand the vote share of the ruling party Expand patronage linkages, especially with key ethnic and religious groups Isolate extremist jihadists and Salafists Respond to women's movement pressures Increase favor among women voters Adhere to ideological principle of gender equality

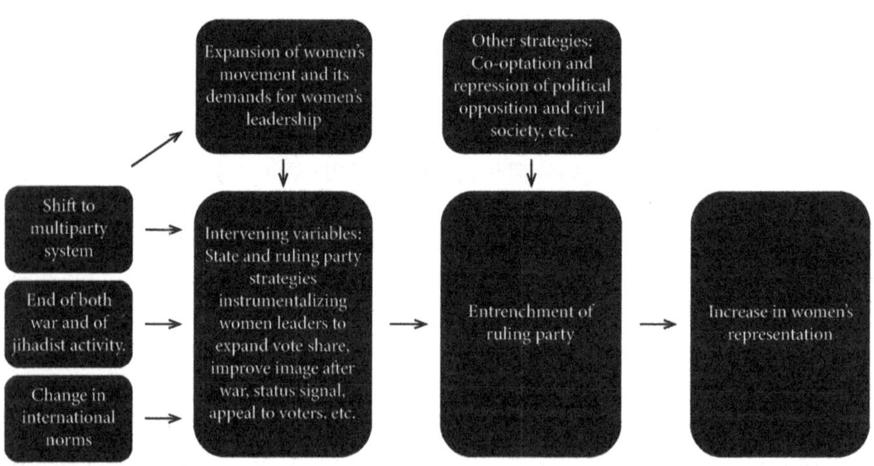

Figure 1.1 Instrumentalizing women leaders for party entrenchment

and other perks. Most of the women's organizations were fairly depoliticized, focusing primarily on developmental and educational activities, handicrafts, sports, and activities to encourage women to become better mothers and housewives. The women leaders may have also used women's organizations to build their powerbase of pro–ruling party voters, and sometimes even advancing policies that harmed women. For example, women leaders tied to the ruling party were complicit in the roundups of single women on the pretext of being prostitutes in Nigeria and Zimbabwe in the 1980s (Abdullah 1993; Dennis 1987). These women leaders promoted the regulation of women's morality in Niger by the Union des Femmes du Niger in the 1960s and in Zambia by the Women's League in Zambia in the 1980s (Cooper 1995; Geisler 1987).

It was not until the 1990s that we began to see strategies to instrumentalize women to compete in electoral politics, resulting in large increases of women in legislatures, local councils, cabinets, and other bodies. Women became more visible in party politics, even starting and leading parties and running for president in some countries. These changes were associated with the shift to multiparty politics, new pressures from women's movements and international agencies, the increased use of gender quotas, and the end of major conflicts.

The Instrumentalization of Women Leaders in Autocracies

In order to remain dominant, ruling parties often instrumentalized women leaders through the use of various strategies like reserved seats for women—a type of affirmative action quota—and appointments to key positions, all the while also attempting to co-opt them and repress women in the opposition. These strategies explain how the shift to a multiparty system, the end of war, and changes in international gender norms contributed to the entrenchment of hegemonic parties. To be clear, these were not the only strategies, but they contributed to this process.

Ruling parties have adopted a number of what I call intervening variables (e.g., efforts to expand vote share, improve regime image, status signal, and appeal to female voters) as stepping stones to the entrenchment of the ruling party and ensuring its hegemony (see Figure 1.1). These mechanisms explain underlying processes and provide a fuller, more detailed explanation of causal relationships.

Some authoritarian countries—though not all—have promoted women leaders and women's rights more generally for economic and/or political reasons through strategies to influence both international and domestic audiences. Countries have signaled their commitment to women leaders by adopting reserved seats or legislated candidate quotas. Others have made political appointments of women to ambassadorial and other prominent visible international positions, mainly targeting countries they wish to influence.

For example, the UAE aspires to become a model of gender equality to the rest of the world and is a major funder of UN Women. Some countries like Rwanda may organize or host global forums like those of the International Parliamentary Union to give greater visibility to their successes in placing women in legislatures, for example. They may promote women in sports to gain international visibility and seek global leadership of women in fields like the sciences, in which women have traditionally been marginalized. Many of these gains are advertised in speeches and press releases of key governmental representatives.

While these reforms may represent genuine gains for women, they can also serve other purposes that have little to do with women's advancement (Table 1.1). Regarding economic strategies, governments may seek international favor to expand trade and foreign direct investment (FDI), as Morocco has done. For others, the interest in boosting foreign aid, especially military aid, looms large, as is the case of Egypt, the largest recipient of US security aid in Africa until September 2022, when this aid was blocked because of human rights violations. Domestically, countries may also want to enhance women's status to increase women's labor productivity, improve key industrial or agricultural sectors, and diversify the economy, which are some of Rwanda's stated goals.

Political strategies are equally important. Globally, countries may seek to soften a country's image after civil war or military rule or as a result of jihadist activity, as we saw in Morocco. They may seek legitimacy against a problematic human rights record. They might virtue signal by showcasing women leaders to assert global or regional leadership (e.g., Rwanda). They may also wish to comply with international and regional targets for women's representation to avoid appearing as laggards. Domestically, authoritarian regimes may instrumentalize women leaders to preserve or expand the vote share of the ruling party, mainly through the use of quotas. Some seek to expand ruling coalitions, especially with key ethnic and religious groups, or they may use women's rights as a way of isolating extremist jihadists or Salafi elements. Finally, they might pursue strategies to increase favor among women voters, although, as Barnett (2023) has shown in the case of Morocco, citizens do not always correctly perceive these strategies and may believe that women's rights reforms are being imposed on a resistant public (Table 1.1).

It should be noted that democracies also instrumentalize women leaders and women's rights, as we see in a limited fashion in the case of Namibia (Chapter 9). This has been true historically in countries where women's rights have aligned with nationalist objectives. Improved child care, parental leave, and specialized training of women have been used as ways of expanding the workforce, which alleviates financial burdens of supporting an aging population (Esping-Anderson et al. 2002). It may also be harnessed to facilitate increased fertility rates in the face of a shrinking population. According to such utilitarian arguments, employing women taps into the talent of a useful and educated workforce and helps curb social exclusion and poverty.

Entrenchment of Dominant Parties

The aforementioned strategies are adopted with the aim of entrenching ruling parties. Entrenched parties in authoritarian contexts are parties that have been in power for at least three electoral cycles or longer. They are also more likely to promote women as leaders (Figure 1.1). As the dominant parties moved from a one-party to a multiparty dispensation, their vote share diminished. The loss of vote share meant they needed to find new ways to maintain vote share. They also needed to find new ways to shore up their rural base, which was generally their primary source of support. The need to find ways to increase legislative representatives happened mostly in nondemocratic countries but also in a handful of democracies. However, in democracies, the need to maintain vote share is less urgent than in autocracies. Moreover, as of this writing, we are beginning to see the dominance of entrenched parties in democracies being seriously challenged in countries like Namibia and South Africa. In democratic Botswana, the ruling party of five decades was toppled in the 2024 elections by an opposition party.

Sartori (1976) defines a dominant one-party system as one in which parties or a political group claim more than three consecutive electoral wins (with a majority of votes in coalition governments). I consider these to be entrenched parties. They generally have higher levels of party institutionalization, which refers to the durability of a party's organizational structures and its ability to function as a stable and effective organization, with clear rules and procedures for succession and decision-making. Generally, clear rules in a party benefit newcomers like women, who can more easily gain support within a party than those with opaque, changing, and arbitrary rules. However, the institutionalization of parties in Africa is weak, even in dominant-party contexts. Yet these parties still manage to remain entrenched by weakening and repressing the opposition. The use of nonviolent means to control the opposition, like the use of reserved seats for women, lessens the cost of maintaining power. The staying power and continued dominance of entrenched parties help explain why women and other newcomers to politics might align themselves with such parties.

The Shift from One-Party Rule to Multipartyism

African countries democratized after the early 1990s as they moved away from single-party to multiparty rule, expanded political space for civil society, experienced declines in military rule, and improved political rights and civil liberties overall. While countries liberalized politically, only a few became democracies. Most remained either semiauthoritarian or fully authoritarian while adopting the trappings of electoral democracy by holding elections. This allowed parties to operate semifreely and opened some space for civil society and freedom of speech, regardless of how limited or unpredictable it was.

The emergence of multipartyism in the early 1990s set in motion a set of dynamics that forced authoritarian regimes to increase vote share to remain in power and become entrenched. One of these measures involved promoting women as leaders through quotas, often through reserved seats, which are exclusively used by authoritarian regimes in Africa. In a move to expand patronage networks, authoritarian countries also expanded the number of districts to increase female representation without excluding men. The shift toward multipartyism led to new independent women's organizations and movements, creating additional internal pressures for reform in both authoritarian and democratic countries. At times, these parties also used co-optation, violence, and repression against their opponents, including women leaders.

Autocracy in Africa

However, by 2005, the tides began to turn, and levels of democracy started declining globally, as democratization leveled off in Africa. A few countries like Côte d'Ivoire, Mauritania, and Liberia improved their levels of democracy after 2005. But many more countries in Africa significantly declined in levels of democracy between 2005 and 2024, including Benin, Burkina Faso, Burundi, Congo Brazzaville, Djibouti, Gabon, Mali, Mozambique, Niger, and Tanzania (Freedom House 2024). Overall, since 2005, there has been a slight increase in authoritarian regimes, while semiauthoritarian countries increased up to 1995 and then declined (see Figure 1.2). More generally, the picture is one in which democratization reached equilibrium after 2010. By 2024, 16 percent (nine countries) in Africa could be considered democratic, 36 percent (twenty-one countries) had hybrid regimes, and 48 percent (twenty-seven countries) were authoritarian, according to Freedom House data.

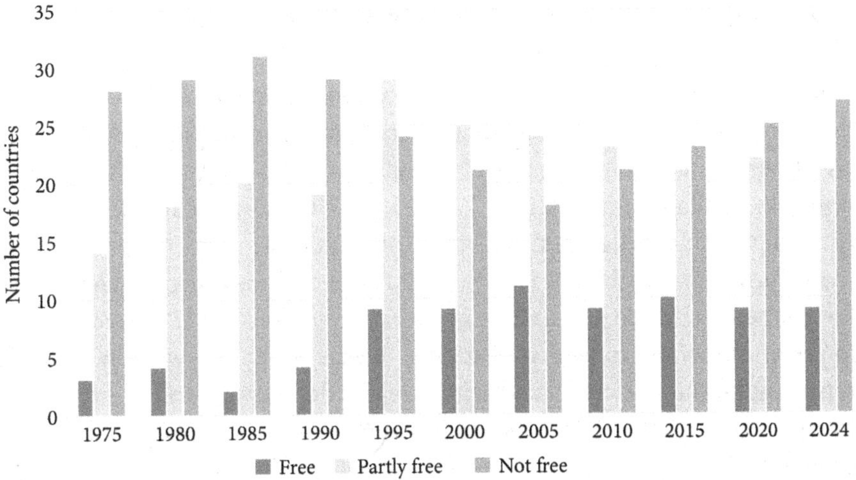

Figure 1.2 Democracy status of African countries by regime type, including North Africa (1975–2024)
Source: Freedom House (2024).

Based on a breakdown of V-Dem (2024) data, electoral integrity was the area most likely to be attacked by authoritarian and semiauthoritarian regimes in Africa. Authoritarian countries experienced increasing repression of civil society, erosion of freedom of expression, harassment and censorship of media and social media, suppression of the political opposition, and increased corruption. There were also renewed efforts to regulate civil society organizations through nongovernmental oversight boards in countries like Malawi, Zimbabwe, and Nigeria.

There are other indications of an erosion of democratic institutions after 2014. After a steady drop in attempted and successful military coups after the 1990s, there has been a trend of increasing military coups since 2020 in Chad, Guinea, Mali, Burkina Faso, Gabon, and Sudan and self-coups in Tunisia in 2021 and Zimbabwe in 2017. Increasing political polarization in Libya, Tunisia, Ethiopia, Egypt, Somalia, Benin, Guinea Bissau, and Sierra Leone has accompanied autocratization. Moreover, there have been continuing efforts to expand presidential term limits through legal means. From April 2000 to July 2018, presidential limits were changed forty-seven times in twenty-eight countries, with at least six failed attempted changes (Mohlamenyane 2021). These trends indicate undemocratic efforts to expand the executive and curtail the legislature's role.

Autocracy and Women's Representation in Africa

While there has been a persistence of authoritarianism and even a slight decline in overall levels of democratization in terms of political rights and civil liberties after 2005, the rate of women's political representation has nevertheless increased (see Figures 1.3 and 1.4). The percentage of women in African parliaments has increased over threefold since 1995. According to the Inter-Parliamentary Union (IPU), by 2024, the average percentage of seats for women in Africa (including in North Africa) was 24.9 percent in the lower house. Numerous cross-national studies show that women's political representation is not correlated with levels of democracy, and it is occurring irrespective of levels of democratization in Africa (Stockemer 2009; Tripp and Kang 2008).

Of the nine African countries Freedom House labeled as "free" in 2022—countries that I would consider democracies—women held on average 25.2 percent of the seats in the lower house of Parliament. In the twenty-seven "not free" countries, which I regard as authoritarian, women held, on average, 27.2 percent of the seats. In the twenty-one partly free or semiauthoritarian countries, the percentage was 22.4 percent.

These patterns of female representation extend globally. In the 2021 Listening to Leaders Survey, leaders and policymakers were asked about their priorities regarding Sustainable Development Goals (SDGs). Among leaders in nondemocratic countries, 25.8 percent identified gender equality as a

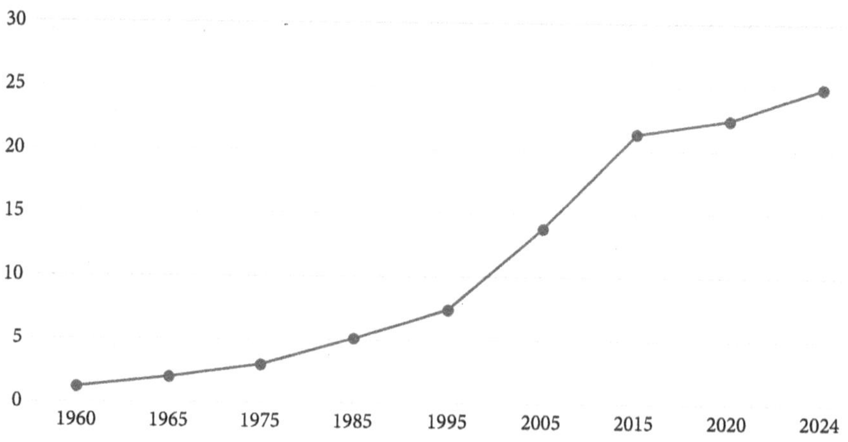

Figure 1.3 Women's legislative representation in African parliaments, including North Africa (1960–2024) (%)
Source: IPU (2024).

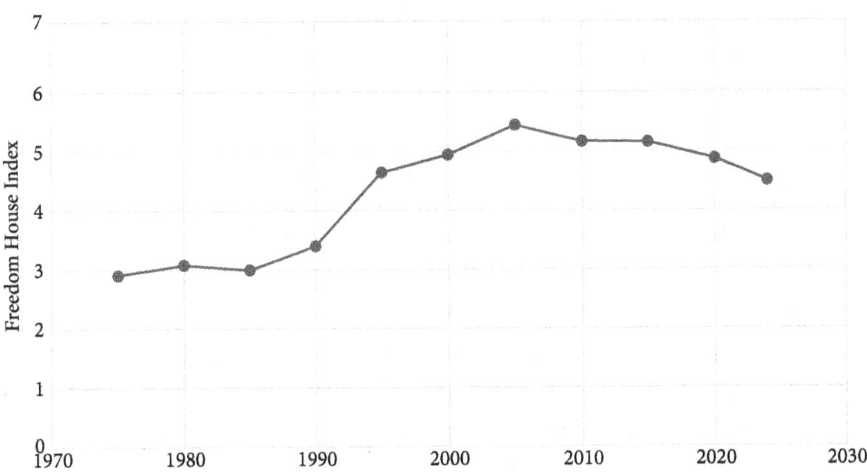

Figure 1.4 Democratization in Africa (1975–2024)

Note: The scale (0–7) is inverted, so higher average scores represent more political rights and civil liberties. The figure includes North Africa.
Source: Freedom House (2024).

priority, while 29.1 percent of leaders in democracies did so.[1] In sub-Saharan Africa, the percentage of leaders who ranked gender equality as a high priority was greater than in other world regions except for the Middle East and North Africa (MENA), which had the highest percentage of leaders ranking gender equality as a priority.

What explains the simultaneous and potentially contradictory trend of women's increased presence in political institutions? Understanding the nature of contemporary autocracies and African regimes more generally is critical to explaining this phenomenon. A less violent and ideological form of competitive authoritarianism that often mimics democracy through institutions like elections has been spreading worldwide, including in Africa. This form of authoritarianism emerged after 1990 as autocratic countries liberalized politically in Africa.

These electoral autocracies may be free of massive fraud. Still, incumbents skew the outcome through a host of other tactics, including abuse of state resources, denying the opposition media coverage, harassing opposition candidates, and even jailing, exiling, or murdering them (Levitsky and Way 2002). Guriev and Treisman (2019) argue that rather than terrorizing or indoctrinating their citizens, autocrats sometimes use the manipulation of information on economic performance and the provision of public services to

[1] https://docs.aiddata.org/reports/listening-to-leaders-2021.html.

soften their image. In this book, part of this sprucing up of the authoritarian image also has involved using women's rights and women leaders to divert attention away from the less savory and more repressive sides of their rule.

Women Leaders and Strategies to Increase Vote Share

One of the main strategies of authoritarian regimes to remain in power includes efforts increase vote share. While competition is accepted, it is almost exclusively under conditions in which the incumbent hegemonic party wins. With the introduction of multipartyism after the 1990s, ruling parties suddenly had to contend with the need to maintain vote share to remain in power. One strategy they pursued, among many others, was the promotion of women leaders in legislative bodies through reserved seats, which they could control. As a result, the face of African politics changed dramatically as more women entered politics after the 1990s.

As of 2024, there were five times more women in Parliament and three times more women ministers than in 1985. Women hold over 50 percent of ministerial posts in Rwanda (54 percent) and Guinea Bissau (50 percent) and over 40 percent of the posts in South Africa, Ethiopia, Seychelles, Mozambique, Malawi, and Angola. The percentage of women in cabinets increased after 2000. African cabinets have proportionately more women foreign ministers than any other world region. In fact, over one-third (ten out of twenty-nine) of all female foreign ministers globally are from Africa. Women are Speakers of the House in one-third of the fifty-four parliaments of Africa (including North Africa), which exceeds the world average of 20 percent. Since 2000, more women have been running for president, more women have been appointed as prime ministers, and more women have been heading parties (Tripp 2021).

Some of these changes can be explained by the opening to political liberalization after the early 1990s and the need for dominant ruling parties to cope with increased competition by maintaining vote share in the Parliament. One way they did this was through the adoption of reserved seat quotas. Before 1995, only six African countries (11 percent) had adopted some kind of quota, while by 2024, 74 percent had a quota. Most countries in Africa adopted quotas after the UN Fourth World Conference on Women, held in Beijing in 1995. The women's leadership goals articulated by this conference were echoed in UN Security Council Resolution 1325, which called for women to be represented in all peacebuilding operations. These goals were incorporated into the UN Millennium Development Goals (MDGs) and targets of the African Union, Southern African Development Community (SADC), and other regional and international bodies.

One strategy of hegemonic parties to maintain control used primarily by autocracies was the expansion of the size of the legislature. In some countries, this was done under the pretext of increasing the proportion of women and other constituencies like youth and people with disabilities in Parliament. The average African legislature increased in size over threefold since 1990: 88.8 percent of African countries have increased seats in legislatures, and 37.7 percent of the countries in the region added an upper house since 1990 (Gerzso and Van de Walle 2022). The decision to increase legislative seats generally originated in the executive branch and has been resisted by the opposition in the legislature. Gerzso and Van de Walle (2022) showed that this aims to weaken the legislature as an institution and expand executive control over it by extending patronage, particularly in authoritarian contexts.

Another strategy for dominant parties to remain in power is the use of reserved seats for women. Many authoritarian party leaders believe they must find a way to increase female representation in a multiparty context without threatening incumbent males, and reserved seats are one way of doing this. Reserved seats are a percentage or number of seats set aside for women candidates of any political party. Democracies generally have voluntary party quotas (in which any political party can introduce a quota for their own lists in elections) and/or legislated candidate quotas (a quota mandated by the constitutions and/or electoral law requiring that all parties have a minimum number or percentage of women candidates). Autocracies and hybrid regimes may adopt party or legislated quotas, but they are the only countries that adopt reserved seats in Africa. This is no accident. Those in power can more easily manipulate the reserved seat systems. Thus, at least sixteen nondemocratic African countries have reserved seats. Reserved seats are one way of eliminating competition between incumbent males and new contenders like women since women primarily compete among themselves for the seats that are dedicated to women.

Authoritarian ruling parties have also adopted other extralegal means of ensuring electoral dominance. Unlike in democracies, ruling parties in authoritarian regimes often use violence to maintain dominance. Violence against the opposition, including opposition women, is one way for the ruling party to ensure its continued dominance. They also de-campaign opposition women candidates in elections and create a political environment of fear as they seek to crush the opposition, sometimes not only figuratively at the ballot box but physically as well.

The case of Uganda (Chapter 3) illustrates these dynamics well. Like many other authoritarian countries, Uganda promoted women's rights and women leaders in the late 1980s. However, it stepped up efforts as part of a strategy to maintain vote share after adopting multipartyism in 2005. It increased the number of women in reserved seats when it expanded the number of districts, thus augmenting the appointments of women in Parliament. The government thus used a variety of strategies to advance women political leaders, simultaneously responding to pressures from the women's movement while seeking to ensure the continued dominance of the ruling party. As the chapter on Uganda shows, opposition women have turned out to be the biggest losers in this process, particularly in gaining reserved seats set aside for women. The discrepancy between the levels of legislative representation of women in the opposition parties relative to opposition male parliamentarians is quite significant, particularly in countries with reserved seats (Table 2.8). It underscores an important feature of authoritarianism in Africa today: The political beneficiaries of reserved seats are almost exclusively women aligned with the ruling party.

Women brought in through quotas or reserved seats are not necessarily different from other women in Parliament. Valdini (2019) points out that "just because women are used strategically, this does not mean that they are unqualified." For example, studies have shown that quota women in Uganda are no different in qualifications from women in open seats, nor are they different from male candidates (Josefsson 2014; O'Brien 2012). There is no shortage of qualified women, even in poorer countries with low female literacy rates. Similarly, the women's movements and coalitions that have pressed for these reforms do not see them as simply a farce, although many see the dangers. Even when women are brought in for utilitarian reasons, they can and have used their positions to promote women's rights, if only for symbolic purposes and as encouragement for other women to run for office and advance themselves in other ways.

Internal Pressures from Women's Movements

The opening up of political space after the 1990s gave rise to new autonomous women's movements in Africa, which, even in authoritarian contexts like Niger, Rwanda, Mozambique, Mali, Sudan, Uganda, and Cameroon, were critical in pressing for women's rights reforms and women's leadership (Burnet 2012; Disney 2008; Kang 2015;Tønnessen and al-Nagar 2013; Tripp et al. 2009; Wing 2008). There appear to be more women in leadership roles in authoritarian countries where women's movements have actively pressed for such changes.

Although this book focuses on state strategies, it also looks at the ways in which women's movements made demands for women's representation and political inclusion with the opening of political space after the 1990s. With the rise of multipartyism, the large mass organizations tied to political parties declined in importance as a wide variety of independent women's organizations representing diverse interests and political tendencies emerged after the 1990s. These new organizations were often a major source of pressure to adopt quotas and increase female representation at different levels of government. They were better resourced than the old mass organizations as they had access to donor funds. Many had leadership training and set goals to increase women's presence in politics. These organizations had greater leverage because they were autonomous from the state and from the ruling party. They selected their own leaders, had their own funds, and had agendas that were not tied to party agendas. They also were able to build coalitions across party lines and across ethnic and other divisions.

The opening of political space allowed for the formation of new women's coalitions in Africa, many of which demanded an increase in women's political representation through the adoption of quotas and promoted leadership training for women (Kang and Tripp 2018). Using a data set of civil society coalitions in fifty African countries (1989–2014), Alice Kang and I show that specific types of mobilization, often multiethnic in character, lead to the faster adoption of quotas. This correlation holds when controlling for international aid and involvement of international women's movements and for whether countries recently emerged out of major armed conflict, complementing recent scholarship that highlights global influences.

Although these coalitions have had a significant impact, the women's movement has often been limited by the entrenched parties, which represent more traditional interests around contentious issues. There has been pushback from ruling parties, for example, when it comes to land and property rights, inheritance rights, abortion, LGBTQ rights, and personal status law. There has also been resistance to policy reforms around marital rape, decriminalizing homosexuality, and abortion.

The case of Zimbabwe (Chapter 4) illustrates the importance of women's movements in pressing for women's rights and leadership. Zimbabwe is an authoritarian country with a strong military presence. It has a repressive government that flagrantly violates human rights and has limited political space for civil society and women's organizations. Even though Zimbabwe was one of the most repressive countries in Africa under President Mugabe, it managed to pass a constitution in 2013 that provided extensive rights to women. These reforms were heavily influenced by an active women's movement, which got 75 percent of its demands incorporated into the constitution. Women in independent associations worked across party lines together with civil society in making these reforms, including a provision for adopting reserved seats for women. Women's movement efforts were bolstered by pressures to maintain vote share. Zimbabwe had been a hybrid regime since independence and took a turn toward full-blown authoritarianism in 2000. Only when the ruling party, ZANU-PF, faced a formidable challenge to its dominance from the opposition in the 2008 elections did it introduce women's rights reforms and promote women as leaders. The constitutional reforms resulted in a significant jump in the representation of women in Parliament from 15 percent to 32 percent in the 2013 elections after introducing reserved seats. With ZANU-PF further entrenched as an authoritarian ruling party facing competition for vote share from an opposition party, it needed to take measures to shut down the opposition to preserve its dominance. Supporting women's rights was one of these measures.

Postconflict Dynamics

The end of the Cold War resulted in the conclusion of many long-standing conflicts, which created opportunities for increased women's representation in postconflict settings (Figure 1.5). These opportunity structures included the establishment of peace accords, constitutional reforms, and electoral reforms, and they were primarily in authoritarian settings. Although much has been written about the relationship between conflict and women's leadership in Africa, the authoritarian character of these regimes has rarely been studied.

In addition to the need to maintain vote share in multiparty contexts, there are other reasons why authoritarian countries are especially keen to promote women leaders. Postconflict authoritarian countries experienced sharper and earlier increases in women's political representation than authoritarian countries that had not experienced major civil conflict. The countries with the biggest jumps in female legislative representation, of 23–24 percent, were primarily postconflict countries or countries that experienced major upheavals, such as Uganda, Burundi, and Rwanda. Of the top ten countries with the smallest gender gap for political participation in Africa, according to the Global Gender Gap Index (GGGI), seven are postconflict countries. Of the top ten countries in Africa in IPU rankings, eight are postconflict countries,

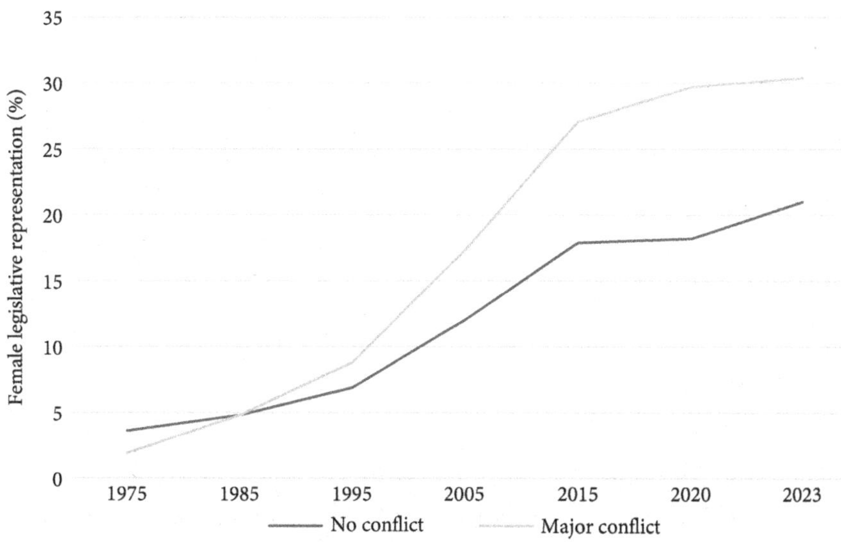

Figure 1.5 Prior conflict and female legislative representation in Africa
Source: IPU (2024).

highlighting the importance of the impact of conflict on women's representation. Quantitative analyses further underscored these observations (Hughes 2009; Hughes and Tripp 2015).

Some postconflict countries increased women's representation over the course of one or two elections. South Sudan was the most recent postconflict country to exhibit this pattern. Following a referendum, the new nation became independent after breaking away from Sudan in 2011. Women now claim 32 percent of the legislative seats and one-third of the ministerial positions, and the speaker of the house and the vice president are women, following postconflict patterns found elsewhere.

This study builds on prior comparative research on women's rights in postconflict Africa (Tripp 2015; Hughes and Tripp 2015) and beyond (Anderson and Swiss 2014; Berry 2018; Hughes 2009). According to my 2015 study, which includes case studies of Angola, Uganda, and Liberia, these patterns are particularly visible in Africa because so many countries—at least nineteen—came out of major conflict after the 1990s and the first decade of the 2000s. However, the pattern was evident before the 1990s, with the end of the liberation wars in the former Portuguese colonies of Angola, Mozambique, and Guinea Bissau, which had higher levels of female representation in the late 1970s than other African countries at the time. Many countries that came out of major conflict have expanded women's rights and political leadership faster

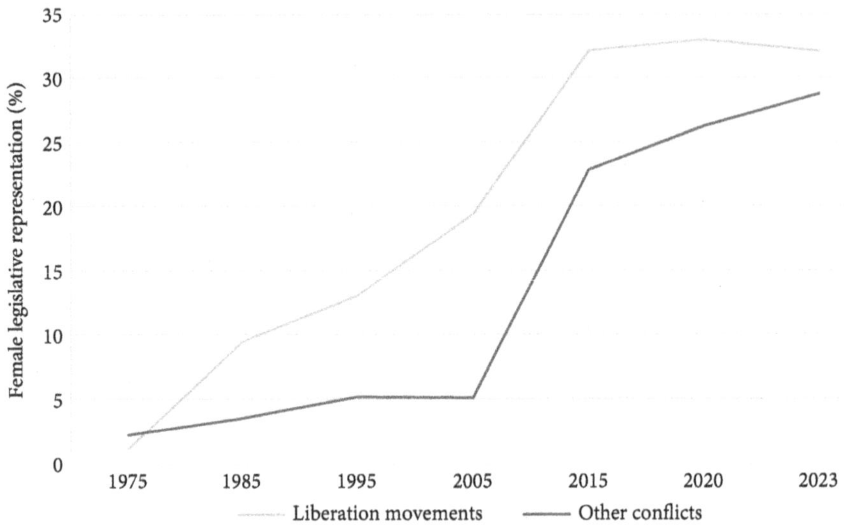

Figure 1.6 Left-leaning liberation movements and female legislative representation in Africa
Source: IPU (2023).

and earlier than countries that had not experienced major conflict in Africa, particularly countries that had armed liberation movements (Figure 1.6). For example, the African countries that first embraced parity in cabinets were all postconflict countries: Rwanda, Ethiopia, Mozambique, and Uganda. They have had substantially higher rates of legislative representation and more women in the executive. The first elected woman president in Africa in 2005 was Ellen Johnson Sirleaf in Liberia, a country that had just come out of a major war. Three factors can account for these differences between postconflict and other countries.

First, the decline of major conflict resulted in changes in political elites, which opened up possibilities for new political actors to assert themselves. Much of the early postconflict effect can be explained by left-leaning liberation movements that ended colonial rule and apartheid. Their impact was especially important from 1985 to 2015 as the consequences of the end of the independence wars began to be felt in constitutions and legislation pertaining to women's quotas.

Second, the decline of conflict created opportunity structures such as peace negotiations and constitution-making exercises that allowed women activists to press for a women's rights agenda and increased representation. Many of these initiatives were funded by UN agencies and foreign donors, allowing them to influence the introduction of gender-related provisions into the various processes.

Third, women's experiences during war gave them common cause. They mobilized around these concerns through their autonomous women's movements. The end of conflict also disrupted traditional gender roles and relations and incentivized women to demand greater rights and representation.

The case of Uganda (Chapter 3) illustrates the postconflict impacts that became especially visible after 2000, when more countries emerged out of significant conflict in Africa. The ruling party, led by Yoweri Museveni, took over the country in 1986, ending a period of military rule and conflict. The big jump in women's legislative representation for women occurred in 1989 in Uganda, and women also became more visible in ministerial positions and in subnational local councils. Museveni and his National Resistance Movement (NRM) adopted reserved seats for women in the national legislative body and within subnational local councils. The NRM adopted this quota before adopting the 1995 Beijing Platform of Action of the United Nations, which spurred countries worldwide to increase women's political representation. In fact, the NRM had already introduced quotas in local Resistance Councils while they were fighting prior to their takeover of the country in 1986. The Ugandan case thus underscores the independent impact of the end of conflict beyond international pressures, something Melanie Hughes and I also found in a cross-national statistical study (Hughes and Tripp 2015). The NRM's promotion of women in politics was part of its strategy to appeal to women in rural areas, where it garnered most of its support.

It should be noted that the postconflict patterns generally are not found during conflict. Countries that are in the midst of conflict or experiencing various forms of instability, such as persistent coups, do not have the wherewithal to focus on enhancing women's rights or women leaders. If the state has collapsed, they are not in the business of seeking to comply with international treaties and paying attention to international gender equality indices. Here, we can point to the situation in Uganda prior to 1986 and the governance vacuum that existed in Uganda during the years of conflict. We can also point to the period of genocide and conflict in Rwanda and the period in Mauritania's recent history when the country was plagued by coups. These are times when the issue of women's leadership was simply not on the table, save a few exceptions. Ruth Perry headed the interim Council of State of Liberia that governed the country after the first Liberian civil war (1989–1996). Agathe Uwilingiyimana served as prime minister of Rwanda from 1993 until her death in 1994 during the Rwandan genocide. Catherine Samba-Panza was also selected as interim president of the Central African Republic in the midst of civil strife in 2014 and served until 2016. Uganda's National Resistance Army formed local Resistance Councils during the conflict in Luwero, in which women held one position out of ten in each council. But these examples are few and far between, and except for the Uganda local councils, they involved only a handful of women in top positions and not in Parliament.

International Gender Norms

Changing international norms regarding women's representation after the 1990s heightened efforts to keep up with these international standards but also to virtue signal around women's leadership globally and in some African states. This was especially true after the 1995 UN Fourth World Conference on Women, held in Beijing, where a Platform of Action was adopted in which member states pledged to increase women's leadership in all areas and at all levels. Most authoritarian countries had more to gain than democracies in seeking to tidy up their tarred image as a result of human rights abuses. Adopting women as leaders was one of the easiest ways to signal this cleanup. Most authoritarian countries in Africa have made some effort to comply with changing international norms regarding women's rights.

This book shows how authoritarian countries that promote women leaders are more likely than other countries to pursue a strategy to soften their international image and for purposes of gaining international and regional stature. Moreover, the internal and external objectives of instrumentalizing women leaders are intertwined, with the former usually being of greater consequence. Nevertheless, interviews in all countries highlighted this international aspect of the instrumentalization of women's rights.

Ruling party strategies to maintain vote share and further institutionalize their hegemonic position coincided with efforts by international and regional organizations like the United Nations, the African Union, and the SADC to pressure governments to increase women's representation. Promoting women leaders became part of an international status-signaling strategy and a way to divert attention from an otherwise dismal human rights record (Bueno de Mesquita and Downs 2005; Pinto 2019). This was much more important for authoritarian countries than for African democracies, and promoting women leaders was a visible way of softening a country's image. As Valdini (2021) has pointed out, the inclusion of women may carry less potential threat than the inclusion of men from traditionally excluded groups. Often, when the ruling party is keen to signal their favor to ethnic or religious constituencies, choosing women leaders from those groups allows the party to achieve two aims at once.

The political costs of promoting women leaders were often lower than adopting other democratic reforms of ensuring civil rights, political liberties, and clean elections, which might threaten the regime more directly. Moreover, it had additional benefits in terms of internal legitimacy. High levels of female leadership, for example, have often allowed the Kagame regime in Rwanda to hide behind the smokescreen of women's rights to win positive international acclaim at a time when its human rights violations and the politicization of ethnicity were increasingly being called into question (Longman 2006). This has implications for human rights activists, who, as in the case of Morocco, often took up women's rights cases because they felt they could make more progress in this area than in other areas of human rights law (Tripp 2019).

Leaders want their countries to appear "progressive" and compliant with international norms regarding women's rights—not only to divert attention from human rights abuses but also to attract investment and trade and maintain overseas development assistance (ODA). Some have argued that the appointment of women leaders has been used for purposes of international status signaling to soften the image of an illiberal regime in the hopes of accessing greater FDI, loans, and foreign aid and of enhancing trade relations (Bjarnegård and Zetterberg 2022; Bush and Zetterberg 2021; Bush et al. 2021; Edgell 2017; Kroeger and Kang 2022). Governments often believe that advancing women in Parliament is a good way to signal gender equity globally since the measure for women's legislative representation is one of the most commonly used measures for indicating such a commitment (Arendt 2018).

Part of what makes international status signaling work is that international donors and institutions themselves use women's rights instrumentally and issue reports evaluating how different countries rank when it comes to various aspects of women's rights (see, e.g., the rankings of the IPU, the World Economic Forum's annual Global Gender Gap Report, the UN Development Programme's (UNDP's) Gender Inequality Index, the African Gender and Development Index, and the World Bank's *Women, Business and the Law* report). International funding agencies often state that women's education is an essential component in the fight against global terrorism. Moreover, funding women's development initiatives is often said to be the key to peace, environmental sustainability, and many other positive developmental outcomes (Cornwall et al. 2008). There is a perception among some donors and governments that women leaders are helpful in combating corruption (Goetz

2007). These feed into general perceptions about women in aid-recipient countries.

However, not all are as sanguine about the relationship between international ranking indices and gender reform. Judith Kelley (2017) has looked at how the United States has used soft power and scorecard diplomacy, ranking countries to embarrass them into taking positive action. Kelley argues that rating, ranking, and block lists can be effective because states generally care about their legitimacy and identity and about preserving their reputation in the international community. However, she found that various measures of aid, trade, and military assistance were not significant in statistical analyses of the effects of scorecard diplomacy. There was no evidence that aid recipients would be more likely to react to scorecard pressure, even if ranked in ways that might threaten aid. Interestingly, image-related concerns were three times more common than material concerns. These findings suggest that there is reason to be cautious in drawing strong conclusions in linking aid, trade, and foreign investment too sharply to these strategies of promoting women as leaders.

International and regional motivators are not equally important in all parts of Africa. Moreover, it is likely that foreign aid correlates more closely with women's rights that are not tied to political pluralism, elections, or repression, as Donno et al. (2022) discovered in a cross-national study. Countries in North Africa that have extensive trade relations with European Union (EU) countries are to a certain degree motivated by external political economy factors and hope to use women's rights to demonstrate that they are not a source of violent jihadism. For countries like Zimbabwe and Uganda, whose main trade partners are the UAE, China, and other African countries, trade does not feature as such an important consideration in their gender strategies. Declining levels of foreign aid to Africa make ODA a less critical consideration. China, which does not pay attention to gender rankings in its foreign relations, has become Africa's largest trading partner, with one-fifth of the continent's exports going to China, and trade with Europe is declining. All of these trends make the need to virtue signal around women's rights less relevant to trade, aid, and investment.

One way of gauging what motivates countries is to look at the timing of the adoption of quotas. Zimbabwe adopted quotas much later than most of the other countries in Southern Africa, suggesting that it was not in any particular hurry to comply with the deadlines set by the regional organization SADC or by pressures from the United Nations that started in earnest after the 1995 UN Fourth World Conference on Women, held in Beijing (Krook 2006). This suggests that it was more motivated by internal factors and the ruling party's competition with the opposition party. Similarly, Uganda adopted quotas *before* the United Nations started pressing for measures to increase women's representation after 1995, pointing toward primarily domestic considerations for introducing reserved seats.

Nevertheless, external considerations play a role and often overlap with internal deliberations. The case of Morocco (Chapter 7) is used to explore the impact of trade partners and foreign aid on women's rights. The EU is Morocco's leading trade partner, accounting for 56 percent of its trade. The EU has an active policy of encouraging Morocco to increase female political representation through a variety of programs, while Morocco has responded by tailoring its policies to signal to the EU countries that it is keen to advance women's rights and women leaders. Thus, Morocco's leaders wish for the country to appear "modern" and compliant with international norms regarding women's rights in order to attract investment and trade.

In countries in North Africa that have the EU as a primary trade partner for both imports and exports (Algeria, Tunisia, Morocco, Egypt, and Libya), women hold on average 18.5 percent of the parliamentary seats compared with MENA countries that trade with other parts of the world, where women hold only 10.5 percent of the parliamentary seats. While this possible relationship is evident in North Africa, it is not as evident in the rest of Africa: Women in countries with EU trading partners in Africa hold 17.3 percent of the legislative seats compared to 23.4 percent for countries that do not trade with the EU. Thus, the need for status signaling with European trade partners may be more evident in North Africa because the concerns around their external image are more salient as a result of the recent history of violent extremism in these countries. Early in the first decade of the 2010s, Morocco and Tunisia became two of the biggest external suppliers of fighters for Daesh.

But even in Morocco, external factors are secondary to internal reasons for promoting women leaders. Women leaders and women's rights have been used for internal purposes of marginalizing violent extremists. Adopting women's rights even became a question of political survival for political parties, which had to please the king, who was keen to advance women's rights as part of his anti–religious extremism strategy (Tripp 2019). It was simultaneously a response to domestic pressures from women's movements, which took advantage of critical junctures, often in the context of a change of leadership or social upheaval, to advance their goals. Thus, the internal and external signaling strategies are often inseparable.

The internal and external objectives are intertwined in Rwanda (Chapter 6), which is an iconic case for international virtue signaling because its rates of female representation are the highest in the world, and the government engages in active global self-promotion around its women's rights record. It became the world leader in descriptive legislative representation of women after the 1994 genocide and civil conflict. Much of the explanation for this surge in female representation in Rwanda can be accounted for by the political calculus of the ruling Front Patriotique Rwandais (Rwandan Patriotic Front; RPF). The number of female legislators jumped from 26 percent in 1994 to 49 percent after the 2003 elections and then to 61 percent in 2022. Rwanda's quota and other women's rights reforms won the country positive international acclaim and visibility, particularly when their human rights violations were increasingly being questioned.

After the genocide, the RPF leadership emphasized women's role in the reconciliation and reconstruction processes and encouraged women to enter public office. This won the RPF considerable support among the female population. The government could, in turn, count on a loyal cadre of supporters who would not challenge RPF authority. Then, in 2003, Rwanda adopted a constitution that reserved at least 30 percent of the seats for women, guaranteeing them an additional loyal constituency. An electoral law of 2010 called for the election of another twenty-four deputies from the country's provinces.

However, the RPF has made sure that in elections, no serious political opposition groups are allowed to participate freely or run for office and has effectively silenced any criticisms or challenges to its authority, including from women. Moreover, the top leadership posts held by women have primarily gone to pro-RPF anglophone Rwandans who had lived in Uganda or elsewhere prior to the RPF takeover of Rwanda (Powley 2003). In Rwanda, the imperative to divert international attention from human rights to women's rights has been a key motivation, although internal factors have weighed more heavily on these calculations.

Factors Militating Against the Promotion of Women Leaders

One finds fewer women leaders in countries without entrenched ruling parties and with an alternation of parties in power, like Nigeria, the Gambia, Liberia, and Sierra Leone. These are mostly hybrid regimes with more competitive elections (see Chapter 2). While in long-standing democracies, competition may facilitate women's representation, in autocracies, it is the least-competitive countries with entrenched parties that are most successful in promoting women's representation because they can crush the opposition and promote loyal women leaders with less resistance from other parties or societal actors. Hybrid regimes are more sensitive to other societal and political actors, which limits their ability to advance women.

The authoritarian countries that have not implemented gender quotas and have not promoted women leaders also tend to be countries plagued by conflict, coups, and coup attempts. This was evident in the case of Mauritania (Chapter 5). After the military became more heavily involved in Mauritania's politics in 1978, the country was plagued by six coups, four of which were successful and the last one of which took place in 2008. This was also the period in which women were largely absent from politics. Given these patterns, the spate of coups in Central and West Africa since 2020 does not bode well for women's representation and rights.

Authoritarian countries with few women in politics are often under personalist or military rule (e.g., Burkina Faso, Chad, Guinea), or they may have large areas controlled by armed groups. Countries that have experienced severe state repression, an absence of democratic institutions like elections or a functioning legislature (e.g., Eritrea), and weak women's movements also fall into the basket of countries that have done less to advance women's status.

Generally, military rule does not allow for the entrenchment of political parties, if they have parties. Thus, it also dampens efforts to advance women as leaders—not just because militarism is generally patriarchal but because of the instability of military rule and the fact that their authority comes from force rather than from popular support through elections. The case of Mauritania (see Chapter 5) illustrates the positive impact of the transition from military to civilian rule on party entrenchment and women's representation. Mauritania is a former French colony that first experienced single-party rule after independence from 1960 to 1978, when Parti du Peuple Mauritanien (Mauritanian People's Party; PPM) was the only legal party. It then came under military rule from 1978 until 1992, when it held its first multiparty elections. Even with the introduction of a multiparty system in the early 1990s, nothing was done to level the playing field for the opposition, and little was done to democratize the country, which remained authoritarian. Consequently, civil society was fragmented and weak until the first decade of the 2000s, when women's organizations began to emerge and became the most organized sector in civil society. The Parti Républicain Démocratique et Social (PRDS) won three elections, followed by a Rassemblement des Forces Démocratiques (RFD) coalition from 2006 to 2009, thus alternating party control.

The Union pour la République (UPR)—which changed its name to Equality Party in 2022—became the ruling party in 2009 and remained in power through three electoral cycles, thus becoming an entrenched party. Women were not visible in politics throughout one-party rule, military rule, and the alternation of various parties during the long period of continued instability. The percentage of women in Parliament increased from 3.7 percent in 2005 to 22.1 percent after the 2006 elections. In 2012, a law was passed that created reserved seats for women. Today, women hold roughly 20 percent of the seats. Women also began to claim positions in political parties and hold ministerial positions. Even though the level of women in politics is still not very high in this hybrid regime, women's gains were not evident until the UPR began to entrench itself. The government began to pursue new strategies to maintain power when the country shifted to multiparty rule from one-party and military rule.

Alternative Explanations for Women's Political Representation in Africa

This book builds on a rich and extensive literature on women's rights and political representation in Africa, much of which was discussed earlier. In keeping with the arguments made in this book, the literature on women's representation in Africa has identified postconflict dynamics (Hughes and Tripp 2015), political opening (Fallon et al. 2012), the adoption of quotas (Bauer 2008), pressure from women's movements (Kang 2015; Kang and Tripp 2018), and international normative pressures (Hughes et al. 2015) as explanations for women's political representation.

Not all alternate arguments comport with my findings. Some early cross-national studies globally have shown that women's rights and legislative representation correlate with higher levels of democracy (Inglehart and Norris 2003a; Inglehart et al. 2002). Some case studies in Africa even make similar arguments for South Africa (Walsh 2011), Ghana (Fallon 2008), and Tanzania (Brown 2001). However, most cross-national studies generally do not show a strong correlation between democracy and women's legislative representation (Kenworthy and Malami 1999; Luciak 2005, Paxton 1997; Reynolds 1999; Stockemer 2009; Tripp and Kang 2008; Viterna et al. 2007). Some studies even find a negative correlation between democracy and women's representation (Stockemer 2011; Yoon 2004). Stockemer (2009) argues that democracies not only have fewer women deputies than nondemocracies, but female representation does not increase as democracies mature. He argues that other factors, like quotas, proportional representation electoral systems, and women's mobilization, are more important. Yoon (2004) argues that trends show that women's representation has increased in both democracies and nondemocracies in Africa. She argues that what is important is the political will of major parties, especially ruling parties, to nominate women.

Some authors suggest that democracy per se is not correlated with women's rights; rather, it is the *process of democratization* that opens up political space for women's mobilization to press for legislative gains (Fallon et al. 2012; Paxton et al. 2010). While this may have been the case in the 1990s and the first decade of the 2000s, the fact that women's representation has increased while countries have become more autocratic suggests that this may have been a temporary phenomenon in Africa related to the shift from one-party to multiparty regimes.

Staffan Lindberg (2004) identifies a mechanism through which democratization is linked to women's representation in Africa, arguing that with each subsequent election after the political opening, the quality of democratic elections improves, as does women's representation. The claim that democratization has led to improved elections has been disputed, particularly since 2005, when democratization trends began to reverse on the continent.

Muriaas et al. (2013) argue that regime type determines how much space women's movements have to maneuver and push for reforms, with democracies allowing for more legislative assertion. However, they argue that "there also may be room to maneuver in nondemocratic settings" to make substantive legislative demands. Bauer and Burnet (2013) compared democratic Botswana with authoritarian Rwandan regarding quota adoption and concluded that "a democratic state is not necessarily more likely to adopt gender quotas or have more women in Parliament than a less democratic one and that there are other factors that are more important in determining both." Indeed, in Africa, as of 2021, 67 percent of authoritarian countries and 59 percent of hybrid regimes have adopted some form of gender quota for women in legislatures, while only 44 percent of democratic countries have done so. But the question remains: Why do we see these patterns?

Numerous other factors have sometimes gained currency in the literature to explain women's representation that have mainly been rejected or have not risen to the level of importance relative to other explanatory factors. These include the hypothesized positive impacts of higher GDP, proportional representation systems, female education levels, and women in the workforce. They also include hypothesized negative impacts of the country's colonial legacy, levels of oil revenue, levels of religiosity among the population, and related negative attitudes toward women's representation. Yet none of these factors explains the change in women's representation after 1995 at any level of significance when quotas and postconflict factors are considered (Hughes and Tripp 2015).

There is a growing body of literature on women's rights in authoritarian countries, which I will build on and discuss at greater length in the following chapter.

Research Design and Methods

This book adopts a comparative approach, looking at how women's representation has evolved in authoritarian and hybrid countries in Africa over time and compares them with each other and with democracies. It looks at case studies, situating them in a broader comparative perspective. It asks, When and why do authoritarian countries promote women as leaders? Do the reasons that authoritarian regimes instrumentalize women leaders differ from those of democracies in Africa, and if so, why? Under what conditions do authoritarian regimes advance women as leaders? What are the consequences of the inclusion of women in politics when women are used to enhance the longevity of an autocratic regime? Is political inclusion an opportunity for women, a means of legitimizing an autocratic regime, or both? Are some women leaders complicit in instrumentalizing women's rights?

The study is heuristic or theory-generating in the sense that I am looking for patterns in authoritarian countries and trying to identify the scope of these patterns and their meanings. The main argument explains why entrenched parties that have remained hegemonic for a long time correlate strongly with women's political representation. I am bringing empirical content to key theoretical observations through case studies. This is an inductive study that adopts a nominal approach, described by Joe Soss (2021) as an approach that asks "how various ways of knowing a thing can generate different kinds of knowledge." A case does not exist in a vacuum; it is given meaning by efforts to theorize the phenomenon.

I incorporate Charles Ragin's (2000) insight that cases can be delineated by their unique combinations of conditions while acknowledging that these factors can combine in diverse ways to generate specific outcomes. In this book, we see regime type interacting with the end of major conflict, with the shift from one-party rule to multipartyism, with the end of military rule, and with changing international norms in a variety of ways to influence women's political leadership. As a result, the cases are not discrete but rather overlapping in multiple combinations, reflecting the messiness of the real world.

While carrying out research, I discovered four different ways to group the various objectives of countries in promoting women leaders. They include economic and political rationales that fall into international and national objectives. Some applied better outside of Africa (e.g., diversifying oil economies), but most explanations covered the range of objectives outlined in Table 1.1. The book, then, attempts to explain the evolution of key processes after the 1990s that resulted in changes in women's political representation in autocracies and democracies. It shows how the outcomes converged and differed based on regime type and took different forms. I also learned that competition and lack thereof play a different role in democracies, hybrid, and authoritarian regimes with respect to women leaders (see Chapter 2).

Case Selection

In this book, I look at changes over time in five authoritarian regimes (Mauritania, Morocco, Rwanda, Uganda, and Zimbabwe), which are contrasted with democracies, with a focus on Namibia and Botswana. This is not a controlled comparative study. I do not use the cases to explore variance among the cases. Instead, I selected the cases to capture a range of different types of authoritarian and democratic regimes and trajectories in order to identify how and why authoritarian countries (and two democracies) promote or don't promote women leaders. I look at variance over time in each case and find the differential impact of military and personalist rule versus party-based rule, as well the negative impact of coups and armed conflict on women's representation.

Because I did not know when I embarked on my study, I selected cases that reflected various differences, including region, colonial legacy, and regime type. In this study, I treat North Africa as part of Africa, and I include Mauritania in West Africa; Uganda in East Africa; Morocco in North Africa; Zimbabwe, Namibia, and Botswana in Southern Africa; and Rwanda in Central Africa. They have different colonial legacies, with Zimbabwe, Uganda, and Botswana being former British colonies, Mauritania and Morocco being former French colonies, and Namibia being first colonized by Germany and controlled by South Africa after World War I. Rwanda was under German East Africa until Belgium took over after World War I. Two of the countries became independent later than most African countries: Zimbabwe in 1980 and Namibia in 1990. Morocco gained independence in 1956, Mauritania in 1960, Uganda in 1962, and Botswana in 1966.

Uganda and Zimbabwe were hybrid regimes with party-based systems that became authoritarian, Uganda in 2014 and Zimbabwe around 2000. Mauritania was a military-led authoritarian regime that became a semiauthoritarian regime around 2019. Morocco is a semiauthoritarian monarchy, while Botswana and Namibia have been democracies since independence. All of these countries hold regular multiparty elections, as do most countries in Africa, with a few exceptions. All except for Botswana and Morocco have entrenched parties today, although this was not always the case in Mauritania. Thus, I capture variance not only among democracies, hybrid regimes, and democracies but also between entrenched and nonentrenched parties through process tracing of these cases over time. There are so few democracies in Africa—nine as of this writing—one has to be careful in generalizing. For this reason, I selected two African democracies, Namibia and Botswana, to investigate in greater detail to see how they differed from authoritarian countries and each other.

Of the selected cases, Mauritania and Morocco are primarily Muslim, whereas Uganda, Botswana, Namibia, Rwanda, and Zimbabwe are primarily Christian. Namibia, Rwanda, Uganda, and Zimbabwe have experienced major conflict, although Morocco and Mauritania were also involved in the conflict in Western Sahara. Botswana is the only country of the group that was untouched by conflict. Some countries had active women's movements (Zimbabwe and Uganda), and others had less-active movements (Mauritania and Botswana).

Methods

The book adopts a historical process tracing methodology, reviews newspapers from the focus countries, and reviews the secondary literature pertaining to these countries. It also includes extensive interviews. Although not ideal, the interviews were mostly carried out using WhatsApp and Zoom because of the prevalence of Covid-19 at the time of the research and my inability to travel. I had extensive prior research experience in Uganda and Morocco, which was helpful. I had research assistants in each country who helped set up the interviews.

This book draws on 188 interviews carried out in Uganda, Zimbabwe, Rwanda, Mauritania, Morocco, Botswana, and Namibia. In each country, I identified people to interview from different parties, representing different sectors of society, young and old, and men and women. The in-depth interviews usually lasted one hour but sometimes more. The interviews were with leaders and members of a variety of women's rights, civil society, and human rights organizations; Members of Parliament (MPs); representatives of the women's parliamentary caucuses, government agencies, and women's ministries; party leaders in both the ruling party and the opposition; academics; journalists; and representatives of donor and UN agencies.

In the interviews, I asked questions about the motivations of political leaders and the goals, accomplishments, and limitations of the government, ruling party, opposition parties, the women's movement, donors, and other societal actors over time. I asked about interactions among these actors, specific events, legislation, or judicial rulings and how they should be interpreted. I asked how each country compared with neighboring countries and other countries in Africa regarding women's rights. I focused on the expertise of the individuals and asked about their areas of concern.

I had already carried out interviews in Morocco for a book on why Arab autocrats in the Maghreb adopted women's rights (Tripp 2019). For this book, I also looked at status signaling through content analysis of the king's speeches in Morocco and five years (2017–2022) of the official press agencies' coverage of women's rights issues and women politicians.

Outline of the Book

The Preface and this introductory chapter set the stage for the analysis and discussion in the subsequent chapters, providing a motivation for the study of authoritarianism and women's leadership. Chapter 1 outlined the research questions and introduced some of the main explanations for the advancement of women leaders in authoritarian regimes and how many authoritarian regimes came to promote women as leaders. It also discusses the research design and methods used in the manuscript.

Because the book was researched and written inductively, each chapter highlights different aspects of authoritarian rule and women leaders in the pursuit of legitimacy by the ruling party. It shows how central the promotion and instrumentalization of women leaders are to the goal of ruling party entrenchment. This book looks at several post–Cold War and postconflict scenarios that led to the instrumentalization of women's representation, especially in authoritarian contexts. Women leaders were used to expand clientelistic patronage networks and to co-opt and weaken the opposition. Sometimes these regimes even weaponized women's rights to their own advantage and against the opposition, especially after the introduction of multipartyism in the 1990s. This happened as the need to maintain party dominance became more pressing, with the loss of vote share, which occurred as most African countries introduced multipartyism.

Chapter 2 provides a comparative overview contrasting autocracies with democracies regarding the political representation of women and quotas, along with other key dimensions of gender reform and with respect to constitutional initiatives to address women's representation throughout the continent. The book then turns to detailed case studies of four authoritarian regimes, including Uganda, Zimbabwe, and Mauritania (Chapters 3–5), to focus on domestic motivations for gender reform in women's representation, many of which apply to multiple countries despite the foci selected for each country. The explanations range from the need to maintain vote share (Uganda) to pressure from women's movements (Zimbabwe) and the need to improve a country's image after military rule (Mauritania). Chapters 6 and 7 focus on international and regional factors that influence gender reform in the cases of Rwanda and Morocco. In Chapters 8 and 9, the book looks at two democracies, one with high rates of female representation (Namibia) and the other with low rates (Botswana). Chapter 10 compares democracies and autocracies, both the case studies and, more broadly, within Africa. The concluding Chapter 11 compares African autocracies with other autocracies globally and historically.

Conclusion

The book focuses on a conundrum: Women's movements have demanded an increase in women's representation and top leadership positions, yet authoritarian regimes have simultaneously used women to legitimize and extend their rule. Thus, countries with entrenched parties have been the most successful in promoting women as leaders.

The book challenges quantitative studies of descriptive women's representation for not paying attention to the dangers of authoritarian rule. It also challenges other studies that lump all authoritarian regimes together under the banner of "genderbashing" and do not sufficiently account for not only the differences among them with respect to women's rights but also the extent to which they promote women leaders and gender-related reforms and all the confounding consequences this brings for women and human rights.

The case studies show that the adoption of women leaders and women's rights is more than genderwashing, although status signaling does occur. The fact that countries that promote women leaders also adopt other women's rights reforms suggests that the advancement of women leaders is not all a facade for purposes of status. Internal motivations are stronger than external ones for adopting women's rights in the cases I studied, although changing international norms do matter. The main challenge authoritarian regimes pose for women's rights is not the performative elements of their use of women but rather the repression of dissent, the lack of political space along with a deficit in political rights and civil liberties. Their instrumentalization of women leaders and women's rights is used to garner greater legitimacy and extend their rule. The suppression of the opposition perspectives makes authoritarian regimes less responsive to societal input than hybrid regimes, thus making it easier for them to adopt reserved seats and other woman-friendly policies.

The book looks at how and why ruling parties in African authoritarian regimes have promoted women as leaders, especially since the 1990s, with both the introduction of multipartyism and the decline in major conflicts, against a backdrop of changing international norms regarding women's rights. These countries have advanced women leaders, often through reserved seat quota systems, to further entrench their rule by instrumentalizing women's rights to their benefit and against the opposition, especially after the introduction of multipartyism. This happened as the need to maintain party dominance became more pressing with the loss of vote share that occurred after most African countries introduced multipartyism in the 1990s.

These patterns are especially evident in countries with dominant-party systems, in which the ruling party, the presidential party, is surrounded by many small, unstable parties. This is the modal party system in Africa. Power is highly centralized in the executive, whose party is in power. The ruling parties in these authoritarian countries are characterized by personal rule. Programmatic and ideological differences do not define them; they are illiberal. This suggests that party entrenchment, rather than simply institutionalized party systems and parties, is critical to the advancement of women in authoritarian systems.

With the introduction of multipartyism in the 1990s in Africa and the simultaneous decline in major conflicts after the end of the Cold War, ruling parties sought new strategies to remain in power to institutionalize their hegemonic position further. These changes coincided with and were influenced by efforts of women's movements and international organizations like the United Nations and the African Union to pressure governments to increase women's political representation. They sought to increase the number of women in parliaments, local government, cabinets, the judiciary, and other bodies. Adopting quotas and especially reserved seats became one mechanism authoritarian leaders adopted to further entrench their parties in power and ensure their regimes remained in power. The longer the ruling party remained in power, the more likely one would see women's rights being advanced. The use of reserved seats became a method found only in authoritarian regimes.

This book also shows that there are limits to the instrumentalization of women's rights, regardless of regime type. Policies for which women's rights are instrumentalized for other purposes may mark symbolic advances, but they may also run the risk of not directly addressing women's rights concerns, of having problematic unintended consequences, of not including women representatives in the crafting of policies, and of not being developed with the interests of women themselves in mind. If they are used to divert attention from human rights violations, they can work at cross-purposes to women's rights, which requirefreedom of association, freedom of speech, free and fair elections, and the right to participate in politics freely to flourish. Policies enacted for expediency and pleasing an external audience may look good on paper, but they may not be implemented or funded at a level that would bring about fundamental changes for women. And finally, those women's rights activists who are associated with these reforms, however sincere they are in their goals, may find themselves tainted by association with a corrupt and dictatorial government, especially once the country democratizes.

2

Women Leaders and the Politics of Party Entrenchment

African countries that have entrenched ruling parties are more successful in advancing women leaders regardless of regime type, although most tend to be authoritarian regimes and regimes with dominant parties. Sartori (1976) defines a dominant one-party system as one in which parties or a political group claim more than three consecutive electoral wins (with a majority of votes in coalition governments). I consider these *entrenched parties*—not only because they have passed the three-election mark but because they have longevity as a ruling party. They became entrenched after the introduction of multipartyism in the 1990s and attained higher levels of women's political representation compared with parties that alternated in power through elections, regardless of how institutionalized they were. Some have argued that party institutionalization drives women's representation in authoritarian regimes (Pelke 2021). Party and party system institutionalization (PSI) are part of the process of entrenchment, but parties are fairly weak in Africa, which is why I focus on *entrenchment*, which describes more specifically the aspect of institutionalization that affects women's representation in authoritarian countries in Africa.

Countries with a single dominant party entrenched in power are more successful in promoting women leaders at all levels—in the executive, in the national Parliament, and at the subnational level—in contrast to countries with histories of instability, coups, and military rule. They also do better with women's leadership when compared with countries that alternate parties in power (e.g., Nigeria, Ghana, and Kenya). Advancing women leaders is part of their strategy to become entrenched, but their stability and staying power also make it possible for them to advance women leaders to further entrench themselves.

This chapter looks at entrenchment and how and why it is correlated with women's representation in authoritarian regimes and to a lesser extent in hybrid regimes. It examines the role of dominant-party-based regimes, party and regime institutionalization, and how they are related to entrenchment

Why African Autocracies Promote Women as Leaders. Aili Mari Tripp, Oxford University Press. © Oxford University Press (2025). DOI: 10.1093/9780197829004.003.0003

as well as the role of competition in various regime types. The chapter also looks at one of the main mechanisms authoritarian regimes use to entrench themselves: reserved seats and quotas more generally. The chapters in this volume on Uganda, Zimbabwe, Mauritania, and Rwanda have all used this strategy, which is promoted by the United Nations.

Hegemonic Party–Based Regimes

Several authors have demonstrated how party-based regimes are more likely to adopt women's economic and political rights than personalistic, military, or monarchist regimes because they can more easily use mechanisms of women's representation, consultation, and mobilization and can co-opt women's organizations and women's party wings (Donno and Kreft 2019). Some argue that quota adoption may be stronger in hegemonic party authoritarian regimes like Tanzania because the dominant parties have more resources and use power-maximizing partisan strategies to a larger extent than the opposition parties (Bjarnegård and Zetterberg 2016).

Figure 2.1 illustrates how different types of authoritarian regimes fare in Africa when it comes to women's legislative representation, using the typology developed by Barbara Geddes with Joseph G. Wright and Erica Frantz. Following work by Donno and Kreft (2019), Figure 2.1 shows that party-based dictatorships in Africa do better than other authoritarian regime types when it comes to advancing women's political representation. This gives further credence to the emphasis on hegemonic-party systems in this book as well as to the unsurprising and lackluster performance of military regimes when it comes to women's leadership in Africa.

On occasion, there have been individual populist leaders who have promoted women as leaders. Populist military regimes, such as Thomas Sankara's in Burkina Faso (1983–1987), utilized women's rights to bolster their image and gain popularity. He placed women in major cabinet positions and in the military and criticized patriarchy, referring to it as a male-imposed system of exploitation perpetuated by the ingrained acceptance of sexist norms. Sankara argued that this inequality was a product of societal conditioning and served as a means of establishing dominance and exploitation. In 1984, he designated September 22 as the Day of Solidarity with Housewives, encouraging men to actively participate in household chores, meal preparation, and child-care responsibilities. Sankara's administration also took steps to promote gender equality through health, education, and family development policies. He established the Ministry of Family Development and

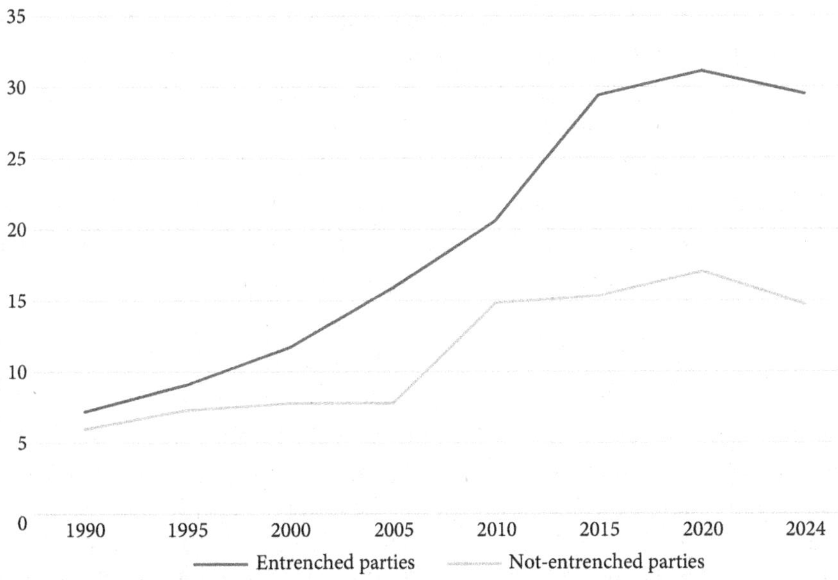

Figure 2.1 Authoritarian regime type and women's representation in Africa
Sources: Geddes et al. (n.d.); IPU (2024).

the Women's Union of Burkina Faso. He implemented measures to curtail polygamy, dowry payments, forced marriages, and female genital mutilation. Furthermore, he granted new legal rights to women, including the introduction of inheritance rights for widows and orphans (Walton 2022). His policies were driven by his populist inclinations rather than a desire to implement structural changes that would have lasted beyond his regime. Sankara's military rule made it impossible for women to participate in parliamentary politics or in most other governance institutions that would have significantly advanced their status. However, most of his innovations did not outlive him, nor are they typical of other military dictatorships.

Pelke (2021) examines why certain authoritarian regimes are more gender inclusive than others and finds, as did Donno and Kreft, that party-based regimes are associated with more political gender equality, but he also finds that the major determinant of gender equality is authoritarian party institutionalization. *Party institutionalization* refers to the durability of a party's organizational structures and its ability to function as a stable and effective organization over time, with clear rules and procedures for succession and decision-making. Generally, the presence of clear rules in a party benefits newcomers like women, who can more easily gain support within a party compared to a party that has opaque, changing, and arbitrary rules (Kittilson 2006).

Some argue that there has been gradual PSI in some countries, even if it is weak (Weghorst and Bernhard 2014). PSI exists where the system is stable and predictable, with a degree of stability in the interactions between parties and an acceptance of the legitimacy of party competition. Mainwaring and Scully (1995) identify four dimensions of PSI: the regularity of competition, stability of the constituency, legitimacy of actors and outcomes, and the existence of programmatic appeals to voters. Rachel Beatty Riedl (2014) argues that party systems in African countries with strong authoritarian parties before 1990 with adequate organizational resources and extensive linkages to society were more likely to survive than party systems in countries with weak parties.

Others, like Meng (2020, 93), look at regime institutionalization, which she defines as "the creation of rules and procedures that structure the distribution of power and resources within the ruling coalition." She shows that since independence and especially after the 1990s, limits were placed on the executive by creating rules and structures that govern the distribution of power and resources within the ruling coalitions. Weak rulers institutionalize power and tie their hands as an accountability mechanism to guarantee access to future rents, while strong leaders don't need to. Almost all leaders in Africa have done this. In the 1990s, over half of African countries had executive constraints; by 2010, over 90 percent had them.

However, in general, party institutionalization and PSI are weak in Africa. Parties may be entrenched not because of party institutionalization or PSI but because they have been adept at co-opting smaller parties and/or repressing them. Thus, entrenched dominant parties are not necessarily institutionalized, although they can be. They have, however, maintained vote share over time and remain dominant within a political system. Ruling parties adapted, with the shift to multipartyism, to find new ways to remain dominant. Meng's executive constraints to institutionalize the regime may be part of this same story.

Particular features of African regimes help explain the ways in which parties become entrenched and how women leaders were instrumentalized. African polities, to a greater extent than other parts of the world, are characterized by hegemonic executive rule that takes the form of personal rule. The modal party system in Africa is characterized by a presidential party system with a dominant ruling party surrounded by many small, unstable parties (Bleck and Van de Walle 2018; Van de Walle 2003). This was the predominant characteristic of authoritarian and hybrid regimes, even as they exited the one-party system and transitioned into multiparty systems in the 1990s. The former single parties used their ties to the state to help establish themselves in this new political order.

As Van de Walle (2003) observed, the ruling parties established their new status by making sure they won the first election in the multiparty system. Programmatic and ideological differences did not define them, and they were illiberal in nature, whether they were authoritarian or hybrid regimes. Van de Walle argued that power was highly centralized in the office of the president, and they were defined by clientelism. Even in democracies and pluralistic parliamentary systems, one often finds a certain level of executive dominance in Africa, as we have seen up until recently in two of the case studies in this book, Namibia and Botswana (Bleck and Van de Walle 2018).

Bleck and Van de Walle (2018) argue that since the 1990s, there has been a very low level of executive alternation. Incumbents get re-elected regardless of their performance, and presidents stay in power because they have more control over clientelistic redistribution. They maintain relationships with donors and other stakeholders. They use incumbency advantage to weaken and fragment the opposition. Multiparty competitive elections are held but with little change in the ruling party and elite.

Some have attributed the longevity of many of these regimes to voting patterns of rural voters who support the incumbents to gain access to resources while not exacting punishment after elections. Thus, the shift to a dominant-party system is associated with a 31 percent higher likelihood of voting for the ruling party (Bratton et al. 2012). Moreover, the opposition is generally weak and has a much lower chance of winning. Bratton et al. (2012) demonstrate that voters tend to associate themselves with incumbent parties since those candidates are more likely to win, and, in turn, voters will be in a better position to access resources and avoid punishment after elections.

Party Entrenchment in Hybrid, Authoritarian, and Democratic Regimes

In Africa, hegemonic parties as described by Bleck and Van de Walle (2018) within institutionalized party regimes (Meng 2020 are most likely to be entrenched. Entrenched parties in Africa generally do more to promote women leaders at all levels than nonentrenched parties (see Table 2.1).

There is a positive relationship between entrenched parties and women's legislative representation, regardless of regime type, in Africa. The percentage of women's representation with entrenched parties is twice that of countries without entrenched parties, and similar patterns are evident at the executive and subnational level (Table 2.1). Since the beginning of the multiparty transition in the 1990s, there has been a growing divide between the average

Table 2.1 Entrenched party impact on levels of representation of women in Africa (2024)

	Ruling party: Entrenched (%)	Ruling party: Not entrenched (%)
Women in legislature	32.1	18.9%
Women in subnational councils	29.6	20.8
Women ministers	26.1	21.0
	$n = 21$	$n = 32$

Sources: IPU (2024); UN Women (n.d.b.); World Bank (2024).

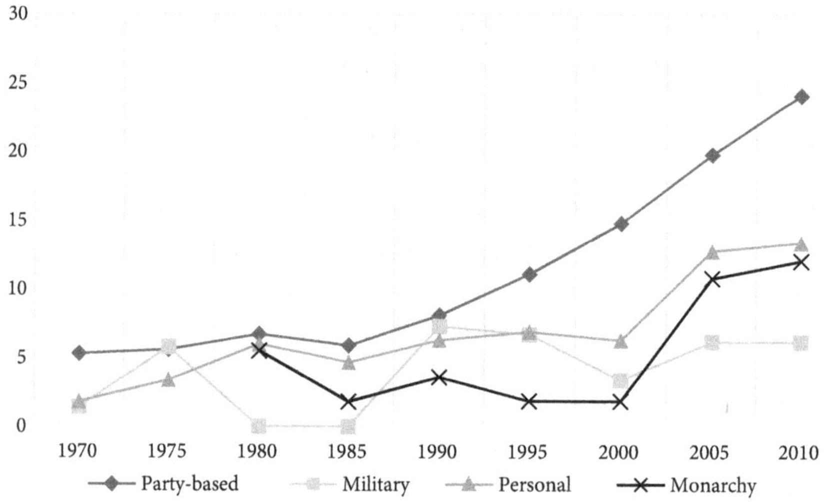

Figure 2.2 Women's parliamentary representation in countries with entrenched and nonentrenched parties in Africa (including North Africa)
Source: IPU (2024).

level of women's representation in countries with entrenched and nonentrenched parties. Overall, the average level of women's representation in African parliaments has steadily increased since the 1990s, but countries with entrenched parties have made increasingly greater gains than those with nonentrenched parties (Figure 2.2).

Party entrenchment is more evident in authoritarian countries and less common in semiauthoritarian hybrid regimes. Party entrenchment is found in only two democracies in Africa out of nine, Namibia and South Africa (Table 2.2). Authoritarian regimes with entrenched ruling parties generally

Table 2.2 Entrenched parties and regime type in Africa (2024)

	Democratic regimes	Hybrid regimes	Autocratic regimes
Entrenched parties	22% (2)	50% (10)	69% (11)
Nonentrenched parties	78% (7)	50% (10)	31% (5)
Total	100% (9)	100% (20)	100% (16)

Note: Excludes military regimes.
Source: Freedom House (2024).

do better with respect to women's representation than hybrid regimes. Their staying power and continued dominance help explain, in part, why women and other newcomers to politics might align themselves with such parties, knowing that they have a good likelihood of winning. In many authoritarian countries the ruling party is able to use reserved seats for women to their own advantage, thereby instrumentalizing women in a new multiparty context. Entrenched parties are effective in backing loyal women and in trouncing the opposition parties and opposition women. They have the resources to co-opt the opposition, including opposition women.

Today, about twenty-three party system countries in Africa have entrenched parties, while twenty-one do not have entrenched parties. Entrenched parties are found in eleven out of sixteen autocracies that have ruling parties (69 percent) (Table 2.2). Hybrid regimes are less likely than autocracies to have entrenched ruling parties and have lower rates of women's representation than full-blown autocracies and democracies (Table 2.3). They have more competition than autocracies, and they may alternate parties as a result of elections (e.g., Kenya). They may be more accommodating to opposition parties, unlike fully authoritarian systems that can use the full force of the party and state to suppress the opposition. But at the end of the day, hybrid regimes are weakly institutionalized and not as likely to be entrenched (Table 2.2). They have weak parties that don't have the advantages of organizationally stronger parties with greater resources and the ability to recruit women candidates. Women who run for office can't rely on strong party affiliation to help garner voter support (Belschner 2022).

Authoritarian regimes, unlike hybrid regimes and democracies, sought to undercut potential threats from other parties in the new multiparty context, especially after the 1990s. They did not attempt to accommodate a variety of societal interests, and therefore they could more easily adopt measures like appointing a cabinet made up of 50 percent women or appointing a woman vice president or prime minister. As Noh et al. (2024) found, when

Table 2.3 Level of women's legislative representation in entrenched parties by regime type in Africa (2024)

	Democratic regimes (%)	Hybrid regimes (%)	Autocratic regimes (%)
Entrenched parties	47.5	25.6	34.2
Nonentrenched parties	10.3	17.6	19.6
Overall	26.4	19.8	28.2

Source: Freedom House (2024); IPU (2024).

quotas legitimate an authoritarian regime, they gain less support from regime opponents. Similar anti–women's rights sentiments were found in Tunisia as a result of former President Ben Ali's pro-women policies (Noh et al. 2024; Tripp 2019). Authoritarian regimes can dramatically increase women's representation in the Parliament without having to negotiate with other political actors. But this also means that they can undo these policies just as easily, as Algeria did when it dropped the quota in 2022.

Donno and Kreft (2019) have argued that in autocracies, "multiparty competition may in fact unleash political forces that only crowd out progress on women's rights and representation, for example, when political contestation has an ethnic dimension." Moreover, women are left out of cabinets when there are many ethnic patrons to be co-opted (Arriola and Johnson 2014; Kroeger and Kang 2022). Challengers to women's representation may be ethnically based, but they may also include conservative societal forces, such as Islamists in Muslim-majority countries, that might use political competition to sideline women.

Political competition, however, works differently in democracies. In fact, political competition in democracies may be linked to the expansion of women's political rights and opportunities like the expansion of women's suffrage (Teele 2018) or the adoption of gender quotas (Fernandes et al. 2024; Weeks 2018). Faced with an electoral threat and the need to garner votes, parties are forced to respond to political competition incentives and adopt reforms they may have previously opposed. Thus, the mechanism for advancing women as leaders is generally different in democracies when compared to autocracies and semiauthoritarian regimes. Competition works against raising levels of women's representation in autocracies and hybrid regimes, whereas it potentially helps this process in democracies.

Most of the studies on political competition and gender quotas have focused on democracies. However, new work in the MENA region suggests the importance of competition for quota adoption, even in autocracies (Shalaby 2025). But even in the Middle East, the big jumps in representation have been found in authoritarian countries because of unilateral state interventions—for example, the UAE, which has no political competition and where appointed women claim 50 percent of the seats in Parliament and 30 percent of the cabinet seats.

Unlike in democracies and even hybrid regimes, the curtailment of competition in authoritarian contexts generally means crushing the opposition. Thus, the goal is to eliminate competition from the system, which allows them the leeway to make grand statements by appointing women leaders without pushback from the political elite. Of course, not all stable autocracies are interested in promoting women leaders. Thus, the relationship between competition and women's representation varies, with higher representation in democracies with high levels of political competition. It is lowest in hybrid, military, and unstable regimes, and high in stable autocracies with almost no competition (Table 2.4).

Dominant entrenched parties use women candidates and the appointment of women at the highest levels to signal to internal constituencies their concern about women's status and to appeal to women voters. Barnes and Burchard (2012) found strong evidence that increasing women's representation in parliaments in Africa influences women's political engagement relative to that of men, and it decreases the size of the political engagement gap in sub-Saharan Africa. They measured political engagement with indicators such as discussion of politics with friends and neighbors,

Table 2.4 Party entrenchment, regime type, and competition

	Party entrenchment/institutionalization	
	Weak	Strong
High competition	**Low women's representation** Hybrid regimes	**High women's representation** Democracies
Low or no competition	**Low women's representation** Unstable autocracies Military regimes Personalist dictatorships	**High women's representation** Stable autocracies

attending a demonstration, interest in public affairs, and contact with a parliamentary representative or political party official. Women also tend to care more about women's leadership than men. In the Afrobarometer Survey Round 9 (2021–2023), which surveyed thirty-nine countries, as many as 80.8 percent of women supported the statement "Women should have the same chance of being elected to political office as men," compared with 70.9 percent of men. Earlier rounds with different countries produce similar gendered outcomes. Women tend to vote at rates slightly lower than men with a few exceptions. The countries where women exceed or are on par with men when it comes to voting tend to have longer histories with democracy (Hern 2020). In the most recent Afrobarometer survey that asked whether the respondents voted in the last election, in Botswana, South Africa, Lesotho, and Senegal more women than men voted, and men and women reported voting at similar rates in Cape Verde and Mauritius. The gender gap in voting was marginal in Malawi and Tanzania (Tripp 2013).

One consequence of the lack of competition in autocracies is the ease with which gender quotas and women leaders can be dropped. There have been relatively few significant reversals in the promotion of women leaders in authoritarian African countries, but the few we observe reveal the instrumental use of women in reverse. The inclusion of women is not a given, and they can potentially be dropped just as easily as they are incorporated for many of the same reasons: because they can ignore societal and opposition party pressures to a greater extent than democracies or hybrid regimes. Sometimes, women are appointed as ministers to clean up a ministry and then dispensed with after they have completed the task. Some women were brought in as heads of state during periods of conflict to help ease tensions because they were detached from warring factions, such as Ruth Perry in Liberia (1996–1997), Catherine Samba-Panza in Central African Republic (2014–2016), and Sylvie Kinigi in Burundi (1993–1994). They were then removed from office when the conflict subsided.

Other times, female leaders are disposed of when it is feared they will become a liability. In Algeria, the percentage of women in the legislature jumped from 8 percent in 2007 to 31.6 percent in 2012 after legal quotas were adopted. Meanwhile, the vote share for the ruling party—Front de libération nationale (National Liberation Front; FLN)—declined dramatically as it faced new challenges from opposition parties, and its fate was no longer assured as it once had been in the past after massive protests rocked the country between 2019 and 2021. The percentage of FLN seats in Parliament dropped from 35 percent in 2007 to 24 percent in 2022, as its vote share fell from 17.35 percent in 2017 to 6.24 percent in 2021. As a result, the political elite quietly stopped enforcing the quota in the 2021 election, and the representation of women plummeted from 25.8 to 8 percent.

Given my theoretical expectations concerning a link between women's representation and party entrenchment, I turn to a linear mixed-effect model to evaluate the effect of party entrenchment on women's representation across fifty-two African countries (Table 2.5). The model relies on data coded in five-year increments from 1990 to 2020 and for the year 2024. The outcome variable is the percent of women in the national legislature. The main explanatory variable is a binary measure indicating whether the ruling party is entrenched or not (i.e., whether the party or the same party by a different name has survived three consecutive election cycles). The model accounts for other covariates that may influence the level of women's representation, including the presence of a gender quota, regime type, GDP per capita, and foreign aid, and postconflict status. The gender quota variable categorizes countries as having either "no quota," "voluntary party quota of the ruling party," "reserved seats," or a "candidate quota." Regime type is measured using the country's Freedom House status, which classifies countries as either "free," "not free," or "partly free," categories that correspond to my democratic, autocratic, and hybrid regime types. GDP per capita is measured in current US dollars as reported by the World Bank. To capture foreign aid, I use the net official development assistance received per capita as reported by the World Bank. Postconflict is a binary variable coded as "1" for countries that have experienced major conflict between 1990 and 2000 with over one thousand annual deaths in any given year within that timeframe, as reported by the Battle Deaths Dataset of the Peace Research Institute Oslo (PRIO). The model includes a random intercept for each country to account for unobserved heterogeneity across countries. It also includes year fixed effects to account for the general increase in women's representation over time. The results are presented in Table 2.5.

In line with my theoretical expectations, the results show a positive and statistically significant relationship between party entrenchment and women's representation. Women's representation is 4.53 percent larger on average in countries with an entrenched party compared to those without an entrenched party, holding constant the other covariates. The results also show that having a quota (candidate, reserved seats, or ruling party quota) increases women's representation compared to countries without a quota. I do not find a statistically significant difference between women's representation in countries that are authoritarian ("not free") compared to democratic ("free"). Women's

Table 2.5 Effect of party entrenchment on women's representation

Variable	Coefficient	Standard Error
Entrenched Party	4.530***	(0.850)
Gender Quota		
Candidate Quota	6.138***	(1.503)
Reserved Seats	10.935***	(1.370)
Ruling Party Quota	11.526***	(1.717)
Freedom House Status		
Not Free	−2.555	(1.576)
Partly Free	−4.041***	(1.445)
GDP per capita	0.0001	(0.0001)
Foreign Aid	−0.002	(0.005)
Post-conflict	2.872**	(1.289)
Constant	−717.209***	(75.029)
Observations	367	
# Countries (Random Effects)	52	
Year Fixed Effects	Yes	

Note: **$p < 0.05$***$p < 0.01$. Reference categories: No Quota (Gender Quota), Free (Freedom House Status)

Source: IPU (2024); IDEA (2024); Freedom House (2024); World Bank Open Data (2024).

representation, however, is lower in countries that are "partly free" compared to "free." Postconflict impacts are also significant, although in this model foreign aid does not appear to reach significance.

Strategies of Entrenchment: Quotas

One of the main ways authoritarian countries used women leaders maintained power by implementing gender quotas. Gender quotas became one of the primary drivers behind the increased representation of women in politics, particularly following the 1995 UN Fourth World Conference on Women, held in Beijing. They are an important way that ruling parties in authoritarian countries are able to cling to power. Before 1995, only seven African countries had adopted quota systems, with some, like Egypt and Ghana, dropping them soon after. However, the landscape has evolved significantly since then, and today approximately 74 percent of all African nations have embraced some type of gender quota. In Africa, 92 percent of authoritarian regimes

Table 2.6 Gender quotas in African legislatures by regime (2024)

Quota type	Democracies	Hybrid regimes	Authoritarian regimes
Legislated candidate quota	3	7	11
Reserved seats	0	5	10
(Ruling) party quota	2	3	4
Total countries with quotas	5	15	25
Countries with no quota	4	6	3
	$n = 9$	$n = 21$	$n = 28$

Note: There is overlap in some countries with two different quota types.
Source: IDEA (2024).

had implemented quotas, followed by 74 percent of hybrid regimes, and 50 percent of democracies (Table 2.6).

It is notable that the outcomes for women's representation are fairly similar regardless of whether the quotas used are legislated, reserved seats, or voluntary party quotas by the dominant party (Table 2.6). *Reserved seats* are seats set aside that only women can run for regardless of political party. *Legislated candidate quotas* are provided through constitutions and/or electoral/party laws requiring that a minimum number of candidates are women. This type of quota is usually binding on all parties that intend to contest parliamentary seats. Sometimes sanctions are imposed to force parties to comply with the quota. *Voluntary party quotas,* in contrast, are self-imposed by political parties without a legal mandate.

In African countries that have instituted quotas, women now hold an average of 28.9 percent of parliamentary seats, whereas in those without such measures, women hold approximately 15.9 percent of the seats (Table 2.7). Notably, a few countries, like Seychelles, had achieved substantial female representation without the use of quotas, boasting a rate of women constituting 43.8 percent of parliamentary seats in 2015. Nevertheless, the countries with the highest levels of female representation tend to rely on quota systems to achieve such outcomes. Even where one finds elevated levels of representation without a quota, it is highly likely that an informal or soft quota is being used.

Generally, nations using proportional representation systems tend to embrace voluntary party quotas, whereas those utilizing plurality/majoritarian systems tend to favor reserved seats, as noted by Laserud and

Table 2.7 Quota types and levels of female representation in Africa (2024)

Quota type	Levels of female representation (%)
Legislated candidate quotas	20.4
Voluntary party quotas*	36.3
Reserved seats	31.9
Quota	28.9
No quota	15.9

*Ruling party has voluntary party quotas.
Sources: IDEA (2024); IPU (2024).

Taphorn (2007). In contrast, in Africa, there does not appear to be a clear-cut connection between the type of quota and the electoral system in use.

Reserved Seats

As mentioned earlier, reserved seats are a type of quota whereby specific seats are designated exclusively for women candidates. Only authoritarian countries use reserved seats in Africa, and all but two of the reserved seat systems are in nondemocratic countries globally (Table 2.8). Reserved seats are often treated as a neutral mechanism in the literature with a few exceptions, devoid of implications beyond promoting women as candidates. Some of the literature on quotas has focused on the positive aspects of reserved seats for women because they are regarded as a mechanism through which to advance a women's rights agenda (Qureshi and Ahmad 2020; Yoon 2013). Reserved seats are seen as a way of encouraging women to participate in politics (Burain 2014; Song 2016), closing the gender gap in political representation, and enhancing gender equality and as evidence for the redress of past imbalances (Nanivadekar 2006), especially in countries that are culturally not amenable to women's public roles. Quotas, including reserved seats, are sometimes viewed as a positive response to pressures from women's movements and coalitions (Kang and Tripp 2018; Krook 2006) and to pressures from international bodies like the United Nations to ensure greater representation of women in political decision-making (Bush and Zetterberg 2021).

More critical accounts have suggested that such quotas represent *autocratic genderwashing* to hide the less savory aspects of authoritarian rule (Allan

Table 2.8 Women parliamentarians in reserved-seats systems: Ruling party versus opposition parties globally (2022)

Country	Freedom House ranking	Women in Parliament	Ruling party women parliamentarians	Opposition women parliamentarians	Independent women parliamentarians
Bangladesh	39 Partly free	20.90%	86% 62	13% 9	1% 1
Burundi	14 Not free	38.20%	76% 35	24% 11	...
China	9 Not free	24.90%	49% (435 est.)	51% (307 est.)***	...
Djibouti	24 Not free	26.20%	93% 14	7% 1	...
Egypt	18 Not free	27.70%	38% 62	54% 91	6% 10
Guyana	73 Free	35.70%	46% 11	54% 13	...
Haiti	37 Partly free	0%	0%	0%	0%
Iraq	29 Not free	29.80%	33% 31	62% 59	5% 5
Jordan	34 Not free	11.50%	...	0%	100% 15
Kenya	48 Partly free	21.60%	56% 39	41% 29	3% 2
Mauritania	35 Partly free	20.30%	60% 12	40% 8	...
Morocco	37 Partly free	24.10%	47%** 45	63% 50	...
Nepal	56 Partly free	32.70%	58% 52	42% 38	...
Niger	48 Partly free	25.90%	...	...	...
Pakistan	37 Partly free	20.20%	45% 31	55% 38	0% 0
Rwanda	21 Not free	61.30%	90% 44	10% 5	...
Samoa	81 Free	9.10%	75% 3	25% 1	0% 0

Continued

Table 2.8 *Continued*

Country	Freedom House ranking	Women in Parliament	Ruling party women parliamentarians	Opposition women parliamentarians	Independent women parliamentarians
Saudi Arabia	7 Not free	19.90%*	...	...	...
Somalia	7 Not free	24.40%*	...	...	...
Tanzania	34 Partly free	36.90%	92% 94	8% 8	...
Uganda	34 Not free	33.80%	42% 61	26% 38	32%* 48
UAE	17 Not free	50%*	...	...	...
Zimbabwe	28 Not free	30.60%	61% 52	39% 33	0% 0

*Appointed
**Ruling coalition
***https://npcobserver.com/2018/03/10/demographics-of-the-13th-npc/.
Sources: Freedom House (2024); IDEA (2024); IPU (2024).

2019; Bjarnegård and Zetterberg 2022). Allan refers to "genderwashing" as the counterpart to "greenwashing" in her study of Morocco and Equatorial Guinea. For her, it represents the abuse of women's rights by authorities, who simultaneously try to convince others "that they are promoting women's empowerment in order to attract investment, increase legitimacy abroad, and divert international attention from the women resisting their actions" (Allan 2019, 10). It serves to silence resistance, and at the same time it works in conjunction with Western states and corporations to hide their collective abuses. Sylvia Tamale (1999, 20) has argued that the reserved seats in Uganda suggest that the leaders do not have a real commitment to women's rights and that they are simply paying "lip service to women's emancipation." Others have argued that reserved seats limit women's meaningful ability to influence policymaking, as in the case of Rwanda (Burnet 2019), and that they also block women from accessing constituency seats (Darhour and Dahlerup 2013).

What generally is not considered are the implications reserved seats have for the strengthening of autocracy, particularly strategies to quell the opposition. But much depends on the political environment in which they are introduced. Targeting opposition women is integral to the strategy of adopting reserved seats. The inclusion of marginalized groups through quotas can lend legitimacy to the political system and enhances the prospects of incumbents winning elections. Herein lies a dilemma: Quotas can be used not only to advance inclusion but also to further entrench autocratic ruling parties.

Quotas are not only a response to pressure from women's movements; they are also a means by which hegemonic ruling parties maintain dominance and longevity in power. Ruling parties thus use women partisans to entrench themselves in power while sidelining opposition women. Bernhard et al. (2020) have argued that incumbent authoritarians opened themselves to the risk of losing when they introduced multiparty competition, but with time, they generally gained legitimacy and regime strength. One way they did this was by ensuring that the opposition remained weak and fragmented. As we have seen elsewhere, incumbent leaders in authoritarian countries have multiple legal and illegal means of excluding opponents from electoral competition (Levitsky and Way 2010; Schedler 2002). The instrumentalization of women's leadership and isolation of opposition women became key legal components of this strategy of entrenching themselves.

As incumbent parties were threatened with the loss of vote share with the introduction of multipartyism in the 1990s in Africa, they sought new strategies to remain in power to institutionalize their hegemonic position further. These threats to vote share coincided with efforts by international organizations like the United Nations and the African Union to pressure governments to increase women's political representation. Adopting reserved seats for women became one quota mechanism authoritarian leaders adopted to further entrench their parties and their regimes in power. They did so particularly after the 1995 UN Fourth World Conference on Women in Beijing, where a Platform of Action was adopted that required member states to take steps to increase women's political representation. The use of reserved seats that they could control took place alongside outright repression, co-optation of opposition women in leadership positions, and attempts to build coalitions with various opposition parties, often through women leaders.

In all the nondemocratic countries that have reserved seats globally, the majority of female representatives can be found in seats controlled by the ruling party and/or parties affiliated with the ruling party. In the remaining countries, the majority of seats are held by the ruling party even if, overall, the opposition parties combined have more seats (Table 2.8). As is evident in the chapters in this volume on Uganda, Zimbabwe, Rwanda, and Mauritania, ruling parties in autocracies prefer reserved seats to other quota systems because, unlike voluntary party quotas and legislated quotas, it is easier for them to control the women running for these seats and keep the opposition women from claiming these seats.

The ruling party also often creates a hostile campaigning atmosphere for women in the opposition in vying for reserved seats. With greater resources, the ruling party can outmaneuver women running in more poorly resourced opposition parties, and sometimes it can co-opt them. Thus, opposition parties have responded by promoting few women parliamentary candidates, making the likelihood of opposition women leaders emerging even more of a rarity.

Conclusion

This chapter argued that entrenched ruling parties in African countries, especially in authoritarian and dominant-party regimes, have been more successful in advancing women leaders than those with more frequent changes in power. This success is partly due to the stability and long-standing dominance of these parties, which allows them to utilize internationally-promoted strategies like gender quotas to secure political legitimacy while promoting women's representation.

Entrenched parties, even if weakly institutionalized, generally show higher levels of women's representation. Entrenched parties are those winning at least three consecutive elections and maintaining longevity. These parties have leveraged their stability to promote female leaders as part of their strategies to maintain dominance and respond to international pressures for gender inclusion. Their stability and longevity make them more likely to promote women in politics, as these rules create structured pathways that can benefit newcomers, including women.

The reason for these patterns has to do with the fact that African political systems often center around dominant presidential parties, with women's inclusion sometimes used to signal legitimacy. Reserved seats are a primary tool for authoritarian regimes to increase women's representation while maintaining control. Reserved seats are found exclusively in authoritarian states in Africa, where they allow the ruling party to control female representation and marginalize opposition women. In contrast to authoritarian regimes, hybrid regimes struggle with women's representation because of weaker party entrenchment and greater competition. Democratic regimes, however, tend to benefit from competition, which pressures parties to adopt inclusive reforms.

Women affiliated with ruling parties in authoritarian regimes have a better chance of electoral success because of resources and political support, while opposition women often face a hostile environment with limited access to campaign resources. These patterns are tied not only to postconflict dynamics and internal and external pressures but also to efforts by the political leadership to instrumentally offset declines in vote share with the introduction of multiparty politics in the 1990s.

PART II

DOMESTIC DIMENSIONS OF AUTHORITARIAN STRATEGIES

3
Preserving Vote Share in Uganda

Electoral authoritarian regimes have used various strategies to remain in power even as they have opened themselves up to competition through multiparty elections. These strategies included numerous measures by ruling parties to maintain vote share. Such efforts became especially important in Africa after the 1990s as most countries adopted multiparty systems. One strategy involved using reserved seats for women, which the ruling party could control through various gatekeeping mechanisms. The other quota mechanisms—legislated seats and voluntary party quotas—give opposition parties more leverage and are not as easily controlled by the ruling party. The dominant party also promoted women leaders to improve the party's image, increase legitimacy, and expand patronage ties. At the same time, it was no accident that opposition party women fared especially poorly in legislatures in reserved seat systems, in contrast to women in ruling parties and compared to male opposition candidates. This was by design, as this chapter shows.

This chapter looks at how Uganda's ruling party, the NRM, has advanced women in the legislature, simultaneously responding to pressures from the women's movement while seeking to ensure its continued dominance. Opposition women in the legislature have become the biggest losers in this process mainly because of the NRM's machinations. In Uganda, women in the opposition are de-campaigned vigorously by the NRM and have often found that running women for reserved seats is a losing proposition. The case of Uganda reveals an essential feature of authoritarianism in Africa today—namely, the use of women's rights to entrench the ruling party in power and maintain vote share. This instrumentalization of women's rights might not seem surprising, but the discrepancy between the levels of legislative representation of women in the opposition parties and the NRM is quite significant. The contrast with democracies like Botswana and Namibia (see Chapters 8 and 9, respectively) is also stark, as these are countries where ruling parties have lost vote share but have not used reserved seats to bolster their position.

Opposition parties globally have not been as successful as ruling parties in capturing women's reserved seats even where, as in Uganda, they have had women in top leadership positions of their parties and have commitments to

Why African Autocracies Promote Women as Leaders. Aili Mari Tripp, Oxford University Press. © Oxford University Press (2025). DOI: 10.1093/9780197829004.003.0004

increase women's representation in Parliament (see Chapter 2). The regime is interested in responding to women's rights activists who demand increased female representation to some extent. But ultimately, its primary goal is to remain in power, and it instrumentalizes women's representation to ensure its dominance.

This chapter[1] builds off of the more general observations about reserved seats in Chapter 2 and provides a background to the Ugandan case, detailing the status of women in the political opposition parties. It then describes the various tactics the ruling party has adopted to maintain vote share, notably after the country shifted to multipartyism in 2005, including the use of reserved seats and independent women candidates as well as tactics of repression, co-optation, and coalition building, to divide the opposition. It shows how the imbalance of opposition women in Parliament has more to do with the ruling party and its tactics and less to do with the opposition parties, despite their weaknesses concerning women's rights. The chapter concludes that these tactics involving women leaders are part and parcel of the ruling party's efforts to maintain vote share and ensure its longevity in power.

The chapter draws on forty-nine in-depth interviews in Uganda in 2021-2022 with women's rights leaders; parliamentarians; ruling and opposition party leaders; journalists; lawyers; academics; members of the judiciary, including a Supreme Court justice and a high court justice; representatives from the ministry of women's affairs; several former ministers, including the first minister of women in development, members of the Constitutional Commission; and many others.

Background

Women's initial foray into legislative politics started under British colonial rule with the Legislative Council (LEGCO). The first two women appointed to the LEGCO in 1954, Barbara Saben and Alice Boase, were British. There was one elected female member, an Asian Ugandan, Miriam Mitha, who served in the LEGCO from 1955 to 1961. At the time, the Uganda African Women's League wrote to the governor, asking that he appoint African women to the LEGCO, and in response, the first African women representatives were appointed, starting in 1956 with Pumla Kisosonkole, followed by four others.

[1] The chapter draws heavily on Tripp (2023).

Even fewer women served at the local level. However, there were a few notable exceptions: Janet Wesonga became mayor of Mbale in 1967, and Miriam Mitha served on the Mbale town council in the early 1950s. The British Barbara Saben served as deputy mayor of Kampala from 1959 to 1960 and was the first female mayor of Kampala from 1961 to 1962.

The National Assembly, which succeeded the LEGCO after independence, held its first direct elections in 1962. Sugra Visram and Florence Lubega were nominated to the National Assembly representing the Buganda legislature (the Lukiiko), and Eseza Makumbi, who was also on the Lukiiko, was nominated to serve on the East African Legislative Assembly, where she remained until 1977.

Only a handful of women were visible in politics during the Idi Amin regime (1971–1979). One of the most noteworthy women was Princess Elizabeth Bagaya Akiiki of Toro, appointed foreign minister by the Ugandan dictator Idi Amin in 1974, having served as ambassador-at-large between 1971 and 1973. Amin subsequently dismissed Bagaya from her position as foreign minister, attempting to humiliate her by portraying her as an immoral woman. Bagaya was a trailblazing advocate and became Uganda's first woman admitted to the bar in 1966. Mary Senkatuka Astles was the other woman leader who gained visibility during Amin's rule. She served as minister of community development (1975–1978) and minister of culture (1978–1979) in Amin's government. Amin also appointed Bernadetta Olowo as ambassador to the Holy See, making her the first woman in the world to hold such a position in nine hundred years. Hajati Kateregа was appointed minister of transport and communication in 1975.

Although military regimes in Africa were generally much less disposed to women leaders and women's rights, one finds that even some of the most repressive regimes passed woman-friendly legislation. Generally, the Parliament was dissolved, as was the case under Idi Amin in Uganda (1971–1979) when he announced that "all legislative powers shall be exercised by me through the proclamation of decrees evidenced in writing under my hand and sealed with the public seal" ("Idi Amin Decrees" 2015). In 1978, the Parliament was reconstituted as a National Consultative Council but served merely as a rubber stamp. However, Amin did manage to issue several decrees affecting women, including the Customary Marriage Act of 1973, which prohibited marriage for women under sixteen and males under eighteen. The Succession Act (Amendment) Decree of 1972 allowed for customary law to govern in many situations and enshrined women's right to inherit from husbands. The Ministry of Public Service and Local Administration Establishment Notice No. 24 allowed female civil servants to take maternity leave starting at the thirty-eighth week of pregnancy or earlier if their health conditions warranted it.

To be clear, Amin was no promoter of women's rights. Amin's regime terrorized, attacked, arrested, tortured, and killed women and their family members. Amin encouraged his Muslim officers to engage in sexual assault against Christian girls with the intent of impregnating them. Additionally, military personnel frequently organized the collection of girls from universities, high schools, training centers, and hospitals for the "entertainment" of Amin's men. In 1978, Amin decreed the establishment of the National Council of Women (NCW) while simultaneously announcing the abolition of all independent women's organizations, including entities such as the Mothers' Union and YWCA (Tripp 2000).

At the same time, Amin also repressed women in other ways. He banned miniskirts, wigs, and trousers, citing concerns about public morality and anticolonial and anti-Western sentiments (Decker 2014). The ban on trousers was later lifted when he discovered that Muslim women in South Asian countries and in parts of the Middle East wore pants. Additionally, he prohibited the use of creams, perfumes, and deodorants. Amin's militia enforced these bans and occasionally used them as a pretext for attacks on women under the guise of maintaining law and order (Akello 1982). As part of his efforts to enforce moral standards, Amin ordered the removal of unmarried women from the city streets, labeling them as alleged "prostitutes." This resulted in deserted streets with only police officers present. His military officers also initiated campaigns to pressure single Ugandan women into marriage, as a component of his morality crusade (Tripp 2000).

After Amin was ousted by Tanzanian troops supported by Ugandan rebels in 1979, an interim government was installed until elections were held in 1980. Rhoda Kalema and Geraldine Bitamazire served as MPs between 1979 and 1980; Theresa Odongo-Oduka served from 1980 to 1985; and she served as state minister of health (1980–1986). Thus, women did not feature in any significant way in authoritarian politics in the early years of postindependence Uganda.

Impact of Conflict

President Yoweri Museveni and his NRM took over the country in 1986 with the end of the Bush War against President Milton Obote that had started in 1980. After the 1989 elections for the National Resistance Council (the

NRM-led legislature), 18 percent of the seats were held by women, mostly as a result of the introduction of reserved seats for women. This followed patterns established during the guerrilla war that brought Museveni to power, in which seats were set aside for women on the local-level Resistance Councils, particularly in the Luwero area.

Museveni's promotion of women as leaders to the Resistance Councils (precursors to the local councils) and to his cabinet won him the support of women, particularly rural women. In the early 1990s, when I was carrying out interviews for my 2000 book *Women and Politics in Uganda*, women talked about the Museveni regime as the "government of enlightenment." Having a woman vice president, regardless of whether she did much for women, was symbolically important because it gave women the sense that they could do anything: They felt they could, for example, start a furniture-making business, become vice chancellor of a university, run an import-export business, or become a race car driver. Women started engaging in public activities in ways that they had not done before. The women's movement succeeded in implementing a 1.5 affirmative action program at Makerere University, which allowed more qualified women to enter university. Today, women receive top scores in university as they graduate. Thus, the changes in women's lives have been palpable.

Popular support for women in politics has also increased with time. The percentage of people who believe women should have the same chance of being elected to political office as men has increased within a decade from 66 percent in 2011 to 77.9 percent in 2021–2023, with women consistently being more supportive of women leaders (Table 3.1).

Table 3.1 Support for women in politics in Uganda

Year of survey	Support for women in politics (%)*	Men (%)	Women (%)
2011/2013	66.0	58.2	73.8
2016/2018	76.4	70.6	82.3
2021/2023	83.4	80.5	86.5
2024/2025	77.9	71.7	84.3

Source: Afrobarometer (2024).
*Response to question: Agree or agree strongly that women should have the same chance of being elected to political office as men.

However, all along, Museveni also instrumentalized women. He introduced a reserved seat system in Parliament, a system that only authoritarian countries use in Africa because it allows the ruling party to control the seats more easily than other quota systems (see Chapter 2). The increase in women's parliamentary representation after 1989 made Uganda one of the first countries in Africa where postconflict effects on women's legislative representation became visible, as Uganda had among the highest rates of female representation in Africa at the time. As explained in Chapter 1, countries that came out of decades of conflict and or experienced extremely intense conflict after the 1990s tended to have significantly higher rates of representation and made more constitutional and legislative gender reforms than countries that did not experience these conflicts. This had to do with changes in political elites, transformations in gender relations, pressures from women's movements, and emerging international norms regarding women's rights (Tripp 2015).

Wishing to further institutionalize the parliamentary quota, women's rights activists demanded reserved seats in the 1995 constitution-making process. Pressure from women lawyers like Miria Matembe and Mary Maitum, who served on the Constitutional Commission, resulted in critical women's rights provisions in the constitution, and pressure from the Women's Caucus and Matembe, who served in the Constitutional Assembly as well, resulted in the reservation of 30 percent of parliamentary seats for women.

Multipartyism and the Double-Edged Sword of Affirmative Action

According to the constitution (ch. 5, art. 42.1), one-third of all political positions should be reserved for women except where it was not practical to do so; however, the NRM only aggressively tried to meet these goals after 2005. A significant change in tactics occurred after Uganda's Parliament adopted multipartyism in 2005 in a quid pro quo arrangement with Museveni that resulted in the lifting of term limits. After this time, the NRM had to start worrying more about maintaining its vote share (Table 3.2). The NRM significantly increased its percentage of women ministers, women in Parliament, and local government at this time.

The women's movement simultaneously pressed Museveni to increase the number of women leaders. As one 2021 petition from an organization called the "Women's Movement of Uganda," explained:

Table 3.2 NRM vote share in parliamentary elections

Year	NRM vote share (%)
1989	100
1996	100
2001	100
2006	67
2011	70
2016	69
2020	64

Source: Uganda Electoral Commission (2021).

Even the harshest critic of the President or the NRM would give credit where it is due and appreciate that under President Museveni's tenure in office, the country has registered some important strides, some of which spring from the affirmative action provisions in the 1995 Constitution. Therefore, we are preaching to the already converted, and our call to you, Mr. President, is to consolidate these gains of your government by ensuring that more women are placed in strategic decision-making positions in the new cabinet, not as a matter of tokenism or sheer gender balance but from recognition of the fact that the women of Uganda have demonstrated excellence and ethical leadership in most places where they have been entrusted with the mantle of leadership (Watchdog Uganda 2021).

The upshot of such efforts was a series of appointments of women to top executive positions and to the cabinet. The main motivation for the ruling party's tactics has been the need to remain in power, notably after the country adopted a multiparty system in 2005. At that time, there was a drop in support for the NRM in parliamentary elections, from 100 percent in the 2001 elections to 67 percent in 2006. Similar rates for the NRM were seen in subsequent elections. Museveni also experienced a drop in support from 69 percent in the 2001 presidential elections to 59 percent in 2005 and 58 percent in the 2020 elections. Even if fractured, the new challenges from the opposition made the maintenance of vote share the paramount goal of the NRM.

In 2024, women in Uganda claimed 47 percent of local government positions, 35 percent of the parliamentary seats, and 43 percent of the cabinet positions. After the 2021 election, women occupied the positions of vice president, prime minister, and deputy prime minister. Speciosa Kazibwe had already held the post of vice president from 1994 to 2003. In 2022, Anita Among secured the position of speaker of the house, a post also held by Rebecca Kadaga from 2011 to 2021. The new appointments were, in part, a way to soften the image of the regime following a particularly violent election in which opposition leaders and followers were brutalized.

These patterns also represent a steady increase in women's representation in Uganda since the NRM took over in 1986. In the most recent parliamentary election, 146 women were elected to reserved seats, one for each district. An additional fourteen women were elected to open seats (out of a total of 353 seats), and thirteen were elected to special interest group seats (out of thirty). The opposition parties combined claimed only one-fifth of the reserved seats for women, far less than their hold on 29 percent of the seats. In contrast, according to the Uganda Electoral Commission, the ruling party controls 69 percent of the vote share and 80 percent of the reserved seats for women. This does not include the other appointed, reserved, and independent seats the ruling party controls.

After President Yoweri Museveni took over in 1986, Uganda was governed by his "no-party" NRM, which was ostensibly a broad-based movement but operated as a de facto single party. Uganda fits the modal African party system in which a hegemonic presidential party dominates the political landscape, surrounded by several smaller parties, including the Uganda People's Congress (UPC) of the former president, Milton Obote, and the Democratic Party (DP). The Forum for Democratic Change (FDC) emerged as the main opposition party in 2004, followed by the National Unity Platform (NUP), which controlled the largest share of opposition seats after the 2021 elections.

However, the NRM's efforts to be inclusive of women also drew criticism from other quarters because the move further entrenched and legitimized the NRM, posing a conundrum for women's rights activists. Miria Matembe, a former parliamentarian and ethics minister and a staunch supporter of the NRM in the past, told me in an interview:

> Museveni intended to offer women an opportunity to get into political structures, and it [his policy] was supposed to motivate them and bring them on board so that their views could be heard that and they would be able to influence the governance agenda. As I talk now, the affirmative action, as you know, it is a double-edged sword. It can be used by those in power . . . to sustain them in power (U32.8.12.20).

Another observer and human rights lawyer pointed out in an interview:

> First, the regime was acutely aware of the global movement for the emancipation of women for the protection of the rights of women and latched onto that global movement to give itself a veneer of legitimacy. Let's not forget that the very first thing President Museveni did when he came to power in 1986 was to ratify international human rights instruments. He latched onto international normative frameworks and development to render himself a veneer of legitimacy. Women's rights became one of the low-lying political fruits that he could pick, and he picked a basketful of them (U7.7.4.20).

Thus, Museveni has been able to play the woman card to great effect with his ultimate goal being to maintain NRM's vote share and staying in power.

Women's Rights Legislation and Constitutional Reforms

Ironically, even though the NRM worked to sideline opposition women, women politicians collaborated across party differences to promote legislation around women's rights. This has taken various forms, most notably through the Uganda Women's Parliamentary Association (UWOPA), the most organized and active caucus within the Ugandan legislature. Women in both reserved and open seats alike have championed a women's rights agenda (Clayton et al. 2017, Wang 2013). Also the Uganda Women's Network (UWONET) and other NGOs have done trainings, provided technical support, and collaborated with parliamentarians on specific advocacy initiatives (U31.6.24.20).

UWOPA has been instrumental in passing a steady stream of legislation affecting women with respect to land (1997, 2010 amended), refugee rights (2006), maternity leave (increasing days off) (2006), employment (2006), sexual harassment (2006), defilement (2007), disability rights (2008), trafficking (2009), domestic violence (2010) and its regulations (2011), female genital cutting (2010), antipornography (2014), and many other concerns. The Medium and Small Enterprise Policy (2015) addresses gender equity as one of its goals. The International Criminal Court Act (2010) criminalized sexual exploitation of women during conflict. In 2006, a law was passed to establish the Equal Opportunities Commission, which was mandated by the 1995 Constitution to oversee the implementation of policies regarding women's rights.

Some of the policies and laws adopted address the political representation of women. The 1995 Constitution provides for reserved seats for women and women's rights to elected office. Beyond this, one of the specific objectives outlined in Uganda's National Gender Policy of 1997 and 2007 is formulating strategies to eradicate discrimination against women in elective and appointed positions within administrative structures. Additionally, the government enacted the Equal Opportunity Commission Act of 2007, which advocates for eliminating gender-based inequalities, particularly those related to sex, and promotes affirmative action policies. The Presidential Elections Act (2000) ensures that both men and women have the opportunity to run for the presidency. Moreover, the Local Governments Act (1997) and the Parliamentary Elections Act (2005) mandate the allocation of 30 percent reserved seats for women at both the national and subnational levels of decision-making, with a strong emphasis on fostering women's participation in politics without any form of discrimination. Within the public service, all officers are governed by the comprehensive Uganda Public Service Standing Orders (2010), which encompass various aspects of public service conduct, including explicit provisions for addressing issues like sexual harassment.

In July 2010, Uganda's Parliament ratified the Protocol to the African Charter on Human and Peoples' Rights on the Rights of Women in Africa (the Maputo Protocol), having faced powerful opposition from the Roman Catholic Church and the Uganda Joint Christian Council. There are still significant gaps in legislation, particularly with respect to marriage, divorce, and land inheritance. The most contentious issues have been around sexual reproductive health and the right to terminate pregnancy, age-appropriate sex education, and the rights of teenage mothers to access contraception. However, the divisions around legislation are not between parties but, rather, they fall along lines age, with younger MPs being more open to these issues (U31.6.24.20).

Women in reserved seats are more active in Parliament in making interventions than women in open seats, even though women in reserved seats differ little from women in open seats in the Ugandan Parliament regarding their qualifications (O'Brien 2012; Clayton et al. 2017). Some have argued that this is because the women in the reserved seats feel accountable to their constituents, the women's movement, and the NRM, but this would be true of women NRM supporters in open seats as well. This study suggests that pressure from both the NRM and women's movement explains the behavior of women parliamentarians in different parties and different types of seats.

Ruling Party Tactics

To maintain vote share, the NRM has been systematically picking off high-profile leaders of opposition parties, including women, while at the same time limiting potential defectors and maintaining a relatively inclusive ruling elite coalition (Khisa 2016). The ruling party uses various forms of co-optation and patronage, from job offers and money to promises not to de-campaign candidates to lure them from the opposition. They also block access to jobs, businesses, or credit, impose unusual tax assessments, dismantle businesswomen's franchise holdings, and carry out direct repression (Muwanga et al. 2020). These efforts to co-opt opposition leaders escalate as elections draw near.

The opposition tends to win in urban areas, but the NRM controls the countryside, where most people live (Bwana 2009). The NRM also merged its party apparatus with the state and, therefore, can harness state resources to gain electoral advantage. These resources give it greater organizational capacity than the opposition parties, especially its use of the local council system, a multitiered system of administrative units that reach the village level. It also uses the Women's Councils for the same organizational end, although they are weak. The NRM can field candidates in almost all districts, including female candidates. It also has the necessary resources to bribe people into supporting the NRM and uses funds diverted from government projects for women, youth, and other groups (Khisa 2018; Muwanga et al. 2020).

Reserved Seats

The NRM's adoption of reserved seats has been one tactic to place women loyalists into the National Assembly. The use of reserved seats to include women in the Parliament is relatively low cost since it does not come at the expense of any seats held by incumbent men. After President Yoweri Museveni took over in 1986, Uganda was governed by his "no-party" NRM, which was ostensibly a broad-based movement but operated as a de facto single party. Uganda adopted a multiparty system in 2005 following a referendum. Uganda has held four elections since that time: in 2006, 2011, 2016, and 2021. The NRM introduced a reserved seat system for women and other groups like the youth, workers, and people with disabilities in 1989. The reserved seat system, which was enshrined in the 1995 Constitution, continued with the country's opening of a multiparty system in 2005. Most of these reserved seats are held by the NRM, with each district represented by one woman (Table 3.3). The use of reserved seats allows the NRM to control the number of women who will be elected without the element of uncertainty that comes from party-list systems or other systems where the outcome is not predetermined.

The reserved seats also proliferate in rural districts, where the NRM can use the local state to coerce women. It is challenging for opposition parties

Table 3.3 Women candidates and winners of reserved seats by party, 2021 general election

Party	Women candidates for reserved seats	Women winning reserved seats	Women winning reserved seats (%)
National Resistance Movement	145	100	69
Forum for Democratic Change	83	8	10
National Unity Platform	86	13	15
Alliance for National Transformation	38	0	0
Democratic Party	26	1	4
Uganda People's Congress	14	2	14
Justice Forum	5	0	0
Ecological Party of Uganda	0	0	0
People's Progressive Party	0	0	0
Social Democratic Party	0	0	0
Independents	361	20	6

Source: Uganda Electoral Commission (2021).

to recruit strong and credible women candidates who can compete against NRM candidates in the rural areas. It is also common for the NRM to use its local machinery, including business supporters, to bribe potential opposition women candidates out of races. Thus, NRM candidates commonly win district women's seats unopposed (communication with Moses Khisa March 16, 2022).

Museveni increased the number of parliamentary seats from 280 in 1989 to 375 in 2011 and then to 529 in 2021. This meant that the NRM could increase the percentage of women in reserved seats without challenging the position of men in the Parliament. Women in Parliament increased from seventy-nine seats in 2006 to 146 in the 2021 election. The NRM vote share (Table 3.2) has decreased since the country went multiparty, but the NRM still holds on to the majority of seats in part because of the reserved seats it claims. The NRM has also increased the number of parliamentary appointees from twenty-five in 2006 to thirty in 2021. If one combines the NRM's elected seats with the NRM women, the appointed seats, and independents who support the NRM, the majority of parliamentarians are NRM supporters. This means that the NRM has maintained its overwhelming majority hold on politics, even with some fluctuations. After the 2006 election, what the NRM lost in overall seats, it recouped with an increase in women's seats, independent seats, and special interest appointees (Table 3.4). Interestingly, even though the number of women from opposition parties holding parliamentary seats is very low, the FDC and the Progressive People's Party both had percentage-wise more women in open seats than the NRM (Table 3.5).

Most notably, there has been an increase in independent candidates from thirteen in 2006 to thirty-two in 2021. Often, individuals who do not win primaries or are not chosen by their preferred party run as independents, giving the NRM even more candidates they can control. Moreover, the majority of women who contested for open seats in 2016 stood as independent candidates. This has helped Museveni maintain the lion's share of votes, even as the NRM vote share dropped from 66 percent in 2006 to 42 percent in 2021. Meanwhile, the opposition parties are increasingly fragmented. Almost two hundred independent women candidates ran for district seats in 2016, thus constituting nearly half of the 405 who ran for Parliament (Electoral Commission of Uganda 2016; Wang and Yoon 2018). Additionally, women make up at least two of ten representatives of the Uganda People's Defense Forces, at least one of five youth representatives, at least one of five representatives of persons with disabilities, and at least one woman in five as workers' representatives and a representative of older adults. And finally, NRM women run for the open constituency seats (Table 3.4).

Repression

A key NRM tactic is to treat opposition leaders violently in order to make an example of them. Museveni won a sixth five-year term in office in the January 2021 elections that his chief opponent, Bobi Wine, claimed were fraudulent. In the 2021 elections, Wine and his NUP supporters came under ruthless repression, as had FDC leaders and members in prior elections. FDC leader Kizza Besigye and an associate were arrested in 2024 in Kenya under mysterious circumstances and spirited back to Uganda to stand trial in a military court. Women opposition leaders and members have not been spared. As

Table 3.4 Women in Uganda's Parliament

Year	Number of districts	Women in affirmative action seats	Women in open seats	Women appointed	Total women MPs	Total MPs	Women MPs (%)
1989*	39	39	2	9	50	280	18
1996*	39	39	8	4	51	276	19
2001*	56	56	13	6	75	304	24
2006	79	79	14	1	100	319	31
2011	112	112	11	8	131	375	35
2016	112	112	18	9	139	426	33
2021	146	146	18	13	167	555	32

Source: Department of Library Services Parliament of Uganda; Nakaweesi-Kimbugwe et al. (2018).
*National Resistance Council.

Table 3.5 Women candidates and winners of open seats by party, 2021 general election

Party	Women candidates for open seats	Women winning open seats	Women winning open seats (%)	Total candidates	Women candidates for all open seats (%)
National Resistance Movement	29	11	38	352	8%
Forum for Democratic Change	5	0	0	212	2
National Unity Platform	6	3	50	182	3
Alliance for National Transformation	6	0	0	110	6
Democratic Party	4	0	0	97	4
Uganda People's Congress	3	1	33	31	10
Justice Forum	1	0	0	14	7
Ecological Party of Uganda	0	0	0	5	0
People's Progressive Party	2	1	50	3	66
Social Democratic Party	1	0	0	1	100
Independents	91	2	2	1040	35

Source: Uganda Electoral Commission (2021).

one activist said to me, "Women are a bit cautious. They're thinking, 'Okay, I really want to participate, but not in this environment. I have children'" (U37.7.28.20). So the risk involved in participating in politics is huge, particularly in opposition politics, especially for newcomers to politics who don't have great resources.

Ugandan police have attacked women in the opposition who have protested government policies. The late Honorable Cecilia Ogwal (1946–2024) was one of the longest-serving female legislators and who once served as the opposition chief whip. She was acting secretary general of the UPC from 1985 to 1992. Ogwal told *The Observer* in 2014 that she had survived twelve attempts on her life. In 2017, she alleged that security operatives beat her and her husband for campaigning against the lifting of the presidential age limit in the constitution. The age limit, which was removed that year, allowed Museveni—then in his fifth term—to run for yet another term and potentially rule indefinitely.

A National Executive Committee member and FDC secretary for the environment, Zainab Fatuma, was stripped in 2015 in a protest (Nyamishana 2015). In 2012, Ingrid Turinawe, then the chairperson of the Women's League and National Political Mobilizer, attended a political rally in Kampala in which she was arrested and a policeman grabbed her breast. She sued the Uganda Police Force and attorney general for suffering and embarrassment and won compensation. The Ugandan government was forced to apologize to her. Betty Nambooze, MP for Mukono Municipality since 2010, had been arrested on numerous occasions on politically motivated charges, and her life was threatened, and she was allegedly poisoned on one occasion. Although she had been a DP stalwart, in 2020, she joined the NUP party.

The NRM even de-campaigned Jessica Alupo in 2021 when she ran for Parliament, and then Museveni turned around and appointed her vice president after she ran as an independent and won. She was a former military officer and had served as a state minister for youth and children's affairs (2009–2011) and minister of education and sports (2011–2015). During her time as minister of education, she introduced many innovations, making the educational system more accessible to poorer children. Alupo ran for Parliament in a race that was marred by violence. She won the primary against another NRM candidate, but election officials allegedly tampered with the vote and announced her opponent's victory. She then ran as an independent in the second round and won (Okello 2020; "Who Is Jessica Alupo" 2021). A longtime NRM stalwart, perhaps she could afford to overlook these machinations for a national executive position.

Co-optation

Co-optation is another common NRM strategy, especially because the party has access to state resources, which it uses to great effect. For example, Anita Among was the deputy treasurer of the FDC but joined NRM in 2020. Two years later, she was appointed to the third most important position in the country as speaker of the house. Beti Kamya-Turomwe was once a member of FDC and served in Parliament from 2006 to 2011. She later formed her own party, Uganda Federal Alliance (UFA), and ran for the presidency in the 2011 elections. She then crossed over to the NRM and served first as minister for the Kampala Capital City Authority (2016–2019) and then as minister of lands, housing, and urban development from 2019 to 2021. She is now the inspector general of government.

The NRM is an equal opportunity co-opter, luring high-profile opposition leaders from all parties. One of the UPC's MPs and wife to the party president, Betty Amongi, is serving as minister of gender, labor, and social development in Museveni's government in 2021. She was appointed minister of Kampala Capital City in 2019 and, before that, minister of lands, housing, and urban development in 2016, even though she was in the UPC at the time. She won the parliamentary seat for Oyam South Constituency. She is married to the UPC president, Jimmy Akena, an MP for Lira Municipality. Akena is the son of Milton Obote, the former prime minister and president of Uganda.

Museveni also appointed Florence Nakiwala Kiyingi, a former DP representative, as minister of state for youth and children in 2016, much to everyone's surprise. He appointed DP candidate for Kampala Sarah Kanyike as state minister for the elderly and the disabled in 2020. She had been the deputy lord mayor of Kampala. Thus, the co-optation of women is a central strategy of the NRM to maintain control.

Coalitions

An important way that authoritarian regimes remain in power is by broadening their ruling coalitions. Since women represent over half of the population, this makes them a key constituency to bring on board politically, especially given their own political aspirations. Women have featured in efforts to build alliances with opposition parties. After 1986, the government had a large number of DP ministers. However, when Museveni's alliance with the DP collapsed around 1994, he sought an alliance with the UPC. He was concerned that he had lost the Buganda region along with the DP and, therefore, needed support from the north, east, and parts of western Uganda to offset these losses. He did not want to give the Baganda, whose kingdom is based in Mengo, federal status because he feared alienating the rest of the country. The Baganda make up 20 percent of the population and are based around the capital. They constitute an economic stronghold in the country and historically were once powerful. When the NRM started courting the UPC, he offered the vice presidency to Cecilia Ogwal, the UPC secretary general. He would have offered other ministerial positions to the UPC, but she rejected the offer, and the talks regarding the entire coalition collapsed. Museveni then appointed a woman, Specioza Kazibwe, as vice president in order to appeal to women, the Basoga, and Catholics. After 2009, Museveni started increasing the number of UPC members in the cabinet and kept only the DP members who were loyal to NRM in the cabinet. In the run-up to the 2016 elections, the UPC formed an alliance with the NRM, and various UPC candidates took money from the NRM. By 2021, the DP was also engaging with the NRM, but the NUP as a party refused, although the NRM courted individuals in NUP.

Some appointments are a form of outreach to win over constituencies traditionally hostile to the NRM. For example, the NRM de-campaigned Jessica Alupo in 2021 when she ran for Parliament, and then Museveni turned around and appointed her vice president after she ran as an independent and won. She and the new female prime minister, Robinah Nabbanja, hail from parts of the country that have been strongholds of the opposition: Alupo from Katakwi in the east and Nabbanja from the western Kibaale area. By the president's own admission, these cabinet appointees were selected in part because of the need to balance religion, region, and ethnicity (Bwire 2021). In the case of Uganda, women are being brought into executive leadership not just because of gender but also because of their ethnicity and regional representation, suggesting that women can be integral to the process of building ethnic coalitions.

Women Leaders in Opposition

NRM's strategy to maintain hegemony by using the aforementioned strategies had an impact on opposition parties. Opposition parties have promoted several notable women leaders over the years. Betty Nambooze served as spokesperson for the DP (2005–2010) and subsequently as MP. In 2021, she won another term representing Mukono Municipality on the NUP ticket. Miria Obote, the wife of Uganda's founding president, Milton Obote, was president of the UPC from 2005 until 2010 and ran for president in 2006. Cecilia Ogwal served as the UPC's acting secretary general between 1985 and 1992. She was active in the Constituent Assembly in 1994 and has been an MP since 1996. Sharon Oyat Arach was appointed as UPC spokesperson in 2020. Of the UPC's top leadership of nine, one-third, or three, are women, including the party spokesperson (Sharon Oyat Arach), National Woman Leader (Miria Muhwezi), and Assistant Woman Leader (Racheal Neluba).

Several women have started parties of their own. Beti Olive Kamya-Turwomwe became the first woman in Uganda to start a political party in 2010, the Uganda Federal Alliance, and was a presidential candidate in 2011. Prior to that, she was a leader of the FDC, although she eventually switched parties to the NRM and, after 2021, became the inspector general of government. She represented the Lubaga North Constituency for the FDC in Parliament from 2006 to 2010.

The leader of the opposition, Betty Aol Ochan, from 2018 to 2021, was an FDC leader from the Gulu District. Alice Alaso was former vice president of the FDC for the Eastern Region and FDC secretary. She then helped form a party that split off from the FDC in 2019, Alliance for National Transformation (ANT), and is now its acting national coordinator. Earlier, she was the women's representative in Parliament for the Serere District, representing FDC from 2006 to 2021. FDC's Winfred Kiiza was leader of the opposition in the Tenth Parliament from 2016 to 2018, having been in Parliament since 2006. One of the best-known FDC women internationally is Stella Nyanzi, a queer rights activist who ran and lost the Kampala women's seat in 2021 but was well known for her outspoken criticism of Yoweri Museveni and public insults (what she refers to as "radical rudeness") that landed her in prison. Dr. Lina Zedriga Waru is the NUP's vice chairperson in Northern Uganda.

Despite the relatively large number of opposition women holding top positions in their parties, the overall number of women from the opposition parties in the National Assembly has been relatively poor, primarily because of aggressive NRM de-campaigning tactics and the use of reserved seats. The FDC had committed to the representation of women at the national level, but they have also advocated for eliminating the quota system because of the advantages it gives the opposition (Muriaas and Wang 2012). Opposition parties have put forward twenty-eight female candidates compared with the NRM's twenty-nine for open seats in the 2021 election, yet they won only five seats this way compared to the eleven won by the NRM (Table 3.4). Opposition women thus had an 18 percent chance of gaining open seats compared with the NRM women's 40 percent chance. Opposition parties put forward 252 female candidates for the reserved seats, compared with the NRM's 145, yet they won only twenty-four seats compared with the NRM's one hundred. Again, opposition women had a 9.5 percent chance of gaining reserved seats compared with the 69 percent chance for NRM women. This does not include the independent seats, most of which are controlled by the NRM. Some may have lost the primary election, causing them to run in the second round of elections as independents, unimpeded by the NRM.

In contrast to women candidates, opposition men vying for open seats (627) won seventy-seven of them (12 percent), 5.3 times less than NRM male candidates, who won 64 percent of the seats. Opposition parties would have had a better chance of winning had they run women for open seats than men, but instead, they ran 2.5 times more men than women. Although NRM's share of parliamentary reserved seats for women has decreased from 73 percent in 2006 to 69 percent today, it has found other ways to maintain an even greater vote share through control of women independents and women in appointed seats (Table 3.6).

The NRM's stranglehold on the reserved seats creates little incentive for opposition parties to field women candidates for these seats. The UPC has committed to a 50 percent quota. But their practice falls far short of these goals. Out of 102 candidates that the UPC nominated for parliamentary seats in the 2011 elections, only three (2.9 percent) were women, and of the 211 nominated for councilor positions, only two (0.9 percent) were women. Of its top leadership of nine, one-third, or three, are women, including the party spokesperson Sharon Oyat Arach; Muhwezi Miria, the National Woman Leader; and Neluba Racheal, the Assistant Woman Leader.

Similarly, the DP committed to increasing the quota for women to 40 percent of the seats in elected positions. However, out of eighty-six DP candidates nominated for parliamentary seats in 2011, only six (7 percent) were women, and of the 151 DP nominees for councilor positions, only three (2 percent) were women. The DP plans to include a clause on affirmative action in their revised constitution, under pressure from the party Women's League and Women's Democracy Network.

In the past, the FDC held the majority of opposition seats for women, but as of 2021, the majority of opposition seats have gone to the NUP, with thirteen reserved seats and three open seats held by women. However, NUP, like the other opposition parties, has experienced difficulties in winning reserved parliamentary seats for its female candidates (see Table 3.6). The DP has only one woman's seat, and the UPC has two. Instead, the parties have focused on other areas of leadership for women.

Opposition women face numerous other hurdles. They tend to compete more successfully in urban rather than rural districts, limiting the areas where they can make inroads. Women in the reserved seats have to represent an entire district rather than a constituency, usually three to four times smaller, placing added financial burdens on them. Women, but especially opposition women, generally have fewer resources. Yet people expect them to pay for children's school fees or hospital bills and make demands on them that they are less likely to make on male incumbents (Segawa 2016).

Most opposition parties do not allocate funds for their women's leagues, so the difference between their policy and practice is stark. As mentioned earlier, they do not see fielding women as a winning strategy in the face of the incumbent's resource advantage, particularly for the reserved seats. The opposition parties cannot meet their targets for women's quotas because they face internal organizational weaknesses and lack finances and human resources.

Table 3.6 Women parliamentarians by party

	1989	1996	2001	2006	2011	2016	2021
National Resistance Movement	100%	100%	100%	66%	49%	49%	42%
National Unity Platform							14%
Forum for Democratic Change				13%	14%	13%	7%
Democratic Party				4%	7%	4%	3%
Uganda People's Congress				4%	3%	2%	2%
Conservative Party				0	0.61%	0	0
Justice Forum				0	0.64%	0	0.25%
People's Progressive Party							0.1%
Others					0	0	0
Independents				13%	26%	31%	32%
	100%	100%	100%	100%	100%	100%	100%
No. total elected constituency		214	295	215	238	289	353
No. appointed		59	12	25	25	25	30
No. women elected	41			79	112	112	146
Women's seats	18%	19%	24%	31%	35%	33%	32%
No. total seats	280	283	295	319	375	426	555

Source: Uganda Electoral Commission (2021).

This means they can't operate functional countrywide party branches and offices, and they are not able to recruit and run effective campaigns for women candidates, especially in rural areas where the political terrain is very rough for opposition candidates (communication with Moses Khisa 3.18.22).

As a result of the defensive posture taken by resource-poor opposition parties in response to the NRM, some women's rights activists place the blame for the lack of women candidates squarely at the feet of the opposition parties. According to one activist, the FDC has not taken gender and women's rights very seriously. As she explained to me in an interview, "You have to have the leaders within the party structures committed to these provisions within their constitution and within their other policies. They'll have policies on paper, but when it comes to resourcing the strategic plan, implementing, monitoring and evaluation, they think they can win elections without focusing on building the party, training candidates" (U37 7.28.20). She and other activists have been critical of parties' lack of commitment to advancing women and for maintaining parties as a "a very patriarchal space," as one put it (U14.7.25.20; U3 6.23.20).

Not surprisingly, women politicians make strategic calculations, knowing they are nearly certain to be vigorously de-campaigned if they run with an opposition party. As newcomers to politics, women often find it easier to align themselves with the ruling party, knowing that they are more likely to win with the party's support. One woman opposition leader said:

> Many women fear to engage on the opposition side because of the incredibly difficult terrain in which we are engaged in currently. Anyone who comes out to oppose the government is seen as an enemy of progress or an enemy of the country. The president doesn't shy away from labeling people like Kyagulanyi, the party leader of NUP, as the country's enemy because he speaks against ills. He speaks about the inequalities that are now very vividly seen. (U10.7.28.20)

The deficit of opposition women in Parliament reveals a glaring imbalance between the opposition parties and the NRM, particularly since many of these parties can easily appoint women to key positions within their parties. While one could attribute the lack of female opposition candidates in parliamentary races to a lack of party commitment to advancing women, as some activists have suggested, a closer look at the NRM tactics of repression and co-optation of women seeking reserved seats reveals a highly imbalanced playing field.

Internal or External Pressures for Gender Reforms?

Most discussions on the adoption of quotas and the promotion of women as leaders in Africa have focused on the changes in international norms and practices after the 1995 UN Fourth World Conference on Women, held in Beijing, and on donor strategies (Bush 2011). However, in Uganda, the reserved seat system started in the late 1980s prior to these international trends, and it was used to strengthen the NRM by reinforcing new patronage structures (Tripp 2000). Sylvia Tamale argues that the affirmative action program of the NRM had multiple possible causes, both domestic and international, that served the purposes of political expediency. Inspired by the example of the Front for the Liberation of Mozambique (FRELIMO) that had promoted women leaders early on, Museveni sought to show the international community after the takeover in 1986 that it was committed to democracy and that it had transcended its military claims to power and garnered greater legitimacy. The policies were also, in part, a reward for the contributions of women to the five-year guerrilla struggle and a response to pressures from the women's movement (Tamale 1999; Tripp 2000). However, as this chapter has shown, the primary beneficiaries of the reserved seats were the NRM itself in its quest to gain legitimacy and entrench its rule, thus remaining in power.

Conclusion

The case of Uganda shows how authoritarian regimes and ruling parties instrumentalize and manipulate the politics of inclusion to entrench themselves in power and to maintain vote share. While much of the literature has treated the adoption of quotas as a response to international and domestic pressures, it has focused primarily on how they are an effort to include women and much less on the ways in which they help perpetuate autocratic rule and exclude the opposition. Reserved seats are primarily a phenomenon found in authoritarian countries, and there is a reason for this. The use of reserved seats (in contrast to legislated seats or party quotas) facilitates the use of women for patronage since they can be treated as a group that owes their positions to the ruling party. At the same time, opposition women and women leaders have turned out to be the biggest losers in this process. This instrumentalization of women's rights might not seem surprising. However, the discrepancy between the levels of legislative representation of women in the NRM and in the opposition parties is quite significant, mainly when one compares the percentage of candidates fielded by the various parties. This is also true more generally (see Chapter 2). Ruling parties in authoritarian countries have often promoted women as leaders through reserved seats in a way that has disproportionately disadvantaged women in the opposition.

While the NRM is the main obstacle to the success of opposition women, their own divisions and weaknesses pose another constraint. Party women have demanded that opposition parties do more to support female candidates. Moreover, while opposition parties do better in promoting women within their party leadership than in elected office, their strength is primarily in urban areas, which limits the districts in which they might expect to win.

The literature on autocracy has looked at how electoral authoritarian regimes entrench themselves even in the face of electoral competition, but it has rarely looked at the gender dimension of these tactics. These tactics are crucial in electoral authoritarian regimes that have opened themselves up to a measure of competition by adopting a multiparty system. However, by using a variety of tactics targeting the opposition and, in particular, opposition women, the incumbents took a goal that had won them international favor—that of increasing women's political representation—and weaponized it against the political opposition through repression and a politics of division and co-optation.

The NRM-led government used reserved seats as a form of patronage. They expanded the number of districts to increase the number of reserved seats for women; they supported NRM candidates who lost out in the primaries and had them run as independents in the second round. They increased the number of appointed seats to increase the number of NRM women and other such special groups in Parliament. This had particularly negative effects on women opposition parliamentarians, who found it nearly impossible to run for office without the threat of being de-campaigned and undermined. This resulted in disproportionately low percentages of opposition women in Parliament and few women opposition leaders in Parliament relative to opposition men and the overall levels of NRM women legislators in Uganda. The opposition itself promoted women leaders at the national level but shied away from fielding many women for parliamentary positions because the system was so skewed against opposition women, who faced being de-campaigned, repression, and co-optation.

The same factors that make it possible for the NRM to advance women and risk opening elections up to challenge also make the opposition hesitant. The issue is not simply the opposition's lack of interest in women's advancement but also the limited possibilities for opposition women when they run for either the reserved or open seats.

The Ugandan case shows the ways in which authoritarian regimes use legal and illegal means of tilting elections in their favor. It shows how a seemingly democratic demand of the women's movement and a goal of global feminist mobilization—to increase women's political representation—can be used for authoritarian ends and can be weaponized against women themselves. This poses a potential challenge to how we understand reserved seats as a source of gender equality and inclusion since the promotion of women in politics primarily serves the political purposes of autocrats rather than the interests of women.

4
The Possibilities and Limits of Women's Activism for Rights in Zimbabwe

Introduction

Zimbabwe is a study of paradoxes. The case of Zimbabwe, like so many authoritarian regimes, requires that we hold contradictory realities in our grasp simultaneously: The same regime that uses the state to repress and sexually assault women in one context passes legislative and constitutional provisions to protect women against violence. The same regime that adopts quotas as a mechanism of inclusion adopts tactics to exclude opposition women. A dictatorial ruler may support some women's rights reforms yet undermine other such reforms. Women leaders tied to the ruling party may simultaneously fight for women's rights and undermine other women leaders and rights.

Zimbabwe checked all the boxes when it came to factors that would predispose it to promoting women's rights. It is a postconflict country; women had played a significant role in the liberation movement; it has an entrenched ruling party; it has been party to international and regional women's rights treaties; and it has an active women's movement, which emerged in the postindependence years, taking advantage of the political space afforded by a hybrid regime. Nevertheless, it took women thirty-three years after independence to gain significant legislative representation. This happened after 2000, when Zimbabwe shifted from being a hybrid regime to a full-blown authoritarian regime with an entrenched ruling party in an effort to further shut down political competition.

This chapter highlights the role of a powerful women's movement, which accounts for the many gains that have been made in a political environment that is otherwise fairly hostile to women's leadership. The chapter simultaneously underscores the role of some key individual women leaders who have taken advantage of women's activism to serve their own purposes.

In other case studies in this book, we have seen the various ways in which governments and ruling parties instrumentalize women's rights for purposes

Why African Autocracies Promote Women as Leaders. Aili Mari Tripp, Oxford University Press. © Oxford University Press (2025). DOI: 10.1093/9780197829004.003.0005

other than advancing the status of women. This chapter complicates women's agency in authoritarian systems in several ways. Most women politicians seek power to advance their political ambitions, women's rights, or other causes. Some may also be complicit in processes of instrumentalizing women's rights even as they promote women's rights. Others go further to use women's rights to enrich themselves and enhance their power—sometimes ruthlessly—and in the process, they advance authoritarian agendas. Some women leaders have engaged in violence to advance their own goals. One purpose of this instrumentalization is to expand the power and personal wealth of leaders. We see in the case of Zimbabwe how top female leaders, who are often related to the male political elite, can use their positions of proximity to state and party power to advance their personal power and wealth.

However, even women who are complicit in the system and try to use it to their own advantage find that playing by patriarchal rules may have negative consequences for themselves as patriarchy can also turn against them. These women leaders may use the party's women's wings or national women's leagues or unions to gain power and instrumentalize women's rights, and they may use women's issues and organizations to advance themselves. They may even end up promoting misogynistic policies to achieve those ends. However, these women are ultimately marginalized and subject to patriarchal pressures.

Women's rights activists have also been constrained by the very leaders who helped bring about some changes for women because of their compromised position. Many women who played key leadership roles in the country's postindependence history were closely associated with those in power through marriage. The women's movement, therefore, has been limited not only by male leaders but also by women leaders who have engaged in patronage politics almost as aggressively as the men, often with dire consequences.

But what makes Zimbabwe especially interesting as a case is that it has had one of the most active autonomous women's movements in Africa, and according to interviewees, their influence has expanded since the early years after independence. The fact that the country was semiauthoritarian until around 2000 facilitated this early emergence of a women's movement. Women played a significant role in the independence movement. They were also a major force in pressing for women's rights reforms and a new constitution, which granted them greater political representation when finally passed in 2013. The odds are seemingly against them, but they have persevered and made important gains alongside setbacks. They have learned to navigate the complexity, ambiguity, and unpredictability of authoritarian governance, and their legislative and constitutional gains are a testament to their ingenuity and resourcefulness.

At the same time, official institutions that were accorded the responsibility for women's rights were loyal to the ruling party and the president. The political elite were more intent on how they could use women leaders and the issue of women's rights to serve their own ends than in advancing women's welfare in Zimbabwe.

This chapter explores the tension between women activists' need for reliance on the ruling party of an authoritarian regime to make gains for women. It shows the limits of institutions like the Women's League that were aligned with the ruling party. It shows how women who were propelled into power by associating themselves with the cause of women's rights could be corrupted by their proximity to the leaders of the ruling party that uses the male rooster as its emblem. It also reveals how some women leaders fell prey to misogynistic politics. It looks at women who broke with the ruling Zimbabwe African National Union–Patriotic Front (ZANU-PF) and joined the opposition, which has an uneven record for advancing women.

This chapter starts with an overview of Zimbabwean politics since independence. It looks at the role of women in the liberation movement and how this shaped their role in postindependence politics. It also explores the cost of resisting the policies of ZANU-PF in the case of a high-profile female leader, Margaret Dongo. The chapter then examines the ambiguous role of the Ministry of Women (in its various permutations) and the ZANU-PF Women's League. The chapter documents how many gender-related legislative reforms were passed as a result of the efforts of the women's movement. It goes on to describe the role of the movement in the two constitutional reform initiatives, one that failed and one that succeeded in 2013. It highlights the gains and limitations of constitutional reform for women in politics. The chapter delves into the roles of leaders at the highest levels, like Grace Mugabe and Joïce Mujuru, in participating in factional politics and using the women's movement to serve their own bids for power. The chapter explores the impact of violence against women in politics and the consequences of this violence for women's rights activists and women politicians. It concludes by examining how the women's movement has dealt with the various challenges the authoritarian regime poses. The overall picture that emerges is one in which the women's movement has persisted against tremendous odds, accounting for pockets of gender reform amid an otherwise checkered political landscape for women's rights.

Background

Zimbabwe is an authoritarian country with a strong military presence. Robert Mugabe led the country for much of its postindependence history. Mugabe headed the Zimbabwe African National Union (ZANU) from 1975 to 1980, when it became known as ZANU-PF. He was one of two liberation movement leaders who had fought against the white minority government since the early 1960s. Joshua Nkomo headed the other party and liberation force, the Zimbabwe African People's Union (ZAPU), from 1961 until 1987. The two parties, which feuded bitterly, merged in 1987 to form ZANU-PF in a Unity Accord after the ethnically and politically motivated Gukurahundi massacres, which led to the killing of approximately twenty thousand people and systematic starvation of people in Matabeleland North and South and Midlands. These areas are home to the Ndebele people, where ZAPU had much of its support (Tendi 2011). ZANU, Mugabe, and his successor, President Emmerson Mnangagwa, have been widely implicated in carrying out the massacres, which have left an indelible imprint on the country and its politics.

Mugabe led the country, first as its prime minister from 1980 to 1987, while Canaan Banana served as president. Mugabe then took over as president from 1987 to 2017 and was also head of the ruling ZANU-PF from 1980 to 2017. The Mugabe regime was characterized as "a militarized form of electoral authoritarianism."[1] Robert Mugabe held on to power for thirty years through violent repression, patronage networks, a wide-reaching party machinery, constitutional and legal manipulation, and an ideology of the right to rule in perpetuity (Bratton and Masunungure 2008, 42). The economy under Mugabe shrank as the country experienced massive inflation, capital flight, and emigration of the labor force. As a result, unemployment and class divisions began to intensify (Z6.7.5.21). These economic hardships placed enormous pressures on women, who shouldered heavy responsibilities for feeding entire families. Many men, in particular, left as migrants to South Africa and elsewhere in search of a livelihood, while women generally stayed behind to care for their households. Men who had once had good jobs often felt disempowered.

There already was discontent regarding Mugabe's 1998 decision to embroil Zimbabwe in the Democratic Republic of Congo (DRC) in a seemingly pointless regional conflict as ZANU-PF generals sought access to the country's diamond sector (Essof 2005). ZANU-PF carried out violent land invasions of

[1] Freedom House ranked Zimbabwe as "partly free" or as what I would call a semiauthoritarian regime from 1978–2000, 2015–2016, and 2018–2019 and as "not free" or authoritarian for other years after 1973 up to present.

1,500 white farms in 2000 in a bid to gain support from the rural peasantry, who remained the base of ZANU-PF support, while the Movement for Democratic Change (MDC) controlled the urban vote. The farms were occupied without compensation. Mugabe believed the issue of land reform would save him. But instead, it further eroded Zimbabwe's international image, displacing thousands and causing further economic decline and hardship.

Hyperinflation became excessive after 2006, as the government printed worthless one hundred trillion dollar bills. Interest rates went through the roof, while unemployment was sky-high. Poverty was on the rise, and fuel shortages had become chronic. The situation continued to deteriorate, and ZANU-PF's support dwindled so that by 2008, ZANU-PF had lost the parliamentary election to the opposition party, MDC.

The MDC was formed in the context of Zimbabwe's unraveling economy in 1999 and helped defeat the constitution in the 2000 referendum. Its leader, Morgan Tsvangirai, lost the 2002 election to Mugabe amid allegations of rigging. Tsvangirai and his followers faced death threats, accusations of treason, imprisonment, and torture. Tsvangirai's bodyguard died in 2007 as a result of injuries sustained during a government crackdown. ZANU-PF lost a significant number of parliamentary seats in the 2008 election but, in the end, scraped through in what was widely considered a pyrrhic victory. In 2008, Tsvangirai won the presidential election, but Mugabe insisted that the election was too close to call and demanded a runoff amid Tsvangirai's claims that he was receiving death threats. Tsvangirai had initially agreed to a runoff but later withdrew from the race, saying that his supporters faced possible death if they went ahead with the election. South African President Thabo Mbeki and the SADC intervened and brokered a peace accord between MDC and ZANU-PF in 2008, and a unity government was created the following year in which Tsvangirai became prime minister. Mugabe continued to make unilateral decisions and remained president.

They were to engage in a constitutional reform process as part of the settlement. There was also considerable pressure from Zimbabwean civic groups, students, women, labor, the Southern African region, and the international community to initiate a constitutional reform process. The Constitution Parliamentary Select Committee (COPAC), charged with drafting a new constitution, was formed with representatives of Movement for Democratic Change–Tsvangirai (MDC-T) and ZANU-PF. A gender quota was introduced along with other vital provisions for women (Z2.4.30.21).

ZANU-PF continued to lose support because of corruption, but the party nevertheless clung to power through the presidency, continuing its efforts to intimidate MDC activists, candidates, and supporters. The unity government ended with the 2013 general election in which Mugabe was elected president, reentrenching ZANU-PF's dominance.

In 2013, because of pressure from women's organizations, Zimbabwe passed a constitution with some of the strongest provisions for women's rights by world standards. After introducing reserved seats, they also significantly increased women's representation in Parliament, from 15 percent to 32 percent in their 2013 elections. Women also gained key posts in cabinets, top parastatals, the judiciary, and university vice chancellorships. These reforms were influenced by an active women's movement that aggressively sought to shape the women's rights agenda, according to the head of the Women's Coalition of Zimbabwe (WCoZ) and CEO of the Zimbabwe Gender Commission, Virginia Muwaningwa. Eventually, the Ministry of Women's Affairs came on board in support of women's leadership. Zimbabwe thus embodies many of the contradictions we find in authoritarian countries. It has a repressive government that flagrantly violates human rights, yet it adopts constitutional and legal reforms around women's rights (Z22.2.3.22).

In 2017, a bloodless coup overthrew President Robert Mugabe, bringing an end to his thirty-year presidency. Emmerson Mnangagwa, the coup's mastermind and a leader in Mugabe's ZANU-PF, was appointed president after the takeover. He won the 2018 and 2023 elections amid cries of foul play by the opposition. He did nothing to improve the rule of law or increase political liberties; instead, he consolidated power. Opposition leaders, human rights activists, and journalists continue to be harassed and arrested, and NGOs have come under greater scrutiny. During the 2023 election campaign, ZANU-PF Vice President Constantino Chiweng promised to crush the opposition party "like lice" and "grind it to the extent that even flies will not eat it." ZANU-PF's Abton Mashayanyika, a bishop, even called for the killing of the opposition presidential candidate Nelson Chamisa. Following the election, accusations of arbitrary arrest, abduction, torture, and killing of political opponents and civil society activists by state actors continued to mount.

Impact of Conflict: Participation of Women in Guerrilla War

To understand the contradictions in Zimbabwe and the role of women in contemporary politics, one has to go back to the war of liberation. Women participated actively in the guerrilla war in Zimbabwe that brought about an end to white minority rule. Some say that as many as one-third of the fighters were women, but the numbers vary (Geisler 1995). The liberation movement had always paid lip service to women's rights. ZAPU, the liberation organization led by Joshua Nkomo, had a strong women's organization in the cities in the 1960s. In 1977, ZANU formed a Department of Women's Affairs, eventually becoming the ZANU-PF Women's League.

Some of the earliest women leaders had fought with ZANU's Zimbabwe African National Liberation Army (ZANLA) in the guerrilla war in the 1970s. Some were primary school teachers like Sheba Tavarwisa, who was among the first women to join these fighters. Later, she became an important political and military leader. Margaret Dongo, who later became an MP, had her beginnings in the guerrilla war, as did Joïce Mujuru (Teurai Ropa Nhongo, also known as Spill Blood), who eventually became vice president. In 1972, women served as porters of military equipment and later as fighters on the frontline of ZANLA. Most women were involved in noncombatant roles, carrying weapons and other materials, cultivating vegetables and maize, cooking, checking food for poison, serving as guards, and engaged in other such tasks. Some taught the children of refugees, while others were in charge of logistics (Lyons 2004). According to Fay Chung, by 1975, there were five hundred female fighters, many of whom were involved in carrying arms from Zambia to Mozambique for hundreds of kilometers, often facing military attacks. Women were trained at a camp called Osibisa. Women guerrillas played an essential part in the military maneuvers in cities, perhaps because they were less likely to be noticed. One woman carried and placed a bomb in a supermarket, Woolworths, in Central Salisbury. Many women gained leadership skills while in exile in Zambia and Mozambique (Z4.2.13.21).

Ruling Party Tactics

After independence, Zimbabwean President Robert Mugabe (1984) acknowledged that the war would not have been won without the help of women. Nevertheless, Zimbabwean women activists were extremely bitter that they were told after the war to wait indefinitely until they could assert their demands (Jirira 1995; Lueker 1998). Worse, in the early 1980s, the government launched Operation Chinyavada or Operation Cleanup to arbitrarily round up thousands of women accused of being "prostitutes," subjecting them to humiliation and abuse. Over six thousand women were arrested, including older women, schoolgirls as young as eleven, and young mothers with babies on their backs. They were sent to the Zambezi Valley resettlement area without legal assistance. In response, the Women's Action Group (WAG) was formed in 1983 to protest the detentions. It involved women of all backgrounds—urban women, professional women, rural women, farmers, factory workers, and nurses—who came together to resist such attacks, support one another, and share their frustrations.

The Case of Margaret Dongo

Women who resisted ZANU-PF were put in their place, as Margaret Dongo learned early on. The consequence of breaking with ZANU-PF in the early years was political oblivion. Long before the emergence of the opposition MDC, Margaret Dongo fearlessly opposed President Robert Mugabe's government in Zimbabwe. Her political journey began in 1975 when she left school and walked three hundred miles to join the liberation army, ZANLA, in Mozambique. After Zimbabwe gained independence, she rapidly ascended through the party's ranks, first working for ZANU-PF and then earning a seat in Parliament and becoming a member of the party's central committee.

In 1989, she cofounded the National Liberation War Veterans Association to demand the rights of war veterans. Throughout her tenure in Parliament, Dongo stood as a lone voice, unafraid to speak out against abuses of power, corruption on the part of the president's family, and state control of the media ("Zimbabwe" 1997). She accused government leaders of betraying the revolution by lining their pockets. Even ZANU-PF parliamentarians asked her to condemn bills they were afraid to attack publicly. One ex-guerrilla said of Dongo, "If I said what Margaret Dongo said, I'd be dead. The party is like an invincible beast. She is the only person in the country who can scream and then be able to leave and hear the echoes of her screaming'" (McNeil 1996).

In 1995, when Margaret Dongo ran as an independent in elections in Harare South, she faced harrowing challenges, including death threats and attacks on her home. Despite these attempts to intimidate her, she persevered and ran a spirited campaign. Mugabe vowed, "There is no way we can allow and have such people winning" (*Reuters* 1995). She initially lost the election when she started criticizing the ZANU-PF political machine. All but two of the sixty-seven independent and opposition candidates running for Parliament lost. ZANU-PF had thrown its full backing behind Dongo's opponent and redrawn Dongo's constituency so that most of her supporters were placed in another district. ZANU-PF groups attacked her supporters. She had petrol bombs thrown at her house and car, traumatizing her. Hundreds of army soldiers in her district had been made to vote a day early and then again on the polling day to ensure her defeat. Dongo contested the election results in court on the grounds of massive irregularities and fraud and won the case.

She then ran successfully in a by-election in 1998 (Meldrum 1995). She thus set a precedent for challenging election outcomes in Zimbabwe.

Despite her long-standing loyalty to ZANU-PF, Dongo eventually reached a breaking point and decided to leave the party. This led her to establish her own political party, the Zimbabwe Union of Democrats, in 1998. In 2000, she spoke out against the land redistribution policy, which she claimed had profited primarily from well-connected individuals close to the political elite. Subsequently, she lost her seat in the 2000 elections, but only after her house was attacked by a group of sixty opponents, who threw rocks through the windows.

Dongo reflected on her experiences as a parliamentarian in an interview:

> When I was elected to Parliament in 1990, my belief was that when you're an elected member of Parliament, even if you belong to a political party, you're going to represent even those [who] don't belong to your party. . . . What is important is to make sure that their voices are heard. So I was very clear on that. With my approach in Parliament, to some extent I became controversial for the party that I belonged to, which was ZANU-PF, and they viewed me as a pseudo-opposition. I was supposed to toe the party line. So I became one of those persons who was regarded as critical and someone who was like a rebel. I was the first person to raise issues to do with corruption when I was still in the ruling party. According to the policy of the party, you cannot wash dirty linen in public. (Z5.6.16.21)

Dongo joined Mujuru's Zimbabwe People First (ZimPF) Party in 2015 and now heads its women's wing. Her story reveals the limits of independent thought within the ruling party.

The Ministry of Women's Affairs

The government created a new Ministry of Community Development and Women's Affairs in 1981, headed by Joïce Mujuru, who was on the central committee of ZANU-PF and also led ZANU-PF's Women's League. The ministry focused on promoting developmental-type activities like adult literacy, forming preschools, and promoting small income-generating projects such as tailoring, handicrafts, and poultry husbandry. The Women's Ministry and the Women's League remained silent in the face of Operation Cleanup, suggesting that they had little independent influence on the ruling party. In this period, the ministry came under tighter oversight of the party and formed the National Women's Council in 1985 to control NGOs and their funding and to serve as an umbrella organization for all NGOs. The council was to implement policies developed by the Women's League (Z22.2.3.22).

In 1988, the Ministry of Women's Affairs was subsumed by the Ministry of Community Development and Cooperatives, and in 1989, it was downgraded to a department within the Ministry of Political Affairs and physically located within the ZANU-PF headquarters. Mujuru lost her position as minister and head of the Women's League, as Mugabe unexpectedly announced that his wife, Sally Mugabe, was taking over the League. The department's functions overlapped with those of the Women's League, but it was to serve the League. Some in the women's movement speculated that this was an effort to bring the ministry under closer party scrutiny and to rein in an increasingly autonomous women's movement (Geisler 1995). 1993, the department was relocated to the Ministry of National Affairs, Employment Creation, and Cooperatives (MNAECC). It was reduced to a women and development unit, coordinated by the president's sister, Bridgit Mugabe, who was ill-equipped to run the unit.

The de facto merger of the department and the Women's League effectively left little room for the women's movement to maneuver. Women not involved with the Women's League had few avenues to influence political decision-making. As one activist explained, "The downgrading of the ministry for women from its autonomous status and its absorption into a weaker ministry in charge of cooperatives, with little political significance, is telling. It indicates the decline of the political and social significance of women to ZANU" (Z6.7.5.21).

By the late 1980s, the ministry had attracted several exceptional technocratic women like Rudo Chitiga and Tendai Bare, who knew how to work the government system to get strong results for women's rights (Z18.12.20.21). As a result, the legal department pushed through a series of laws with the help of pressure from the women's movement.

Eventually, the women who had been active in passing legislation in the Ministry of Women's Affairs migrated to the NGO sector. A women's movement emerged in this period, involving collaboration between black and white Zimbabwean women. For example, the Musasa Project was established in 1988 to address the issue of violence against women. Branches of Women and Law in Southern Africa (WLSA) and Women in Law and Development in Africa (WiLDAF) were formed in Harare in 1989 and 1990, respectively. The Federation of African Media Women Zimbabwe (FAMWZ) was established in 1985, the Zimbabwe Women's Finance Trust in 1989, the Zimbabwe Women's Resource Center and Network in 1990, the Zimbabwe

Women Lawyers Association (ZWLA) in 1992, and Zimbabwean Women in Business in 1995. By 1995, there were over twenty-five registered women's organizations.

One of the constraints on dominant-party regimes is their reliance on women's wings and party-affiliated women's leagues, which have little autonomy from the ruling party. As a result, their agendas have tended to be fairly conservative and have been aimed at building women's support for the ruling party. As donor funds shifted to independent women's organizations, these associations became even more resource-poor as their fortunes waned along with their influence.

Constraints on women's mobilization soon emerged as the government and ruling party renewed efforts to channel mass mobilization of women into the Women's League of ZANU and regulate it. For example, the Association of Women's Clubs, which had been active as far back as the 1960s, reinvigorated itself in the early 1990s, gaining over forty thousand rural members. However, it was suspended under the Private Voluntary Organisations (PVO) Act in 1995. Led by Sekai Holland, it defended the right of an organization to exist autonomously to organize women. They took their case to the Supreme Court in 1996 to challenge the legality of their forced closure and the right to freedom of association and expression. The Supreme Court ruled unanimously in favor of the organization.

Most women's political mobilization in the early years after independence was located in the Women's League, which focused on social welfare concerns and mobilizing women's vote for ZANU. The Women's League provided entertainment for visiting dignitaries and attended ZANU rallies and other events. The depoliticization of the League resulted in the disaffection of professional women and a bifurcation of women's mobilization, with less-educated women being concentrated in the League while professional and better-educated women focused on independent organizations (Geisler 1995). These patterns emerged in other African countries as well.

A new Ministry of Women Affairs, Community, Small, and Medium Enterprises Development was created in 2005 by Oppah Muchinguri, who lost her seat in Parliament and subsequently lost her post as minister. Olivia Muchena succeeded her, serving as minister from 2009 to 2013. She focused on women's economic empowerment, especially women in mining, agriculture, and tourism. She created a women's development loan fund and a women's bank.

As we have seen, the modus operandi of the Ministry of Women's Affairs in its various configurations and the ZANU-PF's Women's League was to comply with the ruling party's edicts. Nevertheless, the women's movement and their representatives within the ministry were able to influence the government's legislative agenda to a certain extent.

Women's Rights Legislation

Initial legislative gains allowed women access to state structures and basic economic rights. The Sex Disqualification Act (1980) allowed women to hold public office. New labor laws allowed for equal pay for equal work and maternity leave. The Legal Age of Majority Act (1982) gave all Zimbabweans legal status as adults at the age of eighteen, and the Matrimonial Causes Act of 1985 equalized divorce. Other legislation was passed with regard to labor relations, the right to work, and the inheritance of property following the death of a spouse or a father or a mother. Zimbabwe's Sexual Offences Act (2001) aimed to protect women from sexual abuse and sex trafficking. A law was passed in 2006 banning marital rape. The law against domestic violence (2007) had far-reaching consequences, addressing physical, emotional, sexual, economic, and emotional abuse. It allowed for protection and relief to survivors of domestic violence and criminalized abuse based on cultural or customary practices that discriminated against or degraded women. Zimbabwe ratified the main international women's rights treaty, the Convention on the Elimination of Discrimination Against Women (CEDAW), in 1991, and it adopted the 1995 African Platform for Action in Dakar, Senegal, and the 1995 Beijing Platform of Action. National gender policy plans were adopted in 2004 and 2008. Zimbabwe also ratified the African Union's Maputo Protocol on women's rights in 2008.

In 2016, Zimbabwe's Constitutional Court outlawed child marriage. It came following a "Not Ripe for Marriage" campaign that highlighted the consequence of early marriage on girls' reproductive health, forced sexual relations, and lack of education, which make it difficult for women to advance in economic and political activities. Katswe Sistahood and other organizations have been advocating for the rights of sex workers. In 2015, the courts issued a court order in favor of the sex workers' forbidding police from arresting sex workers, significantly reducing police harassment and arrests of sex workers. Women's organizations also carried out advocacy around the cost of menstrual hygiene products, and, as a result, in 2018, the Zimbabwean legislature passed a law that removed the 15 percent VAT and import tax on these products.

The women's movement continued to actively press for the Comprehensive Sexual Education Act and reform of the 1977 Termination of Pregnancy Act. Even though Zimbabwe has one of the highest rates of contraceptive use in sub-Saharan Africa, it also has one of the highest maternal mortality rates in the world, and unsafe abortions are a major contributing factor. About 40 percent of pregnancies in Zimbabwe were unintended as of 2016, and 25 percent of all unintended pregnancies resulted in abortion. The rates of such abortions have been increasing (Sully et al. 2018). Dr. Ruth Labode is chairwoman of the Parliament's Portfolio Committee on Health and Child Care, where she has advocated for the review of the Termination of Pregnancy Act, which permits abortion only if there is a serious threat to the mother's life, if the mother is at risk of physical impairment, if the child may be severely disabled, and in cases of permanent impairment to the mother's physical health, grave physical or mental defects, rape, incest, or intercourse with a mentally disabled woman.

Women's rights activists and women's organizations mounted massive campaigns for legal reform, invoking regional and continental treaties and international UN statutes to which Zimbabwe had become a state party. It is unlikely that ZANU-PF would have taken these steps on its own. As one activist-journalist explained, "I want to credit the women's movement because I firmly believe without the women's movement, we wouldn't have as much as 75 or 80 percent of the architecture that we have for women's rights. The other perhaps 20, maybe 15 percent certainly came from a political system that realized that this is the wave that the world is riding, and we need to ride it with the world if we want to look good in regional and international meetings" (Z18.12.20.21).

The extent to which the women's movement has been able to bring about these reforms reveals both the limits and the possibilities for reform within an authoritarian context. It highlights the tension between the women's movement and those within the party and ministry tasked with focusing on the women's rights agenda. The capacity to implement these laws is yet another, even more important, challenge.

The Constitution-Making Process (1997–2000)

The constitution-making process in Zimbabwe revealed another set of ambiguities within Zimbabwean politics, pointing to both the possibilities and the limitations of women's rights activism in an authoritarian context. In 2013, Zimbabwe passed one of the strongest constitutions for women's rights in Africa as a result of pressure from the women's movement. Yet it simultaneously sidelined women's rights activists and women politicians both within the ruling party and in the opposition, revealing once again that its commitment to women's rights did not match the promise of the constitution.

Zimbabwe's first constitution, known as the Lancaster Constitution, was created after overthrowing Ian Smith's white-led government in 1979. It contained only two provisions relating to women: equality and antidiscrimination. Only one woman (A. J. Phillips) was in the British delegation, and one Zimbabwean woman (E. Siziba) represented the Patriotic Front delegation led by Joshua Nkomo and Robert Mugabe at the December 1979 Constitutional Conference at Lancaster House. There were no women in Bishop Muzorewa's interim government delegation. Muzorewa was serving as prime minister at the time.

In 1997, civil society organizations, including women's organizations, created a National Constitutional Assembly to dismantle the 1980 Constitution because it vested too much power in the president. However, the process was entirely government-driven and fraught with tensions between the government and civil society. In this period, opposition parties also started to gain momentum (Z1.7.1.21). A Women's Coalition was formed in 1999, and it came up with the Zimbabwe Women's Charter, demanding numerous constitutional changes. Women's groups felt it retained British colonial-era customary law that allowed for gender discrimination (Muwanigwa 2013).

The women's movement had been heavily engaged in this first constitutional reform process. Initially, two camps formed, one led by the government and the other led by civil society. A feminist, Thoko Matshe, headed up the civil society coalition from 1999 to 2001, and the thirteen largest women's organizations played a vital role in the civic mobilization. State-sponsored violence marred the process (Essof 2005). As one interviewee put it, "That was a very significant moment, where I think the guys in leadership felt threatened that women could actually mobilize and influence political issues to this extent" (Z1.7.1.21). The initial 1999–2000 constitution-making process lacked transparency and resulted in failure, as it eliminated civil society participation. The government's draft 2000 Constitution did not mention women's rights or any of the issues raised by the women's movement, and the Women's Coalition, which mobilized across party lines, strongly rejected it. They campaigned against it in a 2000 referendum, and the "No" campaign garnered 55 percent of the vote. This suggested that a rebuke of ZANU-PF was possible in the 2000 parliamentary elections. Violence and repression followed, and the women's movement retreated (Z1.7.1.21).

Renewed Effort at Constitution Making (2009–2013)

In a second constitution-drafting process (2009–2013), a coalition of twenty civil society organizations (the Group of 20, or G20) formed to draft constitutional provisions and lobby the drafters. This coalition was characterized by its commitment to women's rights that cut across political, religious, ethnic, or other differences, as seen in many other African contexts. By this time, women's mobilization had expanded considerably. UN Women and the UNDP supported Zimbabwean women's rights activists and politicians in forming a lobby group (UN Women 2013). The Women in Politics Support Unit (WIPSU), which worked across party lines, was formed in 2000. In 2001, it initiated the Zimbabwe Women's Parliamentary Caucus (ZWPC), which elected the Honorable Flora Buka as its first chairperson. WIPSU launched several advocacy campaigns, including the 2003 iconic "Vote for a Woman" campaign for the Urban Council's Elections. Other coalitions had emerged, including the Women and Land Lobby Group and, most consequentially, the Women's Coalition of Zimbabwe (WCoZ).

The WCoZ was a group of sixty organizations and eight chapters throughout Zimbabwe. It facilitated and coordinated lobbying and advocacy activities and brought women together to strategize how best to influence the constitution-making process (Mushonga 2011). They started at the time of the Government of National Unity (GNU) in February 2009. The cross-party nature of women's mobilization after 2018 was facilitated by this period of the GNU. Women worked together both within and outside the government in ways that were not possible prior to this period (Z11.7.19.21).

Women made up 30 percent of the COPAC, which included MPs and the senate from different parties. The WCoZ lobbied hard and got a higher percentage of women on COPAC because the percentage of women in Parliament at the time was 16.5 percent. The WCoZ convened a conference in October 2009 attended by two hundred women to discuss the constitution-making process and strategize around women's demands. This resulted in the development of a Women's Constitutional Rapid Response Committee and numerous other strategies, including the development of a Women's Charter to influence the process. They organized provincial consultations with women leaders in four parts of the country to develop a countrywide outreach plan. The WCoZ worked with the Musasa Project in the Midlands and the ZWLA based in Harare to reach rural women at the ward level to educate them about the process. They ran a massive media campaign to disseminate information about the constitution-making process. COPAC solicited input into the process from throughout the country, and the WCoZ facilitated the process of ensuring women participated and provided input (Mushonga 2011).

Women in Zimbabwe had learned from the Kenyan constitutional experience in demanding a quota and adopted some of the tactics the Kenyan women activists had developed. ZANU-PF and MDC women worked across party lines and formed a united coalition, the G20. They coalesced with women from smaller parties, the churches, and the labor movement as well as with female students from the Zimbabwe National Students Union and other groups (Z11.7.19.21; Z1.7.1.21). There was a very extensive and intensive public consultation process with the constitution. It involved public education by the civil society organizations. The commissioners went out to meet people all over the country in rural and urban areas (Z11.7.19.21).

Four years of negotiations resulted in a new 2013 Constitution containing 75 percent of the demands made by women's rights activists (Muwanigwa 2013). It was celebrated as a "remarkable victory for women's rights activists," mainly because it omitted the earlier constitution's exclusionary clause that sealed off customary law from constitutional protections (Bond 2017, 89–90). Also included were provisions for equal land rights for women, protections from domestic violence, equal rights for women in marriage and divorce, and the creation of the Zimbabwe Gender Commission. There was consensus among the people I interviewed that the gains in the constitution were the product of pressure from the women's movement rather than external pressures. As Margaret Dongo explained, "I think the women's movement did a great job. They empowered women in all sectors of life. They empowered women in business, they empowered women in politics, and they empowered women in all social life. So I think the contributory factor [in the constitutional reforms] comes from the NGOs that are representing women in Zimbabwe. They've done a lot" (Z5.6.16.21).

Constitutional provisions included gender balance in appointing ministers and deputies, equal numbers of male and female senators based on a party-list system of proportional representation, and the promotion of gender balance and equality of men and women in all spheres, including politics. The state is to amend legislation to ensure gender equality in all institutions and agencies of government, including equal representation of men and women on commissions. The constitution guarantees full political rights, including the right to vote, form or join political parties, and be elected or hold office. Moreover, according to the constitution, "the State must take all measures, including legislative measures, needed to ensure that . . . women constitute at least half the membership of all Commissions and other elective and appointed governmental bodies established by or under this Constitution or any Act of Parliament." Thus, the constitution provided for 50 percent representation for women in all bodies. In spite of these gains, women activists did not achieve all their goals when it came to implementing the constitution.

Aftermath of Constitution-Making Process

After 2014, the political environment changed in important ways. A woman, Nomalanga Khumalo, became deputy speaker of Parliament, and another woman, Edna Madzongwe, became president of the senate in the GNU, serving from 2013 to 2018. Her deputy, Mabel Chinomona, has been president of the senate since Madzongwe's term ended in 2018.

After the constitution was passed, there has been a process of reconciling the laws with it, often with mixed results. An independent Gender Commission was established in 2016 by a legislative act to assist in the process of legislative reforms, which are to originate in the Ministry of Women Affairs, Community, Small, and Medium Enterprises Development. The commission works closely with women's rights organizations (Z22.2.3.22). Nevertheless, most of the momentum for reform has come from women's organizations.

Some provisions of the Electoral Act were revised to increase women's representation to 30 percent but not to 50 percent, as required by the constitution. The quota system was implemented, but there were few government programs to increase or empower female legislators. The Political Parties Finance Act did not include a provision on campaign financing that would increase the participation of women (Z11.7.19.21). This limited the number of women who could run for office. Parliamentary candidates must pay $1,000 to register to run, compared to $50 in the previous election, and that does not count the amount that candidates spend on vote buying, which seems to be necessary to remain competitive. As a result, in the 2023 elections, there were only seventy female candidates running with 637 male candidates in 210 constituencies. This represented 11 percent of the candidates, down from 14 percent in 2018.

In spite of heavy pressure from women's organizations for 50/50 representation in Parliament as well as in local government, women got sixty additional reserved seats in the lower house, winning 31.5 percent of the seats in 2013, more than doubling the percentage of women that had reached office in the prior election (14 percent). Out of the total eighty senators, sixty senators (six from each of the ten provinces) are elected through a proportional representation system, according to the 2013 Constitution. Male and female candidates are listed alternatively, with every list headed by a female candidate. Only 12 percent were elected directly. In 2013, women won 47.5 percent of the seats in the senate, up from 33 percent in the prior election. Ten years later, in the 2023 election, women took 30.7 percent of the seats in the National Assembly in a race in which only 11 percent of the contestants were women. Women won 45 percent of the seats in the senate. The number of local councillors increased from 17 percent in 2018 to 31 percent in 2023, reflecting a 30 percent subnational quota (Matiashe 2023). At the last minute, a controversial local government quota was introduced in 2021 before the elections, allowing 30 percent of the local government seats for women to be distributed among parties on a proportional representation basis.

Women activists had demanded and won 50 percent representation in the constitution. They felt this was necessary not just because women made up most of the population but also because, as a women's rights activist said, "we have a huge ratio of women who are very capable of taking up positions of authority and decision-making. We want equality. What they've done is just trying to pacify us, to get away from what the constitution says, because the constitution speaks about 50/50 [representation for women]" (Z12.5.31.21).

The reserved seats did not cost ZANU-PF anything, and the women in those seats did not represent any particular constituency. But the extra seats helped ZANU-PF gain in vote share, as is evident in the jump from 46 percent of seats to 63 percent in 2013, an increase of 17 percent (Table 4.1), even as ZANU-PF experienced a drop in support.

Parties relegated women to the quota seats instead of advancing them on party tickets. Some saw this as a problem since the women in the quota don't have a constituency, which means they don't have a lot of influence. For this reason, the quota women are sometimes called *bakosi* (meaning "cheap," "of no value," or "free")[2] MPs (Bhatasara and Chiweshe 2021). By implication, as one activist explained, they are considered worse than sex workers because sex workers at least asked for a fee for a sexual transaction (Z27.2.10.22).

Activists argue that women are silenced not only by party discipline and priorities but also by the perception that they are there as a favor and can't speak against the party that co-opted them into this space. Some argue that the women's movement itself has not only been co-opted but has been infiltrated by people deliberately sent by the government to destabilize it and collect

[2] The term originated in the Basic Commodity Supply Intervention Facility (BACOSI), a 2008 Zimbabwe Reserve Bank initiative that aimed to subsidize basic commodities, most of which were considered substandard (Mangena 2022).

Table 4.1 ZANU-PF vote share, female representation, and seats in Parliament (1980–2023)

Year	ZANU-PF seats in Parliament (%)	Women in Parliament	Seats in Parliament	Women in Parliament (%)
1980	57.0	9	100	8.0
1985	64.0	8	100	11.0
1990	97.5	17	115	12.0
1995	98.3	22	150	14.7
2000	48.47	14	150	9.3
2005	59.59	24	150	16.7
2008	45.84	32	214	15.2
2013	63.16	85	270	31.5
2018	52.35	86	270	31.9
2023	50.03	86	279	30.8

Source: IPU (2024).

information on individuals. Moreover, some women in the movement and Parliament are related to men in the government, limiting what they can do (Z15.2.11.21; Z12.5.31.21).

Some politicians say the picture may not be quite this stark. However, women in Parliament, even opposition parliamentarians, see more room to maneuver. Ruth Labode (Movement for Democratic Change Alliance; MDC-A), chairperson of the Parliamentary Portfolio Committee on Health and Child Care, said that when she started chairing the committee, "I removed my jacket of being in the opposition. I put on the jacket of justice to say the masses must get healthcare, and I will police the central government together with my bipartisan committee. And the only way I could get work done was to ensure that my reports were always bipartisan. I sell my ideas to both my party and the ruling party." However, she admits that it would be more difficult for an opposition parliamentarian to serve on a committee like Justice or Home Affairs, which is more politically sensitive than her health committee (Z9.6.6.21).

Labode has had to be persistent. For example, she lobbied for the removal of restrictions on access to sexual and reproductive health (SRH) services for adolescents. A group of ZANU-PF members of the parliamentary committee immediately rejected her suggestion. She managed to get a few supporters and then created a forum for champions of SRH rights, which included people from other committees, thereby garnering the necessary ZANU-PF support. Similarly, in lobbying around abortion policy, she has had support from the Women's Parliamentary Caucus, including from the chairperson of the caucus, who is a ZANU-PF member, Honorable Kwaramba. One of her biggest successes was getting the minister of justice to back her in successfully repealing Section 79 of the Criminal Law Code, which criminalized HIV transmission in 2022. Such laws discourage people from being tested for HIV and obtaining treatment and prevention services. Zimbabwe became only the second country in Africa to fully repeal its HIV-specific criminal law after the DRC repealed its law in 2018. This law affected women more than men because if women became pregnant, they would be tested and learn their status. Their partners would then report them to the police, claiming that they had been infected by the women, even though it was possible that the men had infected their partners. This law resulted in more women in jail than men on charges of infecting their sex partners.

Notably, despite rivalry and hostility between the political parties in Parliament, there has been considerable cooperation between women MPs through the women's parliamentary caucus. When I asked one parliamentarian why this was the case, she pointed out that the polarization is usually pushed by men, particularly those seeking leadership in their party. However, one can also assume that some collaboration is derived from the common causes women find around critical issues. Thus, women have found ways to advance their goals even in some of the most unlikely circumstances, such as the Parliament. Women's organizations reinforce these collaborations. For example, the Women's Coalition (WCoZ) generally works with all parties and takes a nonpartisan stance. They find they can work well with women across the political and ethnic divide, particularly around issues of political inclusion, civic education, health, abortion, maternal health, reproductive rights, economic literacy among women, access to information, water education, political participation, and leadership training (Z8.3.23.21; Z12.5.31.21). Once again, we see both the constraints and the possibilities for gender reform in the Zimbabwean context.

Women in the Opposition

Women's rights activists from the WCoZ found that they had received considerable support from opposition party leaders like the Honorable Jessie Majome, the Honorable Thokozani Khupe (who had served as deputy prime minister from 2009 to 2013 in the Government of National Unity (GNP), the Honorable Dorcas Sibanda, and the Honorable Tendai Biti.

However, women in the opposition suffer a tremendous amount as a result of the ruling party's efforts to fracture the opposition and infighting within the opposition. Moreover, women in the opposition themselves were not protected from party strategies that marginalized them. The Honorable Jessie Majome, who had served on the National Executive Committee of MDC-T, was ousted from Parliament as well as from her party. She was an MP from 2008 to 2013 and chaired the Parliamentary Committee on Justice, Legal, and Parliamentary Affairs. She also headed COPAC during the constitution-making process from 2009 to 2013. She had served as the country's deputy minister of justice, legal and parliamentary affairs, and deputy minister for women's affairs, gender, and community development at one time. She did not run in 2018 because she accused the MDC-T of manipulating party guidelines and pitting her against another strong leader of the women's movement, Joana Mamombe, in the same constituency.

However, like the ruling party, divisions within the opposition pose an additional constraint on women leaders. Infighting within the MDC leadership made it challenging for the women's movement to ally with them. As one MDC Alliance member and former councilor in Bulawayo explained:

> So now the problem is that at the end of the day, your views, your freedom and whatsoever, you cannot express them. Why? If you stand up today and say, "I'm with Dr. Thokozani Khupe," then the MDC-T will just recall you and say, "Now that you are with Dr. Thokozani Khupe or you are with Nelson Chamisa, you are no longer a member of MDC-T. They'll just automatically recall you from the council. You'll be told what to say. Or someone will be just watching your movement and someone will be just listening to what you'll be saying. So, at the end of the day, you won't be participating freely and you'll be just forced to remain calm. I remember one time we were asked to sign some affidavit saying I'm with President Nelson Chamisa, I'm not with [Douglas] Mwonzora. Once you signed the affidavit, automatically Mwonzora was going to recall you. Whether you love to be in Mwonzora's camp or you don't, you'll just be quiet, you'll be sitting on the fence (Z23.2.8.22)

The Women's Movement, Power Politics, and the Women's League

Some of the sharpest contradictions in Zimbabwe are evident at the highest levels of political power, as some women used women and women's rights to advance themselves politically. The Women's League, in particular, became a powerbase for women relatives of male ZANU-PF leaders. They used it to benefit from patronage and play the same factional politics games as men. However, the outcome for women was far from assured, and the game was much more dangerous for them. Two women who aligned their fortunes with ZANU-PF's leadership epitomize this dynamic: Joïce Mujuru served as vice president, and Grace Mugabe, in particular, had an outsized influence on politics in Zimbabwe.

Joïce Mujuru

Historically, the position of vice president went to a woman. However, when Mnangagwa claimed the presidency in 2017, the ZANU-PF Women's League informed him that no woman was interested in becoming the vice president in anticipation of what they thought the president wanted to hear. This was the consequence of a long sequence of power struggles involving women leaders in ZANU-PF.

The League's reticence to advocate for a woman had its origins in earlier powerplays. For example, in 2004, the ZANU-PF Women's League and a ZANU-PF faction led by General Solomon Mujuru had pressed Mugabe to nominate a woman candidate for the party's vice presidency and the country's post of vice president. General Mujuru had been the military head of ZANLA during the war. He led the integration of ZANLA into the Zimbabwe National Army after independence and was promoted to general. He became one of the most powerful powerbrokers in Zimbabwe.

ZANU-PF congress passed a resolution in 2004 stating that one of the party's two deputy presidents had to be a woman. Six of the party's ten provincial chairs and a militant war veteran leader who opposed the nomination of Mujuru were suspended from the party, and Jonathan Moyo, minister of state for information and former professor at the University of Zimbabwe was publicly reprimanded for his support of Emmerson Mnangagwa, who had been the country's first minister of state security and oversaw the Central Intelligence Organization. Moyo was also expelled from ZANU-PF's powerful central committee at the time.

In the process, the then–Speaker of Parliament, Mnangagwa, was sidelined, and Mujuru's wife, Joïce Mujuru, was nominated by the Women's League, thus claiming the post of vice president of the country and vice president of the ZANU-PF. This set off "the night of the long knives," as the factional fight was referred to. Mujuru remained vice president between 2004 and 2014. As one of the first female commanders in Mugabe's ZANLA forces,

Table 4.2 Heads of ZANU-PF Women's League

Head of ZANU-PF Women's League	Term
Sally Mugabe	1978
Joïce Mujuru	c. 1981–1988
Tsungirirai Hungwe	c. 1990s
Thenjiwe Lesabe	1994–2004
Oppah Muchinguri	2004–2014
Grace Mugabe	December 2014–December 2017
Mabel Chinomona	December 2017–present

she had long been regarded as a potential successor to Mugabe. Two factions emerged, each bidding to eventually succeed Mugabe. One, known as Gamatox, backed Mujuru, and the other, known as Weevils, backed Mnangagwa. Grace Mugabe also entered the fray to oppose Mujuru. She announced her intentions in a 2014 rally in Harare, saying, "People say I want to be President. Why not? Am I not Zimbabwean?" The ZANU-PF Women's League executive secretary then, Oppah Muchinguri, stepped down to allow Grace Mugabe to assume the position in 2014 (Mamvura and Mazuruse 2022; see Table 4.2 for a list of the leaders of the ZANU-PF Women's League).

Grace Mugabe then set out to orchestrate the political demise of Joïce Mujuru. Mujuru was accused of plotting against Mugabe. She was removed from her position as Zimbabwe's vice president and ZANU-PF vice president and was expelled from the party. A few years earlier, in 2011, her husband had died at home in a fire under suspicious circumstances. She blamed political enemies for killing him ("Mugabe Knows" 2016). Some saw General Mujuru's untimely death as an effort to disempower his wife from her political aspirations. Part of the political arsenal trained against her was an effort to discredit her claim to have shot down a Rhodesian helicopter during the liberation war and to promote scandalous stories that minimized her role in the liberation war and made her appear antiwoman. Rumors spread that she defrauded state enterprises (Mangena 2022).

Mugabe and his wife, Grace Mugabe, led attacks against Mujuru, calling her a prostitute. She occupied an ambiguous position in Zimbabwean politics, as she had been vilified for being both a "prostitute" and, as she had also been referred to, a man. After Mujuru's removal from the line of succession to Mugabe, George Charamba (who went by the nom de plume Nathaniel Manheru) described her fall from power while mocking the gender quota, saying,

"She was not bright! Aah, don't forget she came in to represent the women's bloc. . . . It was about representing women; she came from the women and the President had to oblige" (Manheru 2016).

After Joïce Mujuru was removed from the vice presidency in 2014, Grace Mugabe accused her of factionalism in the party. She was denounced for attempting to overthrow and possibly assassinate Mugabe. After her expulsion from the party, she formed her own ZimPF party and ran for the presidency in 2018. Subsequently, she kept a low profile and eventually faded into obscurity.

The upshot of Mujuru's bid for the presidency was that ZANU-PF women were basically told that ambitious women were a problem, especially if they wanted to become president. The clause providing for a female vice president was then removed from the ZANU-PF constitution, and it was replaced with a clause that said the president could choose whomever he wanted. The Women's League initially tried to reinstitute the clause to no avail, and by 2017, the League had completely capitulated, saying that women were not interested in the vice presidency.

Grace Mugabe

Grace Mugabe was similarly sidelined when she used her position as the wife of the aging President Mugabe to claim power. She had been Robert Mugabe's secretary and later married him, in 1996—while his first wife was lying in the hospital dying. Thus she became his second wife and first lady. As one lawyer-activist said, "You find that women just end up caught in the revolving doors" (Z3.3.4.21).

Grace Mugabe, known as "Gucci Grace" because of her extravagant tastes for luxury goods, became head of the Women's League and a member of the ZANU-PF Politburo in 2014 after edging Mujuru out (Allison 2017). Her supporters argue that as head of the League, she sought to ensure that women were beneficiaries of the land redistribution exercise in Zimbabwe. Approximately 20 percent of women received land in the Fast Track Land Reform Program after 2000, and even more have benefited because of changes in inheritance laws (Z24.2.9.22). Grace Mugabe initiated programs for women to get into commercial farming and gold mining. She pushed for the creation of the Women's Bank and helped revamp irrigation schemes in Binga, Manicaland, and Mashonaland Central. She launched a program to distribute farm equipment to women and helped renovate girls' schools. She was also behind the Command Agriculture Program (Z20.11.4.21). Grace Mugabe thus was able to build up a base of support through the Women's League. She drew on the motherhood trope to enhance her political status (Biri 2021).

But she also used her position to get what she wanted. She went after some land in Mazowe, Mashonaland Central, and destroyed some huts associated with the Shona spirit medium, Nehanda Nyakasikana (1840–1898), who had mounted a rebellion against the British settlers and later served as an inspiration for the nationalist liberation movement. As one interviewee observed, "Because I think for women like Grace who come from her own generation, they grew up seeing men bulldozing their way, using the mafia style to get whatever they want in Zimbabwe and using the military and stuff. So Grace is from a generation of women who saw that if you want to have power in politics, you also need to bulldoze your way" (Z27.2.10.22).

She also headed a faction, Generation 40 (G40), that included members of ZANU-PF's Youth League and other politicians ("Kenyatta Team Lacoste" 2017). She feuded with the Lacoste faction of the party, led by then–Vice President Mnangagwa, which had accused the G40 clique of trying to capture the state. As a result, Mnangagwa lost his post as minister of justice, legal, and parliamentary affairs and as vice president in 2017 and fled to South Africa. Many Zimbabwean analysts believe that the first lady was using her proximity to the aging and ailing president to insinuate herself into power to reap material benefits from the position. This was particularly offensive to many Zimbabweans because she was not elected to the presidency (Mamvura and Mazuruse 2022).

Around 2014, Grace Mugabe started to hold "Meet the People" tours or rallies with party loyalists nationwide. The first lady was able to enhance her political visibility through the rallies while reminding people there was "no vacancy in the State House" and that God had chosen Mugabe and would rule the country even beyond the grave. Grace Mugabe highlighted the trope of "mother of the nation" and reminded people that she held power out of virtue of being the president's wife. She also purported to be highly educated in spite of questions raised about her claim to have obtained a doctorate (Mangena 2022).

Together with supporters Jonathan Moyo and Savior Kasukuwere, she was able to isolate the war veterans and put herself next in the line of succession to take over as president (Dendere 2018). In the course of factional fights that she inflamed, she publicly shamed leading men in the Mugabe administration, whom she referred to as her "political children" (Mangena 2022). In response, Mnangagwa, with the backing of the Zimbabwe Defense Forces and members of the Lacoste political faction, masterminded a bloodless coup in 2017 and put both Mugabes under house arrest, forcing the president to resign his post as head of the ZANU-PF and president of thirty-seven years.

Grace Mugabe was expelled from ZANU-PF and banned for life, along with other ministers and prominent personalities ("List of People" 2017). She was accused of running a "cabal" intent on ruining the country (Mudiwa 2017). The upshot of these factional fights involving women was that both Grace Mugabe and Joïce Mujuru were labeled loose women (*hure*) and pompous, loud women (*marujata*). Not only did the Women's League back down from demanding a woman in top leadership, but Mnangagwa's wife, Auxillia Mnangagwa, was forced to resign from her parliamentary seat. The president announced that Auxillia Mnangagwa would become the mother of the nation, telegraphing a clear message that her own personal political ambitions were not to be entertained (Dendere 2018).

After these events, women associated with the Women's League felt they could not seek high positions. Fear seemed to drive this sentiment. As one ZANU-PF woman politician said, "We are not fit for high positions because we have been deemed a problem. This is something that has obviously come from the male side of things. And women have agreed and adopted it even though I know for sure that they [the women] do not believe that. People are afraid. They're afraid to lose positions. They're afraid to get harassed and put in a position where they might be in danger of some sort. So they would rather just toe the male line than to speak their mind. And this is the type of politics that has existed in ZANU-PF for a long time now" (Z20.11.4.21).

Many women find that the only way they can have influence is by aligning themselves with ZANU-PF. As one activist put it, "The problem with Zimbabwe is that everything is political. The medical system is political, the transport, infrastructure, tenders, everything is political. You're only listened to if you're ZANU-PF. And if you're not ZANU-PF, you're literally demonized. Nobody listens to you. Nobody has time for you. And if you [women] do speak, they will make sure that they thwart all your efforts" (Z3.3.4.21).

The Marujatanization of Women in Politics

One way to understand the contradictory treatment of high-level women in politics is to look at some of the cultural tropes surrounding them. Women in Zimbabwe are regarded in two diametrically opposed frames, according to Gibson Ncube (2020). They are simultaneously portrayed as mothers (*amai* in Shona or *umama* in Ndebele), who are to be revered, but also as "whores" (*hure* or *pfambi* in Shona, *nyembesi* in Ndebele slang). One of the slogans during the liberation war was "Forward with the cooking stick," which highlights women's maternal roles (Nhongo-Simbanegavi 2000), which are not viewed as antithetical to being engaged in politics and can even be seen as a basis for political action. This is also a mindset, as one activist pointed out, "that if you are not corrupt and you don't misappropriate government funds, you are a woman. The Shona word for integrity and doing things properly, *kuita mukadzi*, is sarcastically a reference to being feminine" (Z27.2.10.22). This may also explain why people found Grace Mugabe's behavior such an affront; it violated this perception of women as not corruptible. Thus, when women's ambition oversteps the bounds of what is deemed acceptable, they can be seen as "whores," or women of loose morals, as former Vice President Joïce Mujuru found out when she decided to run for president (Bhatasara and Chiweshe 2021; Z27.2.10.22).

When Grace Mugabe, once seen as the "mother of the nation," overstepped her role as her husband aged, she, too, was pushed aside and labeled a "prostitute." Her fall reflected the *marujatanization* of women in politics, which is the association (in Shona) of women as loose, loud, and pompous (Mawere 2017). It is a warning for women to stay in their lane not to try to take over male roles.

The cases of Joïce Mujuru and Grace Mugabe point to the limits of women's pursuit of power at the highest levels. They show that women can play the same patronage game as men and build up their power bases. But they face the added hurdle of misogyny. The cases of Joïce Mujuru and Grace Mugabe additionally show how women's pursuit of power is not necessarily more innocent than that of men but it can also serve the cause of women's rights, while simultaneously serving to further entrench a political party.

Violence Against Women in Politics

One of the most jarring paradoxes in Zimbabwe is the willingness, on the one hand, to pass legislation affecting women and include women in politics, while at the same time repressing and carrying out violence against them when they make demands for the "wrong" reforms. The repression is arbitrary and unpredictable and has a chilling effect on women's mobilization and the types of issues that are adopted. As one gender specialist and lecturer put it, "There are these coercive instruments that the government has put in place to make sure that women's movements are controlled, creating fear of getting into politics and fear of getting into leadership positions" (Z27.2.10.22).

Opposition women leaders and activists are especially targeted. One MDC politician I interviewed explained that she had run away from her home with her sisters and children because of violence: "There was a time that you were not even allowed to put on an MDC T-shirt or have an MDC slogan. And even if they would just suspect that you were an MDC supporter, they'll just hit you. To date, we don't even know where some of the members are" (Z23.2.8.22).

Opposition leaders the Honorable Joana Mamombe, Netsai Marova, and Cecilia Chimbiri were arrested three times in 2020 for protesting the government's Covid-19 policies, including the lack of food and social support. They were initially abducted and subjected to physical and sexual assault and then charged with communicating falsehoods to their relatives, friends, and legal practitioners about their abduction and torture by suspected state security agents in 2022. All three women belong to the Citizens Coalition for Change (CCC), formerly, the MDC-A. ZANU-PF claimed that the women had staged all of the events; it rearrested them and forced Mamombe to undergo psychiatric evaluation.

Women's movement activists offered them support, visited them in prison, and raised funds for them, but they purposefully did not hold marches or engage in public confrontations with the state (Z15.2.11.21). "We are dealing with a really unpredictable government and unpredictable judicial system. We can never be sure what is going to happen," said one of the women, Marova, in an interview with *The Independent* (Oppenheim 2022). In 2023, the High Court acquitted Mamombe and Chimbiri, while Marova went into exile.

There are many other such cases. State security agents also allegedly abducted Jestina Mukoko, director of the Zimbabwe Peace Project, from her home and held her incommunicado while torturing her in 2008. Itai Dzamara of the Occupy Africa Unity Square campaign was abducted in 2015 and has not been heard from since (Changachirere 2020).

Sometimes, the charges can be severe for relatively mundane activities. In one instance, Farirai Gumbonzvanda, a girls' rights activist and community volunteer with the Rozaria Memorial Trust, and Rita Nyampinga of the Female Prisoners Support Trust were arrested along with four other civil society leaders and charged with treason in 2019 for participating in a training workshop on nonviolent action in the Maldives. As often happens, the charges against them were never dropped. Farirai explained to me, "People don't usually have their charges dropped because I think it would be an admission for the government to sort of say that 'we were not supposed to arrest you.' So the best you can get, which is what we got, is you'll be called back in summons. I don't really see a situation where they will drop the charges completely. They do this to threaten and scare people." However, it also has the effect of politicizing women who weren't all that keen about politics to begin with. Farirai pointed out that "sometimes I think it's sort of, it goes against the whole objective. Because I mean, I look at someone like myself: I never used to be that interested in politics in general. I was very passionate about social justice, but I never really paid attention even to the politics happening around the country. But after that experience is when I sort of started tuning into politics" (Z8.3.23.21).

Another woman, Rejoice Nharaunda-Makawa, national vice chairperson of the WCoZ, was arrested for exposing on a radio talk show how older men were exploiting children. She was charged with publishing falsehoods. Because the issue hits personally at those in power, they find the exposure offensive. As Nharaunda-Makawa explained, "What is our main political figure looking like? So if you go into that space, you would find that your typical politician has five wives and that his youngest wife is nineteen. So he's been dating her since she was seventeen. And so are they going to sit down and pass legislation to oust that exploitation of young girls? Maybe not, because they are the perpetrators. However, does that then stop us from having the conversation? No, it doesn't. We get arrested. But do we stop talking? No. We keep pushing, and then we get arrested. So, we keep pushing again, and then we get arrested again. I guess that's what activism is about" (Z12.5.31.21).

Nharaunda and another woman and man were forced off of the Zimpapers Board, which is the oldest and largest publisher of newspapers since 1891, controlling the leading daily newspapers like *The Herald, The Chronicle*, and *H-Metro* as well as two Sunday newspapers. She said she was forced out: "I'm now deemed to be disloyal and untrustworthy because it's now a new dispensation and because I challenge things and I ask questions. There's an expectation that you go in there, and you should continue to ratify and sign off on things without questioning them or using your intellect. And so because the three of us have repeatedly challenged a new board and I will ask for accountability and transparency, there's a huge effort to ensure that I am silenced and bullied into keeping quiet permanently." She felt women were more dispensable and regarded as more problematic when they didn't toe the line, especially when they exposed how someone in a position of power was engaged in wife battering (Z12.5.31.21).

Another form of violence is psychological, which draws on the aforementioned arsenal of cultural tropes regarding women in politics. There are cultural expectations about women that constrain them. According to Hungwe (2006), women were perceived as "undermining Zimbabwean ideological constructions of womanhood, premised on female dependency upon males." For example, "good women" are expected to be at home at 4 p.m., which is an impossibility for a politician. As one university gender specialist I interviewed explained, "Fear was instilled systematically from colonial times into women so that they do not participate in politics. So even if on paper, you are told that you can participate. Women will be in Parliament, but they will be quiet.... If you are a female and you force your way into politics, you are a 'whore.' You are [considered] a 'prostitute' because you want to be in a male space. What are you doing where men spend time? If you are above twenty-five years old and you are not married, and worse, if you get into politics, you are [labeled] a 'prostitute.' And if you get promoted in politics, you obviously have slept with the whole cabinet. That is the dominant narrative" (Z27.2.10.22).

Thus, becoming involved in politics brings women under suspicion of sexual impropriety and of having slept their way into positions of power, and women risk being labeled as "prostitutes." This has served as a significant deterrent preventing women from engaging in politics. As we saw in the cases of Joïce Mujuru and Grace Mugabe, the term "prostitute" is widely leveled against women in politics to delegitimize their involvement in public life (Gaidzanwa 1995).

Women have actively pushed back against such treatment. Thokozani Khupe, the leader of one of the opposition party factions, the MDC-T, and female presidential candidate in 2018 said, "The slut-shaming has actually shifted gender dynamics in a way. Young women are coming out in support of other women. There is an outpouring of sympathy from men, too, and more people are talking about gender stereotyping. We are using it to gain power, not lose it." Her chief election agent, Priscilla Misihairabwi-Mushonga, wore a T-shirt with "#MeToo" emblazoned on the front and the Shona word for prostitute, "Hure," on the back. "That is how we are taking back our power. We can't allow men to use our sexuality to undermine us. It should be ours to use," Misihairabwi-Mushonga later told the Associated Press (Mutsaka 2018).

Given this environment of violence and intimidation, it is not surprising that the Zimbabwe Electoral Commission (ZEC) found that 74 percent of women and 67.2 percent of men were not interested in participating in politics for fear of violence. Overall support for women as leaders is also lower than the overall level of support for the continent, as is evident from a 2024 Afrobarometer survey (see Table 4.3). Misogynistic attitudes still prevail.

Both men and women also lack campaign resources and fear not being qualified, but women also cited the "masculine nature" of politics, the perception of women in politics as "loose women," religious and cultural norms

Table 4.3 Attitudes toward women in office in Zimbabwe

Survey round	Year	Survey response supportive of women in political office (%)[a]		
		All	Men	Women
R3	2005/2006	66.9	58.4	75.5
R5	2011/2013	76.1	69.4	82.7
R6	2014/2015	68	56.8	79.2
R7	2016/2018	69.9	60.9	78.7
R9	2021/2023	74.8	72.8	76.6

[a]"Let's talk for a moment about the kind of society you would like to have in this country. Which of the following statements is closest to your view? Choose Statement 1 or Statement 2. Probe for strength of opinion: Do you agree or strongly agree? Men make better political leaders than women and should be elected rather than women. Women should have the same chance of being elected to political office as men." Afrobarometer R9 2022.

Source: Afrobarometer (2024).

against women as leaders, and the biases and discrimination against women in political parties, which are the gatekeepers to political leadership roles.

Responses to Repression

As a result of repression against women activists, the WCoZ and other activist groups are careful about the issues they take up, although individuals within the coalition have spoken out and have faced arrest and intimidation. As one women's rights activist put it, "The advances we have made around sanitary towels or ending child marriage are because the issues we are dealing with are not considered too political and they are not considered a threat to the political status quo. So the government is okay with us agitating in those fields. It's not like we are directly targeting issues of corruption, nepotism, and stuff like that. We are being strategic about it because we are aware that if we try to be very confrontational, a lot of us will be arrested. I think it's a realization that being very public and very visible is not always the way to get around things" (Z15.2.11.21).

Thus, the movement does not challenge government violence against women. Instead, they focus on domestic or interpersonal violence, fearing that the government will shut down their organizations if they tackle more significant issues. One activist explained in an interview with me that the Zimbabwean government acts like it is war-ready in a country that is not at war. It treats NGOs as antistate, as spies and instigators, even when they speak about "harmless" issues. They are tolerated up to a point. But "when they cross some line in the sand, the government then threatens to withdraw their license," noted one policymaker (Z13.3.4.21). Even when the state threatens to displace people from communal lands, such as the Chilongo community of 13,840, she explained, "you will see the deafening silence of the civil society organizations, and that speaks volumes in terms of the parameters within which they work and how they manage their own security" (see Human Rights Watch 2021a). One does not know who is going to be targeted next, which leads to institutionalized tenure insecurity. These land grabs are particularly harmful to women because customary land is generally the only land available to them. Since customary land is not allowed to be sold, when it is sold on the black market, it means that land falls even further out of reach for women, who often don't have the resources to purchase land. If they manage to buy such land, it can also be more easily disposed of because it is an illegal transaction (Z13.3.4.21).

When working on issues like child marriage and the taxation of sanitary towels that were considered nonpolitical, women's rights activists could collaborate with ZANU-PF politicians like Monica Mutsvangwa and Olivia Muchena, particularly during the GNU. Participating in coalitions with ZANU-PF also provided some immunity for opposition women and women's rights activists. Opposition activists found their collaborations with individuals in the Ministry of Women's Affairs to be productive when developing policies around, for example, less-controversial issues like ending child marriage.

However, there were limits on women in ZANU-PF as they were prevented from going against the party line when it came to gender concerns. As a leading female politician explained, "Shockingly, when certain issues would come up, some women would even stand up against women empowerment" (Z20.11.4.21). Another activist explained, "The silence of ZANU women regarding the abuse of women is telling, and it reflects negatively on ZANU women, indicating their fear and incapacity. It indicates that women within ZANU cannot push or rely on ZANU to champion and defend women's rights in Zimbabwe" (Z6.7.5.21). As a result, women in the opposition were sometimes more vocal about gender equality issues in Parliament than the ZANU-PF women.

One new challenge to the politics of repression may be coming from younger women activists and politicians. Many of the female parliamentarians from ZANU-PF were older adults who were not very well educated and did not know how to articulate issues coming out of the women's movement. They felt threatened by younger women pressing more urgently for reform. There is also "a belief in the Women's League that more seasoned women must take up senior positions, and there's a fear of young women, young blood," according to a veteran woman politician (Z20.11.4.21).

Thus, there is a generational divide between feminists when it comes to politics, with younger feminists being more interested in historically taboo issues like abortion and the rights of sex workers and LGBTQ-identified people. Some are also advocating for 50 percent legislative representation instead of a reserved seat quota that makes them beholden to ZANU-PF. As one younger activist put it, there is a generational divide "in terms of strategy and in terms of what issues are priority. So you find that for young women like me, we are more concerned about political rights. We've been organizing for a number of years now, but things are not changing. We need more women in Parliament, more women in decision-making spaces. For example, it's the women and partly the women's movement also who pushed for this quota system, the sixty seats in Parliament. So now us, the young women, are saying, 'We don't want this quota system; we want 50/50" (Z15.2.11.21).

Limited Role of External Pressures

The Zimbabwean government, which is one of the largest recipients of ODA in Africa, is nevertheless not in a position to virtue signal with its women leaders in the ways described by the genderwashing literature. As one activist explained, "To some extent, they are trying to look good because there are certain processes that hold them to account, like the SADC Gender Barometer. It asks how many women you have in Parliament, how many women you have in decision-making spaces. So you can't make that up if you don't have those women in Parliament." But the activist was quick to point out that "it's not always that we want to look good in the global arena; it's also mounting pressure within the country where there are a lot of young women who are coming up and saying we also want to be in these spaces" (Z.15.2.11.21).

Zimbabwe thus responds to internal pressures from the women's movement but to a much lesser extent, to international and regional actors when it comes to women's rights. This has been especially true since penalties were imposed on Zimbabwe by the European Union (EU), United States (US), and United Kingdom (UK) in 2002 and 2003 for human rights abuses and for the use of legal means as well as violence to repress the country's opposition. US President Biden extended the sanctions in 2023 in light of continuing violations leading up to the elections (White House 2023). These penalties include financial and visa sanctions against selected government representatives, a ban on defense items and service transfers, and a suspension of nonhumanitarian government-to-government assistance. International investors and banks are not keen to do business with Zimbabwe for fear of violating these sanctions. However, the country's inability to borrow money from international financial institutions has more to do with bad debt than with sanctions. By 2000, the World Bank had suspended lending to Zimbabwe because of defaults on debt, and in 2001, the International Monetary Fund (IMF) declared the country ineligible to access its funds. In short, external incentives for gender reform are weak.

Conclusion

Given women's extreme challenges in Zimbabwe, one would be justified in asking whether the fight is worth it. But in listening to the stories of women activists in Zimbabwe, many treasure the opportunities they have claimed, even if there are many hurdles. As one activist explained, "We are gradually educating. We are gradually raising awareness. We are gradually influencing change. We're aware that we're not going to have the impact with the results that we want overnight, but they certainly have shifted from independence. My mother would never have had the voice that I have, and the reason I do the work I do today is because my mother died at thirty-five of cancer. She had been a child bride. She was taken as a bride at thirteen. She had her first child at fourteen, and two children at fifteen. By the time she died at thirty-five, she'd had six children and two miscarriages. She was married to an abusive man, and she didn't have the voice. And so I do the work that I do today because of what my mom went through and what I then went through as a young girl, growing up as an orphan without my mother. There's a whole revolution that's been happening from that time [of independence] in my own personal space. And I can see the difference and I can see the impact. I'm doing stuff that my mother and grandmother would have never dreamed of doing" (Z12.5.31.21).

Another activist pointed to the contradictions that have arisen as a result of women's pressures for reform: "Suddenly women are overtaking everywhere because now there's pressure, not just from the women's groups, but even the government itself is under pressure also, from other governments, to make sure that women are taken care of and women are listened to, and women are taken seriously. So the government obviously puts in place all these policies, but the same government is dominated by men, and these same men don't want these women going into political positions .... [This is why] you will find women who are fighting or who have had to fight to actually be taken seriously as legitimate members of Parliament. This is the stuff that's going on underneath, which you cannot see" (Z27.2.10.22).

The Zimbabwean experience with women's rights is complicated because of the multiple forces pushing for and against gender reform. As a result, the Zimbabwean landscape of women's rights is full of contradictions. This is a country that would not have gained liberation from colonial rule without the efforts of women. Yet one finds, for example, top women politicians undermining women's rights to advance themselves as leaders, the existence of governmental and party institutions dedicated to women's rights silent amid the repression of women, government efforts to open the legislative and constitutional terrain for women while limiting inclusion of certain women, and legislation sponsored by the ruling party to curtail violence against women as the government violently suppresses women activists engaged in noncontroversial activities. The ambiguous picture that emerges can be explained by the fact that the women's movement has persisted against all odds. It has taken advantage of openings and opportunities in the Parliament, in both the opposition and ruling parties, in the Women's League, in the women's ministry, and in politically advantageous moments to advance its agenda.

5
The Challenge of Militarism for Women's Political Representation in Mauritania

Authoritarian countries that have experienced more instability have had fewer women in positions of power than stable countries with single parties that have remained in power for multiple electoral cycles. Countries with military governments that came into power through coups and are ruled by military juntas are not generally disposed to promoting women's rights or advancing women as leaders. Patriarchal politics define military regimes, which are not necessarily seeking legitimacy in conventional ways through elections. They are not generally holding elections unless they are transitioning to an electoral autocracy. Thus, they are not seeking to appeal to domestic constituencies or impress the international community.

This military influence is evident in the case of Mauritania, where the periods of instability and army rule saw little in the way of the advancement of women's status. Only after the country moved from military to civilian government did women gain representation in the elected governments and were appointed at the cabinet level in larger numbers. This is not to say that women's movements have not tried to influence outcomes or that military leaders have entirely ignored women, but compared with other regime types, they have not done as well.

However, it should be noted that all of the authoritarian regimes in this study involve countries where the military played an oversized role in civilian rule, including Mauritania, Zimbabwe, Uganda, and Rwanda. In other words, the same military leaders remained in power in all these countries after conflict or, in the case of Mauritania, after military rule, but they remained in civilian garb. The fact that they had this military legacy meant that they needed to find a variety of ways to recast their image, and bringing women into governance structures was one way to give a new face to their rule. It allowed them to present a softer side to their governments once they had transitioned to civilian rule.

Mauritanian society is a good case to look at because the country's culture is relatively free for many women. This is particularly true of the Bīẓān people

Why African Autocracies Promote Women as Leaders. Aili Mari Tripp, Oxford University Press. © Oxford University Press (2025). DOI: 10.1093/9780197829004.003.0006

(a mixture of Arab and Berber people who refer to themselves as "white"), who make up the political elite. Certain women with political backgrounds or economic influence have used this to their advantage in the political sphere. However, it did not benefit most women in the political sphere until the military rule and the era of coups ended.

It was not until the middle of the first decade of the 2000s—a time when greater stability and regime institutionalization started to take hold—that women leaders and women's rights began to improve markedly in Mauritania. The country has made moderate progress in advancing women as political leaders. Today, it would be considered a hybrid regime, neither fully authoritarian nor democratic. Mauritania began to loosen up on civil liberties and political rights after 2005. However, the country has been an autocracy with long periods of military rule for much of its postindependence history. Even after it shifted to civilian rule in 1991, it could be said that the military held disproportionate power, which continues to constrain women's possibilities for leadership. The alternation of parties in power during the period of the hybrid regime has continued to constrain women's representation, though not as severely as military rule did.

The chapter draws on interviews with a wide range of people, including current and former parliamentarians representing the ruling party, Union pour la république (UPR); the main Islamist party, Parti tewassoul; the Rassemblement des forces démocratiques (RFD); the Union des forces démocratiques (UFP); and Alliance populaire progressiste (APP). The interviews included an adviser to the minister in the Ministère des Affaires Sociales, de l'Enfance et de la Famille, along with the Secrétaire Générale de la Commission Nationale des Femmes de l'UPR, gender experts in the United Nations Development Programme, and a representative of the European Union in charge of funding relating to governance. The interviews also included numerous women's rights, antislavery, and civil society organizations. Interviews also took place with the former minister of women and numerous academics and journalists, among others. The interviewees were with a mixture of Bīẓān, Pulaar, and Wolof-speaking people.

Background

Politics in Mauritania is defined by the president and the major party in power, known as the Equity Party (UPR until 2022). It is also controlled by tribal governance structures as well as race and caste, with vestiges of slavery remaining. The country has a nomadic population that became sedentary as recently as the 1980s (MRT7.6.8.20). Moreover, the Salafi influences that emerged in the 1990s are strong, and they have posed some challenges to women's rights reform, but they are present in other countries in the region that have made more significant gains in gender equality. All of these factors create challenges to advancing women's rights. Still, none is as important as the frequency of coups d'état and the long duration of military rule, especially when considered comparatively.

Mauritania is lodged between the Maghreb and sub-Saharan Africa, and its 3.5 million population are a mosaic of the Bīẓān of Arab or Berber descent, who make up 30 percent of the population, and the H'rāṭīn, who are the former slaves or descendants of slaves of the Bīẓān and who make up 40 percent of the population. The Haalpulaar, Soninké, Wolof, and Bamana are based in the south and constitute the remaining 30 percent of the population. The country abolished slavery in 1981 and criminalized it in 2007. They strengthened antislavery laws in 2015. Although the H'rāṭīn have the same legal rights as other citizens, they remain socially disadvantaged. Thus, the socioeconomic status of women in Mauritania is complex because culturally, some Bīẓān women have a relatively high status within society, but because of continued illegal practices of slavery and discrimination against the H'rāṭīn and other Mauritanians, the advances for women are uneven. There are other hierarchies in Mauritania based on tribe and clan, and some Bīẓān women (and men) occupy a low status in the tribal structure.

Mauritania became part of French West Africa and a colony of France in 1904. In 1960, it gained independence from France and became an Islamic Republic. Mauritania's political history is one of long periods of rule by one party (1960–1978) punctuated by military coups and military rule. Since independence, between 1960 and 2008, the country experienced ten coups d'état, four of which were successful. Military rule lasted from 1978 until 1991 and was followed by alternating ruling parties as a hybrid regime. All of these factors—multiple coups, military rule, and nonentrenched parties—conspired against the possibility of substantially advancing women's rights.

The Mauritanian Progressive Union (UPM) was formed in 1948 and contested in the 1951 French National Assembly Elections. Its candidate, Sidi el-Mokhtar N'Diaye, won a seat in the French Parliament. In 1952, the party, led by Moktar Ould Daddah, won twenty-two out of twenty-four seats in the Territorial Assembly Elections, and in 1957 it won thirty-three out of thirty-four seats. In 1958, the party merged with the Mauritanian Agreement and the black nationalist Gorgol Democratic Bloc to form the Mauritanian Regroupment Party (Parti du regroupement mauritanien; PRM) from 1958 until 1961. Daddah sought to bring together the competing parties in Mauritania to create a united front in the struggle for independence. Fiercely nationalistic, Daddah resisted French efforts to incorporate Mauritania into a greater Morocco or into the Common Saharan Regions Organization (Organization commune des régions sahariennes; OCRS).

After gaining independence from France on November 28, 1960, Mauritania became an Islamic Republic, and its first president, Moktar Ould Daddah, declared it a one-party state in 1964. In 1961, the PRM merged with several other Mauritanian parties to form the Mauritanian People's Party (Parti du peuple mauritanien or PPM). Daddah remained president until 1978, when he was deposed in a coup that brought a series of military leaders to power.

In 1978, all independent associations and political activities were curtailed until 1986, including women's political involvement in an effort to stave off potential threats to the ruling party (Lesourd 2007). Another coup in 1984 brought Colonel Maaouya Ould Sid'Ahmed Taya into power, and he held office until 2005. At that time, women were cut entirely out of politics, which remained in the hands of men, especially tribal chiefs and religious leaders (MRT8.6.10.20).

Kadihine Movement

Although women were not visible in politics during the years of military rule, they did engage politically in social movements, including movements of youth, workers, and, in particular, the Kadihine movement in the 1960s and 1970s. In 1971, women also created a new association of women called the Movement of Mauritanian Democratic Women. This movement was led by its president, Marième Mint Lehweyj (MRT8.6.10.20).

The Kadihine movement emerged out of a 1968 Zouerate workers strike, which the government severely repressed. It opposed the military's role in Mauritanian politics, especially the use of coups. It also opposed the single-party rule of Mokhtar Ould Daddah. It was made up mainly of H'rāṭīn but also included many Black Africans and those marginalized by the caste system as well as women, young people, workers, and peasants. The Kadihine movement launched many political careers in Mauritania, including those of many women's rights activists and politicians. It was led by Marxist intellectuals who opposed the Arab nationalist movement because of its emphasis on Arabization and racial politics. This Arab nationalist faction had been growing since the 1960s. It had been aligned with the Nasserist movement in Egypt and the Baathist movement in

Syria and wanted Mauritania to be exclusively defined as an Arab country aligned with the Arab Maghreb. The Kadihine movement, in contrast, wanted Mauritania to become part of the West African organization Economic Community of West African States (ECOWAS), which was formed in 1978. The Kadihine movement became a party in 1973, Parti des kadihines de mauritanie (PKM), the precursor to the current left-leaning antislavery party, Union of the Forces of Progress (Union des forces du progress; UFP).

Aminetou Mint El Moktar, currently president of the Association of Women Heads of Household (AFCF), and other women like her had their start politically in the Kadihine movement in the 1970s. She was a left-wing activist who campaigned for national unity and equality for men and women. The movement also included women like Sy Lalla Aïcha Ouedraogo and Salka Mint Snid, president of the Network Association of Mauritanian Women Journalists.

The Kadihine party eventually split into several groups because of factional infighting over ideological differences. Some members of PKM joined President Moktar Ould Daddah's PPM party. Another faction formed the National Democratic Movement (MND). It had separate wings for youth and women and operated clandestinely because it was dealing with a military regime that was not favorable to women's movements. Mint El Moktar was in charge of the women's wing. The movement continued until 1991, after which a multiparty system was introduced.

In 1989, conflict broke out between the minority ethnic groups (Haalpulaar, Soninké, and Wolof) against the hegemony of the Arabic-speaking majority (70 percent), and the upshot of this was the repatriation of 80,000–120,000 people to Senegal and Mali under the pretext that they were Senegalese. Their land was claimed by Arabic-speaking Bidhān and H'rāṭīn people (Boukhars 2016). Between 180 and 300 Black Mauritanian soldiers were killed in the Mauritanian army barracks. These incidents became a threat to Ould Taya's legitimacy. In the 1980s, Iraq's President Saddam Hussein made a bid to assume the mantle of Nasser as leader of the Arab world. Ould Taya started to assert that "Mauritania is an Arab country" in the mid-1980s, seeking military support from Hussein, which he received. The Taya regime supported Hussein, who invaded Kuwait in 1990, resulting in a withdrawal of aid by Arab, Western bilateral, and multilateral donors. In 1993, the National Assembly passed an amnesty law for the killing of Black Mauritania troops in 1989–1991 to protect members of the military who had carried out human rights violations. The law is still in effect today.

Impact of Multipartyism

The PPM was the only legal party from 1961 to 1978. It was headed by President Moktar Ould Daddah, who served as president from 1960 until 1978, when he was deposed in a coup. Parties and associations were subsequently banned to control any possible opposition or threats to power, as was the case in one-party states in Africa at the time. Five coups followed in close succession: in 1978, 1979, 1980, 1981 (unsuccessfully), and 1984. Maaouya Ould Sid'Ahmed Taya came to power in a bloodless coup in 1984 and ruled as president until 2005, when he was also ousted in a coup. Taya started a process of liberalization, controlling it all the while. The constitution was rewritten in 1991 during his rule, and the preamble was revised to include the Universal Declaration of Human Rights (1948). It allowed for the formation of parties and freedom of assembly. After 1993, associations were free to form.

President Taya introduced a multiparty system in the early 1990s without leveling the playing field for the opposition. He held a referendum on a new constitution, the installation of a Parliament, and the opening of the press, which nevertheless remained severely curtailed throughout his rule. Taya resigned from the military so he could run as a civilian and was elected president in 1992, becoming the first elected president to run in a competitive election. Municipal elections had already been held in 1986 and 1990. However, the opposition boycotted the legislative elections, which meant that Taya's party, the Parti républicain démocratique et social (PRDS), claimed all the parliamentary seats. Taya was re-elected in 1997 and 2003 in elections that were regarded as flawed, and the opposition boycotted the 1997 presidential elections. The veneer of democracy was obviously thin, yet countries like the United States and France and international financial institutions like the World Bank and International Monetary Fund (IMF) found a way to support the government. Parties were fragmented, and the regime suppressed civil society. People were selected for government positions based on tribal and ethnic affiliations, while democratic institutions were sidelined as incapable of catering to the many regional, tribal, and ethnic interests (Salem 1997).

In 2001, Mauritanians voted in fairly open, competitive national parliamentary and municipal elections for the first time. Eventually, power struggles within Taya's system led to his downfall. There was a failed coup attempt in 2003, but he prevailed in the 2003 elections. There was growing discontent with the security situation in the country as various terrorist groups launched attacks. In the middle of the first decade of the 2000s, major protests broke out between civil society, the opposition parties, various social movements, and the ruling party. They protested the cost of living, unemployment, and other issues. Taya was overthrown in a 2005 coup masterminded by a group of military officers, his two closest advisers and allies (who happened to be cousins of the same tribe), Ould Mohamed Vall and Ould Abdel Aziz, both of whom later became president.

The 2005 coup put Colonel Ely Ould Mohamed Vall into power as the head of the military junta. Hundreds of political prisoners were released, elections were set, and an independent electoral commission was created. Sidi Ould Cheikh Abdellahi ran for president as an independent even though he was seen as a representative of the military junta. He was elected in 2007. He fired four top generals in 2008 and was soon thereafter ousted by the head of the Presidential Guard Haut Conseil Militaire d'État (HCE) led by General Ould Abdel Aziz, who claimed that he would restore civilian rule and democracy. Aziz stepped down from the presidency so he could run in the 2009 elections, and for four months, Ba Mamadou dit Mbaré held the position of president, making him the first Black leader of Mauritania. Aziz won the 2009 elections, bringing the UPR into power. The UPR has remained in power to this day, although it rebranded itself as El Insaf or Equity Party in 2022. In 2024, El Ghazouani was re-elected president. UPR/El Insaf has remained in power through three electoral cycles, thus becoming what I have called an entrenched party. The international community condemned Aziz's 2008 coup, but the reaction was mixed domestically. Aziz won the 2009 election with 53 percent of the vote, though the election was widely regarded as fraudulent. He was re-elected in 2014 in an election that was boycotted by the opposition. Aziz did not run in the 2019 election. Unlike many other presidents on the continent, he did not attempt to change the constitution to allow for a third term. The presidency was won by another member of the UPR, Mohamed Ould Ghazouani, who was Aziz's closest friend and adviser. Subsequently, in March 2021, Abdel Aziz was found guilty of corruption and convicted. He served a sentence of several months in prison as a result of these charges. In 2023, he was sentenced to another five years in prison for money laundering and illegal enrichment charges. The state appealed the sentence, arguing it was too lenient, while Aziz's legal team challenged the ruling, claiming that only a high court of justice had the authority to try a former president. Following these appeals, a Nouakchott court sentenced him to 15 years in prison on corruption charges in May 2025.

Several movements emerged after 2009. A February 25 movement (similar to Morocco's February 22 movement) in 2011 was a result of the diffusion of the influence of the Tunisian Jasmine Revolution and Arab Spring uprisings throughout the Arab region. In Mauritania, it centered around corruption, military involvement in politics, and state repression more generally. A worker's movement also struck for better conditions, especially in the gold mines. The Initiative for the Resurgence of Abolitionism (IRA) in Mauritania and Touche Pas à Ma Nationalité (Don't Touch My Nationality) were also active in this period, even after the 2007 abolition of slavery (Bekoe 2012).

In spite of the decline in violent extremism, improvement in the standard of living, and infrastructure development, the country still suffers from uneven access to resources. There is considerable polarization over racial and ethnic demands for equality and inclusion in positions of power, particularly among the H'rāṭīn, who make up 40 percent of the population and the majority of the military (70 percent). The antislavery movement has been very active, even though the country criminalized slavery in 2007 and replaced those laws with more stringent ones in 2015 (Boukhars 2016). Despite the laws, practices of slavery have continued. Although slavery has a racial dimension, it is also a caste problem. Not all Black Moors were slaves, and some Haalpulaar and Soninké themselves had black slaves. Slavery in Mauritania is an extremely sensitive issue.

In addition to political instability and entrenched inequalities, another element that made it difficult for women to make advances was the increase in violent extremism, particularly between 2005 and 2011, involving a mixture of regional and local extremists, the most well-known of which was al-Qaeda in the Islamic Maghreb (AQIM), a network based in several Sahelian and Saharan countries (Jourde 2007). Most of the groups that made up this network were not very sophisticated and ultimately had little impact. The country stabilized when Mohamed Ould Abdel Aziz took over as president in 2009 as a result of an aggressive counterterrorism strategy. Moderate Islamists launched theological debates to temper the jihadists, and the government sought to persuade Salafists to change their attitudes, especially toward violence. It combined a soft counterterrorism campaign with a harder counterterrorism strategy. It monitored the mosques and arrested people who voiced support for violent extremism (Boukhars 2016).

Women's Status

Historical Legacies

One of the striking features of this country is the relative societal, political, and economic freedom of women historically, notably the Bīẓān, who are women of Arab and Berber descent. In interviews, people frequently reference historic Berber women leaders from the region to explain the special status of Mauritanian women today.[1] They often cite the work of Ibn Batuta, the Moroccan scholar and traveler who visited Oualata in the fourteenth century. In *The Travels* (الرحلة, *Rihla*), he describes how he found himself disturbed because he had to speak with women leaders in the absence of their husbands, which he believed violated Muslim norms of his day, as he explained.[2]

The French explorer René Caillé similarly observed three centuries later that "the Bīẓān women retain more influence over their husbands than our French women . . . . As for the men, they are in no way jealous of their wives" (Tauzin 2001). During the conquest of Mauritania by French troops, officers Colonel Gouraud, Ernest Psichari, and many others were struck by the boldness of the Bīẓān women who "exposed themselves to bullets to encourage the warriors to resist, reload their weapons and bring the wounded to safety." In reflecting on Mauritanian history, El Kettab (2012, 15) observed that "the Beïdaniya has always been interested in politics. She was often the inspiration for expeditions of revenge or war. She exercised an indisputable influence in Djema'a."

Mauritania has been an important center of Islamic religious learning in the region, and women have played leadership roles in religious institutions early on as scholars of logic, linguistics, poetry, philosophy, religious knowledge, and jurisprudence. They were also spiritual guides, poets, and leaders and were active in the Tijaniyyah Sufi *tariqa* or order. Women like Fatma Mint Haj Elbechir of Ouadane in the nineteenth century were known for their roles in the oral transmission of Islamic texts. Women directed institutions for Islamic education, and by the early twenty-first century, women were running one-quarter of Nouakchott's Qur'anic

[1] For example, Khnathe Mint Bakar is the daughter of Bakar Elgoul, the emir of Brakna and founder of the Alouite dynasty in Morocco. She became the first woman minister in all Muslim countries. There are other women like Zeineb Nevzawi, the wife of Aboubekr Ibn Oumar of the Saharan Almoravids. She was divorced and married to Youssouf Ibn Tachefin, and it is thanks to her that the latter staged a coup d'etat against Aboubekr Ibn Amer.

[2] Ibn Battuta also wrote, "The greater part of the inhabitants are merchants. The women are exceedingly beautiful, and more respectable than the men. The character of these merchants is strange enough, for they are quite impervious to jealousy. No one is named after his father, but after his maternal uncle; and the sister's son always succeeds to property in preference to the son: a custom I witnessed nowhere else, except among the infidel Hindoos of Malabar. But these are Mohammedans, who retain their prayers by memory, study theology and learn the Koran by rote. As to their women, they are not shy with regard to the men, nor do they veil themselves from them, although they constantly accompany them at prayers. . . . It is a custom among them that a man may have a mistress, of women strangers to him, who may come and associate with him, even in the presence of his own husband and of his wife. In like manner, a man will enter his own house, and see the friend of his wife with her alone, and talking with her, without the least emotion or attempt to disturb them; he will only come in and sit down on one side till the man goes" (Ibn Battuta 1829, 234).

schools (Wiley 2018). Khnathe Mint Bakar of Brakna organized scholarly salons in the eighteenth century. Ghadije Mint Mohamed El Akel, who lived in the nineteenth century, taught the Koran, religion, and the law. She was renowned for her knowledge of Aristotelian logic, astronomy, and medicine.

Even though Mauritanian society today is patriarchal, historically, the movement of Bidhān women was not constrained, and they did not have male guardians. This can be attributed, in part, to a nomadic lifestyle that supported a semimatrilineal system of lineage, which was transformed into a patrilineal system between 1400 and 1500 (Hall 2016; Zunes and Mundy 2010). Society in this region at that time was secular, as the law of the land was distinct from religious edicts (Camara 2010). Contemporary women and men in Mauritania have come out of this long legacy in which Bidhān women were unusually active in the public sphere, and today, they are well aware of it. Some women even organized caravans; during the colonial period, some expanded their involvement in commerce throughout West Africa. As Aminetou Mint El Moktar, president of the Association of Women Household Heads, put it:

> I believe that the openness of Mauritanian society, particularly Arab society, allows women a certain independence that other Arab women do not have. Our traditions and customs have given women a sort of innate emancipation. We kept this nomadic culture, this culture of the desert where the woman had to take care of her home during her husband's long absences, which makes her quite independent today. We thus take into account the place of women and give it a certain importance because, in the rest of the Arab world, women are under the total control of the patriarchy. The Mauritanian woman has her independence in her family. (MRT8.6.10.20)

Another Mauritanian professor put it this way, referring primarily to Bīẓān women: "It has often been said that the woman takes precedence over the man; she imposes her will; she cannot be polygamous, and when she wants, she leaves the man and she will make a second marriage, which will be for her and her family a new status . . . . For me, women are human beings like any other. There is no difference between men and women" (MRT11.6.11.20).

Almost all interviewees repeated these sentiments: "We women here are free, and in the homes, we are in charge" (MRT7.6.8.20). Interviewees talked about the lack of violence in the traditional nonpatriarchal Bīẓān society, although rape and gender-based violence (GBV) have now become an issue of concern in Mauritania as organizations have been formed to combat GBV and pass legislation around it.

According to El Kettab (2012), "the Bīẓān woman has always had her say in both the public and private spheres. Islamic traditions limit her to a certain role, but our society is also marked by a Berber heritage which advances her status." Many in the interviews talked about the legacy of the Berber past, which was matrilineal and not polygamous. Hence, the incidence of polygamy is relatively low in Mauritania. As historian Ahmed Mouloud explained, "We inherited this very open Berber past, which is disappearing but it is omnipresent in our culture. . . . As far as Bīẓān women are concerned, traditional society is antipolygamous. Traditional society has a certain tolerance for everything that young people do." He went on to say that Salafist and Islamist ideas threatened this traditional way of life and that, unlike traditional society, "these are the people who are against modernization and against women's rights" (MRT16.6.15.20).

Although the contexts today are vastly different from the precolonial and colonial times, it is clear that there has been a long history of women's social, economic, and political agency. Therefore, one would expect more engagement in formal politics today, but the lack of institutionalized politics and a history of coups and military rule has acted as a constraint. By 2024, women constituted one-fifth of the legislature and cabinet and close to one-third of the municipal councils. Moreover, modern-day politics has been subsequently influenced by centuries of religious influences and colonialism and, more recently, by a shift from nomadic to more sedentary lifestyles and Salafist influences, all of which have placed restrictions on women.

Military rule subdued women's political expression. In the 1960s and 1970s, women composed songs and lullabies to express their political demands and condemn political oppression, exile, and military surveillance (Salem Z. Ould 1997). Lesourd (2007, 6) quotes a woman who said, "Of course women are in politics! . . . Their opinion is respected, heard, considered." She quotes other women who talk about how women naturally belong in politics: "Mauritanian women are different! They are strong women! They know politics well!" However, women's participation during this period of military rule was circumscribed. Nevertheless, in this period, women participated in politics through advocacy, networking, talking about politics on the phone and at the market, and visiting each other. They might also circulate leaflets. But some were put in danger and humiliated because of their political activities, Lesourd explains.

Socioeconomic Status of Women Today

Much has changed in Mauritania for women with the end of military coups and as government policies have evolved. Mauritania, for example, has experienced the largest improvement in closing the gender gap in the MENA region since 2006, according to data from the World Economic Forum, which looks at education, health, and political and economic empowerment measures. Nevertheless, maternal mortality is still high at 424 deaths per 100,000 (Office Nationale de la Statistique et al. 2022). In terms of professional integration, unemployment affects women much more than men (44 percent of women are unemployed); moreover, there is discrimination against women when it comes to loans granted by financial institutions, and they are not privileged in the distribution of projects. Violence against women is said to persist through the practice of excision (72 percent of girls undergo this practice), early marriage (19 percent of women were married before the age of fifteen, and 43 percent before eighteen), and the practice of force-feeding, affecting around one-fifth of girls (El Kettab 2012). H'rāṭīn women, in particular, still face restrictions in their access to land, education, employment, and health services.

Mauritania has a ratio of 105 percent of girls to boys in secondary school compared to Africa's overall ratio of 88.4 percent for 2019 and a ratio of 104 percent of girls to boys in primary school, while Africa's overall ratio is 97 percent for 2019. Literacy for adult women, however, is 43 percent compared to 64 percent for men and 59 percent for sub-Saharan women overall, and non-Arab girls are marginalized in the educational system (UN Human Rights Council 2021). This high rate of school completion for girls does not automatically translate into women's visibility in politics. For this reason, we need to look at other factors that have influenced women's representation.

Even though women are more likely to be educated these days, men are still able to secure the best jobs and salaries. Mauritania has low rates of female labor force participation (31 percent in 2019), whereas for Africa, it was 46 percent in the same year. Much of this is constrained by the level of economic growth in Mauritania. Mauritania's GDP per capita for 2020 is $1,673, which is above the $1,600 average per capita rate for sub-Saharan Africa overall and only slightly above the rate for the least-developed countries globally ($1,052), based on World Bank data for 2020.

Nevertheless, women's participation in economic activity has increased through cooperatives, small and medium-size enterprises, and the informal sector, especially in the area of trade (MRT27.6.30.20). In the past, women often remained closer to home and sold small goods, like tea, sugar, and tobacco, in their nomadic camps. Women also worked as midwives and healers and have manufactured goods for trade while men were away trading (Wiley 2018). Today, women are also active in the commercial sector, owning clothing stores, import businesses, hairdressing salons, supermarkets, and other such businesses. They trade globally and have expanded trade to France and the Arab states of the Persian Gulf. Most Mauritanian women are engaged in agriculture, pastoralism, trade, and small-scale artisanal production (El Kettab 2012). Women have considerable say in many homes, and their views are taken into account in the community. Men often control the finances and major decisions because they have easier access to employment and better salaries than women.

As the next section explains, women are increasingly playing more prominent roles in the economy and politics, and there is greater acceptance of women's public roles as women's educational levels have increased. This has come with the shift away from open military rule and the entrenchment of the UPR as a political party. There has been an expansion of women's political participation in Parliament, regional, and municipal councils, especially with the introduction of the quota system. According to Seniya Mint Sidi Haiba, a former minister of women, there has also been increased participation of women in administrative positions (e.g., ministers, ambassadors, administrators), greater visibility of women in political parties, and broad participation of women in civil society organizations working on a wide range of issues (MRT27.6.30.20).

As one parliamentarian of the RFD explained, "With the adoption of these reforms we have made things happen. First of all, everyone now knows that women have rights. These rights are in codes and texts. This is a step forward for me. These laws do not contradict the religious order. The situation of women is becoming a concern of public actors. For the president, the ministers, the situation of women becomes a priority. And when we see that in each ministerial department, we are required to create a gender cell, that is to say that in appointments, in missions, we must involve women. We have more women in schools, in universities. We have more women empowered. We have fewer women slaves and more women sensitized. We have more active women. We have more feminist organizations. So, the status of women is progressing well" (MRT1.6.4.20).

Women and Contemporary Politics

Given the legacy of women's political engagement and freedoms within the homes of the political elite, it is striking but not surprising that women remained in the background during the years of military rule after independence. This highlights the book's overall argument that stability and regime institutionalization affect women's political fortunes.

From 1964 to 1978, the PPM was the only legal party, winning three consecutive elections and 100 percent of the votes in each election. International norms and domestic pressures regarding women in politics did not come until the 1990s. However, there were small openings after independence, and women participated in the PPM national congress in 1964, when women's political rights and the need to integrate women into the party were recognized for the first time.

The first formal Mauritanian women's organization, the National Union of Mauritanian Women (Union nationale des femmes de mauritanie), was formed in 1961 as an auxiliary of the PPM at the initiative of Marie-Thérèse, better known as Meriem Daddah, the (French) wife of the first president of the Mauritanian republic Moktar Ould Daddah (El Kettab 2012). In 1961, Aissata Kane, a Haalpulaar woman and a stalwart of the PPM, helped found the Union and represented it at the pan-African women's 1962 Conference des femmes africaines (Conference of African Women). It became the Mouvement national féminin (National Women's Movement; NWM) in 1966 and was eventually merged into the PPM. The focus of the NWM was child care, nutrition, handicrafts, support income-generating activities, and civic education and literacy training. It remains, however, a movement of mainly urban-educated women.

Aissata Kane was responsible for the publication of the NWM's magazine, *Mariemou*. Educational programs regarding child care and home economics were broadcast via radio to illiterate women. Women began to participate in international conferences—not just in Africa but as far away as Finland, at the International Conference of the Family in 1969. These types of developmentally oriented women's organizations and initiatives were linked to the regime or ruling party, led by the wives of the president or the political elite, and typical of this early one-party period in Africa.

In 1966, women raised the problem of the legal and social protection of the family, and they called for the right to participate without restrictions in political activities. Two years later, the right of the Mauritanian woman to participate without restriction in national activities was recognized. In 1971, the National Congress of the PPM appointed a representative woman in the national political office and increased the number of women in various permanent or temporary bodies of the Party (Gaudio 1978). By the late 1960s, some women gained visibility in the highest ranks of the PPM.

Women held only 2.9 percent of the seats in Parliament in 1976, the same average for Africa as a whole at the time. There was a total absence of women ministers in the 1960s and only one in the 1970s. Because of Aissata Kane's talent as an orator and as an organizer in the leading women's organization, President Moktar Ould Daddah appointed her as the first female minister in Mauritania in 1975 to head up the Ministry of Family Welfare and Social Affairs, a post she held until 1978. Overall, most appointments have been to Bīẓān women. There have only been a handful of black women ministerial appointments, with Kane being the first woman to be appointed minister and Coumba Bâ, Layla Kamara, and Aissata Diallo being the most recent in 2017—all of whom are Haalpulaar.

Kane saw herself as an advocate for women's rights in the Personal Status Code (PSC), fighting against polygamy and female genital mutilation (FGM), promoting the education of girls, and increasing the parliamentary representation of women. She was spared when the 1978 coup landed her fellow male ministers in prison. As she put it, this was "the only time I've been discriminated against as a woman" (Kane 2013). She believed that the winds of reform for women were brutally interrupted by the coup, which was followed by years of military rule under the control of the PRDS.

On July 10, 1978, the Military Committee for National Recovery dissolved all youth and women's organizations, and women's mobilization disappeared for some time as the situation for women deteriorated. Whatever efforts there had been to integrate women into politics dissipated until 1991.

None of the military governments from 1978 onward included women in the cabinet until 1986, when Khadija Mint Ahmed Aïche, a former central bank director, was appointed minister of mines and industry under the first civil government after military rule. Between 1986 and 1997, there were eight shuffles in ministerial positions, and only three women ministers were appointed in this period (Lesourd 2007). Women served mostly in ministries that were thought to be appropriate for women (e.g., the Ministries of Status of Women, Health and Social Issues, Civil Service, and Culture, Sports, and Youth).

After the 1990s, various women's organizations were established. For example, Sy Lalla Aïcha Ouedraogo formed the Committee of Solidarity with the Victims of Human Rights Violations (Le Comité de solidarité des victimes de violation des droits humains; CVSDH) in 1993 in response to the massacres in 1989 of Black Mauritanian soldiers in the army barracks. As she explained in an interview, "In 1989, the state took advantage of this antagonism to claim that Black Africans wanted to make a coup d'état, so they were exterminated. That's why I've always opposed it. This is why I founded the CVSDH in 1993, thanks to a group of women. They were women who had been affected by these events. There were also Bīẓān, H'rāṭīn. . . . Widows, poor people, etc. They all got together to give money to some women to help them." She emphasized an essential feature of women's mobilization that aims to bridge the racial and ethnic differences: "I speak Hassaniya; it is this Mauritania that I want, a united Mauritania, without language barriers. . . . It is by uniting our differences that the country will move forward" (El Kettab 2012).

The first decade of the 2000s had created a pocket of political liberalization that permitted women's organizations to mobilize and press for increased political representation. In fact, 80 percent of civil society organizations were headed by women, according to a World Bank report (El Kettab 2012). Women's organizations sought to improve their legal status in this period, and a PSC was passed in 2001. It provided the legal basis for marriage and for a marriage contract. The age of marriage was raised to eighteen for both men and women to address the practice of early marriage, and marriage required the consent of the woman. Enforcement is still weak, as is awareness of these rights.

After the Taya military regime, Mauritania started signing international conventions like the Convention on the Elimination of all Forms of Discrimination Against Women (CEDAW) in 2001. However, it remained with sixteen reservations, which activists have been trying to lift. In this period, Mauritania also adopted treaties on the Rights of the Child (1991), the Rights of Persons with Disabilities (2012), and Economic, Social, and Cultural Rights (2004) in addition to the International Covenant on Civil and Political Rights and other UN treaties regarding torture, enforced disappearance, racial discrimination, the rights of migrant workers, child prostitution and child pornography.[3] Mauritania also ratified the African Union's Maputo Protocol on women's rights (2005).

Women as Party Leaders

As of 2024, there were twenty-two parties represented in Parliament, with the government group holding the majority of seats (119 out of 176 seats), and the dominant party, El Insaf (Equity Party, formerly the UPR), holding 107 of the parliamentary seats. The second-largest party, a Muslim Brotherhood party, Tawassoul (National Rally for Reform and Development), holds eleven seats as part of an opposition group of twenty-eight. The remainder of the parties

[3] https://tbinternet.ohchr.org/_layouts/15/TreatyBodyExternal/Treaty.aspx?CountryID=110&Lang=EN.

claims smaller numbers of seats. Women hold a few key positions in various parties.

Women constitute the majority of the members and activists of Mauritanian political parties, but their presence in decision-making positions in these parties is not commensurate with their participation as men occupy more of the important positions in the leadership of these parties. Nevertheless, the parties have agreed to raise the slogan of women's emancipation and enshrine it in their programs and speeches. However, the practice often falls short of the promise, especially during candidacies and administrative promotions, according to former Minister of Women Seniya Sidi Haiba (MRT27.6.30.20).

The current secretary general of Tawassoul, the Islamist party, is Aminata Niang, a Haalpulaar woman. In fact, Tawassoul was the first party in Mauritania to present a woman, Zeinabou Mint Dedde, as president of its parliamentary group in 2010. They have also put non-Bīẓān in top positions. Tawassoul is also one of the parties with a very active women's organization. The party has other prominent women leaders such as Hindou Mint Diya and Yaye Ndaw Coulibaly, an ethnic Haalpulaar, who was mayor of the Tevragh-Zeina district of Nouakchott and served as the leader of a Campagne des femmes for Mansour's 2009 presidential campaign. She serves in the senate. According to one leader of Tawassoul, the party "has very active members of Parliament in committees that support women's rights. The current secretary general of the party, our sister Aminata Niang, was a member of the bureau of the parliamentary commission in favor of women's rights. And currently several MPs are calling for the improvement and guarantees of women's rights" (MRT19.6.16.20).

Women have played leading roles in other parties. Naha Mint Mouknass became the first woman in Mauritania to head the foreign ministry when she served as minister between 2009 and 2011. In 2016 she was appointed minister of industry, trade and tourism. Mouknass was the second woman in the Arab world to head a political party. In 2000, she was elected president of the Union for Democracy and Progress (UDP), where she has remained to this day. Mouknass also served as an adviser to the president from 2001 to 2005 and was always seated next to the president during cabinet meetings.

There have been numerous women party leaders in Mauritania. A woman activist, Sahla Bint Ahmed Zaid, claimed the presidency of the Hawwa (Eve) party in 2007 (Africa Research Bulletin 2007). Kadiata Malick Diallo was vice president of the UFP in the middle of the first decade of the 2000s and a deputy in Mauritania's National Assembly. She is a Pulaar woman. The UFP, which has three parliamentary seats, is a left-leaning party that was a cross-ethnic, republican party that promoted social justice and opposed slavery. It has its roots in the Kadihine worker movement of the 1960s and 1970s, which opposed the government of Mokhtar Ould Daddah and military rule and involvement in coups more generally.

Today, there are several female leaders of parties. Lalla Mint Cherif, who served as a cabinet minister, has served as president of Parti du sursaut de la jeunesse pour la nation (PSJN) at least since 2011. The party has three parliamentary seats and is allied with the president. Other parties headed by women include the Republican Party for Democracy and Renewal (PRDR), headed by Mintata Mint Hedeid.

Another woman, Doggie Mint Khattry, former minister of women and children, was vice president of the National Pact for Democracy and Development (ADIL). When a coup took place against the democratically elected President Ould Cheikh Abdellahi in 2008, she made the first statement against the coup on television because she was concerned about the future of the country. But the president of her party called her and told her not to concern herself with the events. Women then went to demonstrate in front of the UN office. They were beaten, teargassed, and harassed, and it was only after they took action that the men in the opposition began to become united against the coup (El Kettab 2012).

The country experienced a brief political opening in the first decade of the 2000s that allowed for the emergence of independent women's organizations, which pressed for and were able to get the quota adopted in 2006. Elites who were concerned with Mauritania's external image supported the adoption of quotas. Women already held 37 percent of the seats in the municipal councils in 2007, but there was only one woman out of twenty-seven ministers, and 18 percent of parliamentarians were women (IRIN 2008). Among the main concerns of women activists in this period were ending violence against women and the practice of female genital mutilation, in addition to promoting women's health and microcredit.

Following the election of President Mohamed Ould Abdel Aziz in 2009, the situation of women saw marked progress with a five-fold increase in women ministers within the span of ten years between 2005 and 2015, although there was a slight dip after 2020 (Table 5.1). After 2023, even one of the five vice presidents was a woman from El Insaf (Fatimetou Mint Habib).

Aisha Bint Jeddane ran for the presidency of Mauritania in 2003 and 2009. Later, Lalla Mariem Mint Moulaye Idriss ran in 2014. There have been other firsts. Fatimetou Abdel Malick became the head of the Regional

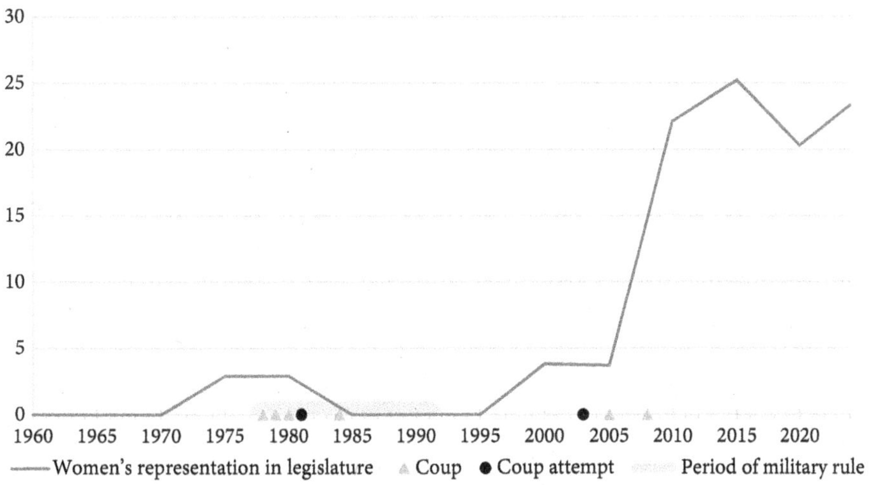

Figure 5.1 Women's representation in the Mauritanian legislature (1960–2024)
Sources: IPU (1995, 2024).

Council of Nouakchott. She was also president of the Network for Locally Elected Women of Africa (2012–2015). Maty Mint Hamady has been mayor of Nouakchott, Mauritania's capital and largest city, since 2014. Prior to this, she was minister of public service, labor, and modernization of administration from 2011 to 2013. Marième Baba Sy was president of the Women's Network parliamentarians from Mauritania.

Women in Parliament

A 2006 decree established a 20 percent quota for women in the electoral lists. It was the product of negotiations between the government and opposition parties, with Seniya Mint Sidi Haiba as one of the main initiators and leaders in establishing the dialogue that led to the quota. At the time, she was an adviser to the prime minister in charge of social affairs and had previously served as a minister of women (El Kettab 2012). As a result, the percentage of women in Parliament increased from 3.7 percent in 2005 to 22.1 percent after the 2006 elections, thus quadrupling the percentage of women in Parliament. At the municipal council level, the proportion of elected women in 2007 was 30.37 percent (1,120 out of 3,688). In 2012, the Law on the Election of Members of the National Assembly was passed, requiring eighteen representatives to be elected from the capital city of Nouakchott, twenty representatives to be elected from a single nationwide constituency, and twenty seats to be reserved for women candidates running in a single national list. These reserved seats, primarily held by the ruling party representatives and those in parties aligned with the UPR, are used by the regime to further entrench its rule.

A Mauritanian Women Ministers and Parliamentarians Network was created in 2007 to press for women's rights legislation. Organizations like the Mauritanian Association of Women Lawyers, the Mauritanian Network for the Promotion of Women's Rights, the Women's Learning Partnership, the Association of Women, and Le Connectingroup-Mauritanie were energized in this period. Among the main concerns of women activists in this period were ending violence against women and the practice of female genital mutilation.

Pressure from the Advocacy Group for the Involvement of Women in Decision-Making and other civil society organizations and international partners resulted in the 2012 electoral law reform. This allowed for women to claim 25 percent of the seats after the 2013 elections. Public figures, religious leaders, the media, women leaders, and political parties joined them. A political dialogue between the government and opposition parties was critical in getting the quota adopted. Seniya Mint Sidi Haiba, secretary of state for the promotion of women in the Taya government (1996–1997), was a key initiator of this dialogue.

The law was amended to create reserved seats, electing eighteen deputies from the Nouakchott constituency, twenty from a single nationwide constituency, and twenty from women running in a single nationwide list. Parties that elect more women than the required number by the quota can increase financial benefits. Moreover, the electoral administration may reject candidate lists that do not meet the quota requirements. Party lists must include a certain number of women and place them preferentially on the list depending on the overall number of councilors.[4] Nevertheless, Wolof, Haalpulaar, and

[4] In constituencies with or less than thirty-one thousand inhabitants, one deputy is elected by absolute majority (two-round system). In constituencies with more than thirty-one thousand inhabitants, two deputies are elected by absolute majority (two-round system). Deputies shall be elected through proportional representation in multi-member constituencies with more than ninety thousand inhabitants.

In constituencies with three seats, candidate lists must include at least one woman candidate in the first or second position on the list. In constituencies with more than three seats, with the exception of the national women's list, each candidate list must be composed of candidates of both sexes in alternating order, taking into account the following two principles (art. 4[A] of the Organic Law Promoting Women's Access to Electoral Mandates and Elective Offices, as amended by Law 2012-034):

- Within each entire group of four candidates, in the order of presentation of the list, there must be an equal number of candidates of each sex;
- The difference between the number of candidates of each sex cannot be greater than one.

Soninké women were especially underrepresented compared to Bīẓān women (Wiley 2018).

After adopting the policy, even though the municipal councils had as much as 32.6 percent female representation in 2012, only 5 percent of the majors were women. However, Maty Mint Hamady has been mayor of Nouakchott since 2014, and Fatimetou Mint Abdel Malick, who had been the first woman mayor of Tevragh-Zeina, was the head of the Regional Council of Nouakchott and also president of the Network for Locally Elected Women of Africa (2012–2015). Diewo Camara was the first woman in her country to hold the position of mayor when she assumed the post in Kaedi in 1991 (Mamadou 2006).

Women now occupy 20 percent of government positions, including prefecture, governor, and ambassador positions. They make up 24 percent of the cabinet positions. Notably, since 2021, the ambassador to the United States has been a woman (Cissé Ould Boide). Women leaders have vowed to seek to extend the quotas to the judicial and civil service. Some have reservations about this quota. While it enabled women to gain access to jobs and electoral seats, especially those who undergo training, some objected to the reserved seat system because it did nothing to change society's perception of women's ability to compete with men and to represent the interests of citizens in the same way as men. As Seniya Sidi Haiba—one of the main architects of the gender quota—pointed out in an interview, the law was passed "in coordination between the political parties that make success their primary objective and the traditional conservative forces that marginalize women, in a clear bargain by adopting the national women's list [reserved seats]. That is why we are seeking, together with groups that advocate for women's issues, to return to the previous mechanism and to increase the share of seats allocated to women to 50 percent in the next elections" (MRT27.6.30.20).

Women can be found in the leadership of important committees: as chair of the Economic Affairs Committee (Zeinebou Mohamed Mahmoud Taghi, from the opposition) and external relations (Marième Adda, UPR) as well as deputy chair of finance (Nanne Cheikhna, opposition) and the Committee of Justice, Defense, and Internal Affairs (Oummoulkhaïry Mohamed Lemine, UPR). The only committees on which women are not in leadership are the Accounts Committee and the Committee on the Islamic Orientation, Human Resources, and Cultural and Political Affairs. Women serve as vice chair of several of the parliamentary groups, including the Tawassoul party group

(Aminata Niang), El Wiam Party[5] (Dr. Cheikna Ould Med Hejbou), Agence Nationale Tadamoun[6] (Cheikha Bouya ould Sheikhna), Wava Mauritanian Party (Elm Betour Mint Abdel Hay), and Parliamentary Group of Coalition Parties (Adama Amadou Sy). Women are not in the leadership of only four parliamentary caucuses.

As one opposition MP pointed out, "Personally I don't feel any distinction between me and my [male] colleagues. There is no difference in treatment between men and women. They have the same role. They [women] are well perceived but their role must increase" (MRT2.6.4.20).

Women have been used by those in power to undercut clan power. For example, President Taya was able to use a member of a former slave caste, Fatma Zeina Mint Sbaghou, to represent his party in Parliament in 1996 as a former minister and an adviser to the prime minister (MRT3.6.5.20). She was a member of a powerful clan, Mechdouf. He put her in Parliament in an effort to humiliate and undercut the head of the clan, Hamoud Ould Ahmedou, and as a warning to other clan leaders not to challenge the state. At the same time, he signaled to the West that Mauritania was addressing the issue of slavery (Hecht 1996). The clan allegedly voted against her because of this move, but she mysteriously won anyway, as did four other candidates whom the clan did not support.

One leader of a women's organization put it, "Today, women in Parliament are more combative than men. They have more ideas. They are more responsible in their struggle than many men. They animate the Mauritanian Parliament a lot. They have taken their courage in their own hands to fight injustice and mismanagement" (MRT8.6.10.20). Another male NGO leader went further to say, "Women in Parliament are the best deputies here. For example, Kadjata Malik Diallo; Nema Mint Mogueya, peace to her soul; Maalouma Mint El Meydah in the senate; Zeinabou Mint Taghi; Aicha Mint Amar Cheine; Saadani Mint Khaitour; and especially Mentate Mint Hedeid. All these women have made their mark in Parliament. So every time we give more to women, our political situation improves. They defend all cases, especially those of the most disadvantaged and victims of injustice. And I cannot forget Maalouma Mint Bilal; she marked the Parliament in a very courageous way" (MRT2.6.20).

A former woman minister of culture, Hindu Mint Ainina, highlighted that even though women who are in politics are brilliant, they can only

[5] Parti de l'entente démocratique et sociale

[6] National Agency for the Fight against the Consequences of Slavery, for Reintegration and for the Fight against Poverty (Agence Nationale de Lutte contre les Séquelles de l'Esclavage, de l'Insertion et de Lutte contre la Pauvreté).

get there because of their connections to men: "Women are in the front row. They speak in a way that is ideal, but they are always held back. Me as a woman I do not have the right to decide my fate. I must follow the will of my father, my brother, or others, and if I refuse, I am *kafir* [a disbeliever], and I fall out of the picture. So I am a model as long as I stay within the conservative and normative framework. The presence of women in an elective position is rarely a personal struggle, it is the result of a combination of circumstances. Women are competent, they are brilliant, they are hardworking, they are extremely imaginative, but they are always there because of someone, through a combination of circumstances that made us chosen, not simply because we are competent" (MRT3.6.5.20).

A former minister of women, Seniya Sidi Haiba, explained, "Some women parliamentarians play an important role, whether it is studying, discussing or proposing bills, or monitoring the work of the government. They are also a role model that motivates other women to get involved in political work and to gain the knowledge needed to do so . . . . Some women parliamentarians have taken strong positions during past and current legislatures by refusing to vote for certain legislation that they have deemed contrary to the country's interest. The position of some of them was even stronger in defending the bill criminalizing rape and violence against girls and women that the National Assembly referred for further study" (MRT30.6.19.20).

Women Ministers

During the thirty years of military control (1978–2009), women appointments to ministries were few and far between (see Table 5.1). In all, there were thirty ministerial appointments involving approximately twenty-five women. Naha Mint Mouknass became the first woman from an Arab country to head up a foreign affairs ministry (see Table 5.2). Today, women hold 20 percent of the seats in cabinet in Mauritania. Most of the ministerial positions held by women have been in the "softer ministries" of women's affairs, education, health, and youth. There were some exceptions. In 1987, Khadijetou Mint Ahmed became minister of mines and industry, and Naha Mint Mouknass became minister of foreign affairs and cooperation (2009–2022) and minister of commerce and industry, handicrafts, and tourism in 2014. Other appointments to critical ministries followed. In 2008, Salma Mint Tegueddi became minister of commerce and industry, and in 2016, Fatma Vall Mint Soueina became the second female minister of foreign affairs and

Table 5.1 Female ministers in Mauritania

Year	Female ministers (%)
1960	0.0
1965	0.0
1970	0.0
1975	8.0
1980	17.0
1985	...
1990	8.0
1995	8.0
2000	10.5
2005	5.6
2010	14.2
2015	26.9
2020	20.0
2025	24.1

Source: World Bank (2024).

cooperation. In 2014, Lemina Mint Kotob Momma was appointed minister of Interior, followed by minister of agriculture.

Some of the women ministers have been recruited from the National Import and Export Corporation (SONIMEX), like Seniya Mint Sidi Haiba, who was deputy general manager of the company from 1991 to 1993, and Maty Mint Hamady, who was once a deputy director of the corporation. Others have been leaders of the gas company Société Mauritanienne de Gaz, better known by its acronym, SOMAGAZ. Many leaders also had family connections with male politicians (Lesourd 2007).[7]

During the presidency of Sidi Ould Cheikh Abdellahi (2007–2008), women began to be represented in a variety of sectors, such as diplomacy with two ambassadors and with judges in the legal field. Mauritanian women took advantage of the political opening early in the first decade of the 2000s to advance their concerns and began to mobilize in earnest.

[7] As Lesourd points out, Khadija Mint Ahmed Aïche, who was appointed minister of mines and industry (1986–1991), is the daughter of a leader of the PPM; Diyé Bâ, minister of health and social issues (1997–2000), is the daughter of a minister under Daddah; Aminetou Mint Mohamed Ould Saleck, secretary of state by the prime minister charged with new technologies, is daughter of Mustafa Ould Salek, a former head of state, who held office under military government in 1979; and Naha Mint Mouknass, advisor to the presidency (2001–2005), is the daughter of a former minister.

Table 5.2 Women ministers in Mauritania (1971–2023)

Name of minister	Position	Tenure in office
Toure Aissata Kane	Minister of Family and Social Welfare	1971–1978
Abdelerahman Khadija Mint Ahmed Aïche	Minister of Mines and Industry	1986–1991
Mariam Mint Ahmed Aicha	Minister of Women's Affairs	1992–1994
Mariam Mint Ahmed Aicha	Secretary of State for Women	1994–1995
Seniya Mint Sidi Haïba Aïche	Secretary of State of Women's Affairs	1995–1997
Diyé Bâ	Minister of Health and Social Issues	1997–2000
Khadijatou Mint Boubou	Secretary of State of Civil Affairs	1997–2005
Achaïtou Mint M'hiham	Secretary of State of Women's Affairs	1997–1998
Mantata Mint Adeid	Minister of Women's Affairs	1998
Mtatem Mint Heyram	Secretary of State of Women's Affairs	1998–2000
Mintata Mint Hedeid	Secretary of State of Women's Affairs	2000–2003
Fatimetou Mint Mohamed Ould Saleck	Secretary of State by the Prime Minister charged with New Technologies	2000–2004
Serka Mint Bilal Ould Yamar	Minister of Public Service and Employment	2000–2005
Naha Mint Mouknass	Advisor to the President	2000–2005
Aïchatou Mint Mahamham	Minister for the Status of Women	2000–2005
Zeinabou Naha Mint Ahmed	Minister for the Status of Women	2000–2005
Ba Diyyé	Head of the Department of Health and Social Issues	2000–2005
Naha Mint Mouknass	Minister Advisor to the Presidency	2001–2005
Salka Mint Bilal Ould Yamar	Minister of Civil Servants and Labor	2003–2005
Zeinebou Mint Mohamed Nahah	Secretary of State of Women's Affairs	2003–2005
Betrigha Mint Kaber Ould Cheikh	Secretary of State by the Prime Minister charged with New Technologies	2004–2005

Continued

Table 5.2 *Continued*

Name of minister	Position	Tenure in office
Mahla Bent Ahmed	Minister of Culture, Sports, and Youth	2005–2007
Nabkouha Bent Tlamid (Noubghouha Mint Ettelamid)	Secretary of State for Women's Affairs	2005–2007
Mognana Sow Deina (Meyena Mohamed Sow Deyna)	Secretary of State in charge of New Technologies	2005–2007
Nebghouha Mint Mohamed Vall	Minister of National Education	2007–2008
Fatimetou Mint Khattri	Minister in charge of Women's Empowerment, Children, and Families	2007–2008
Aicha Mint Sidi Bouna	Vice Minister in charge of the Environment attached to the Prime Minister	2007–2008
Salma Mint Tegueddi	Minister of Commerce and Industry Senator (2002–2008) President of the Law Committee	2008
Messaouda Mint Baham	Minister of Rural Development	2008–2009
Selama Mint Cheikhna Ould Lemrabott	Minister of Social Affairs, Childhood, and Family	2008–2009
Zeinabou Mint Mohamed	Minister of Health	2009
Mariem Baba Sy	Minister of Social Affairs, Childhood, and the Family	2009
Naha Mint Mouknass	Minister of Foreign Affairs and Cooperation	2009–2011
Dr. Coumba Bâ	Minister of Civil Service	2009–2014
Cissé Mint Cheikh Ould Boide	Minister of Culture, Youth, and Sports	2009–2014
Lalla Mint Cherif	La Ministre de la Culture, de la Jeunesse et des Sports	2013
Moulaty Mint El Moctar	Minister of Social Affairs, Childhood, and the Family	2009–2014
Fatima Habib	Minister of Professional Training, Technologies, and Communication	2013–2014
Fatima Habib	Minister of Housing, Urbanism, and Physical Planning	2014
Fatma Vall Mint Soueinae	Minister of Youth and Sports	2014

Lemina Mint Kotob Ould Momma	Minister in the Ministry of Interior	2014
Mekfoula Mint Agatt	Minister Delegate of Foreign Affairs and Cooperation charged with Maghreb and African Affairs	2014
Hawa Tandia	Minister Delegate of Foreign Affairs and Cooperation charged with Mauritanians Abroad	2014
Naha Mint Mouknass	Minister of Commerce and Industry, Handicrafts, and Tourism	2014–2018
Fatima Habib	Minister of Cattle and Livestock	2014–2015
Fatma Vall Mint Soueinae	Minister of Culture	2014–2015
Fatma Vall Mint Soueinae	Minister of Handicrafts	2014–2015
Lemina Mint Kotob Ould Momma	Minister of Social Affairs, Childhood, and the Family	2014–2015
Hawa Tandia	Minister Secretary General of the Government	2014–2015
Nejwa Mint El Kettab	Minister of Communication and Relations with the Parliament	2014–2015
Hindou Mint Haînina	Minister Delegate of Foreign Affairs and Cooperation charged with Maghreb and African Affairs and Mauritanians Abroad	2014–2015
Fatma Vall Mint Soueinae	Minister of Foreign Affairs and Cooperation	2015
Khadijetou M'Bareck Fall	Minister Delegate of Foreign Affairs and Cooperation charged with Maghreb and African Affairs and Mauritanians Abroad	2015
Dr. Coumba Bâ	Minister of Youth and Sports	2015–2016
Fatima Habib	Minister of Social Development, Children, and Family	2015–2016
Vatma Vall Mint Soueinae	Minister of Cattle and Livestock Farming	2015–2018
Lemina Mint Kotob Ould Momma	Minister of Agriculture	2015–2016
Fatima Habib	Minister of Livestock	2016–
Vatma Vall Mint Soueinae	Minister of Culture and Crafts	2016–
Lemina Mint Kotob Ould Momma	Minister of Social Affairs, Children, and the Family	2016–
Hawa Tandia	Minister Secretary General of the Government	2016–
Hindou Mint Aìnina	Minister Delegate to the Minister of Foreign Affairs responsible for Maghreb Affairs, Africa, and Mauritanians Abroad	2016–
Dr. Coumba Bâ	Minister of Civil Service, Labor, and Modernization of Administration	2017–2018

Continued

Table 5.2 *Continued*

Name of minister	Position	Tenure in office
Khadijetou Mbarek Fall	Minister of Trade, Industry, and Tourism	2018
Naha Mint Hamdi Ould Mouknas	Minister of Social Affairs, Childhood, and Family	2018–
Mariam Mint Bilal	Minister of Youth and Sports	2018
Amal Sidi Cheikh Abdallahi	Minister of Higher Education and Scientific Research	2018–2023
Dr. Coumba Bâ	Minister Advisor to the Presidency of the Republic	2019–2023
Naha Haroun Cheikh Sidiya	Minister of Social Action, Children, and Family	2020–2023
Mariem Bekaye	Minister of the Environment and Sustainable Development	2020–2023
Fatimetou Mint Mahfoudh Ould Khattry	Commissioner for Food Safety	2020–2023
Naha Mint Hamdi Ould Mouknass	Minister of Commerce, Industry, Crafts, and Tourism	2020–2023
Aïssata Ba Yahya	Minister Secretary General of Government	2023–2024
Lalya Ali Camara	Minister of Environment and Sustainable Development	2023–2024
Savia Mint N'Tahah	Minister of Social Action, Childhood, and Family	2023–2024
Zeinebou Mint Ahmednah	Minister of Employment and Vocational Training	2023–2024
Naha Mint Mouknass	Minister of Health	2023–2024

Internal or External Pressures for Gender Reforms?

There is a wide range of opinions regarding the reasons why the regime promotes women's rights. One factor has to do with the influence of external pressures, even though the the main impetus appears to be internal. After Taya came to power, pressure mounted domestically to revise Mauritania's legal framework. They also sought to harmonize it with Mauritania's international commitments regarding women but also with respect to human rights more generally. Reforms were made in the PSC of 2001, the Labor Code of 2004, and in laws regarding slavery and women.

Even though these reforms always had an internal motivation, reformers drew on international instruments to strengthen their hand. As former Secretary of State and Minister of Women's Affairs Seniya Sidi Haiba explained:

> In my assessment and experience, leaders work to promote women's rights based on their responsibility to promote and advance society. Because women constitute half or more of that society and because of their pivotal role in the nation-building process, it is natural that they focus the attention of leaders and policymakers not on obtaining funds or external assistance but rather on the development of society and women in particular. International partners play an essential role in achieving these goals. (MRT27.6.30.20)

She saw women's empowerment as a critical state goal that was part of efforts to benefit women and achieve sustainable development.

However, other respondents saw that the pressure came from both Mauritanian society and international laws and that the biggest problem was the lack of implementation of laws, particularly regarding early marriage, forced marriage, child custody, slavery, and its abuses, whether sexual or related to inheritance (Human Rights Watch 2021a; MRT1.6.5.20; MRT 21.6.22.20; MRT5.6.6.20; MRT8.6.10.20; MRT4.6.5.20; MRT2.6.4.20; MRT9.6.11.20). One of the reasons Mauritania has attracted more international attention than many countries is because of the issue of slavery and how it affects women more directly (MRT14.6.14.20). In 2020, authorities arrested Mariem Cheikh, an activist and member of the antislavery campaign group IRA, for her criticism of continued slavery and racial discrimination in Mauritania. Although she was released a week later, IRA members continue to be subject to arrests and harassment, as are other groups like the Alliance for the Refoundation of the Mauritanian State (AREM), which oppose the caste system (Human Rights Watch 2021b). As of 2018, there are ninety thousand people living in modern slavery in Mauritania, or 2.4 percent of the population.

President of the AFCF, Aminetou Mint El Moktar, explained that many women's rights laws can be partly explained by the commitments the country has made to donors and the institutions they are members of: "They are obliged to show the steps taken; there is control, and they have to show their evidence." Brahim Ould Bilal, vice president of IRA-Mauritania, similarly argued, "It is to embellish the image of the country. At the international level, we consider a country advanced when women occupy a good place. In Mauritanian society, we always tend to say that because of religion, women's rights are not respected. But we are still looking to show despite this that we respect these women's rights" (MRT4.6.5.20).

Another journalist explained, "Mauritania is a country that has been harshly criticized during the various sessions of the Human Rights Council in Geneva, and that tarnishes the image of the country. If the international media focuses on slavery in Mauritania, this similarly sullies the image of the country, which is why many laws have been passed to restore the image of the country" (MRT7.6.8.22).

Much of the international focus regarding Mauritania has focused on slavery, which has a particular impact on women and children (MRT7.6.8.22). For example, Michelle Bachelet, the former UN High Commissioner for Human Rights, wrote a letter dated October 8, 2021, to the Mauritanian government imploring it to implement the Law 2015–031 criminalizing slavery and punishing slavery-like practices in Mauritania and to develop a comprehensive national human rights action plan. She called on the government to address the issues of slaves becoming integrated into society because of the lack of identity papers or access to employment, education, or land ownership and who are at risk of returning to situations of slavery (UN Human Rights Council 2021).

One might argue that Mauritania has not only responded to international pressures around women's rights, but it has sought to improve women's rights more generally to polish its international image and divert attention from its more problematic record regarding slavery. Activists point out that there have been greater efforts to respond to the international community around women's rights and also slavery than other concerns, particularly the 1979 women's rights treaty CEDAW (MRT3.6.5.20). Mauritania is a signatory to key UN treaties and the African Union Maputo Protocol. It was also active in the Group of Five for the Sahel[8]—known as G5Sahel—initiatives to bring women into peacebuilding activities. In 2018, Mauritania helped

[8] Burkina Faso, Mali, Mauritania, Niger and Chad

launch the G5 Sahel Women's Platform to convene key leaders, stakeholders, and champions of women's organizations to work together on peace, justice, and security in Burkina Faso, Mali, Mauritania, Niger, and Chad (MRT21.6.22.20). Finally, Mauritania is influenced by the Maghreb countries, both at the governmental level and within civil society. Mauritanian civil society is actively engaged with civil society in the Maghreb, especially in Tunisia and Morocco, and women's rights have been an important area of political lessons (MRT1.6.4.20).

Mauritanian women are generally very active in women's networks not only in North Africa but also in Senegal, Mali, and Côte d'Ivoire. Many women's rights activists pointed out that Mauritanian women are among the most active in the Maghreb and West Africa. For example, Fatimatou Mint Abdel Malick served as president of the Network for Locally Elected Women of Africa from 2012 to 2015 and is president of the Regional Council of Nouakchott (MRT2.6.4.20).

As the head of an NGO said, "For Westerners when they see that there are many women ministers, they say, 'Here it is. It is a country that is developing, at least within the framework of the laws'" (MRT2.6.4.20). However, this virtue signaling is not only aimed at Westerner donors. It is also aimed regionally. For the past ten years, Mauritania has been able to play a significant regional role, holding the chairmanship of the African Union in 2014–2015 and hosting the Arab League summit for the first time in 2016. The increased role of women in the African Union countries, in particular, is being regarded favorably. Thus, while the desire to promote women leaders is domestically driven, the international dimension supports this endeavor and serves additional purposes of virtue signaling.

Continuing Challenges to Advancing Women's Rights

There are numerous continuing challenges that limit women's rights. The Salafists pose one set of challenges at the ideological level. As one women's rights activist explained:

> The main opponents of the [gender] reform are a few radical scholars, especially of the Wahabite or Ṣalafist orientation, who have now become very numerous in Mauritania. These are people whose clock stopped in the fourteenth century. They always live in a time that is not our time. Fortunately, there are other more progressive [religious] scholars who support these reforms. (MRT7.6.8.20)

The same activist also saw the lack of follow-through in enforcing key legislation as another constraint:

> It is not only women's rights that are not enforced—there are many others. Mauritania has ratified a lot of conventions. It has produced a lot of laws, but many of these laws are not applied. Few of them are enforced unless they are there to watch, as is the case with the slavery law. Women today are more aware of their rights and defend them more. They have imposed themselves in all sectors. They are more present in working life. All this is the fruit of an awareness. There is a lot more rape than before, and there is no law to protect women. It is the biggest drama that women have in Mauritania. Apart from that, there is progress everywhere. (MRT7.6.8.20)

Resistance to the Law for the Protection of Women and Girls on violence against women, which has stalled in Parliament since 2016, comes primarily from the Islamist Tawassoul Party and even from some women in the party. The law was brought forward twice and was later withdrawn. One of the reasons women fear reporting rape in Mauritania is the concern of being arrested for the Islamic crime of *zina*, or "fornication," which carries with it a punishment of imprisonment for a minimum of four years. Marietta Diagana, the head of Women's Rights at the Mauritanian office of the UN High Commission on Human Rights, estimates that about six out of ten women prisoners were sentenced to the crime of *zina*. Women who cannot provide adequate proof of rape can be convicted of *zina* (Schenker 2021). Yet charges of *zina* have been used against women found alone with men in public.

As El id Mohameden Mbareck, one of the parliamentarians who brought the bill combating violence against women forward, explained:

> I am a practicing Muslim, and I am attached to my religion; I will say that for every Muslim, this law does not contain any provisions contrary to Islam. But there are actors who want to keep women in this status, and they are the most dangerous actors, and we must fight them. These actors have nothing to do with religion and have nothing to do with human rights. They are people who only defend their particular interests. Because the evolution of women's rights makes them lose all their privileges, like all the countries with which we share religious and legal traditions, we have difficulties, but we have a society that is evolving, and each reform undertaken will undoubtedly have difficulties and obstacles. (MRT1.6.4.20)

The lack of overall freedom remains an impediment to women's mobilization. As a leader of a women's organization explained:

> Today, there is a desire to muzzle people. I held a meeting on the overhaul of laws in Mauritania; there were ten people. Four days later, the Justice Ministry challenged me and asked me, "Did I organize a meeting on secularism? Did I organize a meeting on religion?" I went back and forth to the Justice Ministry for two weeks, and the people who were with me went to jail. So, it is a setback for freedom of expression. The constitution guarantees freedom of assembly. Here, we see meetings of two thousand people for initiatives to support the president, and they are never bothered. But for a meeting of ten people, I am asked, Who funded the meeting? That is ridiculous. So there is a step back. It is difficult to advance human rights because there is no interlocutor. The current president has not honored his commitments to women. He has arrested women like the one who spoke out against the Corona [Covid-19] crisis policy. (MRT8.6.10.20)

Conclusion

Overall, there is progress in Mauritania regarding gender equality compared to the time of military rule in terms of laws passed, international treaties ratified, and the increased number of women involved in politics. However, the challenges remain, many of which are related to the semiauthoritarian nature of the state. As a hybrid regime, the government is sensitive to societal pressures, particularly from the Salafists and Islamists. There is nevertheless much within Mauritanian culture that is conducive to women's rights reforms in spite of the challenges posed by the Islamists and Salafists as well as the undemocratic nature of the regime. The fact that the UPR / Equity Party has emerged and remained in power for over three elections in a regime that is more institutionalized has allowed for some women's rights reforms and the advancement of women as leaders. However, further reforms and enforcement of existing laws are more generally constrained by the limits on freedom of association and political rights.

PART III

INTERNATIONAL DIMENSIONS OF AUTHORITARIAN STRATEGIES

6

International Virtue Signaling and Women Leaders

The Case of Rwanda

In international relations, status can be defined as "collective beliefs about a given state's ranking on valued attributes (wealth, coercive capabilities, culture, demographic position, sociopolitical organization, and diplomatic clout)" (Larson et al. 2014). It relates to a country's standing or rank in a hierarchy of nations (Renshon 2017). Women's status can be one way of ranking nations. As Rumelili and Towns (2022) have observed, states respond to more than just the gap between norms and actual practices. They also respond to being compared to other countries as superior or inferior.

Historically, there has been a perception that women's rights are associated with civilization, modernization, and westernization (Rumelili and Towns 2022). Others have associated women's rights with democratization. The association with westernization has diminished considerably as activists worldwide have helped shape the norms regarding women's rights globally, and the United Nations has been a catalyst in encouraging countries to adopt gender reforms. However, the link between modernity, democratization, and women's rights has persisted. Women's rights—however narrowly defined—have become a general good to aspire to in most parts of the world. Even the most recalcitrant countries, like Saudi Arabia, Qatar, and Kuwait, have sought to give the impression that they are concerned about women's rights in certain areas.

There are several ways that countries carry out status signaling regarding women's rights, often to give the impression of a commitment to modernity, democracy, and many other perceived goods. They can do this through funding allocations to address domestic and international women's rights concerns. They may discuss the status of women's rights in their press statements and diplomatic communications. They may host high-profile conferences on women's status or host athletic events featuring female athletes. They might also highlight their rankings in international indices that compare

Why African Autocracies Promote Women as Leaders. Aili Mari Tripp, Oxford University Press. © Oxford University Press (2025). DOI: 10.1093/9780197829004.003.0007

the status of women in various countries. Alternatively, they might strategically post women ambassadors to other countries interested in advancing women's status. International donors and agencies pay attention to various developmental indices and rankings of women's status, further reinforcing their use in national virtue-signaling endeavors. For example, Sarah Sunn Bush (2011) found that countries adopted gender quotas where international incentives were evident. Moreover, large-scale survey experiments of citizens in Sweden and the United States found that people perceived authoritarian countries as more democratic and were more likely to support granting them foreign aid where they had higher levels of descriptive representation (Bush and Zetterberg 2021). This was also true of development and democracy-promotion professionals, who perceived countries as democratic and worthy of aid if they increased women's economic rights and adopted quotas (Bush et al. 2024).

Governments can tell a "story" about women's status and spin it to avoid inconvenient truths that do not support the desired impression. Signaling also depends on others' recognition of the "story" and how much they buy into it. When they tell their stories, leaders calculate how the story is going to be received and adjust accordingly.

Like foreign donors and multilateral institutions, governments often describe women and women leaders as the key to ending poverty, solving environmental problems, ending conflict, improving household welfare, ending corruption, improving the economy, and promoting democracy. Policymakers, as we see in the cases of Morocco and Rwanda, often draw on the utilitarian language used by foreign donors and the United Nations to explain and justify their policies regarding women.

Because of Rwanda's gender quota policy, the number of female legislators is the highest in the world. According to a leading Rwandan human rights activist, the quota representatives are carefully selected by RPF cadres and have to undergo a long initiation and screening process by the party before and after elections. Nevertheless, the quota and other gender-related policies adopted by the RPF won them positive international acclaim and visibility, particularly at a time when their ethnically based human rights violations were increasingly being called into question.

Like the other countries in this book, Rwanda's primary target audience for its gender policy is its citizens, but it has also engaged in various externally directed status-signaling activities, which are highlighted in this chapter. Countries like Rwanda sought to improve their international image after conflict and genocide, and one way they did this was by advancing women as leaders. Such countries have been particularly sensitive to international perceptions and have sought to carefully curate their international image to assert international, regional, and domestic power. Their international status strengthens their legitimacy at home (Jervis 1989; Lebow 2008; Pu 2017). They tend to focus more on some rights than others, particularly political representation, and measures regarding women's economic empowerment. There has generally been less emphasis on cultural change, reproductive rights, LGBTQ rights, and reforms related to family law. Interestingly and perhaps as a nod to the donor community, even though popular opinion is generally homophobic and there are many anti-LGBTQ policies, Rwanda does not criminalize gay sex, nor does it restrict the discussion or promotion of LGBTQ topics ("LGBT Rights in Rwanda" 2024). The government has stated that it has no plans to criminalize homosexual acts, saying that sexual orientation is a private matter (Musoni 2009).

More so than most African countries, Rwanda has an external strategy for advancing women leaders that responds to donors, investors, trade partners, and the international community. Most authoritarian governments in Africa that instrumentalize women's rights, including Rwanda, do so to strengthen their domestic standing. Like these other countries, Rwanda has promoted women's status and women leaders to enhance internal legitimacy, maintain vote share for the ruling party, co-opt women leaders, and respond to domestic constituencies. But the ruling party in Rwanda has also ensured that no serious political opposition groups are allowed to participate freely in elections or run for office, and it has effectively silenced any criticisms or challenges to its authority, including from women. Nevertheless, Rwanda also gestures to the international community and other African countries to focus on its brighter spots, including economic prowess and women's rights.

How did Rwanda come to embody such massive contradictions as it promotes women's rights and inclusion of women as political and business leaders yet advances a deeply nondemocratic agenda? This chapter looks at the authoritarian nature of the Rwandan Patriotic Front (RPF)-led regime and how the RPF came into power. It then examines the RPF's virtue-signaling strategies and how women and women's rights are part of those strategies. It discusses progress in women's rights and representation as well as the limits of RPF's strategies. Then, it goes into the virtue-signaling strategies, followed by a discussion about how the RPF's domestic concerns relate to its external signaling strategies.

Background

In October 1990, the Rwandan Patriotic Army (RPA), the RPF's armed wing, launched a civil war on Rwanda from its base in Uganda. The RPF and the Rwandan government later signed the Arusha Accords in 1993. During this time, the RPF faced defeat in local elections in northern Rwanda, an area under its military control.

The ceasefire ended on April 6, 1994, when an airplane carrying President Juvénal Habyarimana was shot down near Kigali. Habyarimana and the president of Burundi, Cyprien Ntaryamira, who was flying with him, were killed in the attack. To this day, there is no agreement on who downed the plane: Hutu extremists in the Rwandan government or the RPF. The shooting down of the plane triggered a mass genocide, which targeted primarily Tutsis, resulting in roughly five hundred thousand to six hundred thousand deaths within one hundred days. The precise toll is unknown, and there are debates regarding these numbers (Meierhenrich 2020). The genocide ended when the RPA (and the RPF, by extension) took over the country in July 1994. The RPA was later renamed the Rwandan Defense Forces.

Power has increasingly been centralized since the genocide. The political calculus of the ruling RPF can explain much of the surge in female representation in Rwanda. The most troubling aspect of politics in Rwanda is how the overall political discourse and realities that women parliamentarians face have limited possibilities for democratic debate and are intensifying ethnic tensions. In Rwanda, the executive branch has remained strong compared to other branches of government.

The lack of political choice characterizes the elections in which the RPF wins the lion's share of votes, and the remaining votes go to parties allied with the RPF. The RPF has ensured that no serious political opposition groups are allowed to participate freely in elections or run for office and has effectively silenced any criticisms or challenges to its authority, including from women. In the 2024 presidential elections, Paul Kagame won 99.18 percent of the vote against his opponent, who represented the Democratic Green Party. This party was formed in 2009 and tried to register seven times until it succeeded.

According to Freedom House (2024), parliamentary elections are marked by irregularities, political intimidation, unfair registration, and alleged fraud. They describe Kagame's regime as having "suppressed political dissent through pervasive surveillance, intimidation, torture, and renditions or suspected assassinations of exiled dissidents." Opposition candidates routinely face obstacles in running, including unfair barriers to registration, campaigning, poll monitoring, and media access for opposition parties and candidates. In the 2018 election, the National Electoral Commission (NEC) blocked some opposition candidates from running. The RPF forced people to attend their rallies and vote for President Paul Kagame, who came into power after the 1994 genocide. They were also compelled to attend "solidarity" camps and listen to RPF propaganda. Access to the media and electoral coverage favored the RPF.

Even the former president suffered from this repression. Pasteur Bizimungu, a Hutu, served as president from 1994 to 2000, and Paul Kagame held the post of vice president and defense minister. When Bizimungu left the government to form a political party, he was arrested and imprisoned until 2007, when Kagame pardoned him. The vice president of the Democratic Green Party of Rwanda André Kagwa Rwisereka was found beheaded under suspicious circumstances in 2010, and there are other examples of similar repression.

Extrajudicial killings also continue. As opposition leader Victoire Ingabire explained to me in a 2023 interview, "Today, I have seventy members from my political party [Development and Liberty for All] who are in prison, and I have four who were assassinated, and I have four who are missing until today."

Even musicians are not spared repression. In 2020, Kizito Mihigo, who released a song criticizing the Kagame regime, was arrested near the border while fleeing to Burundi. Several days later, he was found dead in a prison cell. Although it was claimed he had died of suicide, human rights groups suspected murder. Mihigo was a genocide survivor who earlier had been a staunch promoter of the regime.

There are severe restrictions on the freedom of expression and the media, academic freedom, civil society, and even religious institutions that face increased control by the RPF. Journalists are routinely subjected to intimidation and criminal charges for independent reporting. People are accused of "divisionism" or of fomenting ethnic hatred on questionable pretexts. There is ample evidence of a lack of independence of the judiciary.

Women's organizations, like other civil society groups, are only able to operate as long as they do not challenge the RPF agenda. Nevertheless, women are one of Rwanda's most active sectors of civil society. Some groups were already formed in the 1980s, but most were created after 1994, often to deal with problems in the aftermath of the genocide, such as widowhood and the absence of husbands held in prisons. Most women's groups are actively engaged in various areas such as economic development, women's health, and advocating for women's rights. For example, Pro-Femmes (Twese Hamwe) is among the most effective advocacy organizations. It is an alliance of forty women's groups that garnered widespread support for women's issues. Réseau des femmes is another active women's group engaged in development (Smith et al. 2002).

Limits on Women in the Opposition

Like men, women who have spoken out against the regime have faced retribution. One businesswoman, Diane Shima Rwigara, who had attacked the Kagame regime, stood as an independent candidate in the 2017 Rwandan presidential elections. Soon after she announced her candidacy, nude photos of her were circulated to the press to intimidate her. The Electoral Commission disqualified her candidacy on technical grounds. Rwigara, her mother, and four other associates were arrested and charged with "inciting insurrection." Rwigara was later acquitted in 2018, possibly because of international pressure, but her arrest had a chilling effect on other would-be presidential aspirants and those in the political opposition. Earlier, her father, Assinapol Rwigara, had died under mysterious circumstances in 2015, as had her sister, Anne Rwigara, an outspoken critic of the Kagame regime, who died unexpectedly in her home in 2023.

They were not alone. Journalists Agenès Nkusi and Saidati Mukakibibi were sentenced to four years and seven years, respectively, for endangering national security, genocide denial, defamation of the president, and "divisionism" (i.e., issuing statements that could be regarded as divisive and inflammatory). In the period leading up to the 2010 presidential elections, an opposition leader, Victoire Ingabire Umuhoza, was prevented from running, and in October 2012, she was sentenced to fifteen years imprisonment for conspiracy against the country through terrorism and war and genocide denial. Her crime stemmed from her public statement that although Tutsis were the prime targets of the genocide and civil war, there were also Hutu and Twa victims. She had called for recognition of all the victims of the genocide.

Ingabire served an eight-year sentence, five of which were in solitary confinement. Prior to her arrest, she had been a Unified Democratic Forces party candidate for Rwanda's August 2010 presidential elections. She is now the chairperson of a new political party, Development and Liberty for All (DALFA-Umurinzi), which focuses on expanding political space and development. Earlier, she had been the president of a coalition of Rwandan exile opposition groups based in Rwanda, Europe, the US, and Canada.

Like Rwigara, she suffered from a long and drawn-out smear campaign and separation from her family. Several of her close political collaborators were killed or disappeared under questionable circumstances. Ingabire was arrested again in 2025 as part of a trial of political opposition figures. Many other women have suffered a similar fate, having been charged under the country's genocide ideology and sectarianism laws. These examples illustrate how the regime harasses and treats opposition women (and men) and the limits of its women-friendly policies.

The politicization of ethnicity lies behind many of the restrictions on women's political participation. Tutsis are overrepresented in government, while Hutus face discrimination in state employment and accessing scholarships. The top leadership posts held by women have primarily gone to pro-RPF anglophone Rwandans who had lived in Uganda or elsewhere earlier (Powley 2003). Tutsis held 60 percent of executive branch posts in 2016 in a country where 85 percent of the population is Hutu and 14 percent Tutsi. All departments, such as the military, police, and judiciary but not governors, were predominantly Tutsi (De Roeck et al. 2016). Carey Hogg (2009) argues that the ruling party, the RPF, has created a situation in which the women parliamentarians are there to represent women in what she considers an essentialist manner. She argues that this construction has contributed to an ethnic equation that privileges Tutsi over Hutu.

Rwanda's Record on Women's Rights and Leadership

Some have suggested that countries like Rwanda practice genderwashing to help the "regime appear progressive, liberal, and democratic while diverting attention from its persistent authoritarian practices" (Bjarnegård and Zetterberg 2022, 62; see also Allan 2019). But Rwanda, like so many authoritarian countries, has a strong record in advancing women's rights and representation. While one might question the autonomy of the women parliamentarians and other women leaders, Rwanda's gains in many areas are real and compare favorably to those of other countries in the region and globally.

Rwanda became a world leader in women's political empowerment after the 1994 genocide and civil conflict and today holds the highest percentage of parliamentary seats of any country in the world (63.75 percent) (Rwanda Parliament 2024). The percentage of female legislators jumped from 17 percent in 1988, prior to the genocide, to 49 percent after the passage of the 2003

Constitution and the 2003 elections as a result of the adoption of a quota. The number went up to 63.8 percent in 2013 and remained at this level after the 2024 elections (Rwanda Parliament 2024). This increase follows the patterns we have seen in other postconflict African countries (Tripp 2015).

Rwanda implemented a constitution in 2003 that calls for gender equality and for women to occupy at least 30 percent of the positions in decision-making organs (including the lower house and senate), and twenty-four women were to be elected through the electoral college in the Parliament (Chamber of Deputies). As a result, the percentage of women in the cabinet increased from 5 percent in 1996 to 16 percent, 33.3 percent, and 40 percent in 2003, 2005, and 2006, respectively. As of 2024, women held 55 percent of the cabinet posts, and many women were appointed to crucial ministries, including finance and economic planning, justice, public service and labor, and education. At the local level, women held 40 percent of the posts in the local governance committees, although most of the mayors are still men.

Rwanda has also become a hub for innovation, investment, and tourism. It is one of the fastest growing economies in the world. It has become a global leader in environmental policy, cosponsoring a UN resolution to start negotiations on a global agreement on plastic pollution. It has significantly improved health, education, agricultural production, and food security and expanded economic opportunities for its citizens. It ranks in Transparency International indices lower than all but three African countries when it comes to perceptions of corruption. Only Seychelles, Botswana, and Cape Verde have better rankings than Rwanda.

As a result of numerous reforms aimed at creating a more open business environment, Rwanda has increased its ranking by one hundred places on the World Bank Doing Business index over the past ten years. According to the World Bank, it currently ranks as the second-best place to do business in Africa, after Mauritania. It ranks as the thirty-eighth-best place to do business in the world (World Bank 2020). Women in Rwanda hold top financial and business positions, such as the CEO of the Bank of Kigali and the Developmental Bank of Rwanda. According to the World Bank (Wharton School 2021), there are more self-employed women than there are self-employed men in Rwanda. Female-owned enterprises increased from 38 percent in 2017 to 50 percent in 2022, according to a 2023 report by the Rwanda Development Board (2023). In 2022, 39 percent of businesses had at least one female company director (Ashimwe 2023).

Rwanda has actively promoted gender equality in the workplace. It is one of three economies globally that registered gender parity in labor force participation in 2022 (alongside Sierra Leone and Burundi). Rwanda has launched the first National Gender Standards initiative, which sets standards and provides guidance for organizations to adopt workplace policies and practices to improve women's status. It is led by the Rwanda Standards Board (RSB), the Private Sector Federation (PSF), and Gender Monitoring Office (GMO), with support from the UNDP and UN Women. The initiative offers awards like the Gender Equality Seal Certification to companies and public institutions that have successfully established gender-equal working environments.

Rwanda has also encouraged women athletes. Grace Nyinawumuntu is a trailblazing footballer who has claimed visibility along with many other female athletes who have made a name for themselves in basketball, cricket, rally driving, karate refereeing, and chess (Bahizi 2023).

The fertility rate has declined from 6.1 in 2005 to 2.7 in 2019 among women of childbearing age. Maternal mortality rates have dropped significantly. Girls attend primary school at a rate of 98 per 100 boys, while at the secondary level, the parity index stands at 1.13 and 0.78 at the tertiary level. Women's education has seen the most gains at the tertiary level in recent years (National Institute of Statistics of Rwanda 2019). Women also head universities in Rwanda. Thus, Rwanda ranked fifth as the most gender-equal countries in Africa, according to the Global Gender Gap Report of the World Economic Forum (2024), and until 2022 it ranked sixth globally (2022).

Women's Rights Legislation

The Rwanda Women Parliamentary Forum (FFRP) spearheaded several initiatives to improve women's status, including a 1998 inheritance law, which gave women equal inheritance rights and allowed them to maintain separate property within a marriage. It got the gender quotas incorporated into the 2003 Constitution and drafted a bill around GBV, which was passed in 2008. There was also legislation involving the classification of rape among the most egregious crimes (1996), the expansion of the rights of pregnant and breastfeeding mothers in the workplace (1997), the expansion of workplace rights for pregnant and nursing women (1997), and the protection of children from violence (2001). The FFRP has strengthened legal protections for women in relation to succession (2016), discrimination within political parties (2013), access to land (2013), gender-responsive budgeting in the national budget (2013), the sale of children, child prostitution and child pornography (2012) as well as the protection of children (2011), discrimination in education (2011), maternity leave (2016), antitrafficking laws (2018), and many other reforms. A 2009 labor law mandates equal pay, a minimum working age of sixteen for males and females, and enhanced rights for pregnant and nursing women. A new 2023 maternity leave policy extends paid maternity leave from twelve to fourteen weeks.

National policies were developed, such as the National Gender Strategic Plan (2011–2016, 2016–2020), the National Action Plan for the implementation of Security Council Resolution 1325 on Peace and Security (2016–2020), the National Policy Against Gender-Based Violence (2011), and the Legal and Policy Framework for Gender Equality and the Empowerment of Women in Rwanda (2011). Many of the policies have been developed by the executive, including the National Gender Policy (2010) and policies on girls' education (2008), women in agriculture (2010), and reproductive and maternal health (2017).

A substantial number of policies target women in the economy, particularly in export-oriented agriculture. They have created more than forty Isange One-Stop Centers around the country to assist victims of GBV. Various programs have helped improve agricultural productivity and small-scale businesses. The PSF established the Chamber of Women Entrepreneurs to promote women in business. Women entrepreneurs in small- and medium-scale enterprises can access credit from banks and cooperative societies with loan guarantees of up to 75 percent through a government-supported business development fund.

The executive generally develops laws, and the parliamentary role is primarily one of rubber-stamping them. The only laws initiated by Parliament and not the government were the inheritance law, which was passed in 1999 by the transitional National Assembly, a Law No. 59/2008 on the prevention and punishment of GBV, including provisions around marital rape, polygamy, discrimination against pregnant women, and indecent public behavior (London 2020).

Not all policies have benefited women. Some observers are impressed by the cleanliness of Kigali, the capital of Rwanda. However, it has come at a cost to small-scale female traders. Women street vendors have been regularly cleared off the streets of Kigali and imprisoned. Some were single mothers and had to leave their children to fend for themselves. In 2016, there were over nine thousand street vendors; by 2022, there were 3,800 street vendors. Markets were set up where women could sell and were touted in the press as a significant accomplishment of the regime. Local authorities strictly forbade the sale of goods in unapproved locations. While the government portrays these fruit markets as a means of improving the lives of women and petty traders, it is perceived by many as a form of propaganda for the state (R2.3.21.23).

However, not all women can afford to pay for the market stalls, nor are the markets always the best way to reach customers or in proximity to their homes. About 74 percent of women are in informal businesses in Rwanda, many of whom are traders. The government has implemented strict regulations on vendors, and women, in particular, can face arrest for selling fruit on the streets.

The government has also implemented strict regulations around women's reproductive rights. For a while, the prisons were filled with women who had sought an abortion. The Ministry of Gender quietly advocated for a change in the abortion law, which was passed in 2012 (R2.3.21.23). However, abortion is still available only in the case of incest, rape, forced marriage, or if the health of the mother or fetus is in danger. One no longer needs a judge's authorization. However, one does have to get permission from two doctors (Påfs et al. 2020).

Rwanda's Postconflict Virtue Signaling

In spite of the aforementioned limitations when it comes to Rwanda's women's rights agenda, Rwanda's president, Paul Kagame, is seeking leadership in Africa and global recognition for his efforts in improving Rwanda's economy, healthcare, and education and the status of women in Rwanda. The RPF needs to legitimize itself because of how it came to power through force. It can instrumentalize women's rights to divert attention from human rights abuses and the less savory aspects of its regime, including its military ventures into the Democratic Republic of Congo (DRC) and backing of the M23 Mouvement du 23 mars (March 23 Movement) rebel group in the DRC. This helps shift the international focus to its softer image involving women. Foreign diplomats in Rwanda are aware of the lack of democracy and Rwanda's involvement in Congo, but they seem to be willing to overlook these issues for the most part because Rwanda does so well on other fronts, including women's rights. Moreover, Rwanda continues receiving international acclaim, as evidenced by its continued donor funding.

This is not to say that there have been no issues. In 2023, the British government was forced to abandon a plan that would allow it to send immigrants to Rwanda in exchange for $152 million in development funding. However, the Court of Appeal found that Rwanda was not a safe country for asylum seekers as a result of its human rights abuses. The Court of Appeal reversed an earlier ruling by the High Court, which dismissed most legal challenges to the plan.

There have been few economic consequences for Rwanda's human rights record as Kagame continues to win international acclaim. Rwanda has benefited from considerable support from donor countries and agencies to rebuild its economy since the 1994 genocide. It attracts over $1 billion a year in aid, making it the most significant aid recipient in East Africa. Over 40 percent of its national budget is funded by foreign aid (Aikins and Roux 2023).

At times, the United States has balked in its dealings with Rwanda. Until the end of the Biden administration, US relations with Rwanda were defined by $147 million (in the 2021 fiscal year) in bilateral assistance in health, economic opportunity, agricultural production and food security, civil society, electrification, education, and other such programs. The US hosted Rwanda at the Eleventh Annual African Air Chiefs Symposium in 2023. However, Barack Obama cut $200,000 out of its military assistance to Rwanda because of its support for the M23 group ("Rwanda Military Aid" 2012). US Secretary of State Antony Blinken also warned against Rwandese involvement in the DRC and human rights abuses during his 2022 visit to Rwanda (US State Department 2022). Rwanda has dismissed these accusations and has instead claimed that the Congolese government is spurring violence against the minority Banyamulenge population and working with the rebel group called the Democratic Forces for the Liberation of Rwanda, which holds pro-Hutu genocide ideology (Blanshe 2022).

Kagame's Gender Strategy

Rwanda, like Morocco, as explained in the following chapter, uses virtue signaling, which is a form of status signaling. Virtue signaling refers to efforts by a country to reposition itself vis-à-vis countries in their neighborhood to appear more progressive, more democratic, and less threatening (e.g., as a source of terrorism). It can be used by countries seeking to meet their international treaty obligations and to show they are playing by the rules of the international order. The term *virtue signaling* often has negative connotations in psychology, where it originated, as it is associated with individuals taking a moral stance to place themselves in a favorable light. In the global context, it can be seen as an attempt to generate international favor to meet national economic objectives, thereby gaining greater regime legitimacy. In the following sections, I discuss how Rwanda has used women leaders and women's rights as part of a virtue-signaling strategy.

Rwanda's quota and other gender reforms won the country's leadership positive international praise and visibility. When Kagame spoke at the World

Economic Forum at Davos on January 23, 2015, during the launch of a UN Women campaign for gender equality, he was introduced by CNN host Fareed Zakaria as "the man who should get the Nobel Prize for implementation of difficult ideas in a very difficult context." In 2016, Kagame was awarded the Gender Champion Award alongside Nkosazana Dlamini Zuma, the chairperson of the African Union Commission, by the African Women's Movements, a coalition associated with the African Union. He was given the award at a dinner at the Twenty-Seventh African Union summit in Kigali under the theme "African Year of Human Rights with a Special Focus on Women's Rights."

It is evident from the international pronouncements of Rwanda's President Paul Kagame (2014) that he has his eye on the international indices as he works to advance women in politics. For example, in his 2014 speech directed at the Women in Parliaments Global Forum, he talked about meeting the objectives of the United Nations:

> For good reason, the proportion of parliamentary seats held by women is one of the three indicators that were chosen to track progress toward the third Millennium Development Goal of promoting gender equality and empowering women. In Rwanda, we have never seen attainment of this ratio as an end in itself. Consider that nearly two-thirds of the Rwandan legislature is female, even though the constitution only provides for at least 30 percent. It was the citizens of this country who voted to double that. There is an important lesson as we make the final push to achieve the MDG targets by next year and look beyond to the post-2015 framework. Measurements, smart policy, and investment in public goods are crucial tools for driving change. But ultimately, success comes down to the choices made by hundreds of millions of real people every day. (Kagame 2014)

He frames gender equality in various ways as a given, a moral issue, a rights issue, and "a shared responsibility that concerns every member of our society." Kagame puts himself at the center of promoting Rwanda as a global and regional leader of women in politics and hosts many international conferences related to women's empowerment where he speaks. All of this increases his stature at home.

In 2022, Kagame hosted the 145th Assembly of the Interparliamentary Union, which focused on the theme of "Gender equality and gender-sensitive parliaments as drivers of change for a more resilient and peaceful world." Over one thousand delegates, including sixty Speakers and Deputy Speakers of Parliament from across the globe, were in attendance. The Commonwealth Women's Forum was held in conjunction with the biennial Commonwealth

Heads of Government Meeting (CHOGM) in Kigali in June 2022. Their leaders discussed challenges affecting women across Commonwealth countries but also policies and programs that had been developed to help meet gender equality targets. Kigali hosted the Sixth Women Deliver Conference in July 2023, which promotes gender equality and the health, rights, and well-being of girls and women. On March 1, 2023, Rwanda launched the African Women Leaders Network (AWLN) during the Rwanda Women Leaders Network Summit held under the theme "Building the Next Generation of Women Leaders" to kickstart International Women's Month. At this 2023 summit the Rwandan network was merged with the AWLN. At the 2023 Inclusive Fintech Forum in Kigali, Kagame emphasized bringing more women into the financial technolog space to affect women-owned businesses positively. These are just a few of the conferences Rwanda has hosted.[1]

Kagame is signaling to the international community his commitment to women's leadership and advancing women as a means to further development, because women are, as he explained in a speech, "both the beneficiaries and the principal agents of development" (Kagame 2014). He sees the promotion of women's status as a means toward various ends: economic development, improving the welfare of the household and society as a whole, and improving the environment, peace, and other such benefits. As he explained in one speech, women are "the cornerstone of prosperity for society as a whole[,] . . . the key to dealing with climate change, food security, good governance, or health and education, and advances in science and technology. . . . They are in a position to make unique contributions to peace and stability" (Kagame 2010).

He regards women as useful "to catalyze investments to raise labor productivity so that growth results in higher incomes for everyone in society" (Kagame 2014). One of the main ways that women are instrumentalized is through their leadership in the financial and business sectors. Rwanda has adopted numerous reforms to attract investment, and women have been central to these initiatives. The Rwandan government established the Rwanda Development Board, a one-stop investment promotion center and a new investment code. Registering a company takes only a few hours, and obtaining

[1] Rwanda has hosted countless other similar events, including the 2007 Women Parliamentarians International Conference, a 2010 International Conference on the Role of Leadership in Promoting Gender Equality and Women's Empowerment, a 2011 East African Businesswomen Conference, and the high-profile 2019 Global Gender Summit, hosted by the African Development Bank and the government of Rwanda and organized by the Multilateral Development Banks' Working Group on gender to focus on women's access to labor market opportunities. In 2023, Rwanda held the African Women in Media Conference. In 2024, the Remarkable African Women's Leadership Conference was held in Kigali, as was the International Woman Leadership Conference.

an investment certificate takes two days. Permits and documents are easily acquired from the Rwanda Development Board. Government-initiated loan guarantees and liberalization of selected economic sectors also encourage investment (Calabrese et al. 2017). It is no accident that the top executives on this board are all women. Women head up key banks in Rwanda, the Rwanda Convention Bureau, and the Rwanda Social Security Board, among other institutions.

Moreover, to attract foreign investments and aid, Rwanda uses its female ambassadors strategically. One-third of its thirty-three ambassadors are female and deployed to countries like the United States, France, Tanzania, and Sweden. The woman ambassador to Sweden, Amb. Diane Gashumba is also mandated to represent Denmark, Finland, Norway, and Iceland, countries known to favor female leadership. The ambassador, in her introductory letter to the Swedish embassy, unsurprisingly pointed out, "Since the 1994 Genocide against the Tutsi, Rwanda has been on a journey of transformation based on people-centric politics characterized by a series of achievements, i.e., championing gender equality with the highest number of women in Parliament." Other ambassadors routinely highlight Rwanda's achievements regarding women in their diplomatic speeches, referencing their rankings in global indices like the GGGI of the World Economic Forum.

Domestic Considerations

Even though this chapter highlights the external dimensions of Rwanda's strategy, the primary audience and beneficiaries of these policies are, in fact, internal. Rwanda, however, appears to draw on its international approbation to enhance its domestic legitimacy. There are several reasons for this.

One of the most important reasons the RPF brought women into leadership positions had to do with maintaining vote share. Although Rwanda has had a multiparty system since 1991, it has used the women's electoral college as a mechanism to ensure RPF dominance in vote share, as detailed in Chapters 2 and 3. The RPF was able to control the twenty-four seats elected through an electoral college and formed a coalition with smaller parties, which won 74 percent of the votes. The ruling coalition won 79 percent of the votes in 2008, 76 percent in 2013, and 74 percent in 2018. Kagame won 95 percent, 93 percent, 99 percent, and 99 percent of the vote in the 2003, 2010, 2017, and 2024 presidential elections, respectively. The ruling coalition is made up of twenty men and twenty women. If one counts the RPF, the indirectly elected members of the Parliament, and pro-RPF parties, then up to forty-nine out of

Table 6.1 Rwandan Parliament 2018 election results

	Men	Women
Rwandan Patriotic Front coalition		
Rwandan Patriotic Front	18	18
Centrist Democratic Party	0	1
Ideal Democratic Party	1	0
Party for Progress and Concord	0	1
Democratic Union of the Rwandan People	1	0
Indirectly elected members		
Women's representative	NA	24
Youth	1	1
People with disabilities' representative	1	0
Social Democratic Party (supports RPF)	3	2
Democratic Green Party of Rwanda	2	0
Liberal Party (supports RPF)	2	2
Social Party Imberakuri	1	1
Total	30 (37.5%)	50 (62.5%)

Source: Rwanda NEC (2018).

fifty women MPs (98 percent) support the RPF compared with twenty-seven out of thirty men (90 percent) (Table 6.1). It is interesting to note that, like Uganda, of the parties outside of the ruling coalition, women make up only 3 or 6 percent of the representatives, while men make up 5 or 17 percent of these positions, suggesting again that it is more difficult for women to gain parliamentary seats outside of the RPF umbrella even with the quota.

Two of the other parties not formally part of the coalition, the Liberal Party and Social Democratic Party, are effectively allies of the RPF. The Speaker of the House, the Right Honorable Donatille Mukabalisa, is a representative of the Liberal Party, but she does not take positions that diverge from the interests of the RPF. In this way, the RPF has near-total control of the legislative agenda. The National Consultative Forum of Political Organizations vets parties and candidates to ensure that no one overly critical of the RPF can hold seats in Parliament.

There are other reasons besides maintaining vote share that explain the government strategy with women leaders. First, the government seeks to create opportunities for women, in part because women were targeted in the genocide with sexual violence and because hundreds of women fought with the RPF's army during the 1990–1994 war, as they believed that the RPF was an organization that recognized and gave voice to both women and men.

Second, women participated in reconstructing the nation after the genocide, including various social healing and reconciliation programs (Kantengwa 2010). Third, many of the government's strategies have economic goals, particularly to further integrate women into the export-oriented modernized agricultural sector (Andersson 2022).

Fourth, as in other authoritarian countries, the Rwandan government seeks to strengthen the allegiance of women leaders and co-opt them in the hopes that they will bend to the will of the RPF leadership. After the genocide, the RPF leadership emphasized women's role in the reconciliation and reconstruction processes and encouraged women to enter public office. The RPF sought the support and votes of women. The government can count on a loyal cadre of women leaders who will not challenge RPF authority. Thus, the RPF used women to consolidate its control of the country (Burnet 2008; Longman 2006; Reyntjens 2015).

The loyalty RPF seeks to build is along ethnic lines even though the 2003 Constitution calls for the "eradication of discrimination and divisionism based on ethnicity, region or any other grounds" and the "propagation of ethnic, regional, racial discrimination or any other form of division is punished by law." The Rwandan government promotes a view of "Rwandanicity" and national unity to replace ethnic politics. However, about 60 percent of the ministerial positions are held by Tutsis, who constitute 14 percent of the population, compared to the 39 percent of seats held by Hutu, who constitute 85 percent of the population, and Twa, who constitute 1 percent. From 1996 to 2016, Tutsis made up 48 percent of the female ministers and secretaries of state (Guariso et al. 2018), and there is little reason to believe that the ratio has changed much. Moreover, the ratio is probably the same in the legislature. Tutsis are also overrepresented in government, while Hutus face discrimination when seeking public employment or scholarships. These are ways of de facto politicizing ethnicity to solidify loyalty in response to the experience of genocide that targeted Tutsi as a group and their Hutu allies.

Fifth, a large portion of adult men were disqualified from political participation, having been implicated in the genocide. Over 1.1 million people, primarily men, were tried in Gacaca community-based courts that were established because of the large number of accused perpetrators of genocide (*génocidaires*) awaiting trial. This meant that many men who could have potentially been politicians, especially at the local level, were excluded as candidates, thus facilitating women's leadership.

Sixth, women gained legitimacy after the genocide because the dominant national narrative about the genocide often excluded them, even though there is evidence to show that they were sometimes implicated, primarily through indirect acts of violence, such as exposing those in hiding to killers and inciting violence (Brown 2014).

Finally, the policies the RPF adopted toward women's leadership preceded their takeover of Rwanda in 1994 to their time in Uganda, where the RPF was formed in 1987. Later, the RPF appointed women to half their seats in the Transitional National Parliament. The RPF was especially keen to bring women on board to strengthen its legitimacy, particularly among Tutsis who had been exiled in Uganda and elsewhere in the 1980s and who returned to Rwanda after 1994.

Conclusion

The concept of *status* in international relations, encompassing attributes like wealth, culture, and diplomatic influence, has been linked to the perception of women's status as a measure of a nation's progress. Global activism and initiatives from the United Nations and regional organizations have reshaped global norms surrounding women's rights, making it a universal aspiration linked to modernity and democratization (Mageza-Barthel 2015). In its pursuit of international recognition and influence, Rwanda has strategically used women's representation and gender-related policies to project a favorable image on the global stage.

Although most of its reasons for promoting women's rights are domestic, Rwanda has adopted various methods to signal its commitment to women's rights to the international community, such as allocating resources, hosting conferences, featuring women in leadership positions, and highlighting its rankings in gender equality indices. Despite this international signaling, Rwanda remains a country full of contradictions. While it has achieved remarkable success in women's political empowerment, with a high percentage of women in Parliament and key government positions, it also engages in repressive practices by limiting political freedoms and perpetrating human rights violations, primarily directed at the opposition, including women politicians. Rwanda's leaders strategically use women's representation to enhance the country's international standing and domestic legitimacy—a complex strategy combining autocratic governance with progressive gender policies. It appears to be using women's rights as a way of diverting attention away from its human rights abuses.

Despite occasional setbacks, Rwanda continues to attract significant foreign aid and investment, bolstered by its image as a leader in promoting gender equality. Kagame's efforts to advance women's status are seen as a means to achieve various developmental goals, including economic growth, environmental sustainability, and peace. Women's leadership in the financial and business sectors plays a crucial role in attracting investments, and female ambassadors are strategically deployed to countries favoring gender equality to promote Rwanda's achievements in this regard.

The case of Rwanda underscores the need to critically reconsider the link between women's rights and democracy. Rwanda's authoritarian regime has managed to make significant gains in women's rights despite its undemocratic practices. This suggests that gender equality cannot be treated merely as a neutral measurement on an international index. It is essential to consider how authoritarian leaders use women's rights to gain international, regional, and domestic legitimacy to bolster their dictatorship and extend their rule. Indeed, freedom of association and speech—which are protected in democracies—are essential to women's mobilization to influence and shape how women's rights are expressed and which rights are prioritized. Levels of democracy may influence a state's willingness to advance reproductive rights, protections against marital rape, LGBTQ rights, and other more controversial issues. It may also influence the willingness of states to use adequate resources to address key concerns. The fact that a country like Rwanda, which is autocratic, can make important gains in the area of women's rights complicates the picture considerably.

7

Follow the Money

Economic Motivations for Advancing Women's Rights in Morocco

Background

Since 2010, we have seen more women leaders in autocratic countries in the Middle East and North Africa (MENA). While some have associated the status of women in this region with religion, such explanations shed little light on the changes we are seeing today in countries like Morocco, Tunisia, and the United Arab Emirates when it comes to women's representation. This chapter argues that a more fruitful approach is to look at the promotion of women as leaders as part of a symbolic strategy in the service of economic and political gains. Morocco has advanced women leaders and rights partly to sideline religious extremists but also as a way of virtue signaling to incentivize trade relations and attract tourism and FDI. Although trade, aid and FDI are not dominant explanations for the promotion of women leaders in much of Africa, the case illustrates the variety of explanations that account for the promotion of women leaders in authoritarian contexts. It also demonstrates the ways in which internal and external objectives interact. This chapter shows how virtue signaling works in Morocco through the use of thematic analysis of press releases with a focus on economic motivations. The chapter argues that these strategies are more than just window dressing and have become part of the new arsenal of governing strategies of autocrats.

Some have argued that the promotion of women leaders and women's rights by autocrats is merely window dressing aimed at virtue signaling a progressive and modern orientation to the world. However, a closer look at the dynamics behind these changes suggests that many countries adopt such reforms to use women as part of a strategy to strengthen their economies. The case of Morocco illustrates this phenomenon. Women in Morocco hold 35.6 percent of the seats in local councils and 24.3 percent of the seats in Parliament, which is higher than the 17.7 percent rate for the MENA region but lower than the African rate of 27 percent. After 2021, women claimed

Why African Autocracies Promote Women as Leaders. Aili Mari Tripp, Oxford University Press. © Oxford University Press (2025). DOI: 10.1093/9780197829004.003.0008

one-third of the cabinet seats (29 percent), including that of the minister of economy and finance. The appointment of seven women to the cabinet was a first in Morocco's history. All three major cities (Rabat, Casablanca, and Marrakesh) have women mayors, and Morocco has more women ambassadors than any other country in the MENA region. In 2012, Nabila Mounib became the first woman to lead a major political party, the Partie socialist unifié, or the United Socialist Party.

This chapter shows that there is a connection between Morocco's internal and external economic objectives and its women's rights policy. Even though such patterns are evident in North Africa, it is important to underscore that there is no overall correlation between trade and FDI in Africa and levels of female representation because the trading and investment partners of so many countries are primarily China, India, and countries in the Middle East and Africa that do not promote women's rights internationally. Rwanda's main export destinations, for example, include the UAE, the Democratic Republic of Congo, Thailand, the United States, and Ethiopia. There is, however, evidence that foreign aid plays a role in influencing women's representation (Bush 2011; Bush and Zetterberg 2021, Bush and Zetterberg 2024; Donno et al. 2022; Edgell 2017; Kroeger and Kang 2022).

Morocco, under the leadership of King Mohammed VI, describes itself in diplomatic communications as having a new governmental architecture that reflects "a shining image of the progress made by Moroccan women in various fields as well as their active participation in the political, economic and social life of the country" ("Nouveau gouvernement" 2021). What explains this position regarding women's rights? While there have been pressures from women's organizations to increase women's rights and representation, Morocco is also keen to promote trade relations and attract FDI by appearing modern and forward-looking. At the same time, Morocco is trying to shed its image of being a significant source of Daesh fighters in the twenty-first century and respond to its domestic imperative to sideline religious extremists (Tripp 2019). Morocco has also set economic goals that include job creation, strengthening human capital, and promoting inclusive national development that focuses on women and youth employment and improved governance and citizen engagement. This is to be complemented by gender and the digital economy as crosscutting themes (World Bank Group 2024).

Morocco uses virtue signaling involving women's rights as part of its international and regional arsenal to gain favor and achieve these economic ambitions. Yet the Moroccan king himself embodies a key contradiction found in authoritarian regimes: He acts as a primary advocate for progressive women's rights policies yet also promotes an undemocratic form of rule, monarchy.

In the case of Morocco, the external audiences of virtue signaling include primarily EU countries, especially France and Spain, with whom Morocco has extensive trade. In recent years, it has also included African countries, with whom Morocco seeks to expand trade and influence, and to some extent other Arab countries, as Morocco seeks to play a more prominent leadership role in the MENA region. Morocco has played an active role as a moderating force within the MENA region and Africa when it comes to religious extremism. It sees itself as an example of this moderation and has convened meetings bringing together groups representing different Muslim orientations and religions for dialogue. Its women's rights policies are part and parcel of this effort to assert regional leadership.

Increasingly, MENA countries seek to improve their status in Global Performance Indices, often shaped by liberal values and led by the EU and North American countries (Rumelili and Towns 2022). Part of what makes this type of international status signaling work is that international actors and institutions themselves use women's rights instrumentally and issue reports evaluating how different countries rank when it comes to various aspects of women's rights (see, e.g., the rankings of the IPU, the World Economic Forum's annual *Global Gender Gap Report*, the World Bank's *Women, Business and the Law* report, and the UNDP's Gender Inequality Index).

Various development agencies also portray women in instrumental ways. For example, they regard women's education as essential in the fight against global terrorism. Some see women politicians as a key defense in the fight against government corruption. Moreover, women's economic and political empowerment are often seen as key to peace, environmental sustainability, and many other positive developmental outcomes (Cornwall et al. 2008). Recently, states with women leaders have been associated with better management of the Covid-19 pandemic. This is even though countries with more state capacity, stability, wealth, and less corruption are often more likely to promote women as leaders (Piscopo 2020).

Prior Explanations for Gender Reforms in the MENA Region

Much of the literature in the MENA region has focused on religion as a crucial factor undermining gender reforms. Many of the discussions of women's leadership in the MENA region have identified religion as a constraint on female political representation. However, such explanations do not help us understand why we are now seeing improvements in women's status or differences among MENA countries when it comes to female political leadership. Some, like Steven Fish (2002), have even argued that women's subordination helps explain the democratic deficit one finds in the Middle East. However, key improvements in women's status in several MENA countries are not reflected in any loosening of authoritarianism. On the contrary, the improvement of women's rights is being used to strengthen autocratic legitimacy (Müller and Camia 2022; Tripp 2019).

Others have argued that Islam and autocracy provide a potent combination that mitigates against the advancement of women's rights (Inglehart and Norris 2003b). Cesari (2017) suggests that the deficit of women's rights in Muslim countries is tied to religiously based legislation, particularly in countries where the state elevates a dominant religious group with exclusive legal, economic, or political rights and denies these rights to other religions. This is further elaborated on by Dawood I. Ahmed and Moamen Gouda (2015), who argue that the more constitutions in Muslim-majority countries are Islamicized, the less they adhere to women's rights, and the less democratic and politically stable the countries are.

Daniela Donno and Bruce Russett (2004) find these patterns to be more evident in Arab countries but not more generally in Islamic countries. They also argue that these types of relationships are fluid and point out that Catholic countries at one time used to be even more likely to be authoritarian than Islamic ones were, yet this changed after 1990. They speculate that some of the factors influencing women's rights include the role of religious groups, how secular the state is, the role of international and civil conflict, oil, and other such explanations.

Another cross-national study conducted by Mala Htun and Laurel Weldon (2018) argues that the adoption of family law that upholds women's rights depends on whether religion is institutionalized in the state as a doctrine. All Arab countries in the MENA region have a clause in their constitutions stating that Islam is the state religion. However, the institutionalization of a state religion does not tell us enough about the differences between the countries within the MENA region and why some have advanced women as leaders while others have not.

Michael Ross (2008) argues that oil rents suppress female labor force participation in the Middle East, thereby keeping female political representation low. However, this does not account for the use of quotas and appointments to increase the representation of women in oil-producing countries like Algeria, Sudan, and the UAE. Others have shown that the adoption of quotas and the higher descriptive representation of women have an impact on attitudes in donor countries toward electoral autocracies—namely, in seeing them as more democratic and more deserving of foreign aid (Bush 2011; Bush and Zetterberg 2021). Bozena Welborne (2022) looked at the impact of financial globalization and gender rentierism on women's political participation in the MENA region. Some have argued that donor support is crucial in gender quota adoption in the region (Baliamoune-Lutz 2013; Bush 2011; Welborne 2010). Mina Baliamoune-Lutz also found that ODA has increased women's political empowerment in a study of thirteen MENA countries from 2002 to 2010. Valentine Moghadam, Martha Posusney, Homa Hoodfar, and Elizabeth Doumato have done important work on some of the macroeconomic underpinnings of women's political and social mobilization.

This chapter builds on these aforementioned insights, focusing on the role of trade and FDI in instrumentalizing women's rights. In the case of Morocco, the policies driven by the Makhzen (the network of actors close to the palace and associated with the minister of interior) have both an internal and an external audience. The Makhzen has used women leaders to signal to external audiences that Morocco is a modern nation aimed at maintaining or increasing trade and FDI with key partners. The king's related internal goal, which is explored in my 2019 book, *Seeking Legitimacy: Why Arab Autocrats Adopt Women's Rights*, is to push back against extremism and to signal to domestic audiences that as the Commander of the Faithful, he sees the advancement of women as part of his mandate as king, thus seeking internal legitimacy from targeted groups. However, there is also an external element to Morocco's policies regarding women. At the time that Mohammed VI stepped onto the throne in 1999, Morocco found itself dependent on phosphates, tourism from Europe, especially France, remittances from Moroccans living abroad, and agricultural exports.

In this chapter, I look at how Morocco uses women's representation to signal that it is a reliable trade partner. Morocco does this in various ways: through government and diplomatic official statements and speeches, press articles published by the government press agency and progovernment publications often subsidized by the state, and the acceptance of donor support targeted around women's leadership. In this chapter, I examine thematic press coverage of women's rights and women's political leadership in the press aimed at the diplomatic community in Morocco. The chapter situates these political gains for women in the context of the adoption of other women's rights policies. The chapter also looks at the acceptance of Western aid to promote women's rights as evidence of their responsiveness to EU, North American, and UK goals in promoting gender equality and women as leaders.

Having carried out extensive field research and interviews for my aforementioned 2019 book on the Maghreb on Morocco's internal strategies, in this chapter, I am shining a spotlight on its external virtue signaling goals, which require a different methodology. This chapter uses thematic analysis, which involves looking for patterns and themes in data (Braun and Clarke 2006). It uses a constructionist method of analyzing events, statements by prominent individuals, interpretations of events, and the broader social context through which to identify major tropes that explain how Moroccan policymakers think about women's leadership and are presenting it to the world. The chapter draws on an analysis of progovernment sources of French news about Morocco, *Maroc Diplomatique*, which is dedicated to news reporting on political, economic, cultural, and societal concerns as they relate to Morocco's diplomacy. The study involved analysis of critical themes in all the articles (396) between 2013 and 2022 that mentioned women in the title or article description. The analysis involved counting and comparing various categories of issues, types of funders, and types of recipients to get a sense of the issues and concerns in the press. The study then analyzed all sixty articles between 2013 and 2022 from the online site of *L'Agence Marocaine de Presse* (MAP), the official Moroccan press agency, that had substantial content on women in politics. The study identified and analyzed the ways in which various government spokespeople and the monarchy rationalized and talked about why they supported gender equality, the frames they used, and how they have changed from past descriptions. Today's discourse is compared with the discourse that characterized the king's discussion of women's rights from the start of his ascendance to the throne.

Comparative Perspectives Within North Africa

Although the drivers of women's rights reforms are primarily internal, external factors also play a role. Taken as a whole, North African countries have the strongest trade ties and FDI to the EU countries and the United Kingdom compared with other parts of Africa and the MENA region (Table 7.1).

Also, OECD aid directed at women's empowerment in all sectors increased by 36 percent in Morocco, 122 percent in Tunisia, and 65 percent in North Africa between 2010 and 2020 (see Table 7.2). In this same period, it doubled in the MENA region, whereas globally it has increased by only 20 percent. Foreign donors have played a role in supporting gender reforms in the Maghreb primarily through UN and EU agencies and various international

Table 7.1 North African trade and foreign direct investment (2024)

Country	Leading export market	Leading import market	Major source of FDI
Algeria	European Union	European Union	United States European Union
Egypt	European Union	European Union	United Kingdom
Libya	European Union	European Union	European Union
Morocco	European Union	European Union	United States France
Tunisia	European Union	European Union	France European Union

Source: World Trade Organization (2024).

Table 7.2 Political representation of women in North Africa (2024)

Country	Women's representation in legislatures (%)	Quotas	Political empowerment* (2024)	Political empowerment rank globally*
Algeria	7.9	Legislated quota	0.068	135
Egypt	27.7	Reserved seats	0.176	90
Libya	16.5	Legislated quota	. . .	. . .
Morocco	24.3	Reserved seats	0.188	85
Tunisia	15.7	None	0.216	76

*Political empowerment is a composite measure of the World Economic Forum Global Gender Gap that looks at the gap between men and women in ministerial and parliamentary positions as well as in positions of prime minister or president.
Sources: IDEA (2024); IPU (2024); World Economic Forum Global Gender Gap (2024).

NGOs, like the National Democratic Institute, the International Republican Institute, the International Foundation for Electoral Systems, the Konrad Adenauer Foundation, and the Friedrich Ebert Foundation.

Background: The Case of Morocco

The Moroccan king has drawn on women's rights to blunt extremist Islamist trends and to present a modernizing image of their country abroad (Tripp 2019). However, there also emerged the need to soften the image of Morocco as it became a major source of Daesh fighters and to emphasize to the EU countries that it was a reliable partner. The focus on gender equality was one way to do this, and the EU itself was keen to promote women's rights as part of its democratic and human rights emphasis. One sees the synergy between Morocco and the EU in press statements, articles directed at the diplomatic community, diplomatic speeches, joint agreements, and programs documented below that have women's rights and leadership as a central component.

From the point of view of women's rights activists, the main dynamics of gender-related reform are internal to Morocco (M17.3.4.16). This was repeated in interview after interview. Some activists might find it advantageous to minimize references to external influences due to domestic political sensitivities and the importance of maintaining the perception of national policy ownership. Others emphasize the synergies between international norms and domestic objectives. One Moroccan women's rights activists whose organization had received funding from the EU countries explained that "international standards are no longer perceived as an imposed culture. This vision is changing in Morocco, Tunisia, and Algeria. The question is, rather, do they take priority over internal laws?" Her organization was in the business of developing women's rights legislation using integration of international standards as a legal source. They worked with local associations and lawyers to apply international standards (of treaties Morocco was party to) given the legal vacuum in the country. This involved monitoring in order to advocate for a specific law (M2.1.26.16). Her colleague emphasized that most of the progress has been made at the local level even without legislation. For example, in the area of violence against women, women's organizations work on hospital, police, and prosecution procedures, making sure there are support systems in place (M27.11.11.16). In interviews, it was clear that activists saw the international norms and donor funding as aiding them in the activities they were already working on rather than as imposing an external agenda on them (M17.3.4.16).

A leading women's rights activist, Latifa Jbabdi, who had headed the Union of Female Action, was a chief editor of the Arabic-speaking newspaper *8 Mars* (1983–1994), and a founding member of the Moroccan Association for Human Rights, talked about the importance of both CEDAW and the constitution in providing a legal basis for women's rights in Morocco. She described how Leprintemps féministe de l'égalité, a coalition of women's groups, had compiled their demands and petitioned the constitutional commission to include key provisions around women's rights. They won most of them including Article 19, which provides for parity, equality, and all rights and freedoms of a civil, political, economic, social, cultural, and environmental character. She explained that "the constitution prohibits discrimination and provides for the primacy of international conventions over domestic laws. It stipulates the need to harmonize international instruments with domestic laws" (M18.3.4.16).

Morocco's proximity to EU countries is consequential, particularly with the Mediterranean countries, but its relations with Arab and African regions are also important. The relationship with Europe began with bitter colonial domination and has resulted in legacies of migration and population flows, especially to France, coupled with extensive remittances sent from Europe to Morocco. Linguistic colonial legacies include the continued use of the French language and, to a lesser extent, Spanish in North Africa. The French have also historically influenced intellectual legacies, particularly socialist and feminist thinking, and both ideologies have influenced women's rights activism in the region (Tripp 2019). Spain is even more proximate to Morocco and has surpassed France as Morocco's trade partner. To this day, Spain controls two small territories in northern Morocco, Melilla and Ceuta, having relinquished a third territory, Western Sahara, in 1975 to joint Moroccan and Mauritanian control. This led to a war over the territory. In 1979, Mauritania withdrew its claims, and Morocco took control of the entire territory.

European Strategies

The EU sees its role as a global actor encouraging positive gender reforms in Morocco and more broadly in the MENA region through its external policy, through political and financial instruments, and grounding the commitment to women's rights and gender inequality in the institutional basis of regional cooperation (Laperrouze 2018). Trade partners and sources of FDI appear to be critical influences on the positions taken by Morocco regarding women's political empowerment. This is evident from Morocco's statements regarding women's rights directed at these countries. The EU is Morocco's primary source of FDI and main trading partner in exports and imports. The EU accounts for 64 percent of goods and 51 percent of Morocco's imports.[1] Spain is Morocco's major economic partner, followed closely by France, according to the World Bank.[2] Morocco receives more FDI from France than any other country, and Morocco is the largest beneficiary of funding from the French Development Agency (AFD).

Morocco has long been aware of the EU's interest in democracy, human rights, and women's rights. For many years, Morocco believed it would be invited to join the EU, but at its 1993 Copenhagen meeting, the EU adopted

[1] https://www.eeas.europa.eu/maroc/lunion-europeenne-et-le-maroc_fr?s=204#8911.
[2] https://wits.worldbank.org/CountrySnapshot/en/MAR.

the criteria that only democracies and countries that respected human rights would be admitted. Morocco fell far short of these criteria at the time (Binder and Sandberg 2021).

Since the 1990s, much of the focus of the EU and European countries has been on gender-based violence (GBV), women and girls' economic empowerment, and fighting gender stereotypes. It has also focused on promoting gender mainstreaming in sectoral public policies in cooperation with the Ministry of Family, Solidarity, Equality and Social Development and the Ministry of Economy and Finance, which leads the gender-responsive budgeting efforts. The EU has supported the Ministry of Public Service and Modernisation of the Administration and the Ministry of Interior to increase women's representation in senior ministerial positions.

An agreement was signed after the 1995 Barcelona conference on the Union for the Mediterranean. The Barcelona Declaration recognized "the key role of women" and the need to enhance women's social and economic roles along with the importance of education and employment opportunities for women. Morocco had an advanced status with the EU regarding political cooperation, which the 2000 Association Agreement established. Part of this agreement involved resolving serious gender inequalities to achieve the Barcelona Process's objectives (Commission of the European Communities 2000). In addition, cooperation between Morocco and the Council of Europe has focused on critical human rights issues, such as the prevention of and fight against violence against women and children and the fight against trafficking.

Established in 2008, the Euro-Mediterranean Partnership also involved various forms of economic, political, and security ties, including collaborations around women's rights. This partnership is between twenty-five EU countries and ten Mediterranean countries, including Morocco. A 2021 EU policy regarding the Mediterranean was issued, including crucial provisions around women's rights.

Morocco, Tunisia, and Algeria signed a series of new agreements with the EU regarding the promotion of women's rights after the 2011 Arab Spring. The EU has supported Morocco's Government Plan for Equality (Initiatives concertées pour le renforcement des acquis des marocaines) known as ICRAM I (2012–2016) to the tune of €45 million and a second ICRAM II for €35 million (2018–2023). This funding is intended to support efforts to institutionalize gender equality through a series of government budget objectives, results, and performance indicators. Through such programs, the EU has worked with the Moroccan Parliament to promote gender equality and is keen to further promote women's political participation, targeting political parties.

Individual governments have also provided support. The French government, through its AFD, has also provided budget support for gender budgeting. Women's equal political participation is one of the program's expected outcomes, with the EU listing "accrued women's participation in the public sphere (administrative and political)" as a critical indicator of success (EU Democracy Hub 2021, 7). In addition, the program opened a support fund for the promotion of women's representation in advance of the September 2021 election to provide financial incentives to political parties to promote women candidates.

The Moroccan government adopted various institutional measures, including the creation of an independent entity, the Authority for Parity, and the Fight Against All Forms of Discrimination, provided for in Articles 19 and 164 of the constitution, to oversee the implementation of constitutional provisions regarding the discrimination of women. Further, the National Action Plan on Democracy and Human Rights (2018–2012) incorporated women's rights into its mandate.

Aid directed at women's political empowerment (Tables 7.3 and 7.4) reveals how Morocco and other MENA countries have engaged partners around these concerns. These tables show how the EU and EU countries, followed by the United States and Canada, have the most projects related to women in politics in Morocco. The fact that Morocco receives this type of targeted support specifically from the EU countries and, in turn, Morocco signals to the EU its interest in advancing women leaders, suggests that this is one area of synergy between Morocco and its key trade partners.

The Symbolic Politics of the Monarchy

When Mohammed VI ascended to the throne after his father's death in 1999, he launched a program of women's rights reform. The centerpiece of the king's women's rights reforms was the 2004 Personal Status Code (PSC), passed under pressure from secular women's organizations. Most of the subsequent legislation involved hard-won gains by the women's movement facilitated by the king. Gender quotas were adopted in 2002. Women gained equal access to the courts when the Code of Criminal Procedure was reformed in 2002 to allow women to take civil action against their husbands without prior authorization of the court. Amendments to the Labor Code in 2003 prohibited discrimination against women in employment, salaries, and promotion. Paid maternity leave was also increased to fourteen weeks for women working in both the private and public sectors. Sexual harassment was made a

Table 7.3 OECD aid and support for gender equality and women in politics in the MENA region ($ million)

	All sectors gender equality per capita	Women's rights organizations & movements, & government institutions	Democratic participation and civil society	Legislatures and political parties	Elections	Overall support for women in politics per capita
Tunisia	$29.62	$3.421	$43.878	$0.78	$10.436	$4.95
Morocco	$8.45	$32.297	$8.946	$0.071		$1.12
Libya	$12.22	$0.605	$4.052	$1.119	$1.164	$1.01
Egypt	$4.03	$4.656	$2.541	...	$0.021	$0.07
Algeria	$1.49	$0.17	$1.712			$0.04
North Africa	**$6.42**	**$44.016**	**$63.669**	**$3.027**	**$14.714**	**$0.62**
Middle East	**$9.52**	**$44.872**	**$117.769**	**$0.486**	**$9.943**	**$0.4**

Sources: OECD Gross Disbursements (2019, 2022).

Table 7.4 Foreign aid to Morocco for projects related to women in politics (2019)

Source of funds	Number of projects funded
Belgium	2
Canada	8
EU Institutions	11
France	3
Germany	4
Netherlands	2
Spain	2
Sweden	3
Switzerland	2
United Kingdom	1
United States	11
Total projects	49

Source: OECD (2024); UN Population Division (2024).

workplace crime. The Penal Code was modified in 2003 to impose heavier penalties on a spouse who injured their partner. The Penal Code was revised to allow healthcare workers to waive professional confidentiality rules if they suspected violence between spouses or GBV, and they were allowed to report such incidents to judicial or administrative authorities. In 2004, the king also launched a national campaign to combat violence against women. A law allowing children to take not only the nationality of the father but also that of the mother was announced by the king in 2005 and passed by Parliament in 2007.

Following the 2011 Vingt Février movement protests, Morocco's version of the Arab Spring, the king reformed the constitution. Among other things, the 2011 Constitution guaranteed women "civic and social equality with men." The constitution also required the state to promote gender equality and to end sex discrimination. It was to foster women's participation in political, economic, social, and cultural life; to work toward parity between men and women; and to comply with all international conventions ratified by the government. After the constitution's passage, a new legislative gender quota policy was adopted.

The king sought to improve Morocco's image abroad, strengthen Morocco's economic competitiveness and role as a trade partner, particularly in Africa, and have Morocco promote a moderate Islamic vision of religious tolerance in the Muslim world and beyond. He did this through a variety of strategies, including isolating and neutralizing religious extremists in his own country, incorporating political opponents into national politics, playing off political parties and factions against one another, and promoting women's status to drive a wedge between Islamists and secularists.

He drew on his position as Commander of the Faithful to further legitimize his project. The palace successfully co-opted the Islamic Party for Justice and Development (PJD), which was in power from 2011 to 2021. After jihadist bombings in Casablanca in 2003, the king undertook a massive project of restructuring religious authority in Morocco to protect the "spiritual security" of its citizens, which was another way of saying he sought to prevent the ideas of al-Qaeda and the Salafists from taking hold. The king neutralized the Salafis, repressed those who were considered the most threatening, and brought a handful of them into the political process. At the same time, the king marginalized and weakened the largest Islamist movement, al-'Adl wal-Ihsane (Justice and Charity Association; AWI). The PJD eventually came to support the controversial PSC reforms because they said the final text contained references to Islamic values and traditions (Cavatorta and Dalmasso 2009). The king sought to capitalize on the code to gain greater international legitimacy.

A vital part of the king's strategy of promoting "moderate Islam," as he puts it, has been promoting women's rights, including women's education, combating the economic and political marginalization of women, and other such concerns. He has also used women's rights to communicate a new symbolic politics. This is evident in the king's language in his public speeches and declarations. Yasmine Berriane (2013) studied the king's speeches from 1999 to 2004, and I updated this study from 2013 onward using a more systematic methodology but capturing the same types of idioms and tropes.

Mohammed VI's early speeches depict Moroccan women as heroines and victims. On the one hand, women were valorized for their "firm will," "seriousness," "realism," "integrity," and "righteousness," all of which he claimed made women's emancipation necessary for development and democracy, according to Berriane (2013). On the other hand, women appeared both as "vulnerable" and "victims" alongside street children, people with disabilities, older adults, and individuals who suffered from violence, discrimination, injustice, and poverty. Women were typically described as a homogenous category, although they occasionally appeared as "the rural woman" or "heads of deprived families." Mohammed VI commented from time to time on the need to harmonize national legislation with international conventions in order to improve "the image of Morocco abroad," but he also asserted that Morocco should "position itself as an active partner on the international chessboard," according to Berriane (2013).

At the time of the initial PSC reforms, the king vacillated between a feminist frame of reference based on the notion of equal rights and a maternal frame of complementarity in which women play their designated roles in the family, a frame that Islamists generally embrace. He said that concerning the PSC, according to a complementarity perspective, it is in the family that the woman assumes "her duties" in occupying "the place that suits her and of which she is worthy" (Berriane 2013).

By 2013, the speeches had shifted away from the victim trope and from women's role in the family to putting women and men on an equal footing. Much of the language appeared to be adapted from international women's rights and development discourse, drawing on the UN language of gender mainstreaming. Women are portrayed as active and as catalysts of change. They are no longer a member of a vulnerable group, but instead, they are actively contributing to the welfare of vulnerable groups through their women's rights struggle. However, they are still "selfless." Women are linked to independence, modernity, development, and democracy.

By 2021, the king and government officials had placed gender equality at the forefront of the goal of promoting the rule of law, according to my study. They had shifted to portraying women as leaders, moving beyond the focus on economic empowerment for sustainable development ("HM the King Sends Message" 2018; "ICESCO's Year of Women" 2021). The language of parity and gender equality replaced discussions of women, as the king focused on how Islam emphasizes equality between men and women, since it considers women as شقيقات الرجال, which means "the sisters or allies of men," in terms of judgments (الأحكام). The king draws on two traditions, as Kenza El Ghali, Morocco's ambassador to Chile, explained in summarizing the way the king derives legitimacy from advancing women's rights: "[The king's] plan reflects a vision for the future of Morocco, based on a centuries-old history, a national identity rich in diversity and tributaries, as well as the religious values of the Kingdom." She underscored that "Morocco, a secular country, has always been a land of openness and understanding, a country concerned with promoting dialogue to resolve conflicts. In other words, it derives from traditional values of religion as expressed by the King, Morocco's diverse population that is primarily Berber and Arab, but also from newer democratic values" ("Morocco Has Turned Gender Equality" 2022).

This vision simultaneously draws on the "universal values of humankind and international charters" that provide for gender equality without any discrimination. In the rhetoric of the king, human rights are part of the discourse, and women's rights are seen as essential human rights. As he put it in a 2018 speech to the Women in Africa Initiative Summit, "[Women's rights are] not just a fundamental human right; [they are] also a requirement as per the law and a necessity for the achievement of socio-economic development" ("HM the King Sends Message" 2018). The goal is no longer, as it was in 2013, one of building a modern nation, which seems to have fallen out of the government press releases, but instead of promoting inclusion, democracy, and human rights. Parties tied to the Makhzen have also articulated a similar prioritization of women's rights that is cognizant of the importance of women's rights to the king and the fact that women constituted an essential part of the electorate.

There has been renewed debate over the PSC, especially since the king issued a communique to the prime minister in September 2023, asking him to reform the Family Code with broad participatory consultation with civil society and researchers. In spite of its innovations, there were many gaps in the code that perpetuated critical gender inequalities. With the opening provided by the king, feminist organizations were quick to remind the public of the need to consider gender equality in issues related to child custody and legal guardianship, property rights in the family, access to divorce, the need to end marital guardianship (*wali*), polygamy, child marriage, discrimination against children born outside of marriage, and other concerns (MRA [Mobilising for Rights Associates] 2023). Religious authorities, Islamists, and Salafists have expressed concern with this move to reform the PSC.

Content Analysis of Articles: Morocco

It is evident that economic and political concerns relating to women and GBV in Morocco are among the most important issues covered in *Maroc Diplomatique*, a Moroccan publication aimed at influencing the international community. Political concerns are measured by the representation of women in Parliament, as ministers, in local councils, in the judiciary, in the public service, and as diplomats as well as by the adoption of quotas (Table 7.1). The economic concerns pertain to a wide range of issues having to do with women in business, financing women-owned enterprises, sustainable development concerns, and a wide range of secondary issues having to do with employment, equal pay, access to land, and various sectors of society, including the agricultural, industrial, fishing, and artisanal sectors. Covid-19 and health concerns feature prominently, as does women's involvement in a wide range of cultural expression. Reference to the king and the monarchy is also very noticeable.

Women in areas in which they are stereotypically unexpected are also highlighted, such as women in science and engineering, the security sector, sports, and the media. In addition, women who have won prizes and awards, especially in the international arena, are also mentioned. The two southern provinces that constitute Western Sahara, which also has unusually high rates of female representation, are the parts of Morocco that receive the most commentary.

The articles often focus on women's leadership in government agencies where one would not expect to see such large numbers of women, such as the Moroccan Agency for Nuclear and Radiological Security and Safety. The influence of key international organizations on women's status is frequently noted, such as UN Women, the UN Educational, Scientific, and Cultural Organization (UNESCO), the UN Children's Fund (UNICEF), the UN Population Fund (UNFPA), and the UN High Commissioner for Refugees (UNHCR) but also the African Union and the Islamic World Educational, Scientific and Cultural Organization (ICESCO). It appears that Morocco is almost as eager to influence and engage the African Union as it is to engage the EU countries when it comes to women's rights. This collection of articles references European countries most often (110 times), African countries (seventy-four times), and Middle East countries (sixty-eight times). Regarding individual countries, France (thirty-three) received the most mentions, followed by the United States (twenty-five). There are unusually many references to feminism (thirty-one) and other terms used in feminist discourse, such as *equality of men and women*, *discrimination against women*, *parity*, and *women's empowerment*. Notably, there are few references to religion, and most are positive references to religion as facilitating women's empowerment.

In an analysis of sixty-one MAP headlines relating to *women*, *woman*, *female*, or *gender* from April 2017 to April 2022 the contrast is even starker. Among the most cited terms, 1,151 references are to terms relating to politics (e.g., elections, parties, participation, representation) compared with 188 terms relating to economic concerns (e.g., development, economy, imports). Overwhelmingly, the most cited terms had to do with women in politics. It is also noteworthy that the regions mentioned most often in this collection of articles on women's rights and representation are as follows: Europe and North America (sixty-four), followed by Africa (eighty-five), and the MENA (forty). This parallels the findings of the analysis of *Maroc Diplomatique*, and it reflects the direction of Morocco's virtue signaling.

If one looks at the statements made by ambassadors and other government officials regarding women's rights in MAP, it is clear that government officials of the countries Morocco trades with are a primary target of its messaging. The virtue signaling of Morocco with France and the EU is essential for various reasons. The promotion of gender equality in foreign relations has been a priority for the EU since 2010, as is evident in the European Commission policies, like the aforementioned Strategy for Gender Equality and its increased funding to support women's political representation. The synergy between Morocco's virtue signaling around women's leadership and rights and the EU priorities is unmistakable.

Even though Morocco's policies leave much to be desired from the point of view of women's rights organizations in the country (Feather 2022), EU speeches and donor evaluations regard Morocco as a model for other countries in the Mediterranean region when it comes to advancing gender equality. They frequently point to such reforms as the 2004 Family Code, the 2007 National Code, and the 2022 Electoral Code as evidence of its leading role. Morocco was also the first of the MENA countries to repeal the rape-marriage law that allowed rapists to escape prosecution by marrying their victims.

Conclusion

This detailed case study of Morocco suggests that although domestic factors and women's rights activism motivate Morocco's gender policies, women leaders and women's rights are also instrumentalized internationally to meet domestic economic goals and that there is a synergy between internal and external objectives Morocco's gains in advancing female representation and women's rights are a product of hard-fought struggles by women activists and politicians. Virtually all the legislation passed regarding women's rights bears the imprint of various women's organizations. However, women leaders are at the same time used to virtue signal to Morocco's main trade partners and investors in the EU. Moreover, Morocco wishes to portray itself as a progressive country that is actively improving the status of women as part of its efforts to improve the rule of law. Morocco strategically promotes women as leaders domestically to counter religious extremism and as a form of virtue signaling to attract FDI and official development assistance (ODA) and improve trade relations. The strategy is aimed at helping Morocco shed its international image of being a source of terrorist Daesh fighters and of harboring religious extremists. Morocco's focus on women's rights is also part of its bid for regional leadership within the MENA region and Africa, positioning itself as a moderating force in a turbulent region. Thematic analysis of press coverage and official statements suggest a correlation between Morocco's economic goals and its gender policies.

The EU plays a crucial role in promoting gender reforms in Morocco and the broader MENA region through its external policies and financial instruments. As Morocco's primary source of FDI and main trading partner, the EU exerts significant influence on Morocco's stance regarding women's political empowerment. The EU's focus has also included an emphasis on GBV, women's economic empowerment, and combating gender stereotypes. It has also collaborated with Moroccan government ministries to integrate gender mainstreaming into public policies. The EU has financially supported key Moroccan initiatives for gender equality. Additionally, individual EU countries like France have contributed to gender budgeting efforts and promoted women's political participation through financial incentives for political parties.

8
Democracy and Women's Leadership in Botswana

Even though democratic Botswana does much better than most countries in Africa when it comes to crucial gender equality measures, it ranks low when it comes to political empowerment of women. Moreover, unlike authoritarian countries, the governing party lost its vote share but did not pursue authoritarian strategies such as adopting reserved seats to bolster its presence in Parliament. In fact, the ruling party of fifty-eight years lost its vote share so much that it was dramatically voted out of power in the 2024 elections. It was replaced by the Umbrella for Democratic Change party and Duma Boko as the country's new president.

However, unlike Namibia and other countries with entrenched ruling parties, the political empowerment measure for the Global Gender Gap Index (GGGI) ranks Botswana at 128th globally and 36th in Africa. When it comes to women's representation in national legislatures, Botswana ranks 162nd at the very bottom globally, according to the Inter-Parliamentary Union (IPU).

This chapter explores the discrepancy between women's political leadership and other measures of gender equality by showing how political competition may influence women's representation in a democracy. In the case of Botswana, it is evident that a country can achieve greater gender equality in most areas except for politics, even though gender equality in politics generally goes hand in hand with other forms of gender equality. Botswana's government does not feel the need to use women leaders for purposes of legitimation, nor does it use them for purposes of maintaining vote share. Mindful of an electorate that has the potential to unseat them, the parties seek to accommodate the voters in ways we do not see in authoritarian countries, where the state can more easily institute top-down reform measures. Just as authoritarianism can be linked to women's rights, we see from the example of Botswana that democracy can also be delinked from women's rights if the electorate and dominant social forces (e.g., religious or traditional authorities) oppose specific reforms. Thus, in Botswana, some of the most sensitive reforms have been carried out by the courts, such as

Why African Autocracies Promote Women as Leaders. Aili Mari Tripp, Oxford University Press. © Oxford University Press (2025). DOI: 10.1093/9780197829004.003.0009

the reforms regarding LGBTQ organizations and decriminalizing same-sex relations.

At the time of this writing, there are nine democracies in Africa, which makes it difficult to generalize too much about them. Therefore, I chose to examine two democracies: Namibia (Chapter 9), characterized by high levels of female political representation, and Botswana, known for its low levels of representation of women in politics. This comparative analysis aims to shed light on their distinctions in contrast to authoritarian regimes and with each other.

In Botswana, I interviewed Members of the National Gender Commission, human rights lawyers, gender specialists at UN Women, attorneys, feminist activists, academics specializing in gender and political science, journalists, a former and current minister of gender, current MPs, former speakers of the Parliament, the head of the Botswana Democratic Party (BDP) Women's Wing, and other party leaders.

The first part of the chapter provides some background to the country. It looks at the levels of women's representation in Botswana. It then examines popular resistance to constitutional reform and the signing of international treaties that might have propelled Botswana to take measures to increase women's representation. It identifies sources of resistance, including the women's movement, which in the late 1990s was able to move the needle of female representation for a limited time. The chapter also analyzes the ruling party, political parties, and the governmental Department of Women. The chapter then goes on to describe how progress has been made in many key areas of women's rights, pushing Botswana ahead of most countries in Africa, except in political leadership. It shows how the courts have stepped in where legislation has not been possible.

Background

Botswana is relatively wealthy by African standards. According to World Bank data, it has a GDP per capita of $7,250, while Namibia has a GDP per capita of $4,743. This compares favorably to Africa's overall $1,740 GDP per capita. Botswana—a country heavily dependent on diamond mining, which contributes 50 percent to government revenue—receives relatively little foreign aid ($34.03 per capita in 2022) compared to other African countries, according to the World Bank. Most of its foreign investments have come from South Africa, and its largest trade partners are the United Arab Emirates (exports)

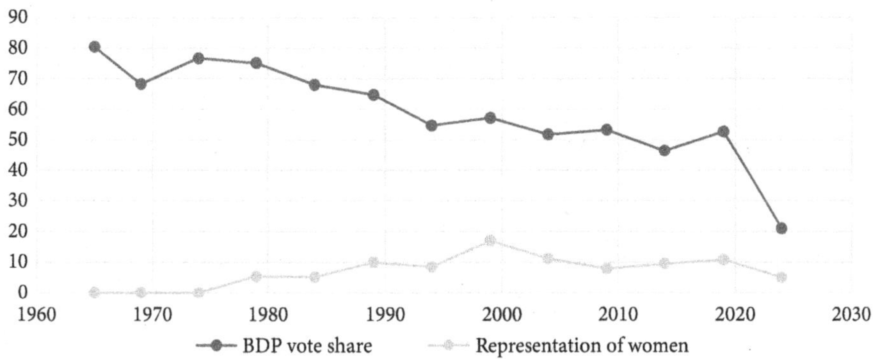

Figure 8.1 Vote share of ruling party and women's legislative representation (%)
Sources: IPU (2024); V-Dem (2024).

and South Africa (imports). A large proportion of its labor force works in South Africa as migrant workers.

Unlike autocracies, Botswana did not introduce reserved seats for women when the ruling party experienced declining vote share, a tactic we saw only in authoritarian countries in Africa like Uganda, Zimbabwe, and Mauritania. Since its independence in 1966, Botswana had an entrenched ruling party, the BDP, until it was voted out of power in 2024. The BDP had already experienced a significant drop of 30 percent in vote share between 1974 and 2014, but then it plummeted by another 31 percent in 2024 (Figure 8.1).

The comparison between Botswana and Namibia with the autocracies shows that even in the face of declining vote share, there hasn't been the same urgency to use women's representation to reclaim legitimacy and party hegemony. Moreover, Botswana has gone on to make major gains in women's rights and ranks at the top of the continent on key gender equality measures, with the exception of women's presence in politics.

Botswana and Namibia are at different ends of the spectrum regarding women's political representation, with Botswana ranking among the lowest and Namibia among the highest in the world. According to the GGGI, which includes composite measures of gender gaps in key areas, Namibia and Botswana were ranked first globally regarding the gender gap in educational attainment and health in 2023. Botswana has the lowest gender gap in health and ranks second in education and economic empowerment in Africa. It ranks ninth in economic empowerment globally (Table 8.1). If it were not for its political empowerment ranking, it would be one of the most gender-equal countries in Africa and the world.

Table 8.1 Global Gender Gap Index Ranking, Botswana (2024)

	Political empowerment	Health	Education	Economic empowerment	Overall
Sub-Saharan Africa ranking	34/35	1/35	2/35	2/35	11/35
Global ranking	125/146	1/146	1/146	9/146	64/146

Source: World Economic Forum (2024).

The country has one of the lowest rates of infant and child mortality and one of the lowest maternal mortality ratios in Africa, with 186 deaths per one hundred thousand live births compared with the Africa-wide ratio of 536, according to World Bank (2020). More girls (93.5 percent) than boys (89.4 percent) complete secondary school. Women have slightly higher adult literacy rates than men. The ratio of females to males in tertiary education is 1.39, which has enormous implications for the placement of women in top positions within the private and public sectors.

In 2022, Botswana's female labor force participation rate stood at 59.9 percent, while the male participation rate was higher at 69.4 percent. Furthermore, women accounted for 52.7 percent of individuals in senior and middle management positions in 2023 (World Bank n.d.). Botswana also has the highest percentage of women in the civil service in Africa, at 60 percent, along with Namibia and Lesotho, but this is not a new phenomenon (UNDP 2022).

Women are powerful actors in the economy, leading the top insurance companies and the private sector enterprises as CEOs as a result of the high levels of education of women. One can point to many highly placed women in Botswana. For example, from 2017 until her untimely death in 2021 owing to Covid-19, the chancellor of the University of Botswana was a woman, Linah Mohohlo, who previously had served as governor of the Bank of Botswana. Increasing numbers of women are playing an essential role on boards, whether in the financial sector, parastatals, private sector, health, universities, technology sector, or even the mining sector, which is the basis of Botswana's economy (B14.7.3.20). For the third year in a row, the 2021 Mastercard Index of Women Entrepreneurs (MIWE) identified Botswana, Uganda, and Ghana as the leading countries in the world in terms of their numbers of women business owners. Remarkably, Botswana secures a place within the top fifteen economies worldwide when advancing business opportunities for women, outperforming high-income and developed nations like Canada, the United States, New Zealand, Switzerland, and Australia. Additionally, Botswana earns a notable position in the MIWE 2021 report for its high scores in "women's labor force participation rates," ranking thirteenth globally (Oluwole 2023).

As many as 78.5 percent of respondents in a 2023 Afrobarometer survey believed that women have equal opportunities to own and inherit land, obtain jobs (82 percent), and be elected to office (86 percent). A greater percentage of women (58 percent) compared to men (52 percent) report that they make independent decisions regarding allocating household finances.

Political Representation of Women

Botswana has dramatically lower levels of female political representation than its neighbors—Mozambique, Angola, Zimbabwe, and South Africa—which, like Namibia, came to independence with the help of armed national liberation movements. (See Chapter 1 for a fuller discussion of the postconflict phenomenon.)

Cabinet Appointments

The very first women entered politics in the 1970s. Dr. Gaositwe Chiepe, popularly known as "the woman of many firsts," was the first member of the cabinet in 1974 and the first female member of the Botswana Parliament in 1979. She served as minister in several key ministries—which was uncommon in Africa at the time—including trade and industry, mines and natural resources, external affairs, and education. Chiepe also held numerous diplomatic posts in Europe, including high commissioner to the United Kingdom and ambassador to West Germany, France, Denmark, Norway, Sweden, and the European Economic Community. She was also the first female educational officer and the first woman to be awarded a postgraduate degree in Botswana. Botswana was able to place many women like Chiepe in top positions before many other countries in Africa because of the large number of highly educated women in Botswana.

By 2022, women in Botswana held 33.3 percent of the cabinet seats, but these appointments dropped to 22 percent with the 2024 elections ("Botswana" n.d.) (Table 8.2). However, these were appointed seats, and

Table 8.2 Women in Botswana's cabinet (1995–2024)

Year	Women in cabinet (%)
1995	11.0
2002	23.0
2006	28.6
2009	19.0
2018	16.6
2022	33.3
2024	22.2

Source: SADC (2024).

Botswana kept up with overall trends in Africa, where, on average, 23 percent of the cabinet posts are held by women. Botswana was the first SADC country to appoint a woman attorney general, Athaliah Molokomme, who served between 2005 and 2016, and there have been two female speakers of the National Assembly: the Honorable Dr. Margaret Nasha (2009–2014) and the Honorable Gladys Kokorwe (2014–2019). The country had one of the first female ministers of defense in Africa, Lesego Ethel Motsumi, who served from 2010 to 2011. Half of the electoral commission members are women. Relative to other SADC countries, Botswana has by far more women magistrates (68.9 percent compared with South Africa and Namibia, which have 50 percent).

Legislative Representation

On average, women hold one-quarter of the parliamentary seats in Africa, which is significantly higher than the rate in Botswana (Figure 8.2). Although women constitute 55 percent of registered voters in Botswana, by 2019, there were only eleven female parliamentary candidates out of a total of 210, accounting for 5 percent of the overall candidates (Chinyepi 2021). In 2024, only three women out of twenty-eight female candidates were elected to a National Assembly of sixty-one members. This marks a significant decline from 2014. Levels of representation in other areas are slightly better. No women have chaired any parliamentary committees, compared with Mozambique, where 44 percent of the committees are chaired by women, Angola (40 percent), South Africa (39 percent), Namibia (38 percent) and Seychelles (38 percent).

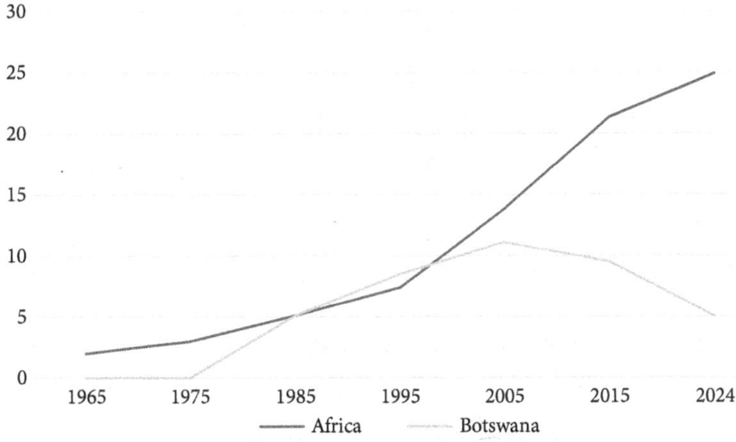

Figure 8.2 Women's legislative representation: Africa and Botswana (%)
Sources: IPU (2024); V-Dem (2024).

Subnational Politics

At the subnational level, the first female mayor of Gaborone was Grace Dambe (1968–1969). Gaborone, the capital city, has had three women mayors. Nevertheless, the pace has been slower in other areas of subnational politics. After the 2019 elections in this first-past-the-post system, women filled 18 percent of local government seats. At the regional level, women hold 23.8 percent of the seats or 117 out of 491 seats (SADC 2022). Women made up only 25 percent of the nominees at the local level in the 2019 elections compared to 75 percent of men (Tables 8.3 and 8.4). The minister of local government and rural development can appoint nominated councilors after each election. As a result, only 18 percent of those elected and appointed were women. Without the appointment of forty women (and seventy-nine men), there would have been only seventy-one women, or 12 percent women. There are generally more women in village development committees, which are a type of community arm of municipalities, and fewer elected and appointed women at municipal level.

Evidence of Resistance to Women's Leadership

Given Botswana's progress in so many other areas of gender equality, it is puzzling that it has done so poorly regarding elected office. There are a number of indicators of Botswana's resistance to adopting measures other African

Table 8.3 Women and men in local government in Botswana (1995–2019)

	1994	1999	2004	2009	2014	2019
Men	341	312	387	399	473	498
Women	60	93	102	88	116	111
Women (%)	15	23	21	18	20	18

Source: Chinyepi (2021).

Table 8.4 Local elections in Botswana (2019)

	Women	Men	Total	Women (%)
Candidates	235	1512	1747	13%
Elected	71	419	490	15
Appointed	40	79	119	34
Total councilors	111	498	609	18

Source: Chinyepi (2021).

countries have taken to increase female representation. One of these is the absence of voluntary party or legislated quotas. One reason for this is the lack of constitutional reform.

Constitutional Reform

Botswana's constitution was written in 1966 and amended in 2016 but it has not undergone a major rewrite like other African countries did after the 1990s. Botswana has a constitutional review process pending, and there is expected to be a strong emphasis on addressing matters concerning gender equality and women's empowerment. However, it has been slower than most African countries to revise these aspects of its constitution. Most African countries changed their constitutions, including autocracies, after the 1990s when they adopted multiparty systems. Botswana was already a democracy and was multiparty, so the impetus to completely revise the constitution was absent.

Botswana's neighbors (Namibia, South Africa, Angola, and Mozambique) were forced to rewrite their constitutions after the end of a major conflict and upheaval that resulted in a new political order and a new set of leaders. Because Botswana did not experience conflict, the urgency to reform the constitution was lessened. This has meant that there were fewer opportunities compared to its neighboring countries for women's rights activists to press for constitutional women's rights reforms.

Although Botswana's constitution has an antidiscrimination clause that mentions sex and refers to people being entitled to fundamental rights and freedoms regardless of sex, it allows for discrimination in matters of "adoption, marriage, divorce, devolution of property upon death and other matters of personal law" in the same clause. Botswana has one of only five constitutions in sub-Saharan Africa that do not incorporate some clause specifically mentioning equality between men and women.

International and Regional Protocols

Unlike most autocracies, Botswana has also been slow to sign protocols or treaties around women's rights. It is one of the only three countries that has not signed the Maputo Protocol on women's rights. Botswana was relatively late in signing the Southern African Development Community's (SADC's) protocol on women's rights in 2015, long after other countries had ratified it. SADC heads of state and government adopted the protocol in 2008, and it came into force in 2013. It is interesting to note that the two countries that had concerns about the SADC protocol were Botswana and Mauritius, two of the most democratic countries in the region. Botswana's foreign minister at the time, Phandu Skelemani, almost signed it in 2008 but backed out at the last minute. Botswana's particular concerns had to do with issues of the age of marriage, the rights of the girl child, and ownership of land (B30.7.16.20). Some parliamentarians were also concerned about inheritance rights, even though Botswana has had equal inheritance since 1970. They were under the erroneous impression that men would not be able to inherit their wife's property if they signed the treaty (B26. 9.9.20).

Similarly, the UN General Assembly adopted the Convention on the Elimination of Discrimination Against Women (CEDAW) in 1979, but Botswana did not ratify it until 1996, long after most independent African countries signed it. Botswana's stance on women's rights in international treaties needs to be located within its broader approach to international human rights instruments. It has also delayed ratifying other human rights treaties. Botswana has taken a cautious approach to all international human rights treaties, including conventions pertaining to disability, child rights, enforced disappearance, migrant workers, abolition of the death penalty, and others, in spite of pressures from activists. The Convention on People with Disabilities got as far as the cabinet but was put on hold because some felt they needed a strategy and funding before they ratified the treaty. Thus, women's rights are not unique in this regard (B34.7.23.20; B14.7.3.20).

Some of the slowness may also be a function of a strong sense of sovereignty. As one activist explained, "They like to make it a point that they own the country, and they make their own laws" as they see fit (B38.8.27.20). Professor of social work Tirelo Modie-Moroka also commented, "It was the mandatory language and the prescriptive language that they were against" (B29.7.15.20).

One lawyer thought that the slowness was due to the need for broad consultation when it came to legal reform and possible resistance from people living in remote areas: "Botswana is a democratic country; one of the key features of democracy is the need for consultation in order for any legal reform to be effected. . . . Sometimes such initiatives are met with a lot of resistance from the grassroots people, and it can really cause a bit of delay . . . This happened when the government introduced the Abolition of Marital Power Act. And that act meant that in order for the husband to engage in any major financial transaction or any major decision that is related to the family, the husband must seek the wife's consent, and the husband no longer has power over the wife, so to speak. That is one of the laws that was met with a lot of resistance, especially by our male counterparts." In the end, the law was passed as a result of pressure from women's organizations (B11.7.30.20).

Political Parties

The concern for how the electorate might respond has informed the conservative stance toward gender equality adopted by most politicians. Interestingly, as the governing BDP party lost vote share, it did not adopt the kinds of strategies involving reserved seats seen in authoritarian countries to maintain their standing relative to other political parties (see chapters 3, 4, 5, and 6 in this volume on Uganda, Zimbabwe, Rwanda, and Mauritania).

The Ruling Party

The former ruling party itself had a history of unity until Ian Khama was elected president in 2009 when the BDP party split into two factions, the A-Team, led by Khama, and the Barata-Phathi. By 2010, the Botswana Movement for Democracy (BMD) was formed. Khama's rule was marked by insecurity as extrajudicial killings increased. As one women's rights activist explained, "I remember the first few years of Ian Khama as president. A lot of people were terrified for their lives because of the killings that happened at the hand of the state. This silenced people" (B3.6.28.20). Inexplicably, a large number of intelligence agencies appeared, including the Directorate of Intelligence and Security, Military Intelligence, the Security Intelligence Services, the Central Intelligence Committee, the Criminal Investigations Department, the Special Branch, the Diamonds and Narcotics Squad, and the Tourism Intelligence Unit (Good 2018). The Mo Ibrahim Foundation noted in 2017 that the government under Ian Khama had become "more dictatorial and less accountable" and that "respect for fundamental human rights is being eroded, while corruption has gone up and the justice system is becoming less effective" ("Mo Ibrahim" 2017).

The BDP had a women's wing, which claimed to be seeking to increase female representation in the political arena, carry out political education, and address issues affecting women and children. However, there has been a lack of will to change the ruling party's constitution to increase female representation, according to activists I interviewed (B30.7.16.20). Moreover, the first-past-the-post electoral system mitigates against female representation. The party itself has not taken steps to create an internal quota the way post-conflict parties as did the South West Africa People's Organization (SWAPO) in Namibia, the ANC in South Africa, and the Frente de Libertação de Moçambique (Mozambique Liberation Front), better known as FRELIMO, in Mozambique.

Presidents who have been from the ruling party have varied in their commitment to women's rights and leadership (see Table 8.5). President Quett Masire made a concerted effort to bring women into politics and help get them elected, whereas President Festus Mogae focused more on women's rights as a development concern (B30.7.16.20; B9.7.6.20). Many feel that the Botswana state is strong enough that if it wanted to sign women's rights treaties and promote women in politics, it could do so, but the hesitance is

Table 8.5 Heads of state in Botswana

Head of State	Years in office
Seretse Khama	1965–1980
Quett Masire	1980–1998
Festus Mogae	1998–2008
Ian Khama	2008–2018
Mokgweetsi Masisi	2018–2024
Duma Boko	2024–present

the result of a lack of political will. As one activist put it, "You really find that it's just natural for political leaders to think, 'No, we [men] deserve the power, we deserve the positions, we've got the right to lead, and the women must just sit and wait. We'll call them when the time's right.' And that time is never going to come, the way I see it" (B38.8.27.20).

Former First Lady Neo Masisi facilitated initiatives to empower women, focusing on the rights of girls and rural women, sexual harassment, and, most of all, gender based violence (GBV) against women, girls, and children more generally. Her husband, the former president from 2018 to 2024, Mokgweetsi Masisi, also made particular reference to gender equality and GBV in his speeches. "I find this is a receptive government. Which is open. But it needs us as citizens, and also the civil society organizations to really push," noted one activist about Masisi's presidency (B14.7.3.20).

Opposition Parties

The political parties in Botswana have done little to promote women's political representation. Although the two opposition parties, the Botswana National Front (BNF) and the Botswana Congress Party (BCP), adopted 30 percent quotas for women candidates in 1999 and the Alliance for Progressives claimed to have a quota, the quotas were not implemented (Global Database of Quotas for Women 2025; Kethusegile-Juru 2002, 8). In 1994, women activists ensured that none of the women's wings of political parties would continue to be headed by spouses of senior politicians (B3.6.28.20).

The opposition parties did not have a woman MP until 2013, when BCP's Habaudi Hubona was elected to Parliament. However, Hubona served for only seven months, losing in the 2014 general elections. Another female opposition member, BNF's Same Bathobakae, was elected into Parliament during the 2014 general elections but died in 2016 (Chinyepi 2021). There have been occasional women in opposition party leadership: Motsei Rapelana headed the BCP for twenty-three years until 2021, and Mpho Pheko is the publicity secretary for the BCP. But women in such positions are few and far between.

During the period of BDP dominance, women found the opposition political parties to be less than welcoming and fraught with internal divisions. Women were treated as decoration, according to activists, as the male contenders fought among themselves. The women's movement had thought it could gain concessions from the opposition parties, but the main opposition block basically disintegrated on the eve of the 1999 elections, giving the ruling party the leeway to get into power in spite of a decline in the actual votes. The women's movement at the time had thought the parties would implement quotas that they had committed to, but with infighting mounting, these hopes faded. The women's wings of the various parties did not call them to account. Botswana's Caucus for Women in Politics was established in 2011 to enable women from all political parties to converge and support each other in their attempts to make their mark in a male-dominated field, but it soon became defunct (B3.6.28.20).

In 2012, the Umbrella for Democratic Change (UDC) was formed by members of the Botswana People's Party and the BMD to unite the opposition for the 2014 elections; in 2017, the BCP joined the coalition, and the BMD left it. The BCP had taken up issues of women's health, education, and affirmative action in politics. But when it joined the UDC, these concerns were dropped. The BCP has a women's league of its own that takes up these concerns, but participating in opposition politics carries its own risk. As one woman opposition leader said, "If you are not part of the ruling party and you participate in politics, you know that your career may be sabotaged. Your employer may be instructed to sack you. I am a new divorcee, so I have two kids that I have to take care of by myself. I still receive messages from my family and calls from my family saying, 'What are you doing in that space? You have young children to raise. What are you going to feed your kids?' It [politics] is still perceived very much as a risky venture" (B25.9.6.20). As of this writing, it remains to be seen what the UDC will do now that it is in power. However, early signs, including appointments to the cabinet and legislative victories, do not bode well for women in politics.

Women's Movement

Alice Kang and I (2018) have shown how women's movements have been critical to the adoption of legislation around gender quotas. Botswana's experience helped underscore the importance of the role of women's movements in pressing for these reforms. In Botswana, there was a period of heightened women's rights activism in the late 1990s, which resulted in numerous women's rights reforms and a temporary increase in women's political representation. However, the movement lost steam by the first decade of the 2000s, resulting in a decline in efforts to increase women's political representation. Subsequently, the movement has become more fragmented and taken new forms and tactics, but it is not as unified as in the 1990s.

Around the time of independence in 1964, the YWCA, Christian Women's Fellowship, the Botswana Council of Women, the Red Cross, and other such religious and welfare organizations were active. Women activists attended UN Conferences in Mexico (1975), Nairobi (1985), and Beijing (1995). The 1995 Fourth World Conference on Women, in Beijing galvanized and helped create new national, subregional, and regional alliances in women's mobilization as in other parts of Africa and the world. Thus, women NGOs first came together nationally in Botswana, forming the NGO Coalition of fifty women's rights organizations. Then, they met with other organizations from the Southern African region to develop an agenda in preparation for an Africa-wide meeting in Dakar, and finally, they attended the meeting in Beijing. The Botswana delegation to Beijing was led by the minister of home affairs and labor, Bahiti Temane, who was very committed to advancing women's rights. The Botswana delegation put the issue of the girl child on the agenda as one of the twelve critical areas of concern in the Platform of Action. It was first adopted by the Southern Africa group and then by the Africa-wide meeting in Dakar. The concerns of the African delegates to Beijing relating to girls ranged from female genital mutilation to early marriage, teenage pregnancy, and the use of girls in agriculture and other forms of labor (B30.7.16.20).

The women's movement was strong by the late 1970s and early 1980s. More radical feminist organizations like Women and Law in Southern Africa research project (WLSA), Women in Law and Development in Africa (WiLDAF), and Emang Basadi came onto the scene (B30.7.16.20). By the 1990s, Emang Basadi was one of the most active organizations. It tackled the discriminatory nature of laws, particularly citizenship, property laws, and marriage laws (see Table 8.6) (B7.7.16.20). The movement also demanded the creation of a women's policy agency, reform of discriminatory laws, and the passage of progressive legislation (Bauer 2011). Even the government itself took the initiative to review all laws because of the influence of the NGOs.

Eventually, the movement took on issues of political empowerment. As a result of the lobbying efforts of women's organizations, after the Beijing conference in 1995, we saw a jump in the percentage of women in Parliament from 10 percent to 18 percent in Botswana. Today, however, there are only pockets of women fighting around different issues, but the broader movement has diminished in strength. The Women's NGO Coalition, which once set the agenda for the movement, no longer exists. The coalition collapse meant there was a lack of coordination in the movement because the movement was no longer speaking with one voice (B30.7.16.20, B38.8.27.20). Because most of the support for NGOs comes from the government, some people felt they could not "bite the hand that feeds them" (B20.8.27.20).

Table 8.6 Women's rights reforms in Botswana (1969–2021)

Legislation	Year	Goal of legislation
Customary Law Act	1969	Aimed to reconcile potential conflicts arising between customary Botswana law and Botswana's common law
Succession Act	1970	Equalized inheritance rights by gender
Employment (Amendment Act) 26	1992	Lifted restrictions on women's night work and ban on women's employment in mining
Universal Pension and Orphan Care Act 1996	1996	Set equal ages for retirement with full pension benefits
Deeds Registry (Amendment) Act 10	1996	Allowed women married in community of property (where assets and debts are jointly owned by the couple) to register immovable property in their names
Penal Code (Amendment Act)	1998	Legislated punishments for gender discrimination, sexual violence, and rape
Affiliation Proceedings Act of 1999,	1999	Provided for the determination of the paternity of an illegitimate child
Public Service (Amendment) Act 14	2000	Set new limitations on employment discrimination and sexual harassment
Marriage (Amendment) Act	2001	Provided new legislation regarding forced and early marriages
Abolition of Marital Power Act 34	2004	Allowed women to be head of household, live in the same way as men, and be employed without permission from their husband. Provided legislation regarding property and inheritance rights.
Marital Power Bill	2008	Set regulations regarding marital relations
Domestic Violence Act	2008	Protected women from domestic and intimate partner violence
Employment (Amendment) Act	2010	Established a minimum pay of half salary for women on maternity leave and prohibited discrimination in the workplace
Section 44 of the Interpretation (Amendment) Act	2010	Set new regulations regarding forced and early marriages
Interpretation (Amendment) Act	2013	Set the legal age of maturity at eighteen, regardless of sex
Legal Aid Act	2013	Gave women better access to justice

Continued

Table 8.6 *Continued*

Legislation	Year	Goal of legislation
Married Persons Property Act	2014	Allowed persons married under customary law to opt for civil law for the administration of their properties
Anti–Human Trafficking Act	2018	Revised the definition of *exploitation*, and increased fines and prison sentences for human trafficking offenses
Amendment to Anti–Human Trafficking Act	2018	Provided new regulations regarding trafficking in persons
Penal Code (Amendment) Act	2018	Introduced stronger penalties for rape and raised the age of consent from sixteen to eighteen
Revision of the Penal Code: Land policy	2020	Allowed women to apply for land and become equal landowners with their husbands
Sexual Offenders Registry Act	2021	Established a sexual offenders registry
Women and Inclusion Act	2021	Promoted women's participation in economic development

Sources: CEDAW Report; Legal Information Institute (2024).

By the twenty-first century, the movement had lost its momentum, in part owing to a drop in donor funding when the United Nations removed Botswana from the least-developed country category (B7.7.16.20; B11.7.30.20; B3.6.28.20; Mokomane 2008). Initially, after the Beijing conference, donors seemed willing to support the women's movement, and they did so vigorously. Scandinavian donors like the Norwegian Agency for Development Cooperation (NORAD) and the Swedish International Development Cooperation Agency (SIDA), the British Council, the US Agency for International Development (USAID), and many other development agencies put money into women's mobilization in the 1980s and 1990s (B35.7.23.20). But by the middle of the first decade of the 2000s, there was a change in the international donor position (B38.8.27.20). The Norwegian, Swedish, and United States donor organizations withdrew because Botswana was deemed a middle-level income country (B14.7.3.20; B20.8.27.20). Even UN Women in Botswana closed in 2020. The diamond-based economy was doing well, and they felt their resources would be better spent in countries that had more significant needs, like Tanzania, Liberia, and Uganda (B30.7.16.20).

The movement also experienced a hemorrhaging of leaders from NGOs to government positions as the government sought to be more inclusive of women (B29.7.15.20; B38.8.27.20; Sebudubudu and Osei-Hwedie 2006). Unity Dow, for example, had been a leader in the women's movement. Then, she took a position as a judge on the High Court and later held several ministerial posts. Even though this movement of women into the government drained the movement, many of these women continued to lobby for changes from within state institutions, as is evident in the steady stream of legislation that continues to be passed (see Table 8.6).

Thus, the women's movement has not gone away but has taken new forms, however it has become more fragmented. The younger generation is seen as more bold but less focused on women's political representation and legislative reform. For this reason, there have been numerous initiatives to focus on mentoring and promoting women leaders, including the Putting Women First Trust, the African Women's Leadership Academy, the African Women Leadership Academy (TAWLA), Letsema Resource Support for Botswana Women in Politics, and the Young Women's Leadership Club at the University of Botswana (Mosime and Dikobe 2021). These initiatives focus on young women becoming activists and building leadership skills (B30.7.16.20). New organizations—such as Kagisano, which did excellent work around GBV, especially during Covid-19 lockdowns—also have continued to emerge.

Young women activists have taken up different issues and are using different tactics that are more direct. As sociologist and activist Elise Alexander said, "They are bolder than we were. They would push the agenda. . . . They say to you straight, 'My body is my body.' In my generation, you couldn't say that. But for them, they decide when they want to have a child. No old woman or no mom should ask them, 'When are you getting married? When are you going to have a child?'" Younger activists engage in a broader range of issues, including LGBTQ issues and other rights-based issues (B9.7.6.20).

In 2018, a petition was submitted to the president against Minister Ngaka of the Ministry of Nationality, Immigration, and Gender Affairs for assaulting his wife in public. The wife also filed a case with the police. The petitioners argued that he was not fit to run a ministry that deals with gender issues. Another young woman was abused by a parliamentarian in northern Botswana, resulting in protests. Younger activists are also more likely to take direct action. A man attacked one young woman because she was wearing a mini skirt on a bus. Another was assaulted in the classroom because somebody said her skirt was too short. Young women demonstrated by saying, "We wear what we want. Nobody's going to tell me what to wear in the public space."

Another older activist confirmed that the tactics of younger activists are "more confrontational" and "more in your face, which is what the older generation doesn't like too much" (B35.7.23.20). The #MeToo movement caught on, and in recent years, there has been pushback in the form of hashtag movements: #IShallNotForget or #WeWearWhatWeWant, and campaigns that say, "We do not accept that older men abuse young girls." These movements were led by both young men and women (B30.7.16.20; B38.8.27.20).

There is also an active Men and Boys for Gender Equality Movement in Botswana. It is based on a strong sentiment that when one talks about GBV and sexual and reproductive health and rights, men need to be involved, educated, and sensitized to the issues involved, according to one activist. Men who are active in this movement want to show that they understand the situation and appreciate the harm done by GBV, but at the same time, the sociocultural environment oppresses them, too. They work against the stigma of reporting domestic and child abuse. It is difficult for men to speak out on many of these issues because of the macho and patriarchal system, according to one women's rights activist (B30.7.16.20).

As women's rights activists became absorbed into government, they continued their activism in these positions. Dr. Margaret Nasha, who was speaker of the National Assembly from 2009 to 2014, was the minister for local government, lands, and housing in the 1990s, and in this position, she strongly advocated for the Abolition of Marital Power Act and helped shepherd it through (B16.7.31.20). Similarly, Sheila Tlou served on the UN Commission on the Status of Women. When she took over as minister of health in 2004, the adult HIV prevalence was at its peak at 24.3 percent nationwide among the adult population (ages ten through forty-nine), according to the UN Programme on HIV/AIDS (UNAIDS), and only 10 percent of the budget had been allocated to health. She told President Mogae, "I'll only be minister if you promise you'll give 15 percent of the budget to health." He told her, "I'm actually giving you 20 percent," which he did. Tlou could not refuse the offer. She made sure that civil society was well funded to mobilize at the community level, allowing them to reduce mother-to-child transmission of HIV and AIDS dramatically. The overall HIV rates also began to drop during her tenure as minister of health.

Thus, the decline in momentum within the women's movement around women's political representation had some impact on women's representation, as did the loss of donor funding for women's NGOs. However, the movement transformed itself as feminists and women's rights activists moved into government positions, where they exerted a different kind of influence. Younger activists took on different issues and changed some of their tactics. Interest in political leadership persisted through a variety of organizations. However, political parties remained key obstacles to the realization of greater political representation of women.

Department of Gender Affairs

Even though "women in power and decision-making positions" (Department of Gender Affairs, Ministry of Nationality) is a stated priority of the Department of Gender Affairs on its webpage, it has not focused as much on women's political leadership as it has on other areas like women's economic empowerment. The department went through a variety of names and ministerial homes over the years. It is presently housed within the Ministry of Nationality, Immigration, and Gender Affairs. The department is responsible for, among other things, reporting on Botswana's progress on CEDAW to the UN Commission on the Status of Women and to SADC on the gender protocol. The Gender Affairs Department also administers a Women's Economic Empowerment Program, which provides seed money to women to start businesses and training in business management, skills development, and technical support.

As mentioned earlier, in the mid-1990s and the first decade of the 2000s, women's rights organizations made a significant effort to push for national policies and the mainstreaming of gender within the national agenda. After the 1995 UN Fourth World Conference on Women, in Beijing, the Ministry of Gender put in place a Women in Development Policy, which was later replaced by a National Policy on Gender and Development in 2015 based on a draft produced by women's organizations and the ministry. They also formulated a National Operation plan adopted in 2018, focusing on promoting women's access to economic, political, social, and educational opportunities and legal protections. The work of the ministry influenced other ministries that sought to mainstream these policies within their own policies and programs. The Ministry of Agriculture was exceptionally energetic and developed its own gender policy within the ministry. Other ministries like investment and trade were much slower (B30.7.16.20).

The Department of Gender Affairs has also been involved in developing a gender component of the national development plan for 2017–2023 and for National Vision 2036. They also helped develop national plans relating to GBV (2014–2020), cervical cancer (2012–2016), poverty eradication (2012), the HIV/AIDS Strategy (2012–2016), inclusive education (2011), child sexual abuse (2010), and other concerns, along with developing key legislation (see Table 8.6).

The government also formed a National Gender Commission in 2022, chaired by Mosadi Seboko, to advise on gender issues, particularly policy development and service delivery. It is developing, for example, a sexual offenders registry, a gender and child protection branch within the Botswana Police Service, and special courts to handle these cases.

Legislative Gains

In sharp contrast to Botswana's sluggishness around women's legislative and subnational representation, Botswana has produced a steady stream of legislation advancing gender equality. The pace of reforms seems to have kept up in spite of the drops in donor funding for women's rights. Equally significant, customary law has undergone alterations because of shifts in statutory law. For instance, customary law no longer tolerates polygyny or male promiscuity, and it has been influenced by the discourse and principles guiding judicial decision-making (Werbner and Werbner 2020).

Thanks to pioneering legislative reforms, Botswana has made significant strides in advancing women's equal rights. One notable example is the 1970

Succession Act, which leveled the playing field by ensuring equal inheritance rights for both male and female surviving spouses. Additionally, the 1992 amendments to the Employment Act removed restrictions on women's ability to work at night and in the mining sector, a key industry in Botswana (see Table 8.6). In 2005, the groundbreaking Abolition of Marital Power Act was enacted, granting women the freedom to choose their place of residence, assume the role of the household head, pursue employment, sign contracts, register businesses, and open bank accounts without requiring their husband's consent. This landmark legislation also conferred equal rights to spouses over immovable property and equal authority in managing marital assets. Further progress was made in 2008 when Botswana introduced the Domestic Violence Act, marking a significant milestone as the country's first piece of legislation aimed at safeguarding women from domestic violence. This achievement is the latest reform recognized by the World Bank's *Women, Business and the Law* report in Botswana's journey toward gender equality.

Given the extent to which the country has adopted other women's rights legislation, it is curious that there has been no effort to introduce legislated quotas. This points to concerns about how the electorate might respond in a country that is a democracy like Botswana. Unlike autocracies, in which leaders can force top-down reforms, this may be harder in a democracy that allows for free political competition. It may also be more challenging in a culturally conservative society to gain acceptance for reforms where lawmakers have to worry about their ability to become re-elected since their constituencies are conservative. As one attorney explained to me, "Here, our MPs, because the elections are constituency-based, I think, in some instances they consider what they think their electorate would think about them if they support a particular bill, for instance" (B16.7.31.20).

Role of the Courts

As a result of these legislative constraints, the courts intervened, particularly when it comes to sensitive cultural issues. As one activist said, they can do so because lawyers "are more exposed to the trends across the continent and across the world, or they're more open to bringing international law comparison to these cases when they're presented in court." They also may be exposed to more trainings and pressure from the women's movement (B22.9.3.20).

The courts have thus played a proactive role in rendering judgments that affect women. Table 8.7 provides some of the key rulings affecting women's status and gender equality. It would have been difficult to pass legislation

Table 8.7 Court rulings on gender equality, Botswana (1992–2019)

Case	Year	Outcome of case
Attorney General v. Unity Dow	1992	The Court of Appeal found that sections of the Citizenship Act discriminated based on gender and violated equal protection and nondiscrimination rights. The law treated children differently depending on whether they were born to citizen mothers or fathers, which was deemed unconstitutional.
Makuto v. State	2000	The Court of Appeal upheld a rape conviction and the penalties associated with it, even when the convicted person was HIV positive at the time of the crime, and considered it a reasonable provision to combat the spread of HIV/AIDS.
Mogodu v. State	2005	The High Court upheld a rape conviction, emphasizing that consent was lacking because of threats and coercion, and discussed procedures for handling criminal trials involving defendants who were minors at the time of the alleged crime but of legal age at the time of trial.
Masusu v. Masusu	2007	The High Court of Botswana at Lobatse ruled in favor of a wife seeking divorce. The court stated that customary law unfairly discriminated against women by faulting them for seeking divorce regardless of their husband's actions. The court ordered the sale of the marital home, with profits going to the wife.
State v. Ketlwaeletswe	2007	The Court of Appeal clarified that sexual intercourse with a girl under twelve years old should be considered rape rather than defilement, in line with common law principles, regardless of consent.
Sekoto v. Director of Public Prosecutions	2007	The court upheld a murder conviction and a twelve-year prison sentence for the appellant, citing the need for stiff sentences to deter domestic violence-related crimes.
State. v. Matlho	2008	The Court of Appeal rejected a challenge to a rape sentence, emphasizing the severity of rape offenses and the need to combat increasing rape rates in Botswana. The appellant argued that the sentence was inhumane, but the court upheld it.
Mmusi v. Ramantele	2013	In a landmark decision, the Court of Appeal upheld the High Court's ruling that Ngwaketse customary law, which prioritized male inheritance of family property, violated women's constitutional right to equality. This case marked the end of patriarchal inheritance practices in Botswana.

Attorney General of Botswana v. Rammoge	2016	The Court of Appeal ruled that the Department of Civil and National Registration's refusal to register the LEGABIBO was unjustifiable and a violation of its members' rights. The court upheld the right of LEGABIBO and other LGBT advocacy groups to promote LGBT rights and advocate for legal reform, dismissing arguments that their objectives went against public morality.
GMJ v. Attorney General of Botswana	2018	The Court of Appeal reversed a High Court decision and allowed a medical negligence claim by a woman who had undergone a procedure resulting in complications. This case clarified legal aspects related to medical negligence and how women can seek legal recourse when their reproductive health rights are violated.
Motshidiemang v. Attorney General	2019	The High Court declared unconstitutional certain sections of Botswana's Penal Code, which criminalized same-sex relations. The court found these sections violated various constitutional rights, including liberty, privacy, and the prohibition of discrimination. The decision modified one section but effectively decriminalized same-sex relations in Botswana.

Source: Legal Information Institute (2024).

about some of the issues addressed in these cases, such as the decriminalization of same-sex relations and women's citizenship rights. One of the first such court challenges was the 1984 Citizenship Act, which denied Botswana's women married to foreign men the ability to transmit their citizenship to their children. The basis for restricting this right to men stemmed from the customary law belief that women were considered minors. It wasn't until Unity Dow brought her case before the High Court in 1991 that the act was overturned, and constitutional provisions regarding citizenship were abolished as a consequence. This marked the first court ruling in Southern Africa that deemed sex discrimination unconstitutional. The government contested the decision, but the Court of Appeals upheld the ruling. Dow built her arguments on the UN CEDAW, to which Botswana only later became a signatory, ratifying it in 1996.

As human rights lawyer Keikantse Phele pointed out, "When you look at the balance of public interest litigation, historically in Botswana, it will give you a highlight on to what judicial activism has done for fundamental human rights in Botswana. And my analysis or observation is that at least every two or three years, civil society in Botswana takes up a matter to the courts as a test matter. And it's almost always successful. So I think [regarding] our courts, the high courts in Botswana, despite our laws being discriminatory or being unequal to some groups of people, the judiciary has come to rescue the interpretation of the law to be more inclusive, to also shine the light on what fundamental human rights are and what they mean to Botswana despite many of them not being in the constitution" (B27.10.27.20).

In another 2016 ruling, the court upheld the right of Lesbians, Gays, and Bisexuals of Botswana (LEGABIBO) and other LGBTQ advocacy groups to promote LGBTQ rights and advocate for legal reform. This was a critical ruling given the relatively large number of organizations that work on LGBTQ rights in Botswana, including Bonela, the Ditshwanelo Center for Human Rights, the Rainbow Identity Association, Men for Gender Justice, the Pal Makambo Center, Friends of Diversity, and Southern Africa Fighting AIDS. The LGBTQ community did a lot to sensitize people, holding meetings with traditional leaders, chiefs, and church leaders who could influence ordinary citizens.

As a member of the LGBTQ community explained that regarding "the LGBT ruling, I would really say that we were fortunate as a movement to have been met with such a progressive panel of judges because the judgment, in and of itself, is an incredible work of art. Their understanding of human rights, the way that they were able to understand the implication of criminalizing consensual, same-sex sexual conduct was very telling of their interaction with society. Yeah. I think it just indicated a level of progress as a society" (B31.7.17.20). Part of what may have also motivated them was the high level of HIV/AIDS in Botswana and the vulnerability of the LGBTQ community to contracting HIV/AIDS. Interestingly, the LGBTQ activists in Botswana actively network with activists in South Africa, Zimbabwe, Kenya, and other parts of Africa and beyond and share strategies. The parallels in strategies suggest that they have learned from the experiences of others and are often operating from the same playbook.

It is possible that concerns about the electorate may be misplaced, especially when one considers public opinion. As many as 86.1 percent believe that women should have the same chance of being elected to political office as men, according to the Afrobarometer survey (2023). This is higher than the average for Africa (75.8 percent) or even neighboring Namibia, which has relatively high rates of women's political representation. However, about 43.2 percent felt that if a woman in their community ran for office, she would be criticized, called names, or harassed by others in the community, and 39.5 percent felt she would face family problems. As many as 79.3 percent think that the government should do more to promote gender equality. Almost 59 percent felt that GBV was the most critical gender issue, with slightly more men than women identifying this as a major problem. A significantly smaller percentage of people emphasized as a major problem the absence of women in influential government roles (14 percent), disparities in workplace opportunities or pay (13 percent), inequitable property rights (6 percent), and unequal educational access as their top concerns.

Conclusion

Botswana trails other African countries in female legislative representation at the national and subnational levels. However, it has made significant gains in other areas of gender equality and is a global leader in lessening the gender gap in education, health, and economic empowerment. It has also passed considerable legislation to advance gender equality.

The country has been slow to sign onto major international and regional treaties that might prompt it to adopt quotas to increase female representation. Unlike most African countries, as of this writing, it has not rewritten its 1966 Constitution, which would have been another opportunity for women's rights reform. It did not rewrite its constitution when most other African countries did, as they moved from one-party rule to multiparty rule because it already had a multiparty system. Additionally, Botswana thankfully has not fallen into a major conflict, but this has also eliminated the necessity for constitutional overhauls seen in postconflict nations. Neither the ruling party nor the opposition parties have made significant efforts to promote women as leaders. Moreover, the women's movement waned in the first decade of the 2000s after losing donor support when the United Nations upgraded the country's ranking from a least-developed country to a middle-income country.

Botswana has consistently advanced gender equality through legislative reforms in inheritance, employment, domestic violence, and more. It is possible that it has not adopted gender quotas because, as a democracy, its leaders are sensitive to perceived electoral consequences. Unlike in authoritarian countries, in democracies it is harder to implement top-down reforms without consequences. Nevertheless, the courts in Botswana have positively affected gender equality with landmark rulings, including decisions regarding the rights of LGBT advocacy groups and the decriminalization of same-sex relations. However, they are not in a position to rule on gender equality in political representation. Hence, this one area of gender equality lags in spite of major gains in almost every other domain.

9

The Difference Democracy Makes

The Case of Namibia

Namibia, previously known as Southwest Africa, was a German colony from 1884 to 1915, after which it was administered by South Africa from 1920 until independence in 1990. It gained independence from South Africa after a protracted war of liberation. Unlike in many of its neighboring autocratic countries, in Namibia elections are regarded as free and fair. There have been no politically motivated killings tied to the ruling party since independence, and there is no repression of the opposition. Journalists and civil society operate freely. The women's movement has been able to use the political space available and has made many important gains. Namibia is also a country that has advanced women politicians at all levels and is a leader in women's rights not just in Africa but globally, ranking first in Africa for its overall small gender gap and eighth globally (Table 9.1). In 2025 it elected a woman president.

Nevertheless, the country is a democracy ruled by a dominant party that has remained in power since independence in 1990. SWAPO, the ruling party, is controlled by the same faction of elders who have dominated SWAPO since the early 1960s and who have a shared history of exile (Melber et al. 2017). Thus, Namibia is a democracy, but it also embodies many of the features of an entrenched dominant one-party system: A ruling party attempts to control

Table 9.1 Global Gender Gap Index Ranking, Namibia (2024)

	Political empowerment	Health	Education	Economic empowerment	Overall
Sub-Saharan Africa Ranking	3/35	1/35	1/35	8/35	1/35
Global ranking	21/146	1/146	1/146	17/146	8/146

Source: World Economic Forum (2024).

Why African Autocracies Promote Women as Leaders. Aili Mari Tripp, Oxford University Press. © Oxford University Press (2025). DOI: 10.1093/9780197829004.003.0010

the party women and use the women's rights agenda to build support and legitimacy. At the same time, the party is subject to resistance from within and from the opposition parties while simultaneously attempting to be responsive to an active women's movement. The result is party policies that reflect a range of interests. This is evident in the evolution of Namibia's 50/50 policy on gender equality in political leadership.

This chapter looks at three sources of Namibia's gender policies: the country's postconflict legacy, the women's movement, and the ruling party's commitment to gender equality. It then examines the evolution of the 50/50 policy and looks at Namibia's gender policy as a product of Namibia's democratic orientation, as imperfect as it might be. The chapter describes how the policy originated in the women's movement and was picked up eventually by the ruling party and government. It shows the ways in which the government is responsive to civil society, even if sometimes in limited ways. The chapter discusses the hesitance of some members of SWAPO to adopt the 50/50 policy, given that the country is shaped by a conservative culture that influences and constrains the ruling party leadership.

The chapter explains how, unlike the ruling parties in the autocracies in this book and much like Botswana's former ruling party, SWAPO did not seek to increase its vote share through the adoption of reserved seats, even when it lost vote share by 15 percent in 2020. It lost another 12 percent of vote share in 2024. Unlike the ruling party in Uganda, SWAPO has not suppressed women in the opposition parties and has even encouraged other parties to increase women's leadership. Parliamentarians and government officials have collaborated with women's organizations, although they have not been responsive on all issues. Civil society, nevertheless, enjoys freedom of speech and organization. All of these factors generally speak to some of the key differences between autocracies and democracies, but they also hint at some of the less democratic tendencies within SWAPO.

For this chapter, I interviewed Namibian activists in the women's and LGBTQ movement, SWAPO Women's League leaders, MPs, regional councilors, academics, journalists, and representatives of UN Women in Namibia.

Namibia's Postconflict Legacies

A comparison between Namibia and Botswana, another democracy (discussed in Chapter 8), reveals a key difference between the two countries that has influenced Namibia's promotion of women leaders—namely, its postconflict legacy. In contrast to Namibia, Botswana has among the lowest levels of representation for women in the world. Like most postconflict countries, Namibia has more women in politics as a result of a major turnover in the political elite and political order at independence, which resulted in the rewriting of the constitution and other legal and electoral reforms.

Unlike Botswana, Namibia has achieved near parity between the genders in Parliament through internal party quotas, reflecting the legacy of a left-leaning liberation movement and postconflict orientation of SWAPO's internal affirmative action policies. Many left-leaning liberation movements in countries that became independent (e.g., Mozambique, Angola, South Africa) have historically had higher rates of representation. The dramatic change in political leadership and the writing of new constitutions opened up new possibilities for women's rights activists to assert their demands.

Women were active participants in the liberation movement, with many joining SWAPO and taking up arms alongside men. Their contributions were crucial to the independence movement's success, laying the groundwork for women's participation in postindependence politics. Even at the time of the war, women lobbied hard for women's empowerment inside SWAPO (Bauer 2004; Soiri 1996).

The relationship between the autonomous women's movement and SWAPO got off to a rocky start in the years leading up to independence when, in 1985, the Namibian Women's Voice (NWV) was formed. The NWV championed a wave of women's community activism that focused on grassroots women's everyday needs such as for child care and income. The SWAPO Women's Council, the Women's Wing of SWAPO that had been established in exile in Tanzania in 1970, only got off the ground in 1980. It felt threatened by the NWV and sought to shut it down (Becker 2019). As one activist explained to me, "SWAPO called us to Lusaka and asked that the Namibian Women's Voice be closed. SWAPO said we were 'watering down the struggle.' I think they were just fearful of the strong women that were coming up then. That closure really had quite a lot of impact on the women. With that closure, strategically we went to open individual organizations. So we established *Sister Namibia* in 1989 as a magazine" (N1.9.29.20).

Meanwhile, the Women's Wing of SWAPO, the Women's Council, was reduced to an organization that catered party events. One former member of SWAPO described how she resented being called at 4 a.m. to sing happy birthday to the president in the early 1990s and mentioned that these activities persist to this day. "They got stuck in the old model of party wings in Africa," she lamented (N1.9.29.20).

Founding President Sam Nujoma tried to push for higher levels of representation of women over the years but was foiled in numerous efforts, as many male ministers felt they would lose out in the process (Mongudhi 2013). Nujoma stated that granting women political positions was a recognition of their major contributions during the guerrilla war against South African domination. He continued to press for women leaders and for a woman president (Tjitemisa 2022), but he did not always have the support of the entire party on this issue. In a country like Namibia, where women make up 53 percent of the voters, many, like Nujoma, believed that SWAPO could ill afford to ignore women ("Namibia Narrowly Misses" 2020).

Transition to Independence

After independence, President Nujoma created a women's desk in his office, which evolved into the Department of Women Affairs. In 2000, it became the Ministry of Women Affairs and Child Welfare, which brought with it a cabinet-level appointment. In 2005, the ministry was renamed the Ministry of Equality, Poverty Eradication, and Social Welfare. It focuses on gender equality and human rights, issues of socioeconomic development, and the integration of women and other marginalized communities. It coordinates with stakeholders and takes up issues like sexual violence, GBV, and child protection.

The 1990 Constitution of the newly independent Namibia made it possible to pass laws to make sure women have equal chances to be involved in all parts of life in Namibia, especially by ensuring that they get paid the same as men for the same work. One of the first legislative changes to promote gender equality in representation after independence came in 1992 with the Local Authorities Act, which mandated that political parties include a specified minimum quota of women on their candidate rosters. This act was a precursor to many legal changes regarding women's representation (Frank 2004; LeBeau 2005). In 1997, the act was amended to require all political party candidate lists in municipal, village, and town council elections to include a minimum of two females if the council has ten or fewer members and at least three females if the council has eleven or more members (see Table 9.2).

As a result of the Local Authorities Act, the 1998 subnational elections saw women take up 43 percent of the elected council positions, a significant stride toward equal representation that can be largely attributed to the affirmative action measures stipulated by the Local Authorities Act. The women's movement pressed political parties to alternate men and women "zebra style" on their candidate lists in order to fully obtain gender balance at the local level (Namibia Women's Manifesto Network 2003). Thanks to this rule, the number of women in local council positions went up to 37 percent

Table 9.2 Gender-related legislation in Namibia

Legislation	Year	Description
Local Authorities Act	1992	Female party candidates in elections for municipal, village or town councils.
Abortion and Sterilization Act	1975	Abortion and reproductive health rights and forced sterilization
Combating of Immoral Practices Act	1980	Sexual violence, rape, and trafficking in persons
Constitution of the Republic of Namibia	1990	Divorce and dissolution of marriage, employment discrimination, forced and early marriage, and gender discrimination
Social Security Act	1994	Employment discrimination
Cooperatives Act	1996	Employment discrimination
Married Persons Equality Act	1996	Divorce and dissolution of marriage, forced and early marriage, gender discrimination, harmful traditional practices, property, and inheritance rights
Affirmative Action (Employment) Act	1998	Affirmative action to address employment discrimination.
Combating Rape Act	2000	Harmful traditional practices, sexual violence, rape, statutory rape, and defilement
Communal Land Reform Act	2002	Harmful traditional practices, property, and inheritance rights.
Maintenance Act	2003	Divorce and dissolution of marriage
Combating Domestic Violence Act	2003	Domestic and intimate partner violence
Children's Status Act	2006	Property and inheritance rights for children born to married couples
Labour Act	2007	Employment discrimination and sexual harassment.
Combating of Trafficking in Persons Act	2018	Aims to implement the UN Protocol on human trafficking, criminalize trafficking and related offenses, protect trafficking victims, and establish coordinated administration of the Act

Source: Legal Information Institute (2024).

after the 1992 elections. Many other legislative gains followed, especially as the women's movement picked up momentum (see Table 9.2). Eventually, a national gender policy was approved in 1997, which sought to ensure women's greater participation in power sharing and decision-making in all positions, which was one of the ten priority areas set by the government.

Namibia adopted all the key international and regional treaties relating to women without delay after independence. It ratified CEDAW in 1992 without any reservations. Namibia also signed the Maputo Protocol on women's rights in 2003 and ratified it a year later. The protocol went into effect in 2005. In 2008, Namibia signed the SADC Protocol on Gender and Development, and other SADC states signed the protocol.

These policies have been bolstered by the fact that public opinion is largely favorable to women in politics. Most Namibians (78 percent) in 2012–2013 supported women having the same chance of being elected to political office as men. This is considerably higher than the 67 percent who agreed with this statement in 2005–2006. Not surprisingly, women were much more positive than men about women's rights, with 82.3 percent of females believing that women should have the same chances as men to run for office, while 73.5 percent of men concurred. However, only 34.4 percent of respondents felt that women who ran for office had equal standing with men, while 46.1 percent felt that women who ran for office faced criticism or harassment, and 39.8 percent felt they faced problems with their families. In other areas, people's own attitudes toward gender equality were much more positive: 83.8 percent agreed that women should have equal rights to land, 75.3 percent agreed that they have an equal chance to own or inherit land, and 73.9 percent felt women had an equal chance of getting a job.

Women's Movement Influences on the 50/50 Policy

A thriving women's movement emerged in Namibia in the late 1990s and early twenty-first century. The coalitions were very diverse and dynamic. Women's rights activists worked within broader civil society, which included high-ranking female politicians and civil servants (Becker 2019). Namibia had been a darling of the donor community, and some considered the United Nations to be its second government.

The women's movement emerged around the need to pass woman-friendly legislation. As Liz Frank (N5.10.20.20) explained, "The Gender Research Advocacy program at the Legal Assistance Centre would present draft bills around combating rape and domestic violence to Parliament. And then when we could see nothing was happening in Parliament, the way we were then organized was through a civil society network called the Namibian NGO Forum, NANGOF. Sister Namibia led many of the efforts of the women's movement within NANGOF." Being involved in this broader civil society umbrella allowed women's rights activists to mobilize all of civil society around antirape legislation and other concerns. The Women's Leadership Centre started in 2004 and included new foci, including work with indigenous women for their rights. They also took up the rights of lesbian women (N4.10.21.20).

The women's movement in Namibia has been a major force in bringing about gender-related reforms, of which the 50/50 policy was just one. Civil society operates freely in Namibia, and this has facilitated the changes we have seen. The women's movement has been instrumental in helping get key legislation passed affecting women in Namibia, like the Maintenance Act (2003), the Children's Status Act (2006), the Married Persons Equality Act (1996), the Combating Domestic Violence Act (2003), and the Labour Act (2007), which provided maternity leave (see Table 9.2). It has also helped influence the judiciary, which, like the judiciary in Botswana, has taken up numerous cases to advance women's rights (see Table 9.3). The relationship between the women's movement and the state and ruling party has evolved over time.

Namibia's state and economic capacities are similar to those of Botswana. Like Botswana, Namibia has a relatively high GDP per capita of $5,750 compared to Africa's overall $1,900 GDP per capita. Namibia derives most of its revenue from mining, fishing, tourism, and agriculture. Namibia receives more foreign aid ($127 per capita in 2022) than the $49 per capita average rate for sub-Saharan Africa and $34 for Botswana.[1] The World Bank reclassified

Table 9.3 Gender-related court rulings in Namibia

Case	Year	Description
S. v. Katamba Supreme Court of Namibia	1999	Sexual violence, rape, statutory rape, or defilement
Chairperson of the Immigration Selection Board v. E. F. and Another Supreme Court of Namibia	2001	Gender discrimination, LGBTIQ
State v. Vries Supreme Court of Namibia	2001	Sexual violence, rape, statutory rape, or defilement
State v. LS High Court of Namibia	2006	Domestic and intimate partner violence
State v. VU High Court of Namibia	2007	Domestic and intimate partner violence, sexual violence, and rape
State v. G. I. High Court of Namibia	2007	Abortion and reproductive health rights
State v. Nkasi High Court of Namibia	2010	Domestic and intimate partner violence, female infanticide, and feticide
F. N. v. SM High Court of Namibia	2012	Divorce and dissolution of marriage, and domestic and intimate partner violence

Continued

[1] https://data.worldbank.org/indicator/DT.ODA.ODAT.PC.ZS?locations=ZG.

Table 9.3 *Continued*

Case	Year	Description
State v. Naruseb High Court of Namibia	2012	Domestic and intimate partner violence, sexual violence, rape, statutory rape, or defilement
State v. Britz High Court	2013	Domestic and intimate partner violence
State v. Waterboer High Court	2013	Domestic and intimate partner violence
Kamaze v. State High Court	2013	Statutory rape or defilement
S. v. Abraham Alfeus High Court of Namibia. Main Division, Windhoek	2013	Domestic and intimate partner violence, femicide, GBV in general
Life Office of Namibia Ltd. (NamLife) v. Amakali Labour Court of Namibia	2014	Employment discrimination, gender discrimination, sexual harassment
Government of the Republic of Namibia v. L. M. and Others Supreme Court of Namibia	2014	Forced sterilization
Paschke v. Frans Supreme Court of Namibia	2015	Gender discrimination, and property and inheritance rights
E. S. v. AC Supreme Court of Namibia	2015	Gender discrimination
S. v. S High Court of Namibia	2015	Divorce and dissolution of marriage, and domestic and intimate partner violence
State v. Nghidini High Court of Namibia	2015	Domestic and intimate partner violence, statutory rape, or defilement
Monomono v. State High Court of Namibia	2017	Sexual violence and rape, statutory rape, or defilement
State v. Dausab High Court of Namibia	2018	Domestic and intimate partner violence, femicide
Gawaxab v. State High Court of Namibia	2018	Femicide, GBV in general, sexual harassment
State v. Swartz High Court of Namibia	2018	Domestic and intimate partner violence, female infanticide, feticide, and femicide
H. D. v. State Supreme Court of Namibia	2018	Statutory rape or defilement
State v. Iipinge High Court of Namibia	2018	Domestic and intimate partner violence

Source: Legal Information Institute (2024).

Namibia as an upper-middle-income country in 2008, and much funding subsequently dried up. As a result, civil society weakened (N8.10.4.20). The leaders ran out of steam as it became harder to get people to volunteer.

The 50/50 policy had its origins in a 1999 workshop, in which a feminist organization, Sister Namibia, highlighted the need for gender parity in every elected governmental role. During this event, women from various sectors—including from government and from NGOs representing various political views—empowered Sister Namibia to spearhead the creation of the Namibian Women's Manifesto. This manifesto would represent a unified stance on gender issues and advocate for a zebra-style approach to candidate lists, promoting equal representation for the National Assembly elections scheduled for the year's end. They formed a Namibian Women's Manifesto Network. Over a six-year period leading up to the 2004 elections, Sister Namibia engaged the Legal Assistance Centre to survey global quota systems and crafted the 50/50 Bill, which outlined necessary revisions to Namibian electoral legislation. They convened women from across the nation's towns and villages to exchange insights, deepen their understanding of women's human rights as enshrined in both national and international frameworks, and cultivate leadership abilities for hosting workshops and championing advocacy within their localities (IKhaxas and Frank 2014).

SWAPO resisted the manifesto initially because it advocated against discrimination based on sexual orientation. Throughout this period, the Namibian Women's Manifesto Network engaged with thousands of women via workshops at the community level. The members made concerted efforts to visit educational institutions, places of worship, local and traditional governing bodies, political organizations, and nongovernmental groups in their communities, disseminating campaign materials and advocating for the 50/50 gender representation message. The 50/50 campaign created a unifying platform whereby women transcended barriers of race, ethnicity, political leanings, class, and sexual orientation to assert their civic rights to free opinion, speech, and assembly and advocated for an inclusive electoral system that would enhance women's participation (IKhaxas and Frank 2014).

The Namibian Women's Manifesto Network launched the "50/50—Women and Men in Government—Get the Balance Right!" campaign after the 1999 National Assembly elections, which had done little to change the gender balance in Parliament. Equipped with posters, a brochure, and a petition drive, activists advocated for legislative reforms to ensure that women hold 50 percent of the elected offices across all tiers of government: national, regional, and local. Garnering over 2,500 signatures in a brief span, they delivered these endorsements to the speaker of the National Assembly following a protest march to the Parliament at the year's close. They were able to gain support from the Ministry of Women Affairs and Child Welfare. Its deputy minister, Marlene Mungunda, highlighted how the campaign aligned with government policy and international development goals in her public statements (Frank 2001).

In 2001, the Namibian Women's Manifesto Network took significant strides to advance the 50/50 campaign by commissioning research on international gender balance initiatives and crafting options for Namibia's electoral laws. These proposals were discussed nationwide, receiving an overwhelmingly positive reception. As a result, the network asked Dianne Hubbard from the Legal Assistance Centre to draft a 50/50 Bill to amend electoral laws for better gender representation at all levels of government (National Assembly, National Council, regional councils, and local authority councils). The goal was to require that all future elections for local authority councils be held on a party-list system with gender-balanced party lists and to amend the Regional Councils Act 1992, the Local Authorities Act 1992, and the Electoral Act 1992 to bring them in line with the 50/50 policy. They created a pamphlet detailing their demands, available in six local languages, which was endorsed by thirty-four NGOs (Frank 2001). As a result of their efforts, the concept of equal gender representation in politics began to gain traction in public discourse.

Sister Namibia worked together on the 50/50 campaign with SWAPO and opposition party women and with other groups like Women Action for Development as well as religious leaders, trade union women, and civil society women. SWAPO initially adopted the 50/50 policy at its congress in 2002 but subsequently waffled on it, adopting resolution after resolution endorsing the policy at various party congresses. When a clause on lesbians was added to a pledge to respect the human rights of all women, SWAPO and the SWAPO-affiliated trade unions pulled out of the 50/50 civil society campaign (N5.10.20.20). SWAPO actively tried to get the lesbian leaders—in particular, Elizabeth IKhaxas and Liz Frank, who were leaders of Sister Namibia—cut out of the campaign. Sister Namibia continued the 50/50 campaign and ran successful trainings in rural areas.

Later, when Namibia was considering signing the SADC Protocol on Gender and Development, SWAPO jumped back on the 50/50 bandwagon and eventually adopted the 50/50 zebra system of alternating men and women on party lists as a party initiative. There was heated debate around this. SWAPO also committed to a zebra system, so that if a minister is a man, the deputy minister will be a woman, and vice versa. The roles would be switched in successive elections (IKhaxas and Frank 2014).

In 2013, SWAPO amended its constitution to require parity in all its leadership positions at section, branch, district, regional, and national levels (Amupanda and Thomas 2019). This policy committed SWAPO to filling half the seats in Parliament with women. However, no official legislated quota was adopted at the national level, even though the topic has come up from time to time, particularly around the time that they were debating the SADC Gender Protocol (Clayton 2014).

The 50/50 policy resulted in heated debates within SWAPO, as some members and leaders pushed back against the policy, citing concerns of meritocracy, fairness, and equal competition (Amupanda and Thomas 2019; "Plans to Expand" 2014). Some claimed that it would lead to reverse discrimination. The decision initially did not have the backing of portions of SWAPO's eighty-three-member central committee, who felt they might be excluded by this policy that would effectively end male domination of the party and the country. Even the ruling Tanga group (leaders who had been exiled to Tanzania and formed the initial leadership of SWAPO) felt insecure. Efforts to reverse the decision failed as former President Hifikepunye Pohamba insisted on staying the course. Some commentators suggested that this policy was a ploy to maintain and centralize SWAPO control (Melber et al. 2017; N4.10.21.20; N9.11.6.20).

The policy was adopted by the Parliament in 2014, stipulating that there should be 50/50 gender representation in all party and governmental structures, including that of the National Assembly elections. The policy received pushback from some of the opposition parliamentarians. One Democratic Turnhalle Alliance (DTA) MP felt it was a plot to allow women to dominate men, that it was undemocratic because it was not based on merit, and that it would discriminate against men. Some in the opposition had demanded a nationwide consultation on the matter. They saw it as a mechanism to strengthen an executive who already wielded too much power. The president already possessed exclusive authority to nominate or remove cabinet members and all leaders of security agencies, including the police, military, and intelligence services. The president appointed the governors of the thirteen regions and the vice president (Melber et al. 2017).

SWAPO stalwarts responded by saying that the policy was in line with the constitution and international conventions Namibia had already signed, calling for the equal treatment and emancipation of women. In 2014, the legislative elections increased the number of seats in Parliament from 72 to 104, including presidential appointees, and this appeased some of the male opponents of the 50/50 policy (N4.10.21.20). One could argue that these debates around the quota are signs of pockets of resistance to women's representation, but they could also be seen as a sign of democracy in that they reflect healthy, open debate within the Parliament and SWAPO.

International and Regional Influences on the Adoption of the 50/50 Policy

Another influence on pro–women's rights reform measures, such as the 50/50 policy, included international and regional pressures. As one activist explained, "We were one of the last African nations to achieve our independence, and so we were like the United Nations' baby for ten years. I think our international image is very important to our government, how we look to the rest of the world" (N8.10.4.20). Another activist observed, "The Namibian government wants to be seen as a progressive country that is upholding human rights" (N4.10.21.20). One activist similarly noted, "I think part of it is to look good to the rest of the world. Part of it is a real political commitment by the leadership" (N3.9.30.20).

Some politicians were reluctant to implement the 50/50 policy until they realized that they only had a few years left before the SADC Gender Protocol and the national gender policy lapsed. This spurred them to take action and formalize the policy (N10.11.5.20). As a result of the adoption of the 50/50 policy, in 2018, the late President Hage Geingob won an award from the Gender Is My Agenda Campaign Network (GIMAC), which is an organization of fifty-five Africa-based national and international civil society organizations that monitor and lobby for gender equality in Africa. The award recognizes Namibia's efforts to create a standard structure for promoting and protecting women's rights. The award was established by the Femmes Africa Solidarité (FAS) and its Panafrican Center for Gender, Peace, and Development together with GIMAC. Namibia has won similar accolades from the World Health Organization, international NGOs like the MenEngage Africa Alliance, and other world leaders like former President Uhuru Kenyatta in Kenya ("Kenyatta Praises" 2019; "Nam Praised" 2014; United Nations 2022).

While Namibia has garnered international recognition for its efforts, women's rights activists are quick to point out that the woman-friendly policies in Namibia have largely been driven by the women's movement, by key women actors in positions of authority, by the desire for women's votes, and by the political commitment of the country's leadership of the country. As a women's rights activist commented, "I think somehow the party has realized that . . . for inclusive democracy, you need to have representation of both women and youth in leadership positions" (N10.11.5.20). The 50/50 policy is seen as a bold statement, and many of the steps taken by the government reflect this effort. There are women in the government who are making a difference. As one bureaucrat explained, "I do think that women have a place in Namibia. It's not wonderful. It's not perfect. But there are very, very strong women in certain sectors who push the women's agenda on different platforms. We are not those types who keep quiet. We recognize the problem, and we talk about it. We talk about patriarchy and how harmful it is" (N3.9.30.20).

Impact of the 50/50 Policy on Legislature

As a result of SWAPO's internal party quota, the percentage of women in the National Assembly increased from 6.9 percent in 1989 to 50 percent in 2024. The deputy speaker of the National Assembly is a woman (the Honorable Professor Loide Kasingo). Women head up half the parliamentary committees, and three of the parliamentary standing committees are chaired by women.

As it became more entrenched, SWAPO's legislative vote share in the lower house increased from 56.9 percent in 1990 to 80.1 percent in 2014. However, it dropped to 68.3 percent in the 2019 elections, when SWAPO garnered sixty-three seats in Parliament (with eight appointed members), down from seventy-seven seats in the 2014 elections. Like the ruling parties in Botswana and other democracies, and unlike the ruling parties in many authoritarian countries, SWAPO did not introduce reserved seats to deal with the drop in vote share (Figure 9.1).

In the upper house (the National Council), the numbers of women are less impressive, as women hold 14.3 percent of the seats. After 2015, a woman, Margaret Mensah-Williams, served as the speaker of the National Council

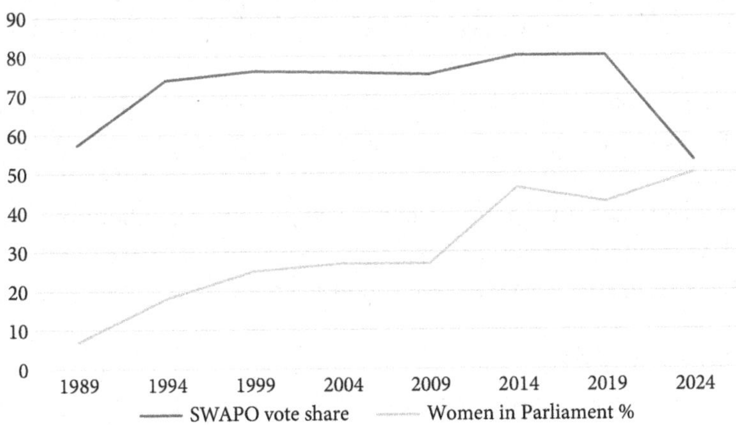

Figure 9.1 SWAPO vote share and women in parliament (1990–2024)

Sources: IPU 2024; Electoral Commission of Namibia 2025.

until her appointment as ambassador to the United States in 2019. In the National Council, there was an increase of women-held seats after the 2004 elections from 7.7 percent to 26.9 percent, but then there was a drop in the 2020 elections to 14.3 percent. Unlike the National Assembly, which is elected by a party-list proportional representation system, the National Council is indirectly elected by the fourteen regional councils (with three members from each council).

Other parties besides SWAPO have fielded women candidates in the spirit of the 2014 parity policy. This departs from the experience of a country like Uganda, which has a reserved seat system and has made it very difficult for women in the opposition to run for office. Unlike the case of Rwanda, where the ruling party targeted opposition women who ran for president, SWAPO encouraged opposition women to run.

Esther Utijua Muinjangue was the first woman to run for president in the 2019 presidential elections. She was also the first woman to head a political party, the National Unity Democratic Organisation (NUDO), which is associated with the Ovaherero ethnic group. Among the SWAPO leaders who came out to congratulate her on being elected to this leadership position was the former president's wife, Monica Geingos, who called it a "milestone." Other SWAPO leaders like MP Pendukeni Ivula-Ithana and MP Doreen Sioka, who is the minister of gender equality and child welfare, congratulated her, as did Elma Dienda, MP of the official opposition, the Popular Movement for Democracy (Amupanda and Marenga 2019).

With the adoption of the 50/50 policy in 2013, SWAPO won the lion's share of seats for women in the 2014 parliamentary elections for the lower chamber of the Sixth National Assembly with thirty-nine out of seventy-one seats, while the DTA had two women and the Republican Party had one. In the Fifth Parliament, there was only one opposition female parliamentarian from the Rally for Democracy and Progress (RDP). However, by 2023, women from other parties were represented to a greater degree as a result of the policy (Table 9.4).

Each of the top five political party lists in the 2019 Namibia elections fielded, on average, 44 percent women candidates. Each party's percentage of women on its candidate list is as follows:

SWAPO: 51 percent
Popular Democratic Movement (PDM): 41 percent
National Unity Democratic Organisation (NUDO): 43 percent
Rally for Democracy and Progress (RDP): 39 percent
All People's Party (APP): 46 percent

Table 9.4 Women representatives in the Namibian National Assembly (2023)

Party	Number of women MPs	Total number of MPs	Women MPs (%)
SWAPO	33	67	49
Popular Democratic Movement (PDM)	7	21	33
Republican Party	2	3	66
All Peoples Party	1	3	33
Landless Peoples Movement	1	4	25
Rally for Democracy and Progress (RDP)	0	2	0
National Unity Democratic Organisation (NUDO)	0	2	0
United Democratic Front of Namibia (UDF)	0	2	0
Namibia Economic Freedom Fighter (NEFF)	0	2	0
Christian Democratic Movement (CDV)	0	1	0
South West African National Union (SWANU)	0	1	0
Appointed by president (nonvoting members)	5	8	63
Total voting members	44	96	45.8

Source: Namibia National Assembly (2024).

Three (PDM, NUDO, APP) of the top five political parties have 20 percent women in top party leadership positions, while SWAPO has the highest at 60 percent, and RDP has 40 percent.

Beyond Descriptive Representation

Because of the enormous gains made by Namibia in advancing women's descriptive representation, some have raised questions about the performance of the women MPs and their commitment to gender equality. Between

2015 and 2018, out of sixty motions, one-quarter (fifteen) were introduced by female parliamentarians, and the majority of them (ten) were introduced by opposition parliamentarians and only five by female SWAPO parliamentarians. Five motions were related to gender equality, and SWAPO female parliamentarians introduced none of these, while opposition parliamentarians introduced three motions. A similar pattern is found in parliamentary questions. In 2017, when women held 45 percent of the parliamentary seats and 49 percent of SWAPO parliamentarians were women, women asked only one-quarter (24 percent) of the questions, and none of SWAPO's backbenchers asked any questions. Only 3 out of 159 questions dealt with gender equality. In a study of parliamentary interventions in the Fourth National Assembly in the Hansard, Amanda Clayton (2014) found that, on average, female participants were less involved in all types of parliamentary debates than their male colleagues, a trend that appeared to be particularly pronounced among female members of the ruling SWAPO Party.

A former MP and chief of the ≠Nūkhoen clan of the Damara people, who was a founding member of the Congress of Democrats Party in 1999, Rosa Namises, confirmed the muted support that SWAPO female MPs give to gender equality issues: "You find that always because they are put into the positions of power, it is dominated mainly by the male. When I was in Parliament, the females in Parliament were very afraid to speak. They were not able to raise their voices, they would send me notes to say, can you speak on this point, can you speak on that point?" (N1.9.29.20). Another activist suggested that there was an element of self-censorship: "If you are a woman from SWAPO, you cannot really just speak up, and speak your mind about whatever you want to say" (N4.10.21.20).

There are a number of explanations for these patterns. SWAPO women may find themselves constrained by party discipline in a party that has a very centralized hierarchical structure. But as one university scholar pointed out, "There's no spontaneous raising of issues around gender unless it's been sort of OK'd by the party hierarchy. That lack of spontaneity I think, inhibits the kind of transformative agenda around gender" (N9.11.6.20). However, in critical debates around the 50/50 policy, some female SWAPO parliamentarians were quite outspoken, perhaps because of encouragement from the party's top brass.

Another way to interpret these findings is that the women are newcomers to Parliament and are not as sure-footed as those who have been seated longer. Women in Parliament also face greater constraints in terms of pushback. Anonymous social media trolls pose a major disincentive for women to be outspoken in politics, as they reveal a deep-seated culture of misogyny that is not unique to Namibia and can be found the world over. It includes derogatory and sexualized hate speech drawing on stereotyped norms (Venditto et al. 2022).

Others have speculated that the silence of SWAPO female parliamentarians might reflect the basis on which they were selected. Some SWAPO female parliamentarians may be selected because they may be fairly loyal to the party and aren't going to challenge SWAPO leadership (Clayton 2014). Many SWAPO male leaders are former exiles who are older, and they may have found that if they could place younger women in critical positions, they would be more malleable and loyal to SWAPO objectives (O'Riordan 2014). Even though women are well represented, some believe women MPs are regarded as token representatives who will not challenge the status quo (Clayton 2014; Hassim and Meintjes 2005). As one opposition MP put it, "There is not really very much of a culture of supporting, recognizing, and embracing women. Even if you are put into Parliament in big numbers, and they support human rights, they are not opening up women's voices in decision-making and in the power corridors. They don't do that, so you end up having almost no voice" (N1.9.29.20).

There may yet be other reasons for the hesitancy of some SWAPO women. When an opposition leader advanced a motion for girls to get free sanitary pads, women parliamentarians and the female deputy minister of gender didn't want to discuss the issue because they were too embarrassed to talk about menstruation in public. Others have used their Christian faith as a reason not to engage key women's movement demands like abortion, even though several ministers of health have advocated for liberalizing abortion laws in Parliament, saying that the state is spending a lot of money on rectifying botched backstreet abortions (N8.10.4.20).

However, these criticisms do not apply to all SWAPO political leaders. Dr. Libertina Amathila—a physician by training who had been minister of health (1996–2005), deputy prime minister (2005–2010), a member of the SWAPO Central Committee, and director of the SWAPO Women's Council—was the first to raise the issue of abortion publicly. Subsequent health ministers, including Dr. Richard Kamwi, Deputy Health Minister Ester Muinjangues, and Dr. Nickey Iiyambo, as well as the late President Geingob have also spoken out about the need for abortion rights.

In 2020, a young woman, Beauty Boois—who had been raped by her uncle as a teenager and sought to perform an abortion on her own, which led to dire consequences—launched a petition to make abortion legal in Namibia and to change a 1975 law imposed by South Africa. Over sixty-three thousand people in a country of 2.6 million signed the petition.[2] Dr. Nickey Iiyambo, who was the first vice president of Namibia and cabinet minister, introduced the motion in Parliament to amend the 1975 law, but it was denied. Religious influences thus weigh heavily on the hesitancy to discuss reproductive health rights for women, and they extend beyond SWAPO (N10.11.5.20).

It may be that more experience, leadership training, and collective strategizing may embolden the quieter female parliamentarians. In April 2023, Namibian women parliamentarians finally established a parliamentary body to advocate for gender equality and other national issues. The caucus aimed to help the female MPs lobby for issues in Parliament and may help overcome some of the hesitancy among female MPs.

Impact of the 50/50 Policy on Other Areas of Leadership

Since its independence, Namibia has had its share of prominent women leaders, such as Nora Schimming-Chase, who was Namibia's first ambassador to Germany (1992–1996). She had initially been a SWAPO member but, in 1999, changed her affiliation to the Congress of Democrats, a party that she helped found. She also served as deputy permanent secretary at the Ministry of Foreign Affairs. The minister of justice, Yvonne Dausab, is often mentioned as one who has stood out in supporting other women. She has built relationships across party lines and adopted strategies to improve access to legal aid and justice for grassroots women. Namibia also has had a woman prime minister, Saara Kuugongelwa-Amadhila, since 2015 and will continue to do so with the new government in 2025. Another woman, Netumbo Nandi-Ndaitwah, was elected vice president of SWAPO in 2017. She served as deputy prime minister in 2015 and then as third vice president after 2024. In March 2023, SWAPO named Nandi-Ndaitwah as the sole candidate for the party in the March 2024 elections, and in December 2024 she became the second elected woman president in Africa with 57.3 percent of the vote. The first had been Ellen Johnson Sirleaf of Liberia.

At the executive level, 38 percent of the cabinet posts are held by women, many of whom head traditionally male-dominated ministries such as foreign affairs, trade, education, and justice. Women make up 71 percent of the deputy ministers. About 26 percent of the ambassadors and consuls general

[2] https://www.safeabortionwomensright.org/news/namibia-a-true-story-of-unsafe-abortion-a-petition-to-make-abortion-safe-and-legal/.

are women, 29 percent of the permanent secretaries are women, and 41 percent of the deputy permanent secretaries are women.

In the judiciary, women make up 33 percent of judges and 49.5 percent of magistrates (SADC 2022). In 2023, the president appointed to the Supreme Court three female justices out of four, and Namibia has a woman minister of justice, Yvonne Dausab.

After the 50/50 Struggle

Adopting the 50/50 policy revealed both the extent of government–civil society collaboration and its limits as the government sought to remove two lesbians from the leadership of the civil society campaign. The issue of sexual minorities has continued to plague state-society relations in Namibia with mixed outcomes, reflecting tensions not only in the state and ruling party but also in society.

After the 50/50 struggle, the movement lost some of its momentum, and it fragmented. Subsequently, a Young Feminist Movement has sought to regain that unified sense of purpose (N4.10.21.20). New forms of mobilization have emerged along with new issues. As one activist explained, "I think the women's movement is gaining momentum. And a lot of the leaders who are involved in the LGBT and sex work movement[s] are also part of the women's movement and are driving a lot of the conversations around reproductive justice, reproductive choice, ensuring that SRHR [Sexual and Reproductive Health and Rights] services are inclusive." She noted that there had been many conversations and events led by national and regional coalitions around abortion, bodily integrity, and bodily autonomy (N2.9.30.20).

There are important areas where the women's movement and the state have differed. There has been frustration at the impasse over key legislation pertaining to the Divorce Act, Customary Marriages Act, abortion law reform, and LGBTQ decriminalization. Some of these differences result from the dominance of SWAPO and conservative elements within SWAPO. This is particularly evident when it comes to LGBTQ rights, which have divided the leadership of the party. In contrast, the Landless People's Movement and the Popular Democratic Movement have been open to having conversations with Out-Right Namibia and other groups on issues pertaining to LGBTQ concerns.

The country's record around LGBTQ rights is uneven. The Supreme Court of Namibia delivered a landmark decision in 2023, affirming the validity of same-sex marriages conducted overseas, although domestic same-sex marriages remain illegal. Foreigners previously faced threats of expulsion and loss of benefits because the government did not recognize their marital status. This historic ruling made Namibia the second African country after South Africa to recognize same-sex marriage, even if in a limited form.

In 2020, Namibia also became the first Southern African nation to explicitly incorporate discussions on homosexuality into its educational program through the comprehensive sexuality education initiative. This decision was a result of lobbying by civil society groups, notably Out-Right Namibia and Lifeline/Childline, as well as the African Youth and Adolescents Network Namibia and the Namibian Family Planning Association. They took the lead in facilitating dialogues aimed at enriching the curriculum's coverage of sexual orientation, resulting in a more open and inclusive approach to these topics within the education system. They faced resistance from cabinet members like the former foreign minister and current president, Netumbo Nandi-Ndaitwah, who were persuaded to support the program only after civil society organizations agreed to rename it "skills-based health education." The Ministry of Education executive director reassured them that the program was not promoting sexual activity among children and was offering age-appropriate education (Haidula 2020). This example shows both the productive engagement of civil society and the Ministry of Education and the conservative nature of many SWAPO leaders in confronting fundamental gender-related issues.

However, efforts to protect same-sex marriage in Namibia failed. There were strong pressures from the Coalition of Christian Churches, which had demanded that same-sex marriages be outlawed in Namibia. SWAPO also put out a statement saying it "strongly condemns and repudiates all kinds of immoral and indecent *acts*" and "other associated *acts* that are either inconsistent with Namibian laws or against public policy." SWAPO said it was instructing its government "to enforce all laws in force that are aimed at preventing and combating such *acts*" (Kavhu 2023).

At the same time, many leading individuals have defied these tendencies in SWAPO. The former first lady, Monica Geingos, an accomplished businesswoman and lawyer who has worked for over two decades in the financial sector, threw her support behind many of the issues raised by young women in the women's movement. She has been extremely vocal on matters pertaining to bodily integrity, bodily autonomy, sex work, sexual violence, GBV, adolescent girls and young women and the need to protect them, and on LGBTQ issues (N2.9.30.20). She launched the #BeFree Movement in November 2016 with the assistance of the UNFPA and the Joint UNAIDS, which focuses on HIV but also promotes "honest and robust dialogue" with young people about drug addiction, teenage pregnancy, psychosocial issues such as suicide, and relationships with parents and caregivers. She has adopted a feminist approach to these issues confronting young people (UN Population Fund 2018).

Interestingly, unlike in Botswana, in Namibia the gap isn't as large between the older and younger generations around issues pertaining to GBV, abortion, and LGBTQ rights (N4.10.21.20; N2.9.30.20; N1.9.29.20; N6.10.2.20). As one activist pointed out, "With the activists that we work with, I think irrespective of age, there usually is one bigger vision holding everyone together. So if it is around abortion, they come together irrespective of age. If it is around LGBT issues, they come together; it doesn't really matter" (N2.9.30.20). However, like in the movement in Botswana, the younger activists use more direct and confrontational action. For example, they hold protests against GBV called "Shut It All Down" and "Enough Is Enough," demanding that the government stop making promises and take action. As one woman middle-aged activist put it, "I think the younger feminists are very radical. They want to pull down statues, they want to burn buildings, and they want to just attack police, and things like that, which, of course, the older feminists are having an issue with. The older feminists are saying, 'We cannot fight the system; we have to work together with the government in order to bring the change because they hold a lot of power.' But the younger women say, 'But we are tired. We are dying; we are being raped. And there's nothing being done. So we need to be really, really radical in our approach'" (N4.10.21.20).

Some older activists have noted that there is also a greater focus on the individual, unlike in the feminism of the past, which had more of a collective orientation (N8.10.4.20). Many organizations, like the Women's Leadership Centre and Open Society Initiative for Southern Africa, focus on building feminist leadership among young women. Since around the 2020s, many young women and men have been claiming a feminist identity, which is something new.

I asked many of the activists I interviewed how they defined feminism. One explained, "For me, feminism is about autonomy and choice and just being you, without any limitations. Feminism, for me, is a theory of a dream that everyone is thriving, that [women's] potential is fully realized. So it's a dream for this world that there's justice, there's no hate, people are thriving in all sectors of their lives." Another answered, "I bring my feminism down to choice. Just have human beings choose to do what they want to be, what they want to do, as long as it is not infringing on the rights of another. Just that human beings choose. Choose to sleep with another woman, to sleep with another man, choose to be an engineer, choose to be a housewife, choose to be a career woman. Just choose and not be criticized for your choice" (N6.10.2.20).

The women's movement and the LGBTQ movement have intersected on numerous occasions and in a variety of campaigns. Many of the leading activists in the women's movement are also leaders of the LGBTQ movement, like Rose Namises, who is now the leader of the sex worker–focused organization Rights Not Rescue Trust, and Liz Frank and Elizabeth IKhaxas, who were both one-time leaders of Sister Namibia and now direct the Women's Leadership Center. As one activist said of them, "These leaders opened up the conversation around patriarchy and heteronormativity during the liberation fight" (N2.9.30.20).

Namibian activists have had a far-reaching impact on LGBTQ concerns within Africa. In 2004, they organized a five-day strategic planning workshop with lesbians from thirteen African countries and founded the Coalition of African Lesbians (CAL). They held leadership institutes for the CAL members and then handed over the activities to a new leadership based in Johannesburg, with up to fifteen staff. They were also key instigators of the effort to conceptualize and pass the UN Security Council Resolution 1325, which requires women to be part of all peacebuilding initiatives at all levels.

In spite of such gains, many feminists see enormous challenges ahead, particularly in traditional institutions. As one put it, "Patriarchal power sits in those traditional courts, in those traditional family structures where women can't breathe, women have no land rights, no right to speak in the court, no right to divorce, and no right to their children. If the man decides [to seek] a divorce, the children are his. So customary laws are completely outrageous, but it's not on the national agenda" (N5.10.20.20).

The Difference Democracy Makes

Although Namibian feminists are critical of SWAPO, the government, and the lack of progress around issues like abortion, LGBTQ rights, sex work, and other concerns, the freedoms of speech and association they enjoy are also palpable, especially when one compares Namibia with its authoritarian neighbors.

When I asked one activist what difference democracy makes, she replied, "I think it definitely makes a difference to me because I know that as a woman or as someone who is gender nonbinary firstly, I advocate for women's issues and I advocate for the LGBTQ community, and I can do so very, very openly. I can do so without any harm coming my way. And I can do that freely in Namibia.

That is one of the freedoms that I do enjoy. And I have a lot of privileges, democratic privileges, our neighboring Zimbabwe does not have. Our press in this country has not been experiencing the same kinds of censorship and violation that you find in Zimbabwe, for example" (N7.10.2.20).

Another activist pointed out, "I think because the one thing that counts in our favor is Namibia is relatively safe, and we can challenge [the status quo] in a more conducive, safe environment. Backlash is often verbal. You won't encounter volatility in rallies and marches. You'll have a lot of feedback on Facebook, Twitter, and radio calls. But not so much in terms of physical threats" (N2.9.30.20).

This chapter has shown through an analysis of the adoption of the 50/50 policy on women's leadership the ways in which a democratic government, led by a dominant party, interacted with the women's movement and SADC, to a lesser extent, in bringing about changes in women's status. It reveals the constraints on the party both internally and from opposition parties. The chapter shows some of the costs and tensions within the party as a result of promoting women's leadership. It also illustrates how maintaining vote share holds less importance in democracies than it does in autocracies, with significant implications for women and the opposition. And finally, the contrast with Botswana illustrates the importance of postconflict legacies in influencing women's leadership outcomes specifically.

10
Comparing Women's Leadership and Rights in African Democracies and Autocracies

As the case studies in this book have shown, democracies and autocracies significantly differ when it comes to the civil and political liberties that surround the advancement of women's rights, with important implications for women's rights activists and their capacity to shape women's rights reforms. However, when it comes to descriptive representation, this chapter demonstrates that in Africa, democracies and autocracies are fairly similar regarding the promotion of women leaders over time, but for different reasons. Autocrats often have had no qualms about repressing women (and men) in the opposition and preventing their advancement as leaders. They use their party hegemony to crush any opposition to the appointment of women to leadership positions. They build legitimacy and entrench their parties for decades, building on the gains they make from women's support and votes.

Democracies and autocracies are both likely to adopt quotas in Africa, although they differ in the types of quotas they adopt, with autocracies leaning toward reserved seats (see Chapter 2). Democracies and autocracies are both likely to adopt constitutional women's rights reforms. Moreover, levels of female representation generally correspond to advancements in women's rights in both democracies and autocracies, but for different reasons. Those countries that support women as leaders are also more likely to support women's rights. On average, both democracies and autocracies have similar outcomes when it comes to gender gaps in education, health, and economic empowerment, and to most other key women's status measures. They diverge when it comes to LGBTQ rights, abortion, and customary law.

Prior work shows that the variance one finds in Africa in women's political representation is more likely to correlate with the adoption of quotas, postconflict outcomes, the growth of civil liberties (Hughes and Tripp 2015),

Why African Autocracies Promote Women as Leaders. Aili Mari Tripp, Oxford University Press.
 DOI: 10.1093/9780197829004.003.0011

and party institutionalization (Pelke 2021). However, these differences do not fall along the democracy/autocracy divide. Civil liberties alone did not influence women's representation in my study with Melanie Hughes, but the expansion of civil liberties did make a difference, suggesting that it opened up opportunities for women's movements to exert pressure for gender equality reform, especially after the political liberalization that occurred after the 1990s in Africa. Surprisingly, proportional representation electoral systems did not influence women's representation in Africa when postconflict factors and quotas were accounted for because so many plurality systems also have high rates of female legislative representation in Africa, often as a result of the use of reserved seats (Hughes and Tripp 2015).

This chapter compares democracies and autocracies in terms of political representation. It then contrasts the two regime types by constitutional reforms and critical measures of women's status. The chapter shows that countries that advance women leaders are equally likely to have positive outcomes in women's rights more broadly defined, regardless of regime type.

Women's Representation

As noted in Chapter 1, most cross-national studies generally do not show a strong correlation between democracy and women's legislative representation (Kenworthy and Malami 1999; Luciak 2005, Paxton 1997; Reynolds 1999; Stockemer 2009; Tripp and Kang 2008; Viterna et al. 2007). Similarly, cross-national studies in Africa have revealed the same patterns when factoring in other variables (Hughes and Tripp 2015).

Figure 10.1 shows that the relationship between women's legislative representation and levels of democracy has varied only minimally over time. Moreover, the levels of female legislative representation are fairly similar regardless of whether one looks at the executive, legislature, or subnational governance structures (Table 10.1).

Figure 10.2 shows the average score on the World Economic Forum's measure of women's political empowerment by regime type.[1] Although countries categorized as "not free" by Freedom House have a higher average score on this measure than "free" countries, the difference is not statistically significant. ANOVA tests reveal no statistically significant difference in the mean

[1] https://www3.weforum.org/docs/WEF_GGGR_2020.pdf.

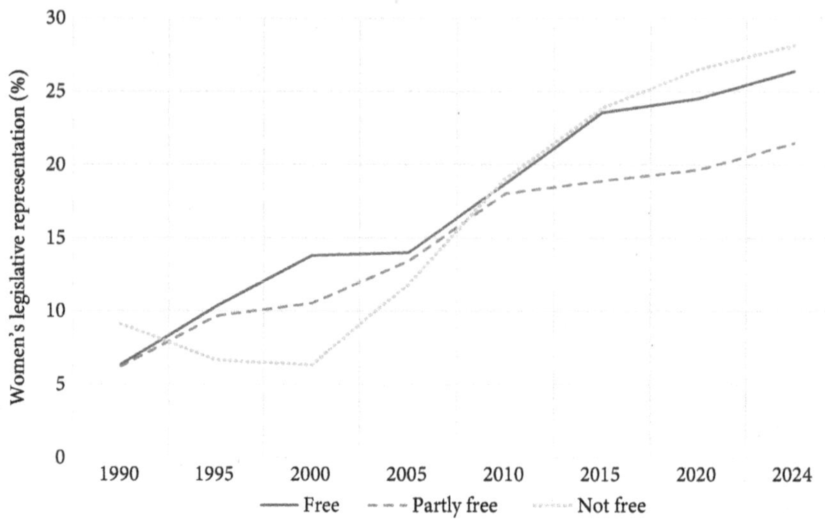

Figure 10.1 Women's legislative representation in Africa (1975–2024)
Sources: Freedom House (2024); IPU (2024).

Table 10.1 Women's political representation in Africa (2023–2024)

Regime type	Legislative representation of women (%)	Women ministers (%)	Women in subnational politics (%)
Democracies	24	26	29
Autocracies	25	25	23

Sources: Freedom House (2024); IPU (2024); UN Women (2025).

score on the political empowerment measure when comparing the group of "free" countries to the "not free" or "partly free" groups.

Figure 10.3 plots the women's parliamentary representation level and the Varieties of Democracy (V-Dem) Electoral Democracy value for each country, with higher levels of the democracy index indicating more elements of electoral democracy. The Pearson correlation coefficient (PCC) of −0.086 and *p*-value of 0.54 indicate that the correlation is not statistically significant. In other words, this simple bivariate analysis does not provide evidence that the percentage of women in Parliament significantly varies by regime type.

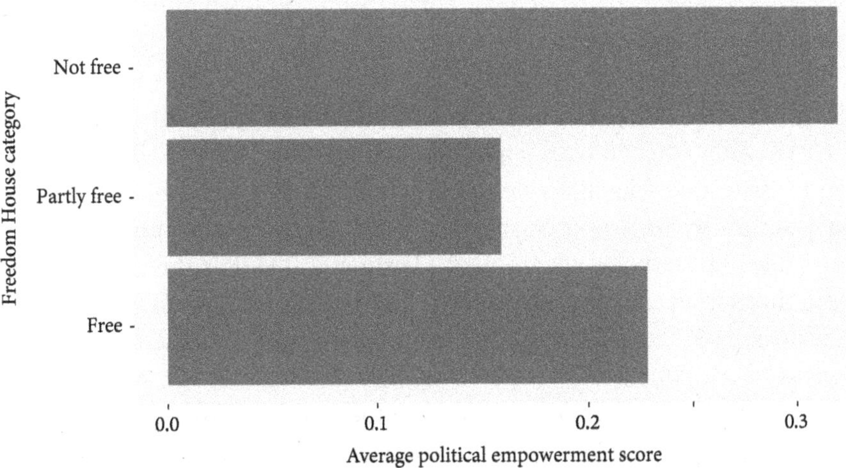

Figure 10.2 Levels of democracy and political empowerment of women in Africa
Sources: IPU (2024); V-Dem (2024).

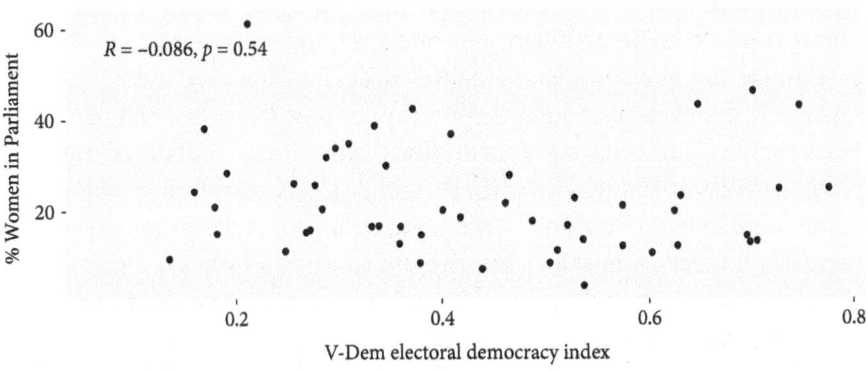

Figure 10.3 Women's representation and V-Dem democracy index for African countries
Sources: IPU (2024); V-Dem (2024).

Women's Rights Reform in African Constitutions

Another way to compare democracies and autocracies is their legal commitment to women's rights. One way to maximize uniformity in comparisons is to look at constitutions. There has been increasing interest in authoritarian constitutionalism in recent years (Barros 2002; Ginsburg and Moustafa 2008; Ginsburg and Simpser 2014), but little has been written about women's rights provisions in authoritarian constitutions. Most of the discussions have involved general comparisons between authoritarian and democratic constitutions.

Constitutionalism has long been viewed as a foundation for state legitimacy. Since the American and French Revolutions, constitutional rule has been virtually equated with legitimate political rule. Liberal constitutionalism is associated with the rule of law, commitments to human rights, and legal constraints on power. Such constitutions represent the opposite of arbitrary rule and despotic government (Tushnet 2014). For this reason, some see authoritarian constitutionalism as a contradiction in terms (Friedrich and Brzezinski 1961; Isiksel 2013). Others have described authoritarian constitutions as "nominal" or "fake" (Loewenstein 1957; Sartori 1962). While one can question the depth and motivation of autocratic commitments to women's rights, many of the operatives within the state may be genuinely committed to women's rights reform. However, as we saw in the case studies, authoritarian structures constrain their goals.

Sometimes, a constitution has been regarded as a way to protect the policymaking process from democratic politics or a way to protect individual liberty from excessive authority. But rarely is it treated as a strategy of political domination or an outcome of power struggles. However, there is nothing inherently democratic about a constitution or how it can be used or abused. For example, authoritarian constitutions subordinate individual rights to public order and national security (Isiksel 2013). A small but growing body of literature looks at how and why authoritarian countries draw on constitutionalism. Indeed, almost all countries use constitutions in symbolic ways to signal their commitment to core values. Some constitutions are aspirational; others hew more closely to actual practice.

Elkins and Melton (2014) argue that democratic and authoritarian constitutions are converging in form, especially in provisions concerning rights and judicial independence. This is especially true regarding women's rights. Constitutions serve numerous functions within authoritarian regimes. Some argue that autocrats use constitutions as window dressing (Gandhi and Przeworski 2007; Law and Versteeg 2013). As a result, constitutions in authoritarian regimes may have extensive lists of protected rights that resemble those of democracies (Ginsburg 2020). They may also include provisions for regular elections, an ostensibly independent judiciary, and other democratic-looking institutions. However, these institutions are structured in ways that legitimately perpetuate the domination of one party or leader. This allows dictators to consolidate both political and related economic power.

Authoritarian constitutions are not there to check the executive or those in power as much as they are a means of distributing power and establishing institutions that control lower-level agents (Ginsburg and Simpser 2014). Thus, numerous constitutional reforms have sought to extend presidential term limits in many African countries.[2]

References to an extensive list of rights, as in North Korea's constitution, make the constitution look like it fits international scripts without risking any expensive constraints. Ginsburg and Simpser (2014) ask why authoritarian countries include these rights if they are window dressing. Przeworski (2014) suggests that it is not so much to fool external audiences as it is a way to normalize the idea that rights everywhere are meaningless. Hollyer and Rosendorff (2011) argue that dictators use the gap between promise and reality to demoralize internal opponents and as a costly signal of the intention to repress or that one can abuse human rights despite the increased cost.

While there is an element of window dressing to authoritarian constitutions in Africa, this implies that they are hiding something. However, many authoritarian regimes in Africa are as successful as African democracies when it comes to women's rights outcomes, as this chapter will reveal, and often they do as well as democracies—for example, in the political representation of women in legislatures, cabinets, subnational government, and judiciaries. Authoritarian countries in Africa fall short of their constitutional provisions and promises, but so do democracies. This raises questions about how we understand the performative element of constitutions—not just in autocracies but also in democracies.

Another use of constitutions in authoritarian countries involves their coordination role or their use as an *operating manual*. They establish government relations with the people, organize governance, and create order (Przeworski 2014). Autocrats often use constitutions as a means of building cooperation and coalitions among elites and as a way to extend their rule (Ginsburg and Simpser 2014). Authoritarian constitutions also create institutions that seek to build trust and describe the functions of various political actors in ways that ensure regime dominance. However, in this role, constitutions can be costly because deviation from the constitution can become a recipe for popular rebellion (Weingast 1997).

Authoritarian countries, like democracies, use constitutions as billboards to advertise their policies both internally and externally (Ginsburg and Semper 2014; Yu 2010). This type of virtue signaling involves efforts by a country to reposition itself vis-à-vis countries in the neighborhood to appear more

[2] Guinea (2001), Togo (2002), Tunisia (2002), Gabon (2003), Chad (2005), Uganda (2005), Algeria (2008), Cameroon (2008), Niger (2009), and Djibouti (2010). See https://osisa.org/termlimits-in-africa/.

progressive, more democratic, and less threatening (e.g., if they have been a major source of terrorists). They can be used by a country that is seeking to meet its international treaty obligations and wants to show it is playing by the rules of the international order. For example, China's reference to "advanced productive forces" in society is a euphemism for capitalists, signaling to international audiences that China is open for business (Ginsburg and Simpser 2014, 6). Law and Versteeg (2014) argue that states attempt to conform to standardized models of explicit and formal constitutional standards to secure recognition from the international community. They found that authoritarian countries were likelier to adopt sham constitutions that contained many rights that were not adhered to in practice.

Authoritarian countries try to become modern and conform to "world society" values to win the international community's acceptance and recognition (Meyer et al. 1997). Law and Versteeg (2013, 2014) suggest that the gap between what a country has in its constitution and what it delivers is much larger in authoritarian states than in democracies. This is even more true in poorer countries.

By enshrining crucial provisions in the constitution, governments take on a normative force to be invoked for rhetorical purposes, but if they remain solely within the constitutional framework, they are nonjusticiable and, thus, more aspirational in nature (Balme and Dowdle 2009). For example, the 2014 Constitution passed under President Sisi in Egypt has many gender-related reforms, including commitments to "achieving equality between women and men in all civil, political, economic, social, and cultural rights." However, women activists in Egypt have come under severe repression. Moreover, Sisi's cabinet approved a bill in January 2021 that would revise the Personal Status Code so that only a guardian could sign the marriage certificate on behalf of the bride. Women would not be able to register their child's birth or travel abroad without a male guardian's consent. The guardian could also apply to annul a marriage within a year if he believes the couple is ill-suited or believes that the dowry is too small. The bill would give fathers priority in child custody cases and allow fathers to prevent mothers from traveling with their children. Thus, the existing legislation and practice in Egypt have not been reconciled with the constitution, but more concerning is that new legislation, in fact, radically departs from the constitution.

Constitutions in authoritarian contexts can also shape social norms and public preferences and stigmatize types of behavior the regime wishes to discourage (Ginsburg and Simpser 2014). Finally, they establish a political frame for the national legal system, whether it is socialist, Islamist, secular, republican, or premised on another ideology. They carry enormous symbolic and ceremonial weight, which means they are generally more entrenched than ordinary law, making them most costly to change (Elkins and Melton 2013).

Empirical studies find few general differences between constitutions written in autocracies and democracies regarding executive power; however, judiciaries have much less autonomy in authoritarian constitutions than in democratic constitutions. There is no difference between the regimes in general when it comes to common rights or inalienable individual rights. However, authoritarian constitutions are much less specific than democratic constitutions (Elkins and Melton 2014). The differences between the regime types, however, are abundantly evident when it comes to the exercise of these rights, particularly political right and civil liberties.

Comparative African Constitutions and Women's Rights

Since 1990, most African countries have fundamentally revised or rewritten their constitutions. These new constitutions in Africa have incorporated women's rights provisions to an unprecedented degree—to the extent that African constitutions, on average, have more references to women's rights than do constitutions in any other world region. They include clauses pertaining to gender equality, discrimination, customary law, violence against women, gender quotas, and citizenship rights. In twenty-six countries, gender-inclusive language has been introduced so that constitutions no longer have exclusively masculine pronouns. Overall, the areas where we have seen the most reforms have to do with general provisions around gender equality and antidiscrimination, as well as with women's political leadership and labor rights, while the areas where we see the most resistance to reform pertain to customary and family law and violence against women (Tables 10.2 and 10.3).

Even though most countries in Africa rewrote their constitutions in the context of political liberalization as they adopted multiparty states and electoral reforms, autocratic and hybrid regimes (neither fully democratic nor fully authoritarian) were more likely than democratic countries to incorporate such women's rights reforms in their constitutions (see Tables 10.4 and 10.5). Moreover, the most significant increase (almost fivefold) in the adoption of women's rights provisions was among hybrid regimes (classified as "partially free" by Freedom House) from the periods of 1960–1989 to 1990–2019. Autocracies (classified as "not free") increased women's rights

Table 10.2 Distribution of gender-related constitutional provisions in Africa

Provisions*	Democracy (%)	Hybrid (%)	Authoritarian (%)	All regimes (%)
Property/land	5	2	2	3
Labor/work	10	9	9	9
Quotas/representation	5	10	10	8
Customary law	4	5	5	5
Equality	17	15	15	16
Antidiscrimination	16	11	11	13
Violence	1	6	6	4
Children citizenship	8	6	6	7
Marriage, motherhood, family	10	12	12	11
Positive rights	4	6	5	5
Mention of international convention	10	13	13	12
Mention of female pronouns	9	5	5	6
	100% $n = 14$	100% $n = 20$	100% $n = 20$	100% $n = 54$

*See explanation in Table 10.3.
Source: UN Women (2025); Global Gender Equality Constitutional Database (2006).

provisions 3.5 times in this same time period while democracies increased their women's rights provisions 2.75 times.

Authoritarian countries have the highest number of gender-related constitutional provisions, followed by hybrid regimes. This adheres to patterns discussed in Chapter 2 and this chapter about some of the differences between authoritarian and hybrid regimes when it comes to women's representation and rights, more generally. Many of these countries emerged from major conflict after the 1990s, and hence, there is significant difference between the constitutions of postconflict countries (8.12 average gender provisions) and countries not postconflict (5.86 gender provisions). As mentioned in Chapter 1, this has to do with changes in political opportunity structures that occurred in the postconflict context after 1990 and especially after 2000 as many major conflicts came to an end; women's rights activists were subsequently able to influence the writing of constitutional and legal reforms that took place after conflict as a result of changes in the political elites (Tripp 2015).

Table 10.3 Description of provisions

Property/land	Provisions for property or land rights for women.
Labor/work	Provisions that guarantee equal pay for women, promote affirmative action in hiring practices, provide maternity care and leave, and prohibit discrimination based on gender in hiring practices.
Quotas/representation	Provisions that call for a quota or percentage of seats that should be allocated to women politicians, or that have language that prevents political parties from discriminating based on gender. This category includes provisions that state an intention to represent women fairly in elected bodies.
Customary law	A provision that the constitution has supreme authority over customary law. Customary law is overridden by the constitution or by state or legislative laws in cases of inconsistency or contradiction. Customary law is only applicable if it is in accordance with the constitution or state's law. Customary laws or customs that harm women or limit their rights or equality are overridden by the constitution.
Equality	A provision that specifically mentions women or equality between both sexes/genders.
Antidiscrimination	A reference to antidiscrimination in relation to women or sexism.
Violence against women	Provisions that specifically provide for the protection of women against violence. This includes provisions that mention combating harmful customs and traditions that undermine women.
Children citizenship	Mention of citizenship being passed onto children through both mothers and fathers.
Marriage, motherhood, family	Provision relating to these terms if the provision specifically mentions the rights of women (e.g., women and men being equal in the family, or the family and mothers being protected by the constitution).
Positive rights	Provisions such as the integration of women in the political, social, and economic spheres of the country; the inclusion of women in the national development plan; and affirmative action provisions (specifically mentioning women) related to encouraging, enabling, or supporting groups that were previously discriminated against (e.g., under apartheid and colonialism). Gender mainstreaming and promotion of gender equality and inclusiveness can also be included under this category.
Mention of international convention or agency to implement convention	Provisions that call for creating a commission of human rights or citing participation in certain international or regional human rights charters.
Mention of feminine pronouns	Whether the constitution consistently uses both masculine and feminine pronouns or whether there is a provision that states that all parts of the constitution apply to both men and women.

Table 10.4 Ratio of the number of women's rights provisions to the number of revised constitutions by regime type in Africa

	1960–1989	1990–2019
Autocracies	2.00	7.05
Hybrid regimes	1.40	6.84
Democracies	2.00	5.50

Sources: UN Women (2025); Global Gender Equality Constitutional Database (2006).

Table 10.5 Correlation between women's rights and V-Dem electoral democracy index

Women's rights measures	Data source	Analysis	
		Pearson Correlation Coefficient	Statistical significance
Education	Global Gender Gap Report	0.21	0.21
Health	Global Gender Gap Report	−0.047	0.78
Workplace index	*Women Business and the Law*	0.21	0.12
Economic empowerment	Global Gender Gap Report	0.023	0.89
Entrepreneurship	*Women Business and the Law*	0.2	0.15
Rights in marriage	*Women Business and the Law*	0.54	2.8e-05***
LGBTQ Legal Index	LGBTQ Legal Index	0.44	0.0011***
Abortion	Guttemacher Institute	0.32	0.018**

Sources: V-Dem (2024); World Economic Forum (2024); World Bank (2024); the LGBTQ Equaldex (2024); Bankole et al. (2020).

Women's Rights Outcomes and Regime Type

Beyond the promise of legal reform embedded in constitutions, which are mainly aspirational, one can also compare how countries fare in terms of women's rights outcomes. As it turns out, in Africa, there is little difference between autocracies and democracies regarding other measures of gender equality outcomes beyond representation. Globally, existing research has shown that authoritarian regimes pass women's rights legislation in economic and social rights at rates that surpass democracies in developing countries. One-third of dictatorships enact a women's rights reform each year compared with 26 percent of democracies because such reforms are less costly politically than opening up the system to political competition, elections, or repressing political opponents (Donno et al. 2022)

Bivariate and correlation analysis did not produce statistically significant differences between democratic and nondemocratic countries when it came to education,[3] health,[4] the workplace index, and entrepreneurship.[5] However, when it came to the legal protection of women in marital relations,[6] LGBTQ rights, and abortion, democracies did better than nondemocracies, with statistically significant results (see Table 10.5).[7]

Only the relationship between democracy and marriage rights remains positive and statistically significant, even after accounting for the level of women's representation in office (see Table 10.5). Authoritarian regimes are more likely to use hot-button LGBTQ issues, abortion, and matters pertaining to family law in a negative way to build their popularity and divert attention from other pressing issues, as we have seen in Uganda's 2023 act criminalizing homosexuality. They may also succumb to international pressures from evangelical Christian movements and global Islamist movements that seek to undermine these rights. This speaks to the unevenness of autocracies when it comes to women's rights reform and the lack of depth to their commitments.

Abortion remains one of the most contentious women's rights issues on the continent. Nevertheless, it should be mentioned that there are new efforts to relax the restrictive colonial-era laws around abortion in Mali, Togo, Chad, Niger, Mauritius, Somalia, and São Tomé and Príncipe. The DRC is also expanding efforts to improve access to safe abortion, and Benin's Parliament voted in 2021 to legalize abortion (Gbadamosi 2022).

Countries promoting women's leadership may still lag in areas such as customary law (e.g., inheritance), abortion, and LGBTQ rights. Some of the issues in these three areas are doctrinal, to use the terminology of Htun and Weldon (2018), who refer to the religious doctrine, cultural traditions, or sacred discourse of a major social group. While

[3] The indicators are women's literacy rate and enrollment in primary, secondary, and tertiary education.

[4] The indicators are the sex ratio at birth and healthy life expectancy.

[5] The indicators are as follows: Can a woman sign a contract in the same way as a man? Can a woman register a business in the same way as a man? Can a woman open a bank account in the same way as a man? Does the law prohibit gender discrimination in access to credit?

[6] The indicators are as follows: Is there no legal provision that requires a married woman to obey her husband? Can a woman be "head of household" in the same way as a man? Is there legislation explicitly addressing domestic violence? Can a woman obtain a judgment of divorce in the same way as a man? Does a woman have the same rights to remarry as a man?

[7] When Freedom House data was used, an ANOVA test, which determines whether there are any statistically significant differences between the means of two or more groups, produced comparable results.

some aspects of customary law may relate to religious doctrine and/or practice (e.g., polygamy, divorce by repudiation), other aspects have little to do with doctrine (e.g., age of marriage). Instead, what these three groups of rights have in common is not so much their affinity to religious doctrine, but, rather, how they represent efforts to control and curtail women's reproductive freedoms. Abortion, contraception, age of marriage, and LGBTQ rights are all potential perceived threats to the reproductive capacity of a nation.

There are a variety of reasons pro-natalist policies are important to countries that include but go beyond religious doctrine. Biological reproduction is essential in agrarian societies and societies that have weak welfare regimes that rely heavily on the labor of the next generation. But it is also important in industrial societies like China, which have plummeting birth rates, yet are not constrained by religious precepts. Some governments wish to increase their population to augment their workforce to pay for an increasingly aging population. Also, war-torn societies that have suffered massive casualties seek to replenish their population by promoting the propagation of children. In the West, selective natalist policies are often used when leaders seek to proliferate certain ethnic/racial groups in the face of migration or of disproportionately sharp demographic increases in others. Not only does one often find racism in various expressions of pronatalist policies, but generally, they also come more directly into conflict with women's autonomy and right to their own bodily autonomy.

In Africa, attitudes toward customary law, reproductive rights, and LGBTQ rights may be shaped by religious institutions and traditional norms of morality—often fueled by foreign religious support. However, they may also be rooted in the practicalities of agrarian life, which rely on children as a source of labor and support for aging parents. For example, raising the age of marriage decreases women's childbearing years, thus generally reducing the number of children born. Limiting rights to abortion and contraceptives will limit women's ability to space their children or choose not to have children. Curtailing the practice of female genital mutilation gives women more control over their own sexuality, which has implications for childbearing. Securing any LGBTQ rights may create a perception that the inclination of people to have children is at risk or falling. These factors help explain, in part, why abortion and LGBTQ rights still have such traction in many societies in Africa, although attitudes are slowly changing as LGBTQ rights activists challenge discriminatory beliefs and practices.

Women's Legislative Influence on Women's Rights Outcomes

Some studies show that having more women in legislative bodies can result in different kinds of agenda setting with more focus on social welfare, the environment, women's rights, and other concerns (Franceschet and Piscopo 2008; Franceschet et al. 2012; Goetz and Hassim 2003). Some have discovered that having gender quotas has influenced government spending in historically feminized policy areas like health. Clayton et al. (2019) found in a survey of more than eight hundred parliamentarians and nineteen thousand citizens across seventeen countries in Africa that women were more likely than men to identify poverty and women's rights as their priority, and 46 percent of women parliamentarians compared with 35 percent of men listed poverty as one of the three most essential issues government needed to tackle. Men tended to prioritize infrastructure.

Nevertheless, sometimes, there is an unrealistic expectation that having more women in Parliament will automatically result in positive gender outcomes. Underlying this may be the notion that women would be naturally inclined to advance women's rights, which, as the studies in this book show, is not entirely unfounded. Women may be more likely to support these rights, but it raises the question, Why should one assume that male politicians are not interested in such reforms? Any women's rights legislation that is passed still overwhelmingly relies on men's votes as long as women parliamentarians are in the minority. This assumption that women are more inclined to support women's rights reforms overlooks questions having to do with the party affiliations of women, party discipline, and party priorities in the legislative arena. Rarely do female or male politicians, for that matter, diverge radically from the policies of their parties.

The case study of Namibia in this book shows that even in a democracy, in which women have near parity in a legislature and in which a ruling party has adopted a 50/50 gender policy in representation, women can still find it difficult to assert their interests. Moreover, it is not even evident in the Namibian case that women parliamentarians necessarily agree on common interests or on progressive gender policies. Much of the impetus may come from women's rights movements and activists rather than simply from women parliamentarians. As my study with Alice Kang (2018) showed, parliamentarians generally are most influential around women's rights when they have a women's movement or broader coalition pushing for change. This has also been born out in global studies of gender reform (Htun and Weldon 2018).

A correlation between policy and women's representation is, therefore, most likely to reflect a country's favorable orientation toward women's rights more generally. I use a series of linear regression models to examine the relationship between women's representation and outcomes for women's rights in African countries. The results are presented in Table 10.6. In this table, I examine women's outcomes in education, health, the workplace, entrepreneurship, labor force participation, abortion, marriage, and LGBTQ rights (see Table 10.5 for details on data sources). I first regress each of these outcomes on an interaction between women's representation in Parliament and the country's Freedom House democracy ranking ("free," "partly free," and "not free"). In the table, "free" is the reference category for the Freedom House categorical variable. The Freedom House categories roughly correspond to democracies, hybrid regimes, and autocracies. Second, I regress each outcome on an interaction between women's representation and the V-Dem democracy index score.

The results in Table 10.6 indicate that, when accounting for the interaction between women's representation and regime type, the relationship between women's representation and nearly all of the outcomes for women fails to reach standard levels of statistical significance. The fourth model in Table 10.6 is the only exception, as it is significant at the .10 level. The results from this model indicate a positive and statistically significant relationship between women's representation in Parliament and marriage rights when accounting for regime type using the V-Dem index. However, women's representation and regime type have no impact on gender equality in education, health, entrepreneurship, labor force participation, abortion, and LGBTQ rights. The interactions between women's representation and regime type fail to reach standard statistical significance levels across all models. Some caution is warranted when interpreting the results in Table 10.6, given the small sample size and the small number of countries categorized as "free" or democratic. Still, the results provide suggestive evidence that by and large, there is little to no relationship between women's political representation and regime type in African countries and women's rights outcomes in other domains. In other words, democracies do not differ from autocracies when it comes to women's rights and representation.

Table 10.6 Women's representation and regime type on outcomes for women in Africa

	Health		Marriage rights		LGBTQ index		Abortion		Education		Entrepreneurship		Women in labor force (%)	
Intercept	0.97***	0.98***	87.61***	-22.89	45.91*	0.64	4.40***	1.25	0.97***	0.76***	73.88***	45.77**	38.81***	30.79***
	(−0.01)	(−0.01)	(−21.54)	(−20.36)	(−17.85)	(−18.22)	(−1.16)	(−1.24)	(−0.08)	(−0.09)	(−16.65)	(−17)	(−6.64)	(−6.57)
Women (%)	0.00	0.00	0.15	1.95 **	0.5	0.62	0.02	0.03	0.00	0.00	0.33	0.67	0.14	0.38
	(0.00)	(0.00)	(−0.77)	(−0.72)	(−0.63)	(−0.64)	(−0.04)	(−0.04)	(0.00)	(0.00)	(−0.59)	(−0.6)	(−0.24)	(−0.23)
Freedom House														
Not free	0.00		−63.24*		−19.24		−1.64		−0.19		−18.61		−1.35	
	(0.01)		(25.42)		(21.39)		(1.37)		(0.10)		(19.65)		7.843	
Partly free	−0.01		−11.87		−10.69		−1.08		−0.16		−2.91		4.6	
	(0.01)		(24.80)		(20.55)		(1.34)		(0.10)		(19.17)		(7.65)	
Women (%) x	−0.00		0.87		−0.31		−0.01		0.00		0.15		0.03	
Not free	(0.00)		(0.91)		(0.76)		(0.05)		(0.00)		(0.70)		(0.28)	
Women (%) x	0.00		−0.50		−0.30		−0.03		0.00		−0.13		−0.10	
Partly free	(0.00)		(0.94)		(0.78)		(0.05)		(0.00)		(0.73)		(0.29)	

Continued

Table 10.6 *Continued*

	Health		Marriage		LGBTQ index		Abortion		Education		Entrepreneurship		Women in labor force (%)	
V-Dem Index														
V-Dem index		−0.02		181.70***		72.26		4.27		0.14		45.8		22.87
		(0.01)		(43.11)		(38.08)		(2.62)		(0.20)		(36.00)		(13.94)
Women (%) x V-Dem index		0.00		−3.56*		−0.68		−0.05		−0.00		−0.73		−0.65
		(0.00)		(1.55)		(1.36)		(0.09)		(0.01)		(1.30)		(0.50)
R^2	0.29	0.20	0.29	0.38	0.16	0.19	0.17	0.12	0.28	0.15	0.10	0.09	0.06	0.07
Adj. R^2	0.18	0.13	0.21	0.34	0.06	0.14	0.08	0.07	0.17	0.07	0.00	0.03	−0.05	0.01
Number observations	37	38	51	52	50	51	50	51	37	38	51	52	50	51

*$p < 0.1$, **$p < 0.05$, ***$p < 0.01$.

Note: For the Freedom House categories “Free” is the reference category. “Women (%)” is the percent of women in parliament.

Conclusion

This chapter compared women's rights and leadership in African democracies and autocracies, showing that both regime types can produce similar outcomes in women's representation and some gender-related rights, although the approach and motives of these regimes differ. Democracies fare better than autocracies when it comes to women's representation in cabinets in Africa and globally (Kroeger and Kang 2022; Nyrup 2024). However, democracies and autocracies in Africa show similar levels of women's representation in other political offices, including legislatures, local governments, and other appointments. Regime type (democracy or autocracy) doesn't strongly predict women's legislative representation, which is instead influenced more by factors like quotas, postconflict conditions, party institutionalization and entrenchment.

African autocracies and hybrid regimes are often as likely if not more so than democracies to include women's rights provisions in constitutions. These reforms, often aspirational, reflect state commitments to international norms. They may also serve as a form of virtue signaling to bolster legitimacy domestically and internationally. In autocracies, constitutions often serve as tools to maintain control, including as symbolic commitments to women's rights that may lack practical enforcement. Despite large gaps between stated rights and enforcement, these provisions can still signal modernity and conformity to international standards.

This study also shows that autocracies and democracies with higher levels of female representation are equally likely to promote women's rights in other areas. However, democracies generally fare better in supporting LGBTQ rights, abortion, and protections within marriage, areas where autocracies are often more restrictive. Overall, the chapter suggests that while regime type shapes motivations and implementation, both democracies and autocracies in Africa can adopt similar women's rights reforms, with autocracies sometimes using them as strategic tools for internal control and external validation.

11
Conclusions

Situating African Countries in Global Perspective

Many ruling parties in authoritarian countries in Africa and beyond have promoted women as leaders as part of a strategy to legitimize their rule to ensure continued domination. As a result, one of the main determinants of whether an authoritarian regime has advanced women in politics is the ruling party's longevity. In Africa, the longer a party has been an entrenched hegemonic party, the more likely it is to have advanced women's rights compared to countries undergoing conflict and coups, countries with hybrid regimes in which there are alternating parties in power, countries under military regimes, and countries under other forms of personalistic rule. Countries that remain with such entrenched parties enjoying uninterrupted power are more likely to promote women as leaders and invest in improving women's status. In contrast, parties in hybrid regimes that alternate parties in power tend to exhibit greater risk aversion when fielding women candidates.

With the shift from one-party to multiparty rule after the 1990s, the hegemonic parties needed ways to maintain vote share. They adopted tactics like co-optation and repression of the opposition as well as intense de-campaigning of opponents in order to maintain their dominance. The use of reserved seats for women was another such mechanism. Reserved seats are a type of quota found only in authoritarian regimes in Africa. These seats are easier to control than voluntary party quotas or legislated quotas that leave candidate selection in the hands of individual political parties. All of these tactics made it more likely that women politicians in authoritarian regimes would align with the ruling party since they knew this had a greater chance of guaranteeing victory. Running on an opposition party ticket was riskier for women than for male candidates in an authoritarian country like Uganda.

This chapter looks at the African experiences from a broader comparative perspective to show where they converge and diverge from patterns in select authoritarian countries in other times and places around the world. The chapter begins by providing an overview of the conditions giving rise to

Why African Autocracies Promote Women as Leaders. Aili Mari Tripp, Oxford University Press.
 DOI: 10.1093/9780197829004.003.0012

women in politics in Africa. It then looks at additional reasons women leaders have been instrumentalized from other parts of the world. The patterns found in Africa generally comport with what one finds in other authoritarian contexts, but the specificities and rationales understandably vary owing to different conditions. The chapter also explores patterns in countries most and least likely to advance women.

The Changing Face of African Politics

The face of African politics changed substantially after the 1990s as larger numbers of women entered legislatures, cabinets, and subnational politics. After 2000, women ran for the presidency in many African countries for the first time; they formed political parties and led them. Women were becoming ministers, not only in the ministries historically associated with women (e.g., community development, youth, sports, education, and health) but also in ministries of defense, finance, and foreign affairs.

This book has suggested a variety of conditions that gave rise to strategies to promote women in authoritarian regimes in Africa. These changes mainly happened after the early 1990s because of a confluence of several factors with the end of the Cold War relating to (a) a shift from one-party to multiparty rule and some opening of political space, which allowed for autonomous women's organizations to press for women's rights reforms, (b) an end to many major conflicts, and (c) changing international norms.

Political Liberalization

After the 1990s, we saw an increase in shifts from one-party to multiparty rule in Africa. In some countries, even in ones that did not fully democratize, the democratization processes themselves gave women activists an entry point into politics and influencing political outcomes. Women's movements played critical roles in demanding women's leadership. There had already been considerable mobilization in Africa leading up to the Nairobi UN Conference on Women in 1985 (Forester et al. 2022) and even more coalition building in advance of the UN Conference on Women in 1995. The case of Zimbabwe shows how an active women's movement successfully pressed for constitutional reforms, establishing a gender quota. In Uganda, pressure from women's organizations helped usher in many women to top executive posts.

However, the book also highlights the contradictions inherent in promoting women because these efforts at establishing legitimacy simultaneously boosted the longevity of the ruling parties.

In some autocracies, the use of reserved seats for women factored into the need to maintain parliamentary vote share after countries transitioned from single-party to multiparty rule in countries like Uganda and Mauritania. The Mauritanian case illustrates how the entrenchment of a political party and its staying power was partially related to the increase in women leaders. It shows how the end of military rule and the decline in coups and attempted coups led to the rise of the Equity Party (formerly, UPR) as an entrenched party, along with advances for women in power. The study of Uganda demonstrated how the need to maintain vote share resulted in efforts to keep opposition parties at bay by making it less likely for opposition women to gain reserved seats in Parliament. The Zimbabwean case revealed how a victory by an opposition party forced ZANU-PF to seek new strategies involving women's rights and leadership to maintain vote share.

The patterns of women's representation in Africa diverged significantly from the outcomes in the former communist countries in Central and Eastern Europe (CEE), Western and Central Asia, and Russia. In these countries, political liberalization and democratization resulted in a dramatic decline in levels of women's representation. For example, in CEE the drop was steep—from a high of 26.14 percent in 1985 to 11.83 percent in 1990 (see Figure 11.1). Similarly, in other parts of the world, like Mongolia, there were drops in women's representation as the country moved away from communist rule. However, the socialist countries that did not democratize (North Korea, China, Vietnam, Laos, Cambodia, Cuba, Nicaragua, and Grenada) had significantly higher levels of representation than did the democracies in their region.

Donno and Kreft (2019) observe that party-based authoritarian systems, like the ones mentioned above, fare better in advancing women's rights than other forms of autocracy (e.g., personalist, military, or monarchic rule). With the decline of socialism, quota systems were dropped, and with multiparty rule, parties sought advantage in other ways. The socialist Soviet Union and the CEE countries, for example, had, on average, higher rates of women's representation than the Nordic countries from the late 1940s until around 1985. It should be noted that these socialist countries did not generally promote women to the highest ranks of leadership, such as the Politburo in the Soviet Union. Some have argued that because of the low levels of representation at the upper echelons of power, the adoption of soft quotas that resulted in elevated levels of representation by world standards were symbolic in nature,

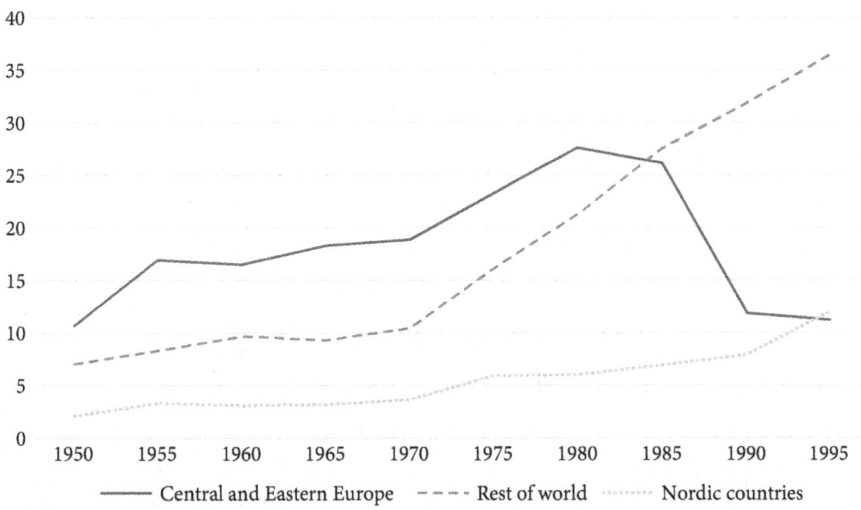

Figure 11.1 Women's legislative representation in Eastern and Central Europe, Nordic countries, and the rest of the world
Sources: IPU (1995).

reflecting the egalitarian ideological goals of the regimes. However, generally, the communist countries also did better than democracies when it came to other measures of gender equality. For example, CEE countries fared well compared to democracies when it came to education, workforce participation, maternity and child-care leave, job security, child care, protections for single mothers, the right to abortion and contraceptives, and other social provisions (Gal and Kligman 2000). Many of these provisions for women were tied to egalitarian ideologies and labor force needs.

However, even some noncommunist autocracies like South Korea after 1987 saw their levels of representation plummet with democratization. In other noncommunist countries like Indonesia, levels of female representation increased, but only incrementally. After democratizing in the 1980s, women's movements across Latin America pushed for greater gender equality in political representation, yielding varied outcomes. Between 1991 and 2000, eleven of nineteen Latin American nations adopted legislated gender quotas. Argentina, which democratized in 1985, led the way by enacting the world's first legislated gender quota law (Ley de Cupo) in 1991, marking a significant milestone for both the country and the region. While the levels of representation rose, they did so slowly and steadily, from 12.9 percent in 1987 to 35.3 percent in 2024 in the Americas, according to the IPU. However, on balance, when examined in relation to cross-national studies (Stockemer

2009; Komer and Tripp 2025), democracy is *not* associated with significantly higher levels of women's representation as compared to nondemocracies.

Postconflict Impacts

In Africa, postconflict nations tend to have higher proportions of women in legislative and ministerial roles. However, countries that experienced liberation wars against Portugal—such as Angola, Mozambique, Cape Verde, and Guinea Bissau—had higher levels of representation in Africa with the end of the Portuguese empire in 1975. Postconflict Namibia, South Africa, and Zimbabwe also stand out as countries with relatively higher levels of women's political representation in the executive and legislature. There was a dramatic decline in the number of conflicts in Africa, especially after 2000, even in countries that had been embroiled in long-standing wars. Countries with prolonged conflicts and major casualties saw some of the biggest changes in women's political representation as new elites entered power at this time.

After conflict, there was generally a change in political elites that allowed new actors, such as women, to enter politics. Women's movements in these countries often took advantage of political opportunities (e.g., peace accords, constitutional and legislative reforms, electoral reforms) that allowed them to press for increased representation. Because women make up more than 50 percent of any given population, their votes can significantly tip the balance in a government. Women were not necessarily the only beneficiaries of these reforms. Often, other groups, like people with disabilities and the youth, also profited from increased seats in Parliament, as was the case in Uganda. In Burundi, ethnic quotas were adopted to better reflect the country's demographics. However, not all marginalized groups have benefited from these developments, as we have seen from the suppression of the LGBTQ population in Uganda, even though they have been very active in mobilizing for their rights.

These same patterns of postconflict increases in women's representation were evident globally, particularly in Asia. In Vietnam after 1975, with the end of the Vietnam War and the reunification of North and South Vietnam, female representation jumped from zero in 1970 to 29.8 percent in 1971. Similar increases occurred later with the end of the conflict in Nepal in 2006 when levels of representation increased from 3.4 percent when the war started in 1996 to 32.8 percent after a quota was adopted at the end of the war in 2009. In Timor Leste, the rate of female representation increased by 136 percent after the country won independence from Indonesia through armed conflict.

Changing International Norms

Finally, international norms regarding women's rights and leadership were changing after the 1990s. Pressures for women's rights reform from international organizations like the United Nations, especially UN Women and the UNDP, regional bodies like the African Union, and subregional organizations like the SADC created incentives for improving gender equality and women's representation but also for status signaling. The use of women leaders was regarded as an exceptionally effective and visible way of signaling gender equality. All of these processes opened up political opportunities for women's movements to press for women's leadership. Adopting quotas, often with the encouragement of UN agencies after 1995, resulted in large increases in women's representation in countries worldwide, more than doubling between 1995 and 2024.

Some countries and parties adopted quotas long before the international norms had changed. The Chinese Communist Party adopted gender quotas as early as 1933 while it was fighting the Nationalist Party for control of China. This was accompanied by woman-friendly policies like marriage reform, land reform, and efforts to bring women into the labor force (Jiang and Zhou 2024). Egypt also adopted a parliamentary quota as early as 1979, which was repealed in 1985 because it had been passed by Anwar Sadat in a presidential decree when a sitting Parliament was in session. Uganda adopted reserved seats in 1989. The first legislated quota was introduced in Argentina in 1991, stipulating that all parties were to present party lists of at least 30 percent women. These quota systems were introduced before 1995, when the United Nations started encouraging member states to increase the representation of women in government institutions. Initially, the United Nations set targets of 30 percent female representation, but by 2015, it had adopted *Planet 50-50 by 2030: Step It Up for Gender Equality*, which envisions full gender equality by removing all legal, social, and economic barriers to women's empowerment.

The Indeterminate Nature of Hybrid Regimes: Responses to Competition

All regime types confront competing agendas, from women's movements and advocates of democracy and human rights to conservative parties, fundamentalist religious (e.g., Christian, Muslim) movements, and people steeped in traditional and customary legal traditions. Regime responses to these pressures vary considerably by regime type. While in democracies, competition may help increase women's representation (Teele 2018), in hybrid regimes, competition and the need to mediate a wide range of societal and party interests—some of which may oppose women's leadership—makes it harder to promote women leaders than in authoritarian regimes. Levels of representation in hybrid regimes are somewhat lower than what one finds in stable authoritarian regimes in Africa, which can repress the opposition and promote loyal women leaders with less regard for differing opinions. Hybrid regimes are more responsive to societal and political actors, which limits their ability to advance women's representation unilaterally as in autocracies.

Hybrid regimes are inconsistent in how they advance women's rights legislation or policies because they are attempting to mediate competing societal interests. This state waffling is thoroughly analyzed in Alice Kang's (2015) *Bargaining for Women's Rights*, which explains how a hybrid Nigerien regime mediated between women's rights activists and Islamists around women's rights reform, with uneven outcomes as a result of pressures from competing societal forces.

The African hybrid regimes resemble autocratizing regimes in other parts of the world, such as Hungary under Victor Orbán, India under Narendra Modi, and Brazil under Jair Bolsonaro in some ways. For instance, Brazil, under Bolsonaro (2019–2022), exhibited a mix of both retreats in women's rights and expansions in welfare provisions that primarily affected women. About seventy of the woman-friendly laws he took credit for were passed by the prior government but went into effect during his time in office. The 2021 menstrual health law was enacted even though Bolsonaro initially vetoed it. He later reinstituted it after a five-month backlash. This law provided free sanitary pads to girls in public schools, women experiencing homelessness or vulnerability, and women prisoners. He also vetoed an increase in pandemic aid for single mothers and was overruled by congress. Femicide and other forms of violence against women increased during his term, even though he talked tough on gender violence (Nugent 2022).

Poland—which started autocratizing early in the first decade of the 2000s and especially after the national-conservative Law and Justice Party came into power—passed restrictive abortion laws in 2021 while simultaneously improving women's representation in Parliament from 20 percent in 2006 to 28.3 percent after the 2019 elections. This figure rose to 29.6 percent in 2023 after the parliamentary elections in which two leading opposition parties took the lead. Poland remains with restrictive abortion and LGBTQ legislation, reflecting the influence of the Catholic Church.

In autocratizing Hungary under President Victor Orbán, same-sex couples do not enjoy the same legal privileges as heterosexual married couples.

The Hungarian government passed a law in 2021 banning gay education and certain advertising labeled as "homosexual and transexual propaganda." However, Hungary has consistently enhanced women's employment opportunities. Between 2013 and 2022, the employment rate for women increased from 52.6 percent to nearly 70 percent, while the female unemployment rate dropped from 10 percent to 3.5 percent. Legislative representation of women never recovered after the drops in representation after socialist rule, when women held 30 percent of the seats in 1980. After 1990, female representation dropped to 7.3 percent; today, it stands at 14.6 percent. Here again, we see an inconsistent commitment to women's rights in an autocratizing regime.

Military Regimes

In this book, I show that military, monarchical, and personalist regimes do not do as well as party-based authoritarian regimes when it comes to women's leadership in Africa. They are more prone to coups and instability, which does not bode well for women leaders. Their leadership culture is overwhelmingly male and patriarchal. This is based on a comparative assessment, but it does not mean that military regimes have never improved women's status, as is evident in Thomas Sankara's Burkina Faso (Chapter 2).

Mala Htun (2003) explores some of the gains made by women under Latin American military juntas. She contends that despite the influence of the Catholic Church on conservative military governments in Latin America, these governments occasionally succeeded in implementing gender-related reforms between 1960 and 1990. They viewed these reforms as a means of alleviating pressure from mobilized popular classes and leftist movements while fostering investment, economic growth, and modernization. For instance, in Argentina during the late 1960s, the military government undertook significant reforms to the civil and criminal codes. These reforms included granting married women expanded property rights, allowing couples to obtain judicial separations through mutual consent, and enacting new laws permitting abortion in cases of rape. In Brazil during the 1970s, the military government legalized divorce, extended equal property rights to married women, liberalized contraception laws, and introduced a national women's health program in 1983. Under the Chilean dictator Augusto Pinochet, changes were made to the civil code in 1989 affording married women full civil capacity. In spite of these examples, generally, progress for women under authoritarian rule has come from party-based systems.

Strategies of Authoritarian Rule

This book has suggested various strategies adopted by authoritarian regimes using women leaders to promote legitimacy and ensure ruling party longevity or entrenchment. These strategies, in turn, led to increases in women's representation. They have included the need to maintain parliamentary vote share in multiparty contexts like Mauritania, Uganda, and Zimbabwe. The Mauritanian case showed how the entrenchment of a political party and the enhancement of its staying power was related to the increase in women leaders. It showed how the end of military rule and the decline in coups and attempted coups led to advances for women in power. The Zimbabwean case showed how pressure from an opposition party forced the ruling party to seek new strategies involving women's rights and leadership to maintain vote share to minimize competition.

Although most of the promotion of women leaders is primarily directed at domestic constituencies, the appointment of women leaders has also been used for purposes of international status signaling to soften the image of an illiberal regime abroad in the hopes of accessing more significant FDIs, loans, and foreign aid. It is a way of enhancing a regime's status internationally and vis-à-vis neighboring countries thereby boosting internal legitimacy. In the case of Rwanda, women's leadership is part of a broader effort by the government to improve the status of women in multiple arenas, particularly the economic sphere. It is also part of an effort to portray the country favorably to paint a positive image of a postgenocidal country externally but also to divert attention from human rights abuses and external interventions in the DRC. Internally, the picture is more complex. As long as one does not resist the government, one can manage and even benefit from the many improvements that Kagame's regime has introduced, but opposing the regime is a recipe for repression.

In Morocco, the efforts to improve women's status and leadership have been part of a strategy to sideline Salafists and moderate internal politics, while responding to women's movement demands. Women's rights are also used to signal to the EU and other potential trade, investment, and aid partners that Morocco is a modern progressive country while leaving behind any lingering associations with jihadist elements.

However, as this book shows, it was not only autocracies that used women's rights in performative ways. Even democracies like Namibia did this but for different reasons. Unlike autocracies, they did not use their record on women's leadership to obscure human rights abuses or enhance ruling party vote share. Like autocracies, the political elite in democracies also may wish to curate their country's domestic and international image, but the pressures to do so by promoting women leaders are not as pressing as they are for autocracies. The case of Botswana illustrates this clearly, as it has felt no pressure to increase its representation of women, even as it has improved its international standing in other areas of women's rights and ranks highly along key measures in Africa and globally.

Genderwashing as a Strategy

Some have suggested that authoritarian regimes are engaged in genderwashing as an attempt to deceive external and internal audiences that their gender policies are a sham. Although they may be engaged in virtue or status signaling, there are several limits to the claims that they are engaged in deception. The main problem with autocracies and their instrumentalization of women leaders is not their effort to create a façade, but rather that they use women leaders as part of a broader strategy to repress the opposition and curtail political choice, freedoms, and rights.

It is unclear whether authoritarian regimes in Africa have adopted women's rights reforms that are any hollower than those of African or other democracies. Countries with the highest rates of female representation in legislatures also have the strongest records of women's rights reform in other areas (Komer and Tripp 2025). Their promotion of women as leaders is part of a broader strategy to address women's rights, even if limited, uneven, and often constrained by a lack of state capacity.

The Case of the UAE

Some countries like the UAE have sought to incorporate women into the workforce and improve women's status as a way of diversifying their economy and moving it away from oil dependence. The UAE, for example, instrumentalizes women's rights for both domestic and external purposes. The UAE is a monarchy that has taken ambitious steps toward becoming one of the world's most gender-equal nations. They have pursued this goal by actively increasing the representation of women in key leadership roles within the government, diplomatic corps, and judiciary. For example, the UAE strives to set an example for gender equality and has become a significant supporter of the UN Women organization. In 2017, Lana Nusseibeh from the UAE assumed the role of president of the UN Women Executive Board. In the UAE today, women occupy 50 percent of parliamentary seats and 30 percent of cabinet positions, and between 2015 and 2019, the speaker of the Parliament was a woman. Women make up 30 percent of UAE ambassadors, and they are taking on numerous high-profile international positions.

The UAE has simultaneously made significant strides in bringing women into the workforce. The UAE positions itself as a global and regional champion of gender equality, often describing itself in press releases as a "stupendous" exemplar for the rest of the world in the realm of women's rights. While one may debate the degree of their success in these endeavors, one of their main motivations is to bring women into the economy to diversify it and move it away from reliance on hydrocarbons. Saudi Arabia is making similar gestures. And while the UAE has made significant gains in promoting women in politics, it does not make any effort to reform family law to promote gender equality.

This type of virtue signaling is unlikely to fool voters or foreign donors. Donors are aware of their partners' records and can determine women's status in these countries. It is not a secret how many women are represented in Parliament or the cabinet. Moreover, in a country like Morocco, citizens, particularly men, misperceive and underestimate their fellow citizen's commitments to gender equality by a large margin, according to work by Carolyn Barnett (2023). This is especially true in countries where there has objectively been moderate progress in women's rights, yet people tend to believe that others are more conservative than themselves. The misperceptions are less pronounced in countries with high or low success levels in advancing women's rights. If people misperceive popular support for government successes negatively, they are probably not being lulled into thinking that there has been major progress on women's rights.

To be sure, if authoritarian regimes have a strong record around women's rights and representation, they may use this record to deflect from a poor human rights record. But that does not diminish their accomplishments in women's rights. Moreover, their accomplishments often result from pressure from women's movements and international actors. Autocracies are no different from democracies in that they may have multiple objectives in promoting women as leaders. Finally, determining autocrats' "real" motives is not likely to be a productive endeavor since multiple state actors are involved with varied and changing concerns. Divining leaders' true objectives would be virtually impossible.

The Case of China

Yet another goal of various authoritarian regimes has been the imperative to increase the workforce by encouraging a combination of natalist policies that simultaneously keep women in the workforce, resulting in a mixture of seemingly contradictory policies. Women constitute one-quarter (24.9 percent) of the National People's Congress in the People's Republic of China. There have only been six women in the Politburo of the Chinese Communist Party (CCP) in its entire hundred-year history, and three were wives of party founders. At this time, there are no women in the Politburo for the first time in twenty-five years (Kapp 2022). There are only eleven women (5.4 percent) in the Central Committee, even though the percentage of women in the CCP has increased from 23.8 percent (20.27 million) in 2012 to 29.8 percent (29.3 million) in 2022 (Statista 2023).

Women make up 45.2 percent of the workforce in China but find themselves discriminated against, especially at the higher echelons of the workforce. Nevertheless, some improvements have been made in the legal environment for women in recent years to address workplace discrimination, sexual harassment, domestic violence, and limited access to education and employment opportunities. China's National People's Congress Standing Committee updated the Women's Rights and Interests Protection Law in 2023, the first amendment in fifteen years. Employers can no longer withhold promotions based on factors like marriage, pregnancy, or parental status, nor can they ask discriminatory questions about a female job applicant's marital or parental status or require pregnancy tests during the hiring process without incurring fines (Interesse 2023).

Perhaps the most important factors driving these new laws are the slowing economy and the aging population, which must be replenished to sustain China's aging population. The one-child policy—introduced in 1980 to facilitate economic growth—had resulted in steep declines in the number of births—from 25.29 million in 1987 to 9.02 million in 2023. It also resulted in a drop in the percentage of women because of male preference and sex-selection practices. The sex ratio at birth went as high as 121.2 in 2004, which is well above the global male–female sex ratio of 1.03–1.07. After China relaxed its one-child policy in 2016, allowing for two children if both parents are only children, the ratio came down to 111.3 (National Bureau of Statistics of China et al. 2023). After 2021, three children were permitted per couple, and the government launched a campaign to encourage women to have more children. At the 2023 National Women's Congress, Xi Jinping exhorted women to "actively foster a new type of marriage and childbearing culture," encouraging them to get married and have babies. The CCP also calls for a return to traditional family values (Stevenson 2023). At the same time, young women are reluctant to get married and have children, given the expense and other challenges of raising a family and working.

Part of the new labor policies, which tackle sexual harassment, may also be a response to China's #MeToo movement, even though the government imprisoned some of the #MeToo activists (Gan 2023). Activists like China's Five Feminist Sisters, who staged protests like "Occupy the Men's Restroom" and "Bloody Bride" to draw attention to daily gender inequality, were detained, effectively silencing protest (Peng 2021). The movement, however, was able to evade China's sophisticated censorship system (the "Great Firewall") through the creative use of emojis and illustrations that were hard to detect (Athlekar 2023).

In African countries, birth rates are decreasing. Still, they are almost four times greater than China's (4.45 children per woman on average in Africa compared with 1.09 in China). Thus, the dynamics and state goals regarding women in Africa are entirely different from those in China. In African countries, the average gender ratio is within the normal range (1.03–1.04), indicating no sex selection. While natalist policies are also present in many African countries, they differ significantly from those in China, taking the form of antiabortion and anti-LGBTQ sentiments. They are motivated by factors that have to do with conservative religious and traditional influences, Western conservative religious influences, the lack of a strong welfare system to care for older adults, postconflict need to replenish the population, and the demands of an agrarian population for labor. The comparison between African countries and China suggests that the sources of pro-natalist ideologies in authoritarian regimes can differ dramatically depending on context. Therefore, although authoritarian regimes may share similar patriarchal orientations, what motivates them may vary considerably.

Repressive Gender Regimes

Finally, we should make mention of the most repressive gender regimes. Some nondemocratic contexts are indeed antithetical to women's rights reforms, including countries living under military or despotic personal rule or where there is continued instability, coups, and conflict. In these countries, the leaders are generally not interested in most forms of policy reform, nor are they generally receptive to pressure from women's movements. At best, they may be selectively interested in some reforms, like girls' education, while flagrantly violating women's rights in other key areas. Some of these countries have formed a bloc within the United Nations called the Group of the Friends of the Family, which has actively worked to undermine progress on women's rights on the international stage. The group includes Russia, Egypt, Iran, Saudi Arabia, and other countries.There are no African countries that are as restrictive and religiously hegemonic as Iran and Afghanistan to mention two examples, although there have been periods and pockets of similar repression. There have been, for example, cases in the recent past of severe restrictions on women in the sharia-controlled states of northern Nigeria around charges of adultery. Algeria also went through its share of extreme subjugation of women during the Black Decade when the Islamists tried to take control. However, these instances are uncommon when compared with the repression women face in countries like Iran or Afghanistan.

Conclusions

Are the advances in women's political representation in autocratic countries opportunities for those interested in improving women's status, or are they part of the broader project of entrenching authoritarianism? This book suggests that they are both. Thus, the instrumentalization of women's rights creates a conundrum that is not easily resolved. On the one hand, it makes sense for women's rights activists to demand power because, with power, they are in a better position to influence women's rights and democratic reforms. On the other hand, they risk providing legitimacy to a regime that is inherently problematic from a human rights perspective, as it seeks absolute dominance over its adversaries. They may help legitimize a regime in ways that enhance its longevity and entrenchment. Authoritarian regimes, by definition, are hostile to democratic rights and liberties and can undermine women's movements that are key generators of reform.

Some women get into politics to advance certain causes. Some women align with the ruling party because it is the only way they can win and have influence. Others align themselves because it is a source of patronage, wealth, and political aggrandizement. Sometimes, women in politics use the same means as autocratic men to remain in power (e.g., violence, corruption). This creates another kind of ambiguity that is difficult to disentangle, as is evident in the Zimbabwean case, in which women autocrats like Grace Mugabe and Joïce Mujuru played the same game as men and used the women's rights agenda to advance themselves.

Political, economic, and symbolic gains for women can be made under authoritarian rule, but they come at a cost. The cost may be steep when women's rights and leaders are instrumentalized to serve goals other than the advancement of the welfare of women and society as a whole. They can come with simultaneous co-optation and repression, particularly of those very same women who are advocating for the right to drive, the right to inherit land, the right to wear what they want to wear, the right to abortion, and the rights of sexual minorities. The top-down appearance of some of these reforms can taint them and make them easy to reject should a new, more democratic government come into power, putting women's rights advocates on the defensive. Thus, the equation is not simple and can be treacherous.

Authoritarian governments may be positively disposed toward endorsing constitutional provisions and legislation concerning women's rights and signing on to international and regional treaties, but they can also be unreliable when it comes to funding and implementing policies. Authoritarian policies can be inverted to serve purposes that have little to do with women's movement goals, as we saw in President Alberto Fujimori's Peru in the 1990s, when he used reproductive rights programs to sterilize poor women, much to the horror of women's rights activists. At this time, Peru had an electoral authoritarian regime.

Key demands can easily be subordinated to other priorities since authoritarian leaders are not as beholden to constituencies as democratic leaders might be, as we have seen in countless ministries of women that have been formed and defunded (Noh 2024). Women's representation and quotas can be reversed as easily as they can be adopted if they are deemed to threaten the dominance of the ruling party, as was evident in the case of Algeria, where a quota law was introduced in 2011 and then, for all intents and purposes, withdrawn in 2021. Women's representation fell from 25.8 percent in 2017 to 7.9 percent in 2021. Women politicians and women's movements run the risk of being co-opted and losing legitimacy if they "fly too close to the sun" by aligning themselves too closely with authoritarian rulers.

The same regime that promotes women leaders may also work against women's welfare in other areas, as we saw in the case of Rwanda, where women vendors have been imprisoned, or in Uganda, where the LGBTQ community has come under dangerous punitive legal constraints. Many regimes in Africa have been hostile to improving women's right to abortion and LGBTQ rights and addressing reforms in family law. Where women's movements have been stronger, we are more likely to see reforms that take women's own welfare and interests as a starting point.

While this book has shown some of the possibilities for women's rights activism in authoritarian regimes, it has also offered a sobering look at their limits. We can see the fickle nature of authoritarian regimes in that they can grant rights as easily as they can remove them. However, we have also seen the resilience of women's rights activists in the face of daunting challenges. One cannot help but be in awe of those who engage in these struggles. As one Zimbabwean activist put it aptly when I asked why she continued to persevere in the face of seemingly unsurmountable odds, "Yes, progress has been made. And my children will be able to do things that I'm not able to do now if we keep pushing, so there is momentum. It will take time. I don't know how much time it will take, but every little step counts" (Z12.5.31.21).

Bibliography

Abbott, Pamela, and Dixon Malunda. 2016. "The Promise and the Reality: Women's Rights in Rwanda." *African Journal of International and Comparative Law* 24 (4): 561–581.

Abdullah, Hussaina. 1993. "Transition Politics' and the Challenge of Gender in Nigeria." *Review of African Political Economy* 20 (56): 27–41.

"Africa: Mauritania Moderate Islamic Parties." *Africa Research Bulletin*, August 1–31, 2007, 17193.

Afrobarometer Survey. n.d. Afrobarometer. Accessed December 1, 2024. https://www.afrobarometer.org/online-data-analysis/.

Ahmed, Dawood I., and Moamen Gouda. 2015. "Measuring Constitutional Islamization: The Islamic Constitutions Index." *Hastings International and Comparative Law Review*.38 (1): 1–74.

Aikins, Enoch Randy, and Alize Roux. 2023. "Could FDI Be Rwanda's Lifeline as Donors Pull the Plug?" *Institute for Security Studies*, April 27.

Akello, Grace. 1982. "Self Twice-Removed: Ugandan Women." *Change (UK) International Reports: Women and Society* 8.

Allan, Joanna. 2019. *Silenced Resistance: Women, Dictatorships, and Genderwashing in Western Sahara and Equatorial Guinea.* Madison: University of Wisconsin Press.

Allison, Simon. 2017. "Grace Mugabe: The Rags to Riches Rise and Fall of 'Gucci Grace.'" *The Guardian*, November 15, https://www.theguardian.com/world/2017/nov/15/grace-mugabe-the-rags-to-riches-rise-and-fall-of-gucci-grace.

Amupanda, Job Shipululo, and Erika Kahelende Thomas. 2019. "SWAPO's 50/50 Policy in Namibia's National Assembly (2015–2018): Full of Sound and Fury Signifying Nothing?" *Strategic Review of Southern Africa* 41 (2): 1–25.

Amupanda, Job Shipululo, and Ralph Marenga. 2019. "The Ascendancy of Esther Utjiua Muinjangue to the NUDO Presidency in Namibia: A Challenge to Patriarchy?" *Journal of Namibian Studies* 26:73–91.

Anderson, Miriam J., and Liam Swiss. 2014. "Peace Accords and the Adoption of Electoral Quotas for Women in the Developing World, 1990–2006." *Politics & Gender* 10 (1): 33–61.

Andersson, K., K. Pettersson, and J. B. Lodin. 2022. "Window Dressing Inequalities and Constructing Women Farmers as Problematic—Gender in Rwanda's Agriculture Policy." *Agricultural Human Values* 39: 1245–1261. https://doi.org/10.1007/s10460-022-10314-5.

Arendt, Christie Marie. 2018. "From Critical Mass to Critical Leaders: Unpacking the Political Conditions Behind Gender Quotas in Africa." *Politics & Gender* 14 (3): 295–322.

Arriola, Leonardo R., and Martha C. Johnson. 2014. "Ethnic Politics and Women's Empowerment in Africa: Ministerial Appointments to Executive Cabinets." *American Journal of Political Science* 58 (2): 495–510.

Ashimwe, Edwin. 2023. "Rwanda Registers Record-High Growth in Women-Owned Businesses." *The New Times*, May 6, https://www.newtimes.co.rw/article/7305/news/women/rwanda-registers-record-high-growth-in-women-owned-businesses.

Athlekar, Prajakta. 2023. "How China's #MeToo Evaded the 'Great Firewall' in the Digital World." *Diggit Magazine*, September 25.

Bahizi, Heritier. 2023. "Top 10 History-Making Rwandan Women Athletes." *The New Times*, June 16, https://www.newtimes.co.rw/article/8311/sports/other-sports/top-10-history-making-rwandan-women-athletes.

Baliamoune-Lutz, Mina. 2013. *The Effectiveness of Foreign Aid to Women's Equality Organizations in the MENA*. UNU-WIDER Working Paper No. 2013/074. Helsinki: UNU-WIDER.

Balme, Stéphanie, and Michael W. Dowdle. 2009. *Building Constitutionalism in China*. Sciences Po Series in International Relations and Political Economy. New York: Palgrave Macmillan.

Bankole, Akinrinola, Lisa Remez, Onikepe Owolabi, Jesse Philbin, and Patrice Williams. From Unsafe to Safe Abortion in Sub-Saharan Africa: Slow but Steady Progress. New York: Guttmacher Institute, December 2020. Figure 1.1. https://www.guttmacher.org/report/from-unsafe-to-safe-abortion-in-subsaharan-africa.

Barnes, Tiffany D., and Stephanie M. Burchard. 2012. "Engendering Politics: The Impact of Descriptive Representation on Women's Political Engagement in Sub-Saharan Africa." *Comparative Political Studies* 46 (7): 767–790.

Barnett, Carolyn. 2023. "Women's Rights and Misperceived Gender Norms Under Authoritarianism." *Comparative Political Studies* 57(14): 1–32.

Barros, Robert. 2002. *The Constitution of Dictatorship*. New York: Cambridge University Press.

Bauer, Gretchen. 2004. "'The Hand That Stirs the Pot Can Also Run the Country': Electing Women to Parliament in Namibia." *The Journal of Modern African Studies* 42 (4): 479–509.

Bauer, Gretchen. 2011. "Update on the Women's Movement in Botswana: Have Women Stopped Talking?" *African Studies Review* 54 (2): 23–46.

Bauer, Gretchen. 2008. "Fifty/Fifty by 2020: Electoral Gender Quotas for Parliament in East and Southern Africa." *International Feminist Journal of Politics* 10 (3): 348–368.

Bauer, Gretchen, and Jennie E. Burnet. 2013. "Gender Quotas, Democracy, and Women's Representation in Africa: Some Insights from Democratic Botswana and Autocratic Rwanda." *Women's Studies International Forum*. 41 (2): 103–112.

Becker, Heike. 2019. "Women in Namibia." *Oxford Research Encyclopedia of African Histories*. https://doi.org/10.1093/acrefore/9780190277734.013.525

Bekoe, Dorina A. 2012. "Political Violence Since 2005" (research report). In *Mauritania: On the Road to Democracy or Just More Violence?*, by Dorina A. Bekoe, Institute for Defense Analyses. https://www.jstor.org/stable/resrep26947.7.

Belschner, Jana. 2022. "Electoral Engineering in New Democracies: Strong Quotas and Weak Parties in Tunisia." *Government and Opposition* 57 (1): 108–125. https://doi-org.ezproxy.library.wisc.edu/10.1017/gov.2020.34.

Bernhard, Michael, Amanda Edgell, and Staffan I. Lindberg. 2020. "Institutionalising Electoral Uncertainty and Authoritarian Regime Survival." *European Journal of Political Research* 59 (2): 465–487.

Berriane, Yasmine. 2013. *Femmes, associations et politique à Casablanca*. Rabat, Morocco: Centre Jacques-Berque.

Berry, Marie E. 2018. *War, Women, and Power: From Violence to Mobilization in Rwanda and Bosnia-Herzegovina*. New York: Cambridge University Press.

Bhatasara, Sandra, and Manase Kudzai Chiweshe. 2021. "Women in Zimbabwean Politics Post-November 2017." *Journal of Asian and African Studies* 56 (2): 218–233.

Binder, Seth, and Eve Sandberg. 2021. *Mohammed VI's Strategies for Moroccan Economic Development*. New York: Routledge.

Biri, K. 2021. "'Munhu wese kuna Amai'? (Everyone to Our Mother): A Pentecostal Perspective on the Deployment of Motherhood in Zimbabwean Politics." In *Personality Cult and Politics in Mugabe's Zimbabwe*, edited by E. Chitando, 148–159. London: Routledge.

Bjarnegård, Elin, and Pär Zetterberg. 2011. "Removing Quotas, Maintaining Representation: Overcoming Gender Inequalities in Political Party Recruitment." *Representation* 47 (2): 187–199.

Bjarnegård, Elin, and Pär Zetterberg. 2016. "Gender Equality Reforms on an Uneven Playing Field: Candidate Selection and Quota Implementation in Electoral Authoritarian Tanzania." *Government and Opposition* 51 (3): 464–486.

Bjarnegård, Elin, and Pär Zetterberg. 2022. "How Autocrats Weaponize Women's Rights." *Journal of Democracy* 33 (2): 60–75.

Blanshe, Musinguzi. 2022. "Rwanda & DRC Accuse Each Other of Using Rebel Groups to Their Advantage." *The Africa Report*, June 10.

Bleck, Jaimie, and Nicolas Van de Walle. 2018. *Electoral Politics in Africa Since 1990: Continuity in Change*. Cambridge, UK: Cambridge University Press.

Bond, Johanna. 2017. "Gender and Post-Colonial Constitutions in Sub-Saharan Africa." In *Constitutions and Gender*, edited by Helen Irving, Edward Elgar, 81–106.

BONELA (Botswana Network on Ethics, Law, and HIV/AIDS). 2016. *BONELA Strategy 2017–2021: A New Era in Health Rights—Fighting Marginalisation*. Gaborone, Botswana.

"Botswana: Gender and Elections." n.d. *Gender Links*, https://genderlinks.org.za/what-we-do/sadc-gender-protocol/advocacy-50/50/botswana-gender-and-elections/. Accessed June 6, 2025.

Boukhars, Anouar. 2016, February 11. *Mauritania's Precarious Stability and Islamist Undercurrent*. Carnegie Endowment for International Peace, Washington, D.C.

Bratton, Michael, Ravi Bhavnani, and Tse-Hsin Chen. 2012. "Voting Intentions in Africa: Ethnic, Economic or Partisan?" *Commonwealth and Comparative Politics* 50 (1): 90–115.

Bratton, Michael, and Eldred Masunungure. 2008. "Zimbabwe's Long Agony." *Journal of Democracy* 19 (4): 41–55.

Braun, Virginia, and Victoria Clarke. 2006. "Using Thematic Analysis in Psychology." *Qualitative Research in Psychology* 3 (2): 77–101.

Brown, Andrea M. 2001. "Democratization and the Tanzanian State: Emerging Opportunities for Achieving Women's Empowerment." *Canadian Journal of African Studies* 35 (1): 67–98.

Brown, Sara E. 2014. "Female Perpetrators of the Rwandan Genocide." *International Feminist Journal of Politics* 16 (3): 448–469. http://dx.doi.org/10.1080/14616742.2013.788806.

Bueno de Mesquita, Bruce, and George W. Downs. 2005. "Development and Democracy." *Foreign Affairs* 84 (5): 77–85.

Burain, Elizabeth. 2014. *Reserved Seats for Women: Encouraging Female Political Participation in the Pacific* 95 (1): 1-4. https://www.pacwip.org/wp-content/uploads/2021/03/Reserved-Seats-for-Women-in-the-Pacific-CPA.pdf

Burnet, Jennie E. 2008. "Gender Balance and the Meanings of Women in Governance in Post-Genocide Rwanda." *African Affairs* 107 (428): 361–386.

Burnet, Jennie E. 2012. *Genocide Lives in Us: Women, Memory, and Silence in Rwanda; Women in Africa and the Diaspora*. Madison: University of Wisconsin Press.

Burnet, Jennie E. 2019. "Rwanda: Women's Political Representation and Its Consequences." In *The Palgrave Handbook of Women's Political Rights*, edited by Susan Franceschet, Mona Lena Krook, and Netina Tan, 563–576. London: Palgrave Macmillan UK.

Bush, Sarah. 2011. "International Politics and the Spread of Quotas for Women in Legislatures." *International Organization* 65 (1): 103–137.

Bush, Sarah Sunn, Daniela Donno, and Pär Zetterberg. 2024. "International Rewards for Gender Equality Reforms in Autocracies." *American Political Science Review* 118 (3): 1189–1203. https://doi-org.ezproxy.library.wisc.edu/10.1017/S0003055423001016.

Bush, Sarah Sunn, and Pär Zetterberg. 2021. "Gender Quotas and International Reputation." *American Journal of Political Science* 65 (2): 326–341.

Bwana, Charles N. 2009. "Voting Patterns in Uganda's Elections: Could It Be the End of the National Resistance Movement's (NRM) Domination in Uganda's Politics?" *Les cahiers d'Afrique de l'est: The East African Review* 41:81–93. https://journals.openedition.org/eastafrica/582.

Bwire, Job. 2021. "Museveni: New Cabinet Members Are Loyal, Hardworking." *The Monitor*, June 10, https://www.monitor.co.ug/uganda/news/national/museveni-new-cabinet-members-are-loyal-hardworking-3432746.

Calabrese, Linda, Phyllis Papadavid, and Judith Tyson. 2017. Rwanda: Financing for Manufacturing. London: Supporting Economic Transformation. https://set.odi.org/wp-content/uploads/2017/06/Financing-for-Manufacturing-Rwanda-June-2017.pdf.

Camara, Fatou Kiné. 2010. "States and Religions in West Africa: Problems and Perspectives." In *Law and Religion in the 21st Century: Relations Between States and Religious Communities*, edited by Rinaldo Cristofori and Silvio Ferrari. London: Routledge.

Cavatorta, Francesco, and Emanuela Dalmasso. 2009. "Liberal Outcomes Through Undemocratic Means: The Reform of the *Code de statut personnel* in Morocco." *Journal of Modern African Studies* 47 (4): 487–506.

Central Statistical Bureau. 1985. *Tsentral'noye Statisticheskoye Upravleniye USSR, Zhenschchiny i Deti SSSR: Statisticheskii Sbornik, Moskva, Finansy i Statistika, 1959, 1967, 1985* [Central Statistical Bureau of USSR, Women and Children in USSR: Statistical handbook, Moscow, finances and statistics, 1959, 1967, 1985]. Moscow: Central Statistical Bureau of USSR.

Cesari, Joycelyne. 2017. "Introduction." In *Islam, Gender and Democracy in Comparative Perspective*, edited by Jocelyne Cesari and José Casanova. Oxford: Oxford University Press, 15-45.

Changachirere, Glanis. 2020. "The Gendering of Violence in Zimbabwean Politics." *African Arguments*. https://africanarguments.org/2020/12/the-gendering-of-violence-in-zimbabwean-politics/.

Charrad, Mounira M. 2001. *States and Women's Rights: The Making of Postcolonial Tunisia, Algeria, and Morocco*. Berkeley: University of California Press.

Chenoweth, Erica, and Zoe Marks. 2022. "Revenge of the Patriarchs: Why Autocrats Fear Women." *Foreign Affairs* 101:103–116.

Chinyepi, Chigedze Virginia. 2021. *Situation Analysis of Women's Political Participation in Botswana*. International IDEA. https://genderlinks.org.za/wp-content/uploads/2021/06/Bots-Situation-Analysis-LR.pdf.

Clayton, Amanda. 2014. *Namibia at a Crossroads: 50/50 and the Way Forward*. Windhoek, Namibia: Embassy of Finland.

Clayton, Amanda, Cecilia Josefsson, Robert Mattes, and Shaheen Mozaffar. 2019. "In Whose Interest? Gender and Mass–Elite Priority Congruence in Sub-Saharan Africa." *Comparative Political Studies* 52 (1): 69–101.

Clayton, Amanda, Cecilia Josefsson, and Vibeke Wang. 2017. "Quotas and Women's Substantive Representation: Evidence from a Content Analysis of Ugandan Plenary Debates." *Politics & Gender* 13 (2): 276–304.

Coffé, Hilde. 2012. "Conceptions of Female Political Representation: Perspectives of Rwandan Female Representatives." *Women's Studies International Forum*. 35 (4): 286–297.

Commission of the European Communities. 2000. "Communication on 'Reinvigorating the Barcelona Process.'" September 6(COM (2000) 497).

Cooley, Alexander. 2015. "Authoritarianism Goes Global: Countering Democratic Norms." *Journal of Democracy* 26 (3): 49–63.

Cooper, Barbara M. 1995. "The Politics of Difference and Women's Associations in Niger: Of 'Prostitutes,' the Public, and Politics." *Signs: Journal of Women in Culture and Society* 20 (4): 851–882.

Cornwall, Andrea, Elizabeth Harrison, and Ann Whitehead. 2008. *Gender Myths and Feminist Fables: The Struggle for Interpretive Power in Gender and Development.* Vol. 38. Malden, MA: Wiley-Blackwell.

Darhour, H., and D. Dahlerup. (2013). "Sustainable Representation of Women Through Gender Quotas: A Decade's Experience in Morocco." *Women's Studies International Forum*, 41 (Part 2): 132–142. https://doi.org/10.1016/j.wsif.2013.04.008.

De Roeck, Mathias, Filip Reyntjens, Stef Vandeginste, and Marijke Verpoorten. 2016. "Institutions in Burundi and Rwanda: A 20-Year Data Overview." In *L'Afrique des grands lacs: Annuaire 2015–2016*, edited by Filip Reyntjens, Stef Vandeginste and Marijke Verpoorten, 9–50. Antwerp: University Press Antwerp.

Decker, Alicia. 2014. *In Idi Amin's Shadow: Women, Gender, and Militarism in Uganda.* Athens: Ohio University Press.

Dendere, Chipo. 2018. "Finding Women in the Zimbabwean Transition." *Meridians* 17 (2): 376–381.

Dennis, Carolyne. 1987. "Women and the State in Nigeria: The Case of the Federal Military Government 1984–85." In *Women, State and Ideology: Studies from Africa and Asia*, edited by Haleh Afshar, 13–27. Berlin: Springer.

Department of Gender Affairs, Ministry of Nationality, Immigration, and Gender Affairs, Government of Botswana, https://www.gov.bw/subsidies/financial-support-women-policy-guidelines. Accessed June 6, 2025.

Devlin, Claire, and Robert Elgie. 2008. "The Effect of Increased Women's Representation in Parliament: The Case of Rwanda." *Parliamentary Affairs* 61 (2): 237–254.

Disney, Jennifer Leigh. 2008. *Women's Activism and Feminist Agency in Mozambique and Nicaragua.* Philadelphia: Temple University Press.

Donno, Daniela, Sara Fox, and Joshua Kaasik. 2022. "International Incentives for Women's Rights in Dictatorships." *Comparative Political Studies* 55 (3): 451–492. https://doi.org/10.1177/00104140211024232.

Donno, Daniela, and Anne-Kathrin Kreft. 2019. "Authoritarian Institutions and Women's Rights." *Comparative Political Studies* 52 (5): 720–753.

Donno, Daniela, and Bruce Russett. 2004. "Islam, Authoritarianism, and Female Empowerment: What Are the Linkages?" *World Politics* 56 (4): 582–607.

Dube, Mqondisi. 2024. "Activists Want More Women in Botswana's National Assembly." *Voice of America*, November 7, https://www.voanews.com/a/activists-want-more-women-in-botswana-s-national-assembly/7855206.html.

Edgell, Amanda B. 2017. "Foreign Aid, Democracy, and Gender Quota Laws." *Democratization* 24 (6): 1103–1141.

El Kettab, Nejwa. 2012. *Engagement politique et associatif des femmes en Mauritanie: Le "négoféminisme maure"; entre stratégies féminines et pratiques informelles du pouvoir politique.* Master 2 sociology, Université de Picardie Jules Verne.

Electoral Commission of Namibia, https://www.ecn.na/. Accessed June 16, 2025.

Electoral Commission of Uganda. 2016. *2016 General Elections Summary.* https://www.ec.or.ug/2016-general-elections-summary.

Elkins, Zachary, and James Melton. 2014. "The Content of Authoritarian Constitutions." In *Constitutions in Authoritarian Regimes*, edited by Tom Ginsburg and Alberto Simpser, 141–164. Comparative Constitutional Law and Policy. Cambridge, UK: Cambridge University Press.

Equaldex. "LGBT Equality Index." Accessed June 6, 2025. https://www.equaldex.com/equality-index.Erdman, Joanna N., and Paola Bergallo. 2024. "Abortion Law Illiberalism and Feminist Politics in Comparative Perspective." *Annual Review of Law and Social Science* 20 (October): 273–291. https://doi.org/10.1146/annurev-lawsocsci-041822-030149.

Esping-Andersen, Gøsta, Duncan Gallie, Anton Hemerijk, and John Myers. 2002. *Why We Need a New Welfare State.* Oxford: Oxford University Press.

Essof, Shereen. 2005. "She-Murenga: Challenges, Opportunities and Setbacks of the Women's Movement in Zimbabwe." *Feminist Africa* 4:29–45.

European Democracy Hub. EU Support for Women's Political Participation and Leadership under the EU's Gender Action Plan: A Case Study on Morocco. 2021. https://epd.eu/content/uploads/2023/08/GAP-Morocco.pdf.

Fallon, Kathleen M. 2008. *Democracy and the Rise of Women's Movements in Sub-Saharan Africa.* Baltimore: Johns Hopkins University Press.

Fallon, Kathleen M., Liam Swiss, and Joyceln Viterna. 2012. "Resolving the Democracy Paradox: Democratization and Women's Legislative Representation in Developing Nations, 1975 to 2009." *American Sociological Review* 77 (3): 380–408.

Farris, Sara R. 2017. *In the Name of Women's Rights: The Rise of Femonationalism.* Durham, NC: Duke University Press.

Feather, Ginger Reeves. 2022. "Towards a Feminist Foreign Policy? New Approaches to the EU as a Global Actor." In *The Gendered Politics of Crises and De-Democratization: Opposition to Gender Equality*, edited by Bianka Vida. Colchester, UK: ECPR Press, 67–90.

Fernandes, Jorge M., Mariana Lopes da Fonseca, and Miguel Won. 2024. "Political Competition and the Effectiveness of Gender Quotas: Evidence from Portugal." *The Journal of Politics* 86: (1). 183–198.

Fish, Steven. 2002. "Islam and Authoritarianism." *World Politics* 55 (October): 4–37.

Forester, Summer, Kaitlin Kelly-Thompson, Amber Lusvardi, and S. Laurel Weldon. 2022. "New Dimensions of Global Feminist Influence: Tracking Feminist Mobilization Worldwide, 1975–2015." *International Studies Quarterly* 66 (1). https://doi.org/10.1093/isq/sqab093

Franceschet, Susan, Mona Lena Krook, and Jennifer M. Piscopo, eds. 2012. *The Impact of Gender Quotas.* Oxford: Oxford University Press.

Franceschet, Susan, and Jennifer M. Piscopo. 2008. "Gender Quotas and Women's Substantive Representation: Lessons from Argentina." *Politics & Gender* 4:393–425.

Frank, Liz. 2001. "Where There Is Political Will, There Is a Way: A Report on the 50/50 Campaign." *Sister Namibia* 13 (5–6): 6.

Frank, Liz. 2004. "Working Towards Gender Balance in Elected Positions of Government in Namibia." In *The Implementation of Quotas: African Experiences*, edited by Julie Ballington, Quota Report Series. Stockholm: International IDEA, 88-95.

Freedom House. 2022. https://freedomhouse.org/.

Freedom House. 2024a. "Freedom in the World: Rwanda." https://freedomhouse.org/country/rwanda/freedom-world/2024.

Freedom House. 2024b. "Countries and Territories." https://freedomhouse.org/countries/freedom-world/scores.

Friedrich, Carl Joachim, and Zbigniew K. Brzezinski. 1961. *Totalitarian Dictatorship and Autocracy.* New York: Praeger.

Funk, Nanette. 2014. "A Very Tangled Knot: Official State Socialist Women's Organizations, Women's Agency and Feminism in Eastern European State Socialism." *European Journal of Women's Studies* 21 (4): 344–360.

Gaidzanwa, Rudo. 1995. "Land and the Economic Empowerment of Women: A Gendered Analysis." *Southern African Feminist Review* 1 (1): 1–12.

Gan, Nectar, and Chinese Human Rights Defenders. "China #MeToo Journalist and Labor Activist Expected to Appear in Secret Trial as Crackdown Deepens." Chinese Human Rights Defenders, September 21, 2023. https://www.nchrd.org/2023/09/china-metoo-journalist-and-labor-activist-expected-to-appear-in-secret-trial-as-crackdown-deepens/?tztc=2. Accessed June 16, 2025.

Gal, Susan, and Gail Kligman. 2000. *The Politics of Gender After Socialism: A Comparative-Historical Essay.* Princeton, NJ: Princeton University Press.

Gandhi, Jennifer, and Adam Przeworski. 2007. "Authoritarian Institutions and the Survival of Autocrats." *Comparative Political Studies* 40 (11): 1279–1301.

Gashumba, Diane. n.d. "Ambassador's Message." Rwanda in Sweden. https://www.rwandainsweden.gov.rw/

Gaudio, Attilio. 1978. *Le dossier de la Mauritanie.* Paris: Nouvelles éditions latines.

Gbadamosi, Nosmot. 2022. "How a US Abortion Ban Would Impact Africa." *Foreign Policy*, June 1.

Geddes, Barbara, Joseph Wright, and Erica Frantz. 2018. *How Dictatorships Work: Power, Personalization, and Collapse.* Cambridge, UK: Cambridge University Press.

Geddes, Barbara, Joseph Wright, and Erica Frantz. n.d. Autocratic Regimes Dataset. Accessed December 1, 2024. https://sites.psu.edu/dictators/.

Geisler, Gisela. 1987. "Sisters Under the Skin: Women and the Women's League in Zambia." *The Journal of Modern African Studies* 25 (1): 43–66.

Geisler, Gisela. 1995. "Troubled Sisterhood: Women and Politics in Southern Africa; Case Studies from Zambia, Zimbabwe and Botswana." *African Affairs* 94 (377): 545–578.

Gerzso, Thalia, and Nicolas van de Walle. 2022. "The Politics of Legislative Expansion in Africa." *Comparative Political Studies* 55(14): 2315-2348.

Ginsburg, Tom. 2020. "Authoritarian International Law?" *American Journal of International Law* 114 (2): 221–260.

Ginsburg, Tom, and Tamir Moustafa. 2008. *Rule by Law: The Politics of Courts in Authoritarian Regimes.* New York: Cambridge University Press.

Ginsburg, Tom, and Alberto Simpser. 2007. "Political Cleaners: Women as the New Anti-Corruption Force?" *Development and Change* 38 (1): 87–105.

Ginsburg, Tom, and Alberto Simpser. 2014. *Constitutions in Authoritarian Regimes.* New York: Cambridge University Press.

Global Database of Quotas for Women. 2025. https://www.idea.int/data-tools/data/gender-quotas-database. Accessed June 6, 2025.

Goetz, Anne Marie. 2007. "Political Cleaners: Women as the New Anti-Corruption Force?" *Development and Change* 38 (1): 87–105.

Goetz, Anne Marie, and Shireen Hassim. 2003. *No Shortcuts to Power: African Women in Politics and Policy Making.* Vol. 3, *Democratic Transition in Conflict-Torn Societies.* London: Zed Books.

Good, Kenneth. 2018. "Bad Khama: The Corruption of the Botswanan Presidency." *Democracy in Africa (DiA).* https://democracyinafrica.org/bad-khama-corruption-botswana-presidency/ Accessed June 6, 2025.

Guariso, Andrea, Bert Ingelaere, and Marijke Verpoorten. 2018. "When Ethnicity Beats Gender: Quotas and Political Representation in Rwanda and Burundi." *Development and Change* 49 (6): 1361–1391.

Guriev, Sergei, and Daniel Treisman. 2019. "Informational Autocrats." *Journal of Economic Perspectives* 33 (4): 100–127.

Haidula, Tuyeimo. 2020. "Civil Society Wins CSE Fight." *Namibian Sun*, December 3, https://www.namibiansun.com/news/civil-society-wins-cse-fight-2020-12-03/?fbclid=IwAR3eZkzvYjvQCP9KmUQiWr7sFsJjf_ZnMkvxVi3_rmW8ODnAS5ZEyIwJdzY.

Hall, Bruce S. 2016. "The Question of 'Race' in the Pre-Colonial Southern Sahara." In *The Sahara: Past, Present and Future*, edited by Jeremy Keenan. London: Routledge.

Hassim, Shireen, and Sheila Meintjes. 2005. "Overview Paper." Presented at the Expert Group Meeting on Democratic Governance in Africa: Strategies for Greater Participation of Women, Arusha, Tanzania. 6–8 December 2005. https://aarhusclearinghouse.unece.org/resources/expert-group-meeting-democratic-governance-africa-strategies-greater-participation-women

Havstad, Lilly. 2022. "Indígena or Não-Indígena? The Gendered Politics of Assimilation in Colonial Mozambique, 1917–61." *Gender & History* 34 (2): 420–436.

Hecht, David. 1996. "In a Nation with Slaves, a Woman Wins a Voice." *Christian Science Monitor*, October 23, 6.

Hern, Erin Accampo. 2020. "Gender and Participation in Africa's Electoral Regimes: An Analysis of Variation in the Gender Gap." *Politics, Groups, and Identities* 8 (2): 293–315. https://doi.org/10.1080/21565503.2018.1458323.

"HM the King Sends Message to Participants in 2nd 'Women in Africa' Initiative Summit." 2018. *Maroc diplomatique*, September 27, https://maroc-diplomatique.net/haca-appel-a-une-mobilisation-efficiente/.

Hogg, Carey Leigh. 2009. "Women's Political Representation in Post-Conflict Rwanda: A Politics of Inclusion or Exclusion?" *Journal of International Women's Studies* 11 (3): 34–55.

Hollyer, James R., and B. Peter Rosendorff. 2011. "Why Do Authoritarian Regimes Sign the Convention Against Torture? Signaling, Domestic Politics and Non-Compliance." *Quarterly Journal of Political Science* 6 (3–4): 275–327.

Htun, Mala. 2003. *Sex and the State: Abortion, Divorce, and the Family Under Latin American Dictatorships and Democracies.* Cambridge, UK: Cambridge University Press.

Htun, Mala, and S. Laurel Weldon. 2018. *The Logics of Gender Justice: State Action on Women's Rights Around the World.* New York: Cambridge University Press.

Hughes, Melanie M. 2009. "Armed Conflict, International Linkages, and Women's Parliamentary Representation in Developing Nations." *Social Problems* 56 (1): 174–204.

Hughes, Melanie M., Mona Lena Krook, and Pamela Paxton. 2015. "Transnational Women's Activism and the Global Diffusion of Gender Quotas." *International Studies Quarterly* 59:357–372.

Hughes, Melanie, and Aili Mari Tripp. 2015. "Civil War and Trajectories of Change in Women's Political Representation in Africa, 1985–2010." *Social Forces* 93 (4): 1513–1540.

Human Rights Watch. 2021a. Human Rights Watch Submission to the Committee on the Elimination of Discrimination *Against* Women Review of the Islamic Republic of Mauritania's Periodic Report for the 80th Pre-Session. https://www.hrw.org/sites/default/files/media_2021/02/202102mena_mauritania_CEDAW_80_0.pdf.

Human Rights Watch. 2021b. Mauritania Events of 2020. https://www.hrw.org/world-report/2021/country-chapters/mauritania#.

Human Rights Watch. 2021c. "Zimbabwe: Thousands of Villagers Facing Eviction: Planned Displacements to Make Way for Commercial Venture." https://www.hrw.org/news/2021/03/06/zimbabwe-thousands-villagers-facing-eviction.

Hungwe, C. 2006. "Putting Them in Their Place: 'Respectable' and 'Unrespectable' Women in Zimbabwean Gender Struggles." *Feminist Africa* 6:33–47.

Ibn Battuta. 1829. *The Travels of Ibn Batuta.* London: Oriental Translation Committee. Samuel Lee (Translator)

"ICESCO's Year of Women: Situation of Moroccan Women Has Shifted from Empowerment to Leadership—Ministers." 2021. March 11. Moroccan News Agency, Maghreb Arabe Presse (MAP). https://www.mapnews.ma/en/actualites/social/icescos-year-women-situation-moroccan-women-has-shifted-empowerment-leadership

"Idi Amin Decrees on Mini-Skirts, Gonorrhea and Wigs." 2015. *Daily Monitor*, Saturday, May 30, 2015. https://www.monitor.co.ug/uganda/magazines/people-power/idi-amin-decrees-on-mini-skirts-gonorrhoea-and-wigs-1612806.

IKhaxas, Elizabeth, and Liz Frank. 2014. "50/50: Claiming Space for Women's Citizenship." *Sister Namibia* 26 (2): 14–15.

Inglehart, Ronald, and Pippa Norris. 2003a. *Rising Tide: Gender Equality and Cultural Change Around the World*. Cambridge, UK: Cambridge University Press.

Inglehart, Ronald, and Pippa Norris. 2003b. "The True Clash of Civilizations." *Foreign Policy* 135:62–70.

Inglehart, Ronald, Pippa Norris, and Chris Welzel. 2002. "Gender Equality and Democracy." *Comparative Sociology* 1 (3–4): 321–345.

Inter-Parliamentary Union (IPU). 1995. *Women in Parliaments, 1945–1995: A Worldwide Statistical Survey*. Geneva: Inter-Parliamentary Union.

Inter-Parliamentary Union (IPU). 2024. "IPU Parline: Monthly Ranking of Women in National Parliaments." Accessed November 30, 2024. https://data.ipu.org/women-ranking?month=1&year=2024.

Interesse, Giulia. 2023. "China Takes Steps to Empower Women: Latest Developments in Women's Protection Law." *China Briefing*, March 8.

International Federation for Human Rights. 2012. "Rwanda: Victoire Ingabire Sentenced to Eight Years Imprisonment After a Trial Marred by Irregularities and a Lack of Transparency" (press release), August 8. https://www.fidh.org/en/region/Africa/rwanda/Rwanda-Victoire-Ingabire-sentenced-12399.

IRIN. "Lack of Legal Status Hinders the Progress of Women." 2005. UN Integrated Regional Information Networks. 18 August. Available online at http://www.irinnews.org/PrintReport.aspx?ReportId=55910, accessed 22 May 2008.

Isiksel, Turkuler. 2013. "Between Text and Context: Turkey's Tradition of Authoritarian Constitutionalism." *International Journal of Constitutional Law* 11 (3): 702–726.

Jervis, Robert. 1989. *The Logic of Images in International Relations*. New York: Columbia University Press.

Jiang, X., and Y. Zhou. 2024. "When Socialist Legacy Meets International Norms: Gender Quota Adoption and Institutional Change in China." *Journal of Contemporary China* 33 (1): 1–20. https://doi.org/10.1080/10670564.2023.2299964.

Jirira, Kwanele Ona. 1995. "Gender, Politics and Democracy: Kuvaka Patsva (Reconstructing)—the Discourse." *Southern African Feminist Review* 1 (2): 1-29.

Josefsson, Cecilia. 2007. "Constructing Representations of the 'Global War on Terror' in the Islamic Republic of Mauritania." *Journal of Contemporary African Studies* 25 (1): 77–100.

Josefsson, Cecilia. 2014. "Who Benefits from Gender Quotas? Assessing the Impact of Election Procedure Reform on Members of Parliament's Attributes in Uganda." *International Political Science Review* 35 (1): 93–105.

Jourde, Cédric. 2007. "Constructing Representations of the 'Global War on Terror' in the Islamic Republic of Mauritania." *Journal of Contemporary African Studies* 25 (1): 77–100.

Kagame, Paul. 2010. "President Kagame Presents Candidature at National Electoral Commission." PaulKagame.com, June 24. https://www.paulkagame.com/dent-kagame-presents-candidature-at-national-electoral-commission-kigali-24-june-2010/.

Kagame, Paul. 2014. "Keynote Address by President Paul Kagame at the Women in Parliaments Global Forum—Joint Session with MDG Advocacy Group, Kigali, 3

July 2014." Paul Kagame Official Website. https://www.paulkagame.com/keynote-address-by-president-paul-kagame-at-the-women-in-parliaments-global-forum-joint-session-with-mdg-advocacy-group/.

Kane, Bakala. 2013. "Interview de Aïssata Kane: 'J'aurai fait voté une loi instituant le quota' à l'éducation nationale au gouvernement et au parlement en faveur de la femme mauritanienne." *Seneweb*, October 19, https://www.seneweb.com/blogs/bakalakane/interview-de-aissata-kane-laquo-j-rsquo-aurai-fait-vote-une-loi-instituant-le-quota-raquo-a-l-rsquo-education-nationale-au-_b_44.html.

Kang, Alice J. 2015. *Bargaining for Women's Rights: Activism in an Aspiring Muslim Democracy*. Minneapolis: University of Minnesota Press.

Kang, Alice, and Aili Mari Tripp. 2018. "Coalitions Matter: Citizenship, Women, and Quota Adoption in Africa." *Perspectives on Politics* 16 (1): 73–91.

Kantengwa, M. Juliana. 2010. "The Will to Political Power: Rwandan Women in Leadership." *IDS Bulletin* 41 (5): 723–80.

Kapp, Caroline. 2022. "Women This Week: Female Representation Regresses in China." *Council on Foreign Relations*, October 28.

Kavhu, Sharon. 2023. "Fight for LGBTIQ Rights in Namibia Goes on After Landmark Court Ruling." *Open Democracy*, June 30.

Kelley, Judith G. 2017. *Scorecard Diplomacy: Grading States to Influence Their Reputation and Behavior*. Cambridge, UK: Cambridge University Press.

Kethusegile-Juru, B. M. 2002. "Intra-Party Democracy and the Inclusion of Women." In Workshop: Electoral Perspectives and the Process of Democratization in DRC: Lessons from SADC. Johannesburg: EISA Research Report.

Kenworthy, L., and M. Malami. 1999. "Gender Inequality in Political Representation: A Worldwide Comparative Analysis." *Social Forces* 78 (1): 235–268.

"Kenyatta Praises Namibia's Gender Policy." 2019. *APA Report*, March 22, https://apanews.net/kenyatta-praises-namibias-gender-policy/.

"Kenyatta Team Lacoste vs. G40: ED 'Poisoning' Triggers Vicious Fight." 2017. *The Standard*. September 10.

Khisa, Moses. 2016. "Managing Elite Defection in Museveni's Uganda: The 2016 Elections in Perspective." *Journal of Eastern African Studies* 10 (4): 729–748.

Khisa, Moses. 2018. "The Limits of Renting Support." *The Observer*, October 10.

Kittilson, Miki Caul. 2006. *Challenging Parties, Changing Parliaments: Women and Elected Office in Contemporary Western Europe*. Columbus: The Ohio State University Press.

Komer, Monica C., and Aili Mari Tripp. *Women's Rights and Representation in Authoritarian Regimes*. Prepared for Politics & Gender Conference, Rutgers University, May 28, 2025.

Kroeger, Alex, and Alice J. Kang. 2024. "The Appointment of Women to Authoritarian Cabinets in Africa." *Government and Opposition* 59 (4): 1206–1229. https://doi.org/10.1017/gov.2022.32.

Krook, Mona Lena. 2006. "Reforming Representation: The Diffusion of Candidate Gender Quotas Worldwide." *Politics & Gender* 2 (3): 303–327.

Laperrouze, Jeanne. 2018. "Morocco: Advancing Women's Rights." *The Parliament Magazine*. June 28.

Lapidus, Gail Warshofsky. 1978. *Women in Soviet Society: Equality, Development, and Social Change*. Berkeley: University of California Press.

Larson, Deborah Welch, T. V. Paul, and William C. Wohlforth. 2014. "Status and World Order." In *Status in World Politics*, edited by T. V. Paul, Deborah Welch Larson, and William C. Wohlforth. Cambridge, UK: Cambridge University Press, 3–30.

Laserud, Stina, and Rita Taphorn. 2007. "Designing for Equality: Best-Fit, Medium-Fit and Non- Favourable Combinations of Electoral Systems and Gender Quotas?" International Institute for Democracy and Electoral Assistance.https://www.idea.int/sites/default/files/publications/designing-for-equality.pdf. Accessed June 4, 2025.

Law, David S., and Mila Versteeg. 2013. "Sham Constitutions." California Law Review 101 (4), 863–952. https://www.jstor.org/stable/23784322.

LeBeau, Debie. 2005. "Multiparty Democracy and Elections in Namibia." *Journal of African Elections* 4 (1): 1–26.

Lebow, Richard Ned. 2008. *A Cultural Theory of International Relations.* Cambridge, UK: Cambridge University Press.

Legal Information Institute. 2024. "Botswana." https://www.law.cornell.edu/women-and-justice/location/botswana.

Lesourd, Céline. 2007. "Femmes mauritaniennes et politique: De la tente vers le puits?" *L'année du Maghreb* 3:333–348.

Levitsky, Steven, and Lucan A. Way. 2002. "The Rise of Competitive Authoritarianism." *Journal of Democracy* 13 (2): 51-65.

Levitsky, Steven, and Lucan A. Way. 2010. *Competitive Authoritarianism: Hybrid Regimes After the Cold War.* Cambridge, UK: Cambridge University Press.

"LGBT Rights in Rwanda." n.d. *Equaldex.* Accessed October 16, 2024. https://www.equaldex.com/region/rwanda.

Lindberg, Staffan I. 2004. "Women's Empowerment and Democratization: The Effects of Electoral Systems, Participation, and Experience in Africa." *Studies in Comparative International Development* 39 (1): 28–53.

"List of People Expelled from ZANU-PF Following Central Committee Meeting." 2017. *Pindula,* November 19, https://news.pindula.co.zw/2017/11/19/list-people-expelled-zanu-pf-following-central-committee-meeting/#google_vignette

Loewenstein, Karl. 1957. *Political Power and the Governmental Process.* Chicago: University of Chicago Press.

London, Nicole. 2020. "Women in the Rwandan Parliament: Exploring Descriptive and Substantive Representation." MSc thesis, London School of Economics and Political Science, London.

Longman, Timothy. 2006. "Rwanda: Achieving Equality or Serving an Authoritarian State?" In *Women in African Parliaments,* edited by Gretchen Bauer and Hannah E. Britton. Boulder, CO: Lynne Rienner., 133-150.

Luciak, I. A. 2005. "Implementing Gender Equality Provisions: Lessons from the Central American Peace Accords." *Critical Half: Bi-Annual of Women for Women International* 3 (1): 14–19.

Lueker, Lorna L. 1998. "Fighting for Human Rights: Women, War, and Social Change in Zimbabwe." *INSTRAW News* 28:34–44.

Lyons, T. 2004. *Guns and Guerilla Girls: Women in the Zimbabwean National Liberation Struggle.* Trenton, NJ: Africa World Press.

Mainwaring, Scott, and Timothy Scully. 1995. *Building Democratic Institutions: Party Systems in Latin America.* Stanford, CA: Stanford University Press.

Mageza-Barthel, Rirhandu. 2015. *Mobilizing Transnational Gender Politics in Post-Genocide Rwanda.* Farnham, UK: Ashgate.

Mama, Amina. 1995. "Feminism or Femocracy? State Feminism and Democratisation in Nigeria." *Africa Development/Afrique et développement* 20 (1): 37–58.

Mamadou, Thiam. 2006. "Femmes et élections." CRIDEM, November 23. https://cridem.org/C_Info.php?article=5909.

Mamvura, Zvinashe, Mickson Mazuruse, and Innocent Mupandasekwa. 2022. "The Toponymic Undoing of Grace Mugabe and the G40 Narrative in the New Dispensation." In *The Zimbabwean Crisis After Mugabe: Multidisciplinary Perspectives*, edited by Tendai Mangena, Oliver Nyambi, and Gibson Ncube. London: Routledge, 79–96.

Mangena, Tendai. 2022. "Narratives of Women in Politics in Zimbabwe's Recent Past: The Case of Joice Mujuru and Grace Mugabe." *Canadian Journal of African Studies* 56 (2): 407–425.

Manheru, Nathaniel. 2016. "Mujuru: The Story of Scattered Wisdom." *The Herald*, October 8, https://www.herald.co.zw/mujuru-the-story-of-scattered-wisdom/.

"Morocco Has Turned Gender Equality into 'Pillar for Rule of Law' (Ambassador)." *Maroc diplomatique*. April 21, 2022. https://maroc-diplomatique.net/haca-appel-a-une-mobilisation-efficiente/

Matiashe, Farai Shawn. 2023. "Zimbabwe's Election Widens Gender Gap in Politics." *IPS*, November 3, https://allafrica.com/stories/202311060277.html.

Mawere, T. 2017. "The Toxic Masculinity That Fueled Mugabe's Reign in Zimbabwe—and Ended It." *Mail and Guardian*, December 11, https://mg.co.za/article/2017-12-11-the-toxic-masculinity-thatfuelled-mugabes-reign-in-zimbabwe-and-ended-it/.

McNeil Jr., D. 1996. "Zimbabwe Opposition: Ex-Guerrilla Is a One-Woman Tempest." *New York Times*, May 13, A4.

Meierhenrich, Jens. 2020. "How Many Victims Were There in the Rwandan Genocide? A Statistical Debate." *Journal of Genocide Research* 22 (1): 72–82. https://doi.org/10.1080/14623528.2019.1709611.

Meldrum, A. 1995. "Rubber-Stamp Parliament." *Africa Report*, 40 (3): 60–63.

Melber, Henning, Daniela Kromrey, and Martin Welz. 2017. "Changing of the Guard? An Anatomy of Power Within Swapo of Namibia." *African Affairs* 116 (463): 284–310.

Meng, Anne. 2020. *Constraining Dictatorship: From Personalized Rule to Institutionalized Regimes; Political Economy of Institutions and Decisions*. Cambridge, UK: Cambridge University Press.

Meyer, John, John Boli, George Thomas, and Francisco Ramirez. 1997. "World Society and the Nation-State." *American Journal of Sociology* 103:144–181.

"Mo Ibrahim Gives Khama's Presidency the Thumbs Down." 2017. *Sunday Standard/Telegraph*, December 5.

Mohlamenyane, Lerato. 2021. "Presidential Term Limits in Africa: What Should Be Done?" Open Society Initiative for Southern Africa, September 2.

Mokomane, Z. 2008. "Late Marriage and Less Marriage in Botswana." In *Changing Family Systems: A Global Perspective*, edited by T. Maundeni, L. L. Levers, and G. Jacques, 288–311. Gaborone: Bay Publishing.

Mongudhi, T. 2013. "Iivula-Ithana Says 50/50 Is Her Highlight." *The Namibian*, June 27.

Moses, Joel. 1977. "Women in Political Roles." In *Women in Russia*, edited by Dorothy M. Atkinson, Gail Warshofsky Lapidus, and Alexander Dallin. Stanford, CA: Stanford University Press, 324–351.

Mosime, Sethunya, and Maude Dikobe. 2021. "Candidate Training Programmes in Africa—a Waste of Resources or Pedagogies of the Oppressed? Experiences from Letsema Training Workshops in Botswana (2013–19)." In *Gendered Institutions and Women's Political Representation in Africa*, edited by Diana Højlund Madsen, 73–102. London: Zed Books.

MRA (Mobilising for Rights Associates). 2023. Proposals for *Reforms* to the Moroccan Family Code Memorandum. https://mrawomen.ma/wp-content/uploads/doc/Family%20Code%20Advocacy%20Chart%20of%20Recommendations%20Nov%2023.pdf?fbclid=IwAR359qJ4Giq9ZFypROVTxgb-GHajZSup

Mudiwa, Rudo. 2017. "Coups and Phalluses." *Africa Is a Country* (blog), November 28. https://africasacountry.com/2017/11/on-grace-mugabe-coups-phalluses-and-what-is-being-defended/.

"Mugabe Knows What Happened to My Husband, Joice Mujuru Insists." 2016. *News24*, December 9, https://www.news24.com/News24/mugabe-knows-what-happened-to-my-husband-joice-mujuru-insists-20161209.

Mugabe, Robert. 1984. "An Opening Address by the President of ZANU(PF)." Presented at Women's League Conference, March 15–17, Harare, Zimbabwe.

Müller, Henriette, and Christin Camia. 2022. "Between Uniformity and Polarization: Women's Empowerment in the Public Press of GCC States." *Politics & Gender* 19 (1): 166–194. https://doi.org/10.1017/S1743923X21000465.

Mumporeze, Nadine, Eom Han-Jin, and Dominique Nduhura. 2021. "Let's Spend a Night Together, I Will Increase Your Salary: An Analysis of Sextortion Phenomenon in Rwandan Society." *Journal of Sexual Aggression* 27 (1): 120–137. https://doi.org/10.1080/13552600.2019.1692920.

Muriaas, Ragnhild L., Liv Tønnessen, and Vibeke Wang. "Exploring the Relationship Between Democratization and Quota Policies in Africa." *Women's Studies International Forum* 41, part 2 (November–December 2013): 89–93.

Muriaas, Ragnhild L., and Vibeke Wang. 2012. "Executive Dominance and the Politics of Quota Representation in Uganda." *The Journal of Modern African Studies* 59 (2): 309–338.

Mushonga, Netsai. 2011. "Advocacy and Lobbying for Policy Change in Zimbabwe: Women's Lobbying for a Gender-Sensitive Constitution." *The Philanthropist* 23 (4): 247–253.

Musoni, Edwin. 2009. "Rwanda: Govt Cannot Criminalise Homosexuality—Minister." *The New Times*, December 19.

Mutsaka, Farai. 2018. "Zimbabwe's Few Female Candidates Face Scathing Abuse." *Philadelphia Inquirer*, July 27.

Muwanga, Nansozi K., Paul I. Mukwaya, and Tom Goodfellow. 2020. "Carrot, stick, and statute: Elite strategies and contested dominance in Kampala", in Tom Goodfellow, and David Jackman (eds), Controlling the Capital: Political Dominance in the Urbanizing World (Oxford, 2023; online edn, Oxford Academic, 23 Nov. 2023), https://doi.org/10.1093/oso/9780192868329.003.0003.

Muwanigwa, Virginia. 2013. "Zimbabwe: New Constitution Gives Hope to Women and Girls." *Gender Links* (blog), April 8. https://genderlinks.org.za/programme-web-menu/zimbabwe-new-constitution-gives-hope-to-women-and-girls-2013-04-08/.

Nakaweesi-Kimbugwe, Solome, Maria Magezi, Tinah P'Ochan, and Jay Abang. 2018. Country Analysis: Leadership in Advancing Women's Rights in Public Decision-Making Processes in Uganda. Robert Bosch Stiftung. https://www.bosch-stiftung.de/sites/default/files/publications/pdf/2019-08/Uganda%20Country%20Analysis_0.pdf.

"Nam Praised for 50/50 Gender Representation." 2014. The Namibian, July 22, https://www.namibian.com.na/nam-praised-for-50/50-gender-representation/.

"Namibia: Decision to Overturn 'Sodomy' Laws Is a Victory for Human Rights." 2024. *Amnesty International*, June 21, https://www.amnesty.org/en/latest/news/2024/06/namibia-decision-to-overturn-sodomy-laws-is-a-victory-for-human-rights/.

"Namibia Narrowly Misses 50% Women in Parliament." 2020. *Gender Links*, March 24. https://genderlinks.org.za/news/namibia-narrowly-misses-50-mark-after-special-appointments/ Accessed June 6, 2025.

Namibia National Assembly. 2024. https://www.parliament.na/national-assembly/.

Namibia Women's Manifesto Network. 2003. "50/50: Women and Men in Local Government—Get the Balance Right!" *Sister Namibia* 15 (4). https://www.proquest.com/docview/194839225?sourcetype=Scholarly%20Journals.

Nanivadekar, Medha. 2006. "Are Quotas a Good Idea? The Indian Experience with Reserved Seats for Women." *Politics & Gender* 2 (1): 119–128. https://doi.org/10.1017/S1743923X06241011.

National Bureau of Statistics of, China, UNICEF China, and UNFPA China. 2023. "What the 2020 Census Can Tell Us About Children in China: Facts and Figures." UNICEF. https://www.unicef.cn/en/reports/population-status-children-china-2020-census.

National Institute of Statistics of Rwanda. 2019. *National Gender Statistics Report.* Kigali, Rwanda: National Institute of Statistics of Rwanda, Republic of Rwanda, and UN Women.

Ncube, Gibson. 2020. "Eternal Mothers, Whores or Witches: The Oddities of Being a Woman in Politics in Zimbabwe." *Agenda* 34 (4): 25–33.

Nhongo-Simbanegavi, Josephine. 2000. *For Better or Worse: Women and ZANLA in Zimbabwe's Liberation Struggle.* Harare: Weaver Press.

Noh, Yuree. "Public Opinion and Women's Rights in Autocracies." 2024. *Politics & Gender* 20 (1): 241–245. https://doi.org/10.1017/S1743923X22000514.

Noh, Yuree, Sharan Grewal, and M. Tahir Kilavuz. 2024. "Regime Support and Gender Quotas in Autocracies." *American Political Science Review* 118 (2): 706–723. https://doi.org/10.1017/S000305542300059X.

"Nouveau gouvernement: Sept femmes aux commandes." 2021. *Maroc diplomatique,* October 8, https://maroc-diplomatique.net/nouveau-gouvernement-sept-femmes-aux-commandes/.

Novikova, Natalia. 2007. "Communism as a Vision and Practice." *Aspasia* 1 (1): 202–206.

Nugent, Ciara. 2022. "Brazilian Women May Deny President Jair Bolsonaro a Second Term." *Time,* September 16.

Nwankwor, Chiedo. 2021. "Women Cabinet Ministers' Substantive Representation in Africa." *Social Politics: International Studies in Gender, State & Society* 28 (1): 241–264.

Nyamishana, Prudence. 2015. "Outrage After Ugandan Police Strip a Female Opposition Official Naked in Public." *Global Voices,* October 13, https://globalvoices.org/2015/10/13/outrage-after-ugandan-police-strip-a-female-opposition-official-naked-in-public/.

Nyrup, Jacob, Hikaru Yamagishi, and Stuart Bramwell. 2024. "Consolidating Progress: The Selection of Female Ministers in Autocracies and Democracies." *American Political Science Review* 118 (2): 724–743. https://doi.org/10.1017/S000305542300062X.

O'Brien, Diana Z. 2012. "Quotas and Qualifications in Uganda." In *The Impact of Gender Quotas,* edited by Susan Franceschet, Mona Lena Krook, and Jennifer M. Piscopo, 57–71. New York: Oxford University Press.

OECD. n.d. "OECD Data." Accessed December 1, 2024. https://www.oecd.org/en/data.html.

Office Nationale de la Statistique, Ministère de la Santé, et Inner City Fund. 2022. *Enquête démographique et de santé en Mauritanie 2019–2021: Rapport de synthèse.* Nouakchott, Mauritanie: National office of statistics, Ministry of Health.

Okello, Dickens. 2020. "Former Minister Alupo to Contest on Independent Ticket." *Chimpreports,* October 16, https://chimpreports.com/former-minister-alupo-to-contest-on-independent-ticket/.

Oluwole, Victor. 2023. "African Countries Leading the Way in Female Entrepreneurship." *Business Insider Africa,* September 17.

"ONU: Pour le Maroc, la promotion des droits des femmes est une 'priorité nationale.'" 2022. *Maroc diplomatique,* March 16, https://maroc-diplomatique.net/onu-pour-le-maroc-la-promotion-des-droits/.

Oppenheim, Mays. 2022. "Zimbabwean Activist Who Alleges Harrowing Torture by Suspected State Security Now Living in Terror in Europe." *The Independent,* December 21, https://

www.independent.co.uk/news/world/netsai-marova-zimbabwe-torture-allegations-first-interview-b2249303.html.

O'Riordan, Alexander. 2014. "Namibia's 'Zebra' Politics Could Make It Stand Out from the Global Herd." *The Guardian*, July 8, https://www.theguardian.com/global-development/2014/jul/08/namibia-gender-equality-zebra-politics.

Påfs, Jessica, Stephen Rulisa, Marie Klingberg-Allvin, Pauline Binder-Finnema, Aimable Musafili, and Birgitta Essén. 2020. "Implementing the Liberalized Abortion Law in Kigali, Rwanda: Ambiguities of Rights and Responsibilities Among Health Care Providers." *Midwifery* 80 (January): 102568. https://doi.org/10.1016/j.midw.2019.102568.

Paulson-Smith, Kaden, and Aili Mari Tripp. 2021a. "Constitutional Reform and Women's Rights in Africa." *African Affairs* 120 (480): 365–389.

Paulson-Smith, Kaden, and Aili Mari Tripp. 2021b. "Replication Data for Women's Rights and Critical Junctures in Constitutional Reform in Africa (1951–2019)." *Harvard Dataverse*. https://doi.org/10.7910/DVN/DOSEBX.

Paxton, Pamela. 1997. "Women in National Legislatures: A Cross-National Analysis." *Social Science Research* 26:442–464.

Paxton, Pamela, Melanie Hughes, and Matthew A. Painter II. 2010. "Growth in Women's Political Representation: A Longitudinal Exploration of Democracy, Electoral System and Gender Quotas." *European Journal of Political Research* 49 (1): 25–52.

Pelke, Lars. 2021. "Party Institutionalization, Authoritarian Regime Types and Women's Political Equality." *Contemporary Politics* 27 (4): 461–486.

Pinto, Vânia Carvalho. 2019. "Signalling for Status: UAE and Women's Rights." *Contexto Internacional* 41 (2). https://www.scielo.br/scielo.php?pid=S0102-85292019000200345&script=sci_arttext.

Piscopo, Jennifer. 2020. "Women Leaders and Pandemic Performance: A Spurious Correlation." *Politics & Gender* 16 (4): 951–959.

Pitkin, Hanna. *The Concept of Representation*. Berkeley: University of California Press, 1967.

"Plans to Expand Parliament Afoot ... to Accommodate 50/50." 2014. *The Namibian*, June 23.

Powley, Elizabeth. 2003. *Strengthening Governance: The Role of Women in Rwanda's Transition*. Women Waging Peace Policy Commission. https://www.inclusivesecurity.org/wp-content/uploads/2012/08/10_strengthening_governance_the_role_of_women_in_rwanda
_s_transition.pdf. Accessed June 9, 2025.

Przeworski, Adam. 2014. "Ruling Against Rules." In *Constitutions in Authoritarian Regimes*, edited by Tom Ginsburg and Alberto Simpser. New York: Cambridge University Press, 21–35.

Pu, Xiaoyu. 2017. "Ambivalent Accommodation: Status Signalling of a Rising India and China's Response." *International Affairs* 93 (1): 147–163.

Qureshi, Abeeda, and Sara Ahmad. 2021. "Reserved Seats for Women in Pakistan: Reinforcement of Patriarchy and Powerlessness (2002–2018)." *Women's Studies International Forum*, 94, 102629.

Reuters. "African Women's Hard, Dangerous Life in Politics." December 4, 1995.

Ragin, Charles C. 2000. *Fuzzy-Set Social Science*. Chicago: University of Chicago Press.

Renshon, Jonathan. 2017. *Fighting for Status: Hierarchy and Conflict in World Politics*. Princeton, NJ: Princeton University Press.

Reynolds, Andrew. 1999. "Women in the Legislatures and Executives of the World: Knocking at the Highest Glass Ceiling." *World Politics* 51 (4): 547–572.

Reyntjens, Filip. 2015. "Rwanda: Progress or Powder Keg?" *Journal of Democracy* 26 (3): 19–33.

Riedl, Rachel Beatty. 2014. *Authoritarian Origins of Democratic Party Systems in Africa.* Cambridge, UK: Cambridge University Press.

Roggeband, Conny, and Andrea Krizsán. 2024. "Autocratization and Gender Politics." In *The Routledge Handbook of Autocratization*, edited by Aurel Croissant and Luca Tomini, 397–412. Routledge International Handbooks. Abingdon: Routledge. https://doi.org/10.4324/9781003306900-32.

Ross, Michael. 2008. "Oil, Islam, and Women." *American Political Science Review* 102 (1): 107–123.

Ruedin Didier. 2012. "The Representation of Women in National Parliaments: A Cross-National Comparison." *European Sociological Review* 28 (1): 96–109. https://doi.org/10.1093/esr/jcq050.

Rumelili, Bahar, and Ann E. Towns. 2022. "Driving Liberal Change? Global Performance Indices as a System of Normative Stratification in Liberal International Order." *Cooperation and Conflict* 57 (2): 152–170.

Rwaka, Gaston K. 2023. "Rwanda: Government Markets Save Women the Wrath of Local Security." *Panorama*, April 15.

Rwanda Development Board. 2023. "Building Resilience for Sustained Economic Growth" (annual report). https://rdb.rw/ar/2023-RDB-AR.pdf.

"Rwanda Military Aid Cut by US over DR Congo M23 Rebels." 2012. BBC, July 22, https://www.bbc.com/news/world-africa-18944299.

Rwanda NEC (National Electoral Commission). 2018. http://nec.gov.rw/uploads/media/URUTONDE_RW_ABADEPITE_BEMEJWE_BY_AGATEGANYO.pdf. Accessed June 6, 2025.

Rwanda Parliament. n.d. "Women Representation." Accessed November 9, 2024. https://www.parliament.gov.rw/women-representation.

Saarinen, Aino, Kirsti Ekonen, and Valentina Uspenskaia. 2014. "Breaks and Continuities of Two 'Great Transformations.'" In *Women and Transformation in Russia*, Edited By Aino Saarinen, Kirsti Ekonen, Valentina Uspenskaia, 1–28. London: Routledge, Taylor & Francis.

SADC (Southern African Development Committee). 2022. *SADC Gender and Development Monitor 2022.* Gaborone, Botswana: SADC.

Salem Z. Ould, Ahmed. 1997. *Le prétexte de la berceuse: Femmes, poésie populaire et subversion politique en Mauritanie—annuaire de l'Afrique du Nord.* Paris: CNRS Éditions.

Sartori, Giovanni. 1962. "Constitutionalism: A Preliminary Discussion." *American Political Science Review* 56:53–54.

Sartori, Giovanni. 1976. *Parties and Party Systems.* Cambridge, UK: Cambridge University Press.

Schedler, Andreas. 2002. "Elections Without Democracy: The Menu of Manipulation." *Journal of Democracy* 13 (2), 36–50.

Schenker, Elizabeth. 2021. "Mauritania's Failure to Adapt Gender-Based Violence Laws." Jadaliyya. https://www.jadaliyya.com/Details/42348.

Schwindt-Bayer, Leslie A., and William Mishler. 2005. "An Integrated Model of Women's Representation." *The Journal of Politics* 67 (2): 407–428.

Sebudubudu, David, and Bertha Z. Osei-Hwedie. 2006. "Pitfalls of Parliamentary Democracy in Botswana." *Africa Spectrum* 41 (1): 35–53.

Segawa, N. 2016. "Woman Opposition Leader Aims to Shake Up Ugandan Politics." *Global Press Journal*, November 20.

Sengupta, Somini. 2017. "On Europe's Far Right, Female Leaders Look to Female Voters." *New York Times*, March 2.

Shalaby, Marwa. 2025. *Varieties of Power: Women's Political Representation and Authoritarianism in the Middle East and North Africa.* New York: Columbia University Press.

Smith, Zeric Kay, Timothy Longman, Jean Paul Kimonyo, and Théoneste Rutagengwa. 2002. Rwanda Democracy and Governance Assessment. November. USAID. https://pdf.usaid.gov/pdf_docs/Pnacr569.pdf.

Soiri, Iina. 1996. *The Radical Motherhood: Namibian Women's Independence Struggle.* Uppsala: The I Africa Institute.

"#SomeoneTellKayihura Part 2: Joint Press Statement on the Dehumanizing and Degrading Treatment of Women in Active Politics by the Uganda Police Force." 2015. *Dear CEO ... From One CEO to Another* (blog), October 13, https://jackieasiimwe.wordpress.com/2015/10/13/someonetellkayihura-part-2/.

Song, Yu. 2016. "Institutionalizing Rural Women's Political Participation in China: Reserved Seats Election for Women." *Asian Women* 32 (3): 77–99.

Soss, Joe. 2021. "On Casing a Study Versus Studying a Case." In *Rethinking Comparison: Innovative Methods for Qualitative Political Inquiry*, ed. Erica Simmons and Nicholas Rush Smith, 84–106. Cambridge, UK: Cambridge University Press.

Statista. 2023. "Number of Chinese Communist Party (CCP) Members in China from 2012 to 2022, by Gender."

Stevenson, Alexandra. 2023. "China's Male Leaders Signal to Women That Their Place Is in the Home." *New York Times*, November 2, https://www.nytimes.com/2023/11/02/world/asia/china-communist-party-xi-women.html.

Stockemer, Daniel. 2009. "Women's Parliamentary Representation: Are Women More Highly Represented in (Consolidated) Democracies than in Non-Democracies?" *Contemporary Politics* 15 (4): 429–443.

Stockemer, Daniel 2011. "Women's Parliamentary Representation in Africa: The Impact of Democracy and Corruption on the Number of Female Deputies in National Parliaments." *Political Studies* 59:693–712.

Sully, E. A., M. G. Madziyire, T. Riley, A. M. Moore, M. Crowell, M. T. Nyandoro, B. Madzima, and T. Chipato. 2018. "Abortion in Zimbabwe: A National Study of the Incidence of Induced Abortion, Unintended Pregnancy and Post-Abortion Care in 2016." *PLoS One.* 13 (19). https://doi.org/e0205239.

Tamale, Sylvia. 1999. *When Hens Begin to Crow: Gender and Parliamentary Politics in Uganda.* Boulder, CO: Westview Press.

Tauzin, Aline. 2001. *Figures du féminin dans la société maure (Mauritanie).* Paris: Karthala.

Teele, Dawn Langan. 2018. "How the West Was Won: Competition, Mobilization, and Women's Enfranchisement in the United States." *Journal of Politics* 80 (2): 442–461.

Tendi, Blessing-Miles. 2011. "Robert Mugabe and Toxicity: History and Context Matter" *Representation* 47 (3): 307–318.

Thomas, Sue, and Clyde Wilcox, eds. 2005. *Women and Elective Office: Past, Present, and Future.* 2nd ed. New York: Oxford University Press.

Tjitemisa, Kuzeeko. 2022. "Nujoma Hopes for Woman President ... Calls for Youth, Merit-Based Deployment." *New Era Live*, May 11, https://neweralive.na/posts/nujoma-hopes-for-woman-president.

Tønnessen, Liv, and Samia al-Nagar. 2013. "The Women's Quota in Conflict Ridden Sudan: Ideological Battles for and against Gender Equality." *Women's Studies International Forum* 41 (2): 122–131.

Tremblay, Manon. 2007. "Democracy, Representation, and Women: A Comparative Analysis." *Democratization* 14 (4): 533–553.

Tripp, Aili Mari. 2000. *Women and Politics in Uganda.* Madison: University of Wisconsin Press.

Tripp, Aili Mari. 2011. "The Uses and Abuses of 'Women's Rights' in International Donor Discourse." Joint Nordic Conference on Development Research, Copenhagen Business School, Copenhagen, Denmark, November 25.

Tripp, Aili Mari. 2013. *Women's Political Participation in Sub-Saharan Africa.* Report produced for the Conflict Prevention and Peace Forum, March.

Tripp, Aili Mari. 2015. *Women and Power in Postconflict Africa.* Cambridge Studies in Gender and Politics. New York: Cambridge University.

Tripp, Aili Mari. 2019. *Seeking Legitimacy: Why Arab Autocrats Adopt Women's Rights.* Cambridge, UK: Cambridge University Press.

Tripp, Aili Mari. 2021. "The Gendering of Peacebuilding: African Cases." In *Women & Peacebuilding in Africa*, edited by Affi Ladan, Liv Tønnessen, and Aili Tripp. African Issues Vol. 42. Suffolk, UK: Boydell & Brewer.1-28.

Tripp, Aili Mari. 2023. "The Instrumentalization of Women Opposition Leaders for Authoritarian Regime Entrenchment: The Case of Uganda." *Politics and Governance* 11 (1): 152-163.

Tripp, Aili Mari, and Alice Kang. 2008. "The Global Impact of Quotas: On the Fast Track to Increased Female Legislative Representation." *Comparative Political Studies* 41 (3): 338–361.

Tripp, Aili, Isabel Casimiro, Joy Kwesiga, and Alice Mungwa. 2009. *African Women's Movements: Transforming Political Landscapes.* New York: Cambridge University Press.

Tushnet, Mark. 2014. "Authoritarian Constitutionalism." In *Constitutions in Authoritarian Regimes: Comparative Constitutional Law and Policy*, edited by Tom Ginsburg and Alberto Simpser. New York: Cambridge University Press, 36-50.

Uganda Constitution 1995. 2017. Constitute Project. http://https://www.constituteproject.org/constitution/Uganda_2017

Uganda Electoral Commission. 2021. https://www.ec.or.ug/2021-general-elections.

UN Children's Fund (UNICEF). n.d. "UNICEF Data Warehouse." Accessed November 30, 2024. https://data.unicef.org/dv_index/.

UN Human Rights Council. 2021. "Universal Periodic Review—Mauritania." OHCHR. https://www.ohchr.org/en/hr-bodies/upr/mr-index.

UN Integrated Regional Information Network. 2008. "Moves Towards Political Empowerment of Women." *Africa News*, 1 April.

UN Population Division. n.d. "World Population Prospects." World Bank. Accessed September 1, 2022. https://data.worldbank.org/indicator/SP.POP.TOTL.

UN Women. 2013. "Zimbabweans Say Yes to New Constitution Strong on Gender Equality and Women's Rights." April 19. https://www.unwomen.org/en/news/stories/2013/4/zimbabweans-say-yes-to-new-constitution-strong-on-gender-equality-and-womens-rights.

UN Women, Women in Politics: 2025. https://www.unwomen.org/en/digital-library/publications/2025/03/women-in-politics-map-2025. Accessed June 3, 2025.

UN Women. n.d.a. "Global Gender Equality Constitutional Database." Accessed November 30, 2024. https://constitutions.unwomen.org/en.

UN Women. n.d.b. "Global Gender Equality Constitutional Database: Women's Representation in Local Government." Accessed November 30, 2024. https://localgov.unwomen.org/data?indicator=Value&year=2023®ions=212&.

UN Women. n.d.b. "Global Gender Equality Constitutional Database: Women's Representation in Local Government." Accessed June 4, 2025. https://localgov.unwomen.org/data?indicator=Value&year=2023®ions=212&.

UNDP (UN Development Programme). 2022. *Where Are Women? Gender Equality in Public Administration in Africa.* https://www.undp.org/sites/g/files/zskgke326/files/2022-03/UNDP-UPitt-2022-Gender-Equality-in-Public-Administration-Africa-EN1.pdf.

UN Population Fund (UNFPA). 2018. "First Lady Takes #BeFree Movement to Ohangwena and Omusati Regions." July 3.

United Nations. 2022. *Experts of the Committee on the Elimination of Discrimination Against Women Congratulate Namibia on the Adoption of Its First National Action Plan on Women, Peace and Security, and Ask Questions About Gender Parity in Politics and Early Marriage.* OHCHR, June 17. https://www.ohchr.org/en/news/2022/06/experts-committee-elimination-discrimination-against-women-congratulate-namibia.

US State Department. 2022. "Secretary Antony J. Blinken and Rwandan Foreign Minister Vincent Biruta at a Joint Press Availability." August 11.

V-Dem (Varieties of Democracy). 2022. https://www.v-dem.net/.

Valdini, Melody E. 2019. *The Inclusion Calculation: Why Men Appropriate Women's Representation.* Oxford: Oxford University Press.

Van de Walle, Nicolas. 2003. "Presidentialism and Clientelism in Africa's Emerging Party Systems." *The Journal of Modern African Studies* 41 (2): 297–321.

Venditto, Bruno, Beatha Set, and Rachel Ndinelao Amaambo. 2022. "Sexualization and Dehumanization of Women by Social Media Users in Namibia." *Sexes* 3:445–462.

Viterna, Jocelyn, Kathleen M. Fallon, and Jason Beckfield. 2007. "Development, Democracy, and Women's Legislative Representation: Re-Visiting Existing Explanations of Gender Variation in the World's Parliaments." Working Paper #288, East Lansing, MI: Women and International Development, Michigan State University. https://gencen.isp.msu.edu/files/1214/5202/6820/WP288.pdf

Walsh, Denise M. 2011. *Women's Rights in Democratizing States: Just Debate and Gender Justice in the Public Sphere.* Cambridge, UK: Cambridge University Press.

Walton, Adele. 2022. "The Revolutionary Feminism of Thomas Sankara." *Jacobin*, March 8.

Wang, Vibeke. 2013. "Women Changing Policy Outcomes: Learning from Pro-Women Legislation in the Ugandan Parliament." *Women's Studies International Forum* 41:113–121.

Wang, Vibeke, and Mi Yung Yoon. 2018. "Recruitment Mechanisms for Reserved Seats for Women in Parliament and Switches to Non-Quota Seats: A Comparative Study of Tanzania and Uganda." *The Journal of Modern African Studies* 56 (2): 299–324.

Watchdog Uganda. 2021. "Open Letter to President Museveni: The Case for More Women in Cabinet and a Female Speaker of Parliament." https://www.watchdoguganda.com/op-ed/20210522/114308/open-letter-to-president-museveni-the-case-for-more-women-in-cabinet-and-a-female-speaker-of-parliament.html.

Waylen, Georgina. 2007. *Engendering Transitions: Women's Mobilization, Institutions, and Gender Outcomes.* Oxford: Oxford University Press.

Weeks, Ana Catalano. 2018. "Why Are Gender Quota Laws Adopted by Men? The Role of Inter- and Intraparty Competition." *Comparative Political Studies* 51 (14): 1935–1973.

Weeks, Ana Catalano, Bonnie M. Meguid, Miki Caul Kittilson, and Hilde Coffé. 2023. "When Do Männerparteien Elect Women? Radical Right Populist Parties and Strategic Descriptive Representation." *American Political Science Review* 117 (2): 421–438.

Weghorst, Keith R., and Michael Bernhard. 2014. "From Formlessness to Structure? The Institutionalization of Competitive Party Systems in Africa." *Comparative Political Studies* 47 (12): 1707–1737.

Weingast, Barry R. 1997. "The Political Foundations of Democracy and the Rule of the Law." *American Political Science Review* 91 (2): 245–263.

Welborne, Bozena. 2010. "The Strategic Use of Gender Quotas in the Arab World." William and Kathy Hybl Democracy Studies Fellowship Paper. Washington, DC: IFES.

Welborne, Bozena. 2022. *Women, Money, and Political Participation in the Middle East.* New York: Palgrave Macmillan.

Werbner, Pnina, and Richard Werbner. 2020. "Adultery Redefined: Changing Decisions of Equity in Customary Law as 'Living Law' in Botswana." *PoLAR: Political and Legal Anthropology Review* 43 (1): 136–152.

Wharton Social Impact Initiative. 2021. "The Transformative Power of Women Leaders in Rwanda." The More Than Ever Tour panel convened by Dean Erika James and led by Vice Dean Katherine Klein. Wharton School University of Pennsylvania, March 18.https://alumni.wharton.upenn.edu/all-stories/alumni/the-transformative-power-of-women-leaders-in-rwanda/ Accessed June 9, 2025.

White House. 2023. "Message to the Congress on the Continuation of the National Emergency with Respect to Zimbabwe." March 1. https://www.whitehouse.gov/briefing-room/presidential-actions/2023/03/01/letter-to-the-congress-on-the-continuation-of-the-national-emergency-with-respect-to-zimbabwe/.

"Who Is Jessica Alupo, Uganda's Vice President Designate?" 2021. *The Independent*, June 10, https://www.independent.co.ug/who-is-jessica-alupo-ugandas-vice-president-designate/.

Wiley, Katherine Ann. 2018. *Work, Social Status, and Gender in Post-Slavery Mauritania*. Bloomington, IN: Indiana University Press.

Wing, Susanna. 2008. *Constructing Democracy in Transitioning Societies of Africa: Constitutionalism and Deliberation in Mali*. New York: Palgrave Macmillan.

World Bank. 2020. *Doing Business 2020*. Washington, DC: World Bank.

World Bank. 2021. *Women, Business and the Law, 2021*. Washington, DC: World Bank.

World Bank Open Data. https://data.worldbank.org/. Accessed June 5, 2025.

World Bank. 2024. "Proportion of Women in Ministerial Level Positions (%)." https://genderdata.worldbank.org/en/indicator/sg-gen-mnst-zs. Accessed June 4, 2025.

World Bank. n.d. "Gender Data Portal: Sub-Saharan Africa." https://genderdata.worldbank.org/en/regions/sub-saharan-africa#:~:text=536%20women%20die%20per%20100%2C000,2000%20to%20536%20in%202020. Accessed June 5, 2025.

World Bank Group. n.d. "The World Bank in Morocco." Accessed November 9, 2024. https://www.worldbank.org/en/country/morocco/overview#2.

World Economic Forum. 2022. Global Gender Gap Report 2022. https://www3.weforum.org/docs/WEF_GGGR_2022.pdf.

World Economic Forum. 2023. Global Gender Gap Report 2023. https://www.weforum.org/publications/global-gender-gap-report-2023/.

World Economic Forum. 2024. Global Gender Gap Report 2024. Accessed December 1, 2024. https://www3.weforum.org/docs/WEF_GGGR_2024.pdf.

World Trade Organization. 2024. Country Profile. 2024. BIS international banking statistics. Accessed September 1, 2024. https://www.bis.org/statistics/consstats.htm.

Yoon, Mi Yung. 2004. "Explaining Women's Legislative Representation in Sub-Saharan Africa." *Legislative Studies Quarterly* 24 (3): 447–468.

Yoon, Mi Yung. 2013. "Special Seats for Women in Parliament and Democratization: The Case of Tanzania." *Women's Studies International Forum* 41 (2): 143–149.

Yu, Guanghua. 2010. "The Other Roles of Law: Signaling, Self-Commitment and Coordination." *Australian Journal of Asian Law* 12 (12): 106–137.

Zheng, Wang. 2005. "'State Feminism'? Gender and Socialist State Formation in Maoist China." *Feminist Studies* 31 (3): 519–551.

Zhou, Yunyun. 2019. "'Being a Good Daughter of the Party'? A Neo-Institutional Analysis of the All-China Women's Federation Organisational Reforms in China's Xi Era." *China Perspectives* 2019 (2): 17–28.

"Zimbabwe: MP Lambasts Government over Corruption." 1997. *The Zimbabwe Independent*, October 3, https://allafrica.com/stories/199710030110.html.

Zunes, Stephen, and Jacob Mundy. 2010. Western Sahara: War, Nationalism, and Conflict Irresolution. Syracuse studies on peace and conflict resolution. Syracuse, NY: Syracuse University Press.

Index

For the benefit of digital users, indexed terms that span two pages (e.g., 52–53) may, on occasion, appear on only one of those pages.

Tables and figures are indicated by an italic *t* and *f*.